THE
CHURCH HYMNARY

Third Edition

THE
CHURCH HYMNARY

Third Edition

WITH MELODY LINE

OXFORD UNIVERSITY PRESS

Oxford University Press, Ely House, London W. 1

GLASGOW   NEW YORK   TORONTO   MELBOURNE   WELLINGTON
CAPE TOWN   IBADAN   NAIROBI   DAR ES SALAAM   LUSAKA   ADDIS ABABA
DELHI   BOMBAY   CALCUTTA   MADRAS   KARACHI   LAHORE   DACCA
KUALA LUMPUR   SINGAPORE   HONG KONG   TOKYO

Selection, Preface, Introduction,
Introductory Notes to the Music
© The Church Hymnary Trust, 1973

First printed 1973
Third impression 1975

Printed in Great Britain by
Morrison & Gibb Ltd, London and Edinburgh

PREFACE

IN 1963 the General Assemblies of the Church of Scotland, the Presbyterian Church of England, the Presbyterian Church in Ireland, and the Presbyterian Church of Wales authorized the preparation of a new edition of *The Church Hymnary*, the previous editions having appeared in 1898 and 1927. The Joint Committee appointed to undertake this task invited the United Free Church of Scotland to be represented on the Church Hymnary Revision Committee.

In the selection and preparation of the contents of *The Church Hymnary : Third Edition* the Committee has been helped by discussion in successive General Assemblies of the participating Churches, and also by the careful scrutiny of its work by the Presbyteries of these Churches, leading to many useful alterations and improvements. Moreover, much specialized knowledge, biblical, theological, liturgical, hymnological and literary, generously shared with the Committee, is gratefully acknowledged.

The General Assembly of the Church of Scotland gave general approval to the draft of *The Church Hymnary : Third Edition* in 1968, and similar authorization was received from the General Assemblies of the Presbyterian Church in Ireland, the Presbyterian Church of Wales, the United Free Church of Scotland, and also the Presbyterian Church of England, which on 5 October 1972 was united with the Congregational Church in England and Wales to become the United Reformed Church.

The Committee had corporate responsibility for the selection and preparation of the music, but acknowledges its debt to those appointed as Music Consultants, Dr. Kenneth Leighton, Mr. Herrick Bunney, Mr. John Currie, and Mr. David Murray; also the late Mr. Guthrie

Foote who, in addition to professional competence, had wide experience in the publication of music. Mr. Ian Barrie also assisted.

Grateful acknowledgement is also made of the professional help so unsparingly given by the staff of Oxford University Press in the whole preparation of this hymnary.

The Church Hymnary : Third Edition is sent out in the prayerful hope that it may enrich the worship of congregations to the greater glory of God.

In the name of *The Church Hymnary* Revision Committee:

THOMAS H. KEIR, D.D.
Convener

R. STUART LOUDEN, D.D.
Vice-Convener

F. N. DAVIDSON KELLY, S.S.C.
Hon. Secretary

INTRODUCTION

Worship and Hymns

A Church hymn book is essentially designed for Christian worship.

Christ's earthly life and self-giving on the Cross was itself the one offering of perfect worship to the Father whose will he fulfilled. Through Word and Sacrament, as in daily obedience, his faithful disciples are united with him as his Body in the continuing offering of this worship.

Hence each action in Christian worship has a double significance. It is indeed Christ's people who pray and who praise the Father. Nevertheless they do so as the baptized community whose life is so grounded in Christ and bound up with his life that in worship he, as Head, exercises always his authoritative office as Prophet, High Priest, and King.

Through the Church's worship, therefore, Christ fulfils today in the life of his people what he did on earth 'once and for all'. When Scripture is read and preached, it is not the words of the Minister the congregation awaits but the Word of Christ who is the Word of God. Through the rites of initiation, Holy Baptism and Confirmation together with Holy Communion, Christ calls his people and establishes them in the covenant of grace. In Baptism he makes the person, whether infant or adult, a member of his Body. In Confirmation he strengthens and blesses the baptized, who profess their faith, as members of his Body with both privileges and responsibilities. In the Holy Communion Christ's eternal self-giving is present still in and through his Church. So, in every action of worship, including what is sung, Christ fulfils his ministry as Prophet, Priest, and King in order that through his Church he may be known as Lord by the world he came to save.

Study of the hymns offered in this book will, it is hoped, make these points clear.

The Cultural Context

It has at all times been necessary for the Committee, in the selection of material, to be aware of the special nature of its responsibility: to provide the means for high and holy worship, and at the same time to recognize the cultural limits within which this can be done.

On the one hand Christ, the Lord of the Church, is active in the midst of his worshipping people. It follows that as the spoken language used in church must be true and faithful to the Word of Christ, so the musical language also must be true to it. The Committee therefore had to take care, with what success only experience will show, to ensure that tunes are true to the words to which they are set. It is hoped, moreover, that in many instances the offer of a different tune to already well-known words will enable the words to yield up their meaning more fully.

On the other hand, this faithfulness to the Divine in worship must be balanced by a concern that the music is appropriate to the variety of emotions involved in the people's worship as well as to their musical ability. The Committee therefore had to keep in view the requirements of a number of somewhat differing communities not only in Britain but overseas. It also found it necessary to include a number of hymns of more or less local provenance or use, to meet the specific needs of some particular branch of the Church. Thus it has tried to ensure that every congregation will find in the Hymnary a sufficient number of tunes it can use.

The Contents and their Order

In selecting the *contents* of the Hymnary every effort has been made to present the essential elements in the Biblical revelation as adequately as liturgical necessity demanded and available resources permitted. Since a Church hymnal is essentially a liturgical book the Committee, in determining the *order* in which the hymns are arranged, has borne in mind that the Order of Holy Communion is normative for worship in the Reformed Church, and that where there is no regular weekly celebration of Holy Communion, the service should still follow the eucharistic pattern.

The Order of Common Worship

The central act of Christian worship from the beginning was understood as a unity, the structure of which involved a double action: (*a*) the 'Liturgy of the Word' based on the reading and exposition of the Scriptures; and (*b*) the 'Liturgy of the faithful', sometimes called 'the Liturgy of the Upper Room'—that is, the Holy Communion or Lord's Supper.

Part I: The approach to God

In the early centuries, Christian worship seems normally to have commenced with reading and preaching. Later, however, it became customary to commence the service with brief acts of approach to God. This comprises *the first part of the service* (Part I of the Hymnary).

Part II: The Word of God

Following his people's approach, God speaks to them through his Word in Holy Scripture and sermon. This 'Liturgy of the Word' is *the second part of the service* (Part II of the Hymnary).

Part III: Response to the Word of God

The third part, to which all else leads, is the 'Liturgy of the Upper Room'—the Holy Communion.

Even where the sacramental elements are not present, there follows response to the Word of God in the Church's outpouring of faith, adoration, thanksgiving, dedication, and intercession, culminating in her rejoicing in the communion of saints and the hope of glory (Parts III and IV of the Hymnary). Thus, recommissioned, the Church returns to her work in the world.

Using the Book

It will be noted that there is a certain correspondence both in style and content between the earlier portions of Parts I and III of the Hymnary, the former acknowledging the greatness of God, the latter providing acts of adoration and thanksgiving. Clearly certain hymns in Part III may with perfect propriety be used for the opening of worship, while some in Part I will provide on occasion suitable acts of response to what God has spoken in his Word. Nevertheless the distinction between the two parts of the book remains valid since the hymns in Part III do on the whole express the heightened adoration and thanksgiving which faithful worshippers are more prepared to offer after the Divine Word has been heard. This again is characteristic of the Communion Service.

The Table of Contents indicates the shape of the service both in its broad pattern and in its variable details; while cross-references at the end of the sub-sections in the body of the book point out certain cognate hymns to be found in other parts of the Hymnary.

The value of arranging a hymn book in this way, both to ministers in selecting a praise list and to congregations at worship, will, the Committee trusts, prove itself in practice.

Psalms and Paraphrases

From the beginning the Psalter had an integral place in Christian worship. Having regard to this and also to the traditional use of metrical versions in the Reformed

Church, the Committee hopes, by including a selection of psalms, both prose and metrical, to promote a fuller use of the riches of the Psalter and that the range of selection may be widened.

The selections from the Psalter and Scottish Paraphrases are normally placed first in the appropriate section or sub-section of the Hymnary.

Hymns for Children

In selecting hymns for use by children, it should not be forgotten that in this, as in other fields, it is better that a child's reach should exceed his grasp than that he should be encouraged to sing what is banal or below his best capacity. Many of the great hymns of the Church are admirably suited for children's enjoyment and use, so that their omission from children's worship is a serious lack.

Hymns suitable only for children and for younger children are placed according to the same principle as the other hymns, hymns of approach to God in Part I and so on, except that they are invariably last in the sub-section. These hymns are designated in a distinctive way in the Index of First Lines.

The Contribution of the Centuries

Each age, including our own, has contributed something new and of value to the rich treasury of the Church's hymnody, and this is reflected in the contents of the book, which contains a number of hymns and tunes written this century, as well as a significant corpus of specially commissioned music.

Congregations will gain both in the variety and the devotional fullness of their worship by extending the range of their hymnody.

So far as possible the dates of author, composer, and source are given.

INTRODUCTION

Thus the Church is constantly reminded that her inheritance and her promise are alike ageless, because they are from God the Eternal;

TO WHOM, FATHER, SON, AND HOLY SPIRIT, ONE GOD, BE GLORY IN THE CHURCH TO THE AGES OF AGES

INTRODUCTORY NOTES TO THE MUSIC

The Selection of the Music

IN the selection of music, three guiding principles have been followed:

1. that the tunes and settings should in general be easily learned and readily singable by the average congregation, and that tunes should be thoroughly suited to the words they are to serve;

2. that where a familiar tune has to be omitted, it should wherever possible be replaced by another familiar tune, or else a cross-reference given to such a tune occurring elsewhere in the book;

3. that a fine tune may well be employed more than once, thus bringing into use certain hymns previously unfamiliar because the tune was unknown or uninspiring, and also providing a known tune for special hymns only rarely required—for example at weddings, funeral services, consecration of churches, and so on.

The Style and Interpretation of Congregational Music

SINGING

Every hymn has its own style, and the manner of its performance will vary, depending on a number of practical considerations—the occasion, the size of the congregation, the acoustics of the building. Consequently, few indications of *tempo* are offered, but it is hoped that the use of the crotchet instead of the mimim as the standard pulse will assist towards lively musical interpretation.

The end of the verbal line in a hymn is generally indicated by the sign. ″ in the musical setting.

Unison verses should be used at times to highlight the words.

Amen has been excluded where it is not appropriate, and should be sung only where it is printed.

ACCOMPANIMENT

It is recognized that the organ will not always be the accompanying instrument. The following points are for general guidance.

(*a*) *The congregation* will best hear notes of at least an octave higher, or lower, than their own voices. Hence organ upper-work and pedals, piano lower and upper octaves, double bass, and strings and woodwind in upper octaves will prove most helpful in leading singing.

(*b*) *The accompaniment* should clearly indicate the mood for each verse, while avoiding too precious an interpretation within the verse itself.

(*c*) *Tunes* should be played over at the speed intended for singing. Normally it is only necessary for the first phrase to be played over. The practice of playing first and final phrases is to be discouraged.

MUSICAL SETTINGS

Some tunes have been revised to a limited extent. Others have been strengthened by more sweeping alterations in the harmonic structure.

A few settings more suitable for a choir than for the average congregation have been included.

Children's hymns and those recommended for unison singing have generally been given accompaniments which are both effective and readily playable.

PROSE SETTINGS

To encourage a wider and more varied use of speech rhythms four musical styles have been included.

1. In *Anglican chanting* the spoken word should always be the guide, the words being sung at the speed of clear speech with the stresses and rhythms of normal speech. Certain details of the pointing have been left to the individual choirmaster's own initiative and preference.

2. *Psalms or Canticles in the style of Gelineau* (e.g. No. 67) are designed to be sung with the rhythm of natural speech bound only by one slow pulse in each bar. The organist must be careful to supply this pulse clearly and regularly. Further details will be found in the introductions to *The Psalms of Joseph Gelineau*, published by the Grail Press.

3. By the introduction of *chanted psalms using only a few chords* (e.g. No. 66) it is hoped that congregations who have not yet attempted to sing prose settings will be encouraged to do so. The short series of chords or 'chant' is used once to each verse. The melodic note changes on the syllable or word marked with an acute accent. These settings may be sung in unison or in harmony.

4. In classical *plainchant* the syllables should be sung with even spacing, but without stiffness. Where possible the singing should be unaccompanied. If, however, a keyboard accompaniment is used it should contain as few chord changes as possible, and the choice of harmony should be governed by the accepted style for the accompaniment of modal music.*

The following symbols, occurring in the music or in

---

* Further guidance may be found in J. H. Arnold, *The Accompaniment of Plainsong* (O.U.P., reprinted by Waltham Forest Books); and in *A Manual of Plainsong*, edited by H. B. Briggs and W. H. Frere, revised and enlarged by J. H. Arnold (Novello).

the verbal text as the case may be, will be found sufficient
to direct the singing of the tones.

[]   Notes enclosed in a *bracket* are used only for the
first verse of the psalm; succeeding verses commence on the reciting note.

| A *vertical* indicates the point at which the reciting
note is quitted. Occasionally it will be found that
at the end of the half-verse a note is left over, for
which there is no verbal syllable remaining; in
such instances the note is simply omitted. This
is termed the 'abrupt mediation'. In No. 166
(Psalm 2) for instance, this happens a number of
times. Notes are also omitted if necessary from
the traditional endings.

:   A *colon* at the end of the half-verse corresponds
with the bar-line in the music, at which point
a short silence occurs, the duration of which is
approximately equal to the two previous syllables.
There should, however, be no break between
verses, but the first syllable of each new verse
should maintain without interruption the flow of
notes from the last syllable of the previous verse.

⌒   A *tie* indicates that two syllables are to be sung at
the same pitch. In other words, the note of the
first syllable is simply repeated.

∙∙   A *double dot* above the text is used where one
syllable requires two notes of the chant.

——   A *long dash* indicates that the reciting note is
omitted altogether.

The method of chanting is as follows. The first half-verse
of a psalm should, if possible, be chanted by one or two
solo voices, the second half of the verse being sung by the
choir or congregation or both. Thereafter complete verses
should be sung alternately by, for example, the choir
(verse 2) and congregation (verse 3) and so on; or else by

a chanter (verse 2) and choir (verse 3). Or some other similar pattern may be followed, such as the ladies' voices of the choir (verse 2) being answered by the men's voices (verse 3), always provided that the alternation is that of complete verses. Only the first verse should be divided between voices or sections of singers at the half-way point.

ACKNOWLEDGEMENTS

THE Church Hymnary Trust wishes to thank the following who have given permission for copyright material to be printed. *A blank in the second column indicates that the author or composer is also the owner of the copyright.*

MELODIES

COMPOSER	OWNER OF COPYRIGHT	NO. OF HYMN
Anderson, J. S.	Oxford University Press	306
Baring-Gould, S.	Mr. G. Hitchcock	653
Barrett-Ayres, R.		425, 470
Berkeley, L.		50(i), 54(i)
Bonner, C.	National Christian Education Council	386
Booth, J.	Oxford University Press and The Church Hymnary Trust	475
Broadwood, L. (mel.) and R. Vaughan Williams (har.)	Oxford University Press	17, 212, 220, 502, 618, 630
Brown, A. H.	Oxford University Press	79, 448
Buck, P. C.	Oxford University Press	329, 330, 366, 662(v)
Buck, P. C.	Stainer & Bell Ltd.	542
Cocker, N.	Oxford University Press	538
Cundell, E.	Cambridge University Press and The Estate of Edric Cundell	679, from *The Cambridge Hymnal*
Dalby, M.		149, 433(i), 647
Davies, Sir H. Walford	Trustees of the late Sir Walford Davies	598(i)
Davies, Sir H. Walford	Oxford University Press	143(ii), 156, 213, 318(i), 433(ii), 602, 631
Davies, M. W.	Union of Welsh Independents	150(ii)
Dorward, D.		340
Editors of *Hymns Ancient and Modern*	The Proprietors of *Hymns Ancient and Modern*	77(i)
Elliott, K.		*Arrangements*: 114(ii), 116, 140(i), 205, 250, 307, 314, 321(i), 370, 584(ii)
Ferguson, W. H.	Oxford University Press	300(ii), 645
Finlay, K. G.		124, 508

ACKNOWLEDGEMENTS

COMPOSER	OWNER OF COPYRIGHT	NO. OF HYMN
Foote, G.	Oxford University Press	155, 583, 655
Forbes, S.		141, 678(i)
Gardner, J.		209, 511, 629
Gelineau, J.	A. P. Watt & Son	67, 350, 389
Greatorex, W.	Oxford University Press	440
Griffith, W.	Oxford University Press	100, 685
Harris, W. H.		572
Harwood, B.	Executors of Dr. Basil Harwood	12, 146(i), 361(ii), 424, 434, 506
Hay, E. N.	Mr. K. Armour	288(ii)
Hedges, A. J. (arr.)	National Christian Education Council	226
Holst, G.	Oxford University Press	178, 336(i)
Howells, H.	Novello & Co. Ltd.	405(ii), 509
Howells, H.	Oxford University Press	146(ii)
Hughes, J.	Mrs. D. Webb	89(ii)
Hutchings, A.	Oxford University Press	110
Ireland, J.	Mrs. N. Kirby	95, 207, 224
Joubert, J.		401(i)
Joubert, J.	Novello & Co. Ltd.	367(i)
Langlais, J.	Secrétariat des Editeurs de Fiches Musicales	469
Leighton, K.	The Church Music Society	60, 560, 561, 563
Leighton, K.		44, 62, 486, 576(i), 672, 690
Ley, H. G.	Oxford University Press	204(ii)
Ley, H. G.	Mrs. H. Ley	400
Lomax, J. (mel.)	Essex Music Ltd.	427
Mann, A. H.	Dr. E. R. Goodliffe	131
Mann, A. H. (har.)	Novello & Co. Ltd.	193
Mathias, W.		292
Moore, J.		401(ii)
Morris, R. O.	Mr. H. Ferguson	194(i)
Murray, A. G.		240
Naylor, E. W.	Mr. B. Naylor	441
Nicholson, S. H.	The Proprietors of *Hymns Ancient and Modern*	550
Nyberg, H.	Suomen Lähetysseuran	666
Oldham, A.		177, 300(i)
Poole, C. W.	Dr. J. Horder	444
Popple, H.	Oxford University Press	633
Poston, E.	Cambridge University Press	277, 308, from *The Cambridge Hymnal*
Rimmer, F.		576(ii)
Röntgen, J.	Mr. F. E. Röntgen	282, 454(ii)
Routley, E.		361(i), 689(i)
Rowlands, W. P.	Mr. G. A. Gabe	473

ACKNOWLEDGEMENTS

COMPOSER	OWNER OF COPYRIGHT	NO. OF HYMN
Rusbridge, A. E.	Mrs. A. R. Rusbridge	186
Sharp, C. and R. Vaughan Williams	Mr. L. Swinyard and Oxford University Press	536
Shaw, M.	Roberton Publications	112, 154, 423
Shaw, M.	Oxford University Press	222, 303, 529
Sibelius, J.	Breitkopf & Härtel, Wiesbaden	673
Slater, G.	Oxford University Press	674
Smith, A. M.		68, 458
Smith, K. D.	National Christian Education Council	622
Somervell, A.	Executors of the late Sir Arthur Somervell	238(ii)
Somervell, A.	Oxford University Press	479(ii)
Stanford, C. V.	Stainer & Bell Ltd.	297, 345(d)
Stanton, W. K.	Oxford University Press	201, 403, 442(ii)
Stocks, G. G.	The Governors of Repton School	53(i), 339
Swann, D.		105
Taylor, C. V.	Oxford University Press	92, 145(ii), 334, 593
Thalben-Ball, G.	Oxford University Press	349(i), 432, 455(i), 594
Thatcher, R. S.	Oxford University Press	503, 523
Thiman, E.	United Reformed Church	500
Thiman, E.		688
Westbrook, F.		152
Williams, R. Vaughan	Oxford University Press	from *The English Hymnal* 115, 144, 157, 172, 328, 335, 439, 443, 447, 534, 619, 623 from *Songs of Praise* 111, 196, 283, 624
Williams, R. Vaughan (har.) and L. Broadwood (mel.)	Oxford University Press	17, 212, 220, 502, 618, 630
Williamson, M.	Josef Weinberger Ltd.	114(i) (*adpt. by Composer*)
Wilson, T.		13, 86, 556(iii)
Wood, C.	Mr. E. M. S. Wood	398
Wood, C.	A. R. Mowbray & Co. Ltd.	271, 341

The following are the copyright of The Church Hymnary Trust and Oxford University Press: 21, 61, 66, 164, 325, 399, 411, 453.

ACKNOWLEDGEMENTS

WORDS

AUTHOR	OWNER OF COPYRIGHT	NO. OF HYMN
Adams, J.	National Adult School Union	444
Agnew, E.	© W. L. Jenkins 1953	230 lines 1-12, from *Songs & Hymns for Primary Children*
	© The Geneva Press 1972	230 lines 13-16, from *Teachers' Guide Book Revised*
Alexander, J. N. S.		162, 203
Alington, C. A.	The Proprietors of *Hymns Ancient and Modern*	120, 270, 555, 593, 599
Alston, A. E.	Mr. C. Alston	31 (tr.)
Andrew, Father	A. R. Mowbray & Co. Ltd.	252
Arlott, J.		619
Armitage, E. S.	United Reformed Church	553
Baring-Gould, S.	Mr. G. Hitchcock	423, 480, 653
Barkley, J. M.		595
Barnard, W. E.		625
Bax, C.	A. D. Peters & Co.	84
Bayly, A. F.		141, 426, 458, 503 (alt.), 554 (alt.)
Bell, G. K. A.	Oxford University Press	474
Blatchford, A. N.	Ascherberg, Hopwood & Crew Ltd.	148
Bourne, G. H.	Oxford University Press	583
Bowie, W. Russell	Abingdon Press	255, 509
Bridges, R.	Oxford University Press	55, 57, 119, 251, 335, 403, 405, 408, 472(i), 642
Briggs, G. W.	Oxford University Press	215, 219, 452, 505, 572
Brownlie, J.	Mr. A. Rutherford Brownlie	95
Buchanan, V.		327
Chesterton, G. K.	Oxford University Press	520, from *The English Hymnal*
Christierson, F. von	Hymn Society of America	133
Clarkson, E. M.	Inter-Varsity Press	337, 592
Cropper, M.		228, 467
Crum, J. M. C.	Oxford University Press	278, from *The Oxford Book of Carols*
Darbyshire, J. R.	Oxford University Press	260
Dearmer, P.	Oxford University Press	341, from *The Oxford Book of Carols*
		43, 111, 515, 588, from *The English Hymnal*
		128, 416, from *Songs of Praise*

ACKNOWLEDGEMENTS

AUTHOR	OWNER OF COPYRIGHT	NO. OF HYMN
Draper, W. H.	Roberton Publications	30
Dudley-Smith, T.		164
Dugmore, E. E.	Mr. E. M. Mills	451
East, J. T.	Methodist Youth Department	222
Editors of *The BBC Hymn Book*	Oxford University Press	305
Ferguson, J. M. Macdougall	Religious Education Press	631, 654
Fletcher, F.	Oxford University Press	309
Fosdick, H. E.	Mrs. E. Fosdick Downs	88
Frere, M. Temple	The National Society	622
Gelineau, J.	A. P. Watt & Son Ltd.	67, 350, 389
Gill, D. M.		384
Gillett, G. G. S.	Oxford University Press	328
Green, F. Pratt	Oxford University Press	152
Greenaway, A. R.	The Proprietors of *Hymns Ancient and Modern*	244, 248
Head, B. P.	The Revd. A. Hanbury Head	339
Housman, L.	Oxford University Press	196, 507
Hoyle, R. Birch	World Student Christian Federation	279
Huey, M. E.	© W. L. Jenkins 1963	17, from *Songs & Hymns for Primary Children*
Hull, E.	Chatto & Windus Ltd.	87 (coll.)
Hunter, A. M.		399
Hunter Clare, T. C.		513
Ikeler, C. R.	© W. L. Jenkins 1963	427, from *Songs & Hymns for Primary Children*
Jackson, F. A.	National Christian Education Council	281, 621, 630, 633
Jeffries, C.	Joint Action for Christian Literature Overseas (Feed the Minds)	468
Jones, A. M.	United Society for Christian Literature	340
Kipling, R.	A. P. Watt & Son Ltd.	446
Kirkland, P. M.	The Misses Kirkland	283
Lacey, T. A.	Oxford University Press	472(ii)
Littlewood, R. Wesley	Methodist Youth Department	528
Lowry, S. C.	Oxford University Press	454
Macalister, E. F. Boyle	National Christian Education Council	16, 557
Macalister, R. A. S.	Oxford University Press	129, 401
Macnicol, N.	Trustees of the late Helen Macnicol	82

ACKNOWLEDGEMENTS

AUTHOR	OWNER OF COPYRIGHT	NO. OF HYMN
Masterman, J. H. B.		508
Mathams, W. J.	Oxford University Press	100
Mathews, B. J.	Oxford University Press	501
Mealy, N. and M.	Seabury Press Inc.	155, from *Sing for Joy*
Merrill, W. P.	*The Presbyterian Outlook*	477
Milner-Barry, A. M.	The National Society	280
Moore, J. Boyd		601
Moore, J. E.	United Church Press	466, from *Pilgrim Bible Stories for Children*
Newbolt, M. R. and Kitchin, G. W.	The Proprietors of *Hymns Ancient and Modern*	550
Niles, D. T.	East Asia Christian Conference	415
Oxenham, J.	Westminster Bank Ltd. and Miss T. Dunkerley	425
Parker, W. H.	National Christian Education Council	124
Perkins Brown, J. E.	United Church Press	157, from *As Children Worship*
Phillips, A. N.		506
Phillips, E. M.		690
Piggott, W. Charter	Oxford University Press	134, 538
Pitt-Watson, I.		64, 68, 126 (paraphrased from *The New English Bible*)
Quinn, J.	Geoffrey Chapman Ltd.	175, 276, 308, 568 (adpt.), 581, 589
Reed, E. M.	Evans Bros. Ltd.	186
Rees, T.	A. R. Mowbray & Co. Ltd.	334, 473
Roberts, K. E.	Oxford University Press	185, from *The Oxford Book of Carols*
Roberts, R. E.	Oxford University Press	330
Scott, R. B. Y.		511
Shields, E. McE.	© Presbyterian Board of Christian Education 1935 and 1963	229
Shillito, E.	Oxford University Press	292
Skemp, A.	National Christian Education Council	156
Smith, F. M.	The National Society	447
Snow, G.		91
Stevenson, L.	Oxford University Press	375
Struther, J.	Oxford University Press	92, 206
Terry, R. R.	Oxford University Press	652, from *The Oxford Book of Carols*
Tucker, F. Bland	The Church Pension Fund	242, 297, 522, 586 (alt.)

ACKNOWLEDGEMENTS

AUTHOR	OWNER OF COPYRIGHT	NO. OF HYMN
Tweedy, H. Hallam	Hymn Society of America	499
Tynan Hinkson, K.	Search Press Ltd.	524
Waddell, H.	The Girls' Auxiliary	486
Watt, L. MacLean	Mr. A. L. MacLean Watt	666
Wilkinson, K. Barclay	Mr. D. R. Gould	432
Winslow, J. C.		51, 428
Woodward, G. R.	A. R. Mowbray & Co. Ltd.	187, 271
Woodward, G. R.	Schott & Co. Ltd.	604, 640, from *The BBC Hymn Book*
Wren, B.	Oxford University Press	469
Wright, W.	Young Men's Christian Association	614

The Church Hymnary Trust also wishes to thank Dr. Bernard Rose for carrying out the pointing of the psalms set to PLAINSONG CHANTS in this book: Nos. 63, 158, 166, 231, 232, 239, 262, 284, 310, 326.

The pointing is copyright and may not be reproduced in any form without application in the first instance to Oxford University Press.

CONTENTS

CONTENTS

CONTENTS

I

APPROACH TO GOD

APPROACH TO GOD

THE HOUSE OF GOD

1 OLD 100TH L.M.   *French–Genevan Psalter*, 1551

A-men.

PSALM 100

ALL people that on earth do dwell,
Sing to the Lord with cheerful voice.
Him serve with mirth, his praise
   forth tell,
Come ye before him and rejoice.

2 Know that the Lord is God indeed;
Without our aid he did us make;
We are his folk, he doth us feed,
And for his sheep he doth us take.

3 O enter then his gates with praise,
Approach with joy his courts unto:
Praise, laud, and bless his Name
   always,
For it is seemly so to do.

4 For why the Lord our God is good,
His mercy is for ever sure;
His truth at all times firmly stood,
And shall from age to age endure.

5 *To Father, Son, and Holy Ghost,*
The God whom earth and heaven adore,
Be glory, as it was of old,
Is now, and shall be evermore. Amen.

2 OLD 100TH L.M.   *French–Genevan Psalter*, 1551

BEFORE Jehovah's awesome throne,
Ye nations, bow with sacred joy;
Know that the Lord is God alone;
He can create, and he destroy.

2

2. His sovereign power, without our aid,
   Made us of clay, and formed us men;
   And, when like wandering sheep we strayed,
   He brought us to his fold again.

3 We are his people, we his care,—
   Our souls and all our mortal frame:
   What lasting honours shall we rear,
   Almighty Maker, to thy Name?

4 We'll crowd thy gates with thankful songs,
   High as the heavens our voices raise;
   And earth, with her ten thousand tongues,
   Shall fill thy courts with sounding praise.

5 Wide as the world is thy command,
   Vast as eternity thy love;
   Firm as a rock thy truth must stand,
   When rolling years shall cease to move.

Isaac Watts, 1674–1748,
and John Wesley, 1703–91
From Psalm 100

3 (i)   JOHN ALCOCK, 1715–1806

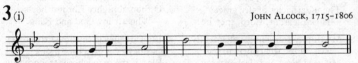

(ii)   FREDERICK A. GORE OUSELEY, 1825–89

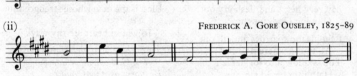

PSALM 100
Jubilate Deo

O BE joyful in the Lord | all ye | lands:
   Serve the Lord with gladness   and come before his | presence | with a | song.

2 Be ye sure that the Lord | he is | God:
   It is he that hath made us and we are his own   we are his | people · and the | sheep of his | pasture.

3 O go your way into his gates with thanksgiving   and into his | courts with | praise:
   Be thankful unto him and speak | good | of his | Name.

4 For the Lord is gracious   his mercy is | ever- | lasting:
   And his truth endureth from gener- | ation to | gener- | ation.

Glory | be to the | Father :
   And to the Son | and to the | Holy | Ghost ;

As it | was in the be- | ginning :
   Is now and ever shall be | world without | end. A- | men.

3

APPROACH TO GOD

4 HARINGTON (RETIREMENT) C.M.

HENRY HARINGTON,
1727-1816 (altered)

A - men.

PSALM 84, verses 1-5

HOW lovely is thy dwelling-place,
   O Lord of hosts, to me!
The tabernacles of thy grace
   How pleasant, Lord, they be!

2 My thirsty soul longs vehemently,
   Yea faints, thy courts to see:
My very heart and flesh cry out,
   O living God, for thee.

3 Behold, the sparrow findeth out
   An house wherein to rest;
The swallow also for herself
   Hath purchasèd a nest;

4 Even thine own altars, where she safe
   Her young ones forth may bring,
O thou almighty Lord of hosts,
   Who art my God and King.

5 Blest are they in thy house that dwell,
   They ever give thee praise.
Blest is the man whose strength thou
      art,
   In whose heart are thy ways.

6 *To Father, Son, and Holy Ghost,*
   The God whom we adore,
Be glory, as it was, and is,
   And shall be evermore. Amen.

5 GRÄFENBERG C.M.

Crüger's *Praxis Pietatis Melica*,
1647 edn. (rhythm altered)

A - men.

PSALM 15

WITHIN thy tabernacle, Lord,
   Who shall abide with thee?
And in thy high and holy hill
   Who shall a dweller be?

2 The man that walketh uprightly,
   And worketh righteousness,
And as he thinketh in his heart,
   So doth he truth express.

4

3 Who doth not slander with his tongue,
   Nor to his friend doth hurt;
Nor yet against his neighbour doth
   Take up an ill report.

4 In whose eyes vile men are despised;
   But those that God do fear
He honoureth; and changeth not,
   Though to his hurt he swear.

5 His coin puts not to usury,
   Nor take reward will he
Against the guiltless. Who doth thus
   Shall never movèd be.

6 *To Father, Son, and Holy Ghost,*
   The God whom we adore,
Be glory, as it was, and is,
   And shall be evermore. Amen.

6 LONDON NEW C.M.

Scottish Psalter, 1635, as adapted in
Playford's *Psalms,* 1671

A-men.

PSALM 36, verses 5–9

THY mercy, Lord, is in the heavens;
   Thy truth doth reach the clouds:
Thy justice is like mountains great;
   Thy judgments deep as floods:

2 Lord, thou preservest man and beast.
   How precious is thy grace!
Therefore in shadow of thy wings
   Men's sons their trust shall place.

3 They with the fatness of thy house
   Shall be well satisfied;
From rivers of thy pleasures thou
   Wilt drink to them provide.

4 Because of life the fountain pure
   Remains alone with thee;
And in that purest light of thine
   We clearly light shall see.

5 *To Father, Son, and Holy Ghost,*
   The God whom we adore,
Be glory, as it was, and is,
   And shall be evermore. Amen.

5

7 MARTYRS C.M.

Scottish Psalter, 1615 (1635 rhythm)

A - men.

PSALM 43, verses 3-5

O SEND thy light forth and thy
truth;
  Let them be guides to me,
And bring me to thine holy hill,
  Even where thy dwellings be.

2 Then will I to God's altar go,
  To God my chiefest joy:
Yea, God, my God, thy Name to
praise
  My harp I will employ.

3 Why art thou then cast down, my
soul?
  What should discourage thee?
And why with vexing thoughts art
thou
  Disquieted in me?

4 Still trust in God; for him to praise
  Good cause I yet shall have:
He of my countenance is the health,
  My God that doth me save.

5 *To Father, Son, and Holy Ghost,*
  The God whom we adore,
Be glory, as it was, and is,
  And shall be evermore. Amen.

8 ST. FLAVIAN C.M.

Melody of Psalm 132 in *English Psalter,* 1562
(first half only), adapted 1599 and later

A - men.

A version with the earlier form of rhythm is at No. 225

PSALM 116, verses 1-7

I LOVE the Lord, because my
  voice
And prayers he did hear.
I, while I live, will call on him,
  Who bowed to me his ear.

2 The cords of death on every side
  Encompassed me around;
The sorrows of the grave me seized,
  I grief and trouble found.

3 Upon the Name of God the Lord
  Then did I call, and say,
Deliver thou my soul, O Lord,
  I do thee humbly pray.

4 God merciful and righteous is,
  Yea, gracious is our Lord.
God saves the meek: I was brought
    low,
He did me help afford.

5 O thou my soul, do thou return
  Unto thy quiet rest;
For largely, lo, the Lord to thee
  His bounty hath expressed.

6 *To Father, Son, and Holy Ghost,*
  The God whom we adore,
Be glory, as it was, and is,
  And shall be evermore. Amen.

9 LOBE DEN HERREN
(HAST DU DENN, JESU)   14 14 478

Praxis Pietatis Melica,
1668 edition

Lobe den Herren

PRAISE to the Lord, the Almighty, the King of creation;
O my soul, praise him, for he is thy health and salvation;
    All ye who hear,
    Now to his temple draw near,
Joining in glad adoration.

2 Praise to the Lord, who o'er all things so wondrously reigneth,
Shieldeth thee gently from harm, or when fainting sustaineth;
    Hast thou not seen
    How thy heart's wishes have been
Granted in what he ordaineth?

3 Praise to the Lord, who doth prosper thy work and defend thee;
Surely his goodness and mercy shall daily attend thee;
    Ponder anew
    What the Almighty can do,
Who with his love doth befriend thee.

4 Praise to the Lord! O let all that is in me adore him!
All that hath life and breath, come now with praises before him!
    Let the Amen
    Sound from his people again:
Gladly for aye we adore him.

Joachim Neander, 1650-80
Tr. Catherine Winkworth, 1827-78, and others
From Psalms 103, 150

10 WESTMINSTER ABBEY
(BELVILLE) 8787 87

From the concluding Alleluias
in an anthem
by HENRY PURCELL (c. 1659–95)

A-men.

Alternative tune, TANTUM ERGO SACRAMENTUM (GRAFTON), No. 373

Angularis fundamentum lapis Christus missus est

CHRIST is made the sure founda-
tion,
   Christ the head and corner-stone,
Chosen of the Lord, and precious,
   Binding all the Church in one,
Holy Sion's help for ever,
   And her confidence alone.

2 To this temple, where we call thee,
   Come, O Lord of Hosts, today:
With thy wonted loving-kindness,
   Hear thy servants as they pray,
And thy fullest benediction
   Shed within its walls alway.

3 Here vouchsafe to all thy servants
   What they ask of thee to gain,
What they gain from thee for ever
   With the blessèd to retain,
And hereafter in thy glory
   Evermore with thee to reign.

4 *Laud and honour to the Father,*
   Laud and honour to the Son,
Laud and honour to the Spirit,
   Ever Three and ever One,
One in might, and One in glory,
   While unending ages run. Amen.

Latin 7th or 8th century
Tr. John Mason Neale, 1818–66 (altered)

11 ADSIS, JESU 6565

WILLIAM HENRY MONK, 1823–89

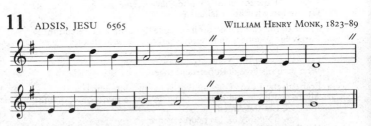

JESUS, stand among us
   In thy risen power;
Let this time of worship
   Be a hallowed hour.

2 Breathe the Holy Spirit
   Into every heart;
Bid the fears and sorrows
   From each soul depart.

3 Thus with quickened footsteps
    We pursue our way,
  Watching for the dawning
    Of eternal day.

William Pennefather, 1816–73

12   LOWER MARLWOOD   8484 884   BASIL HARWOOD, 1859–1949

Macht hoch die Thür, das Thor macht weit

LIFT up your heads, ye mighty gates,
    Alleluia!
Behold, the King of glory waits;
    Alleluia!
The King of kings is drawing near,
The Saviour of the world is here.
    Alleluia!

2 O blest the land, the city blest,
    Alleluia!
Where Christ the ruler is confessed.
    Alleluia!
O happy hearts and happy homes
To whom this King in triumph comes.
    Alleluia!

3 Redeemer, come! with us abide,
    Alleluia!
Our hearts to thee we open wide,
    Alleluia!
Thy presence with us let us feel,
Thy grace and love in us reveal.
    Alleluia!

Georg Weissel, 1590–1635
Tr. Catherine Winkworth, 1827–78 (altered)

13 RUTHERGLEN S.M.   THOMAS WILSON

Lux alma Jesu mentium

LIGHT of the anxious heart,
  Jesus, thou dost appear,
To bid the gloom of guilt depart,
  And shed thy sweetness here.

2 Joyous is he with whom,
    God's Word, thou dost abide,
  Sweet Light of our eternal home,
    To fleshly sense denied.

3   Brightness of God above,
     Unfathomable grace,
   Thy presence be a fount of love
     Within thy chosen place.

c. 1200
Tr. John Henry Newman, 1801–90

14 LUTHER'S HYMN   Later form of a melody in *Geistliche Lieder*,
    (NUN FREUT EUCH)   8787 887   Wittenberg, 1533 or earlier

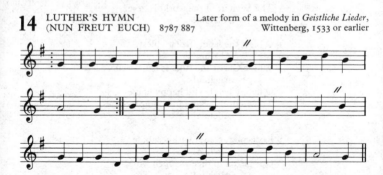

WE come unto our fathers' God;
  Their Rock is our Salvation;
The eternal arms, their dear abode,
  We make our habitation;

We bring thee, Lord, the praise they
  brought;
We seek thee as thy saints have
  sought
   In every generation.

THE HOUSE OF GOD

2 The fire divine their steps that led
    Still goeth bright before us;
The heavenly shield around them
    spread
    Is still high holden o'er us;
The grace those sinners that sub-
    dued,
The strength those weaklings that
    renewed,
    Doth vanquish, doth restore us.

3 Their joy unto their Lord we bring;
    Their song to us descendeth;
The Spirit who in them did sing
    To us his music lendeth;

His song in them, in us, is one;
    We raise it high, we send it on,—
    The song that never endeth.

4 Ye saints to come, take up the strain,
    The same sweet theme endeavour;
Unbroken be the golden chain;
    Keep on the song for ever;
Safe in the same dear dwelling-place,
Rich with the same eternal grace,
    Bless the same boundless Giver.

Thomas Hornblower Gill, 1819–1906

15 QUAM DILECTA 6666   HENRY LASCELLES JENNER, 1820–98

WE love the place, O God,
    Wherein thine honour dwells;
The joy of thine abode
    All earthly joy excels.

2 It is the house of prayer,
    Wherein thy servants meet;
And thou, O Lord, art there,
    Thy chosen flock to greet.

3 We love the word of life,
    The word that tells of peace,
Of comfort in the strife,
    And joys that never cease.

4 We love to sing below
    For mercies freely given;
But O we long to know
    The triumph song of heaven!

5 Lord Jesus, give us grace,
    On earth to love thee more,
In heaven to see thy face,
    And with thy saints adore.

William Bullock, 1798–1874, and
Henry Williams Baker, 1821–77

11

16 SURREY (CAREY'S) 8888 88 HENRY CAREY, *c.* 1687–1743

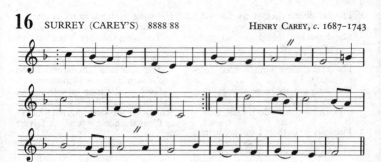

For younger children

LORD Jesus, be thou with us now,
As in thy house in prayer we bow;
And when we sing, and when we pray,
Help us to mean the words we say,
Help us to listen to thy word,
And keep our thoughts from wandering, Lord.

Edith Florence Boyle Macalister, 1873–1950

17 SHIPSTON 8787 English Traditional Melody, collected by
LUCY BROADWOOD, 1858–1929

For younger children

SERVE the Lord with joy and gladness,
Come into his gates with song;
Serve the Lord with loving-kindness,
Love and praise him all day long.

Mary Elizabeth Huey
Based on Psalm 100, v. 2

18 MAINZ 6666
(MARIA JUNG UND ZART)

Geistliche Kirchengesäng, Cologne, 1623,
as in *Psalteriolum Harmonicum*, 1642
(rhythm slightly altered)

For younger children

THIS is God's holy house
And he is here today;
He hears each song of praise,
And listens while we pray.

Louise M. Ogelvee

THE MAJESTY OF GOD

19 IRISH C.M.   *A Collection of Hymns and Sacred Poems*, Dublin, 1749

A-men.

PSALM 95, verses 1–6

O COME, and let us to the Lord
    In songs our voices raise,
With joyful noise let us the Rock
    Of our salvation praise.

2 Let us before his presence come
    With praise and thankful voice;
Let us sing psalms to him with
      grace,
    And make a joyful noise.

3 The Lord's a great God and great
      King,
    Above all gods he is.
Depths of the earth are in his hand,
    The strength of hills is his.

4 To him the spacious sea belongs,
    For he the same did make;
The dry land also from his hands
    Its form at first did take.

5 O come and let us worship him,
    Let us bow down withal,
And on our knees before the Lord
    Our Maker let us fall.

6 *To Father, Son, and Holy Ghost,*
    The God whom we adore,
Be glory, as it was, and is,
    And shall be evermore. Amen.

20 (i)   GEORGE ALEXANDER MACFARREN, 1813–87

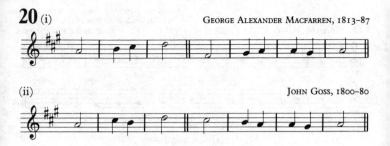

(ii)   JOHN GOSS, 1800–80

PSALM 95, verses 1–7

Venite, exultemus

O COME let us ' sing unto · the ' Lord:
Let us heartily rejoice in the ' strength of ' our sal- ' vation.

2 Let us come before his ' presence with ' thanksgiving:
And show ourselves ' glad in ' him with ' psalms.

3 For the Lord is a ' great ' God:
And a great ' King a- ' bove all ' gods.

4 In his hand are all the ' corners of the ' earth:
And the strength of the ' hills is ' his ' also.

5 The sea is ' his and he ' made it:
And his hands pre- ' pared the ' dry ' land.

6 O come let us ' worship and fall ' down:
And ' kneel be · fore the ' Lord our ' Maker.

7 For he is our God and ' we are his ' people:
He is our ' shepherd and ' we are his ' flock.

Glory ' be to the ' Father:
And to the Son ' and to the ' Holy ' Ghost;

As it ' was in the be- ' ginning:
Is now and ever shall be '   world without ' end. A- ' men.

THE MAJESTY OF GOD

21

JOHN CURRIE

For an explanation of the pointing system see
Introductory Notes to the Music

PSALM 95, VERSES 1–7

Venite, exultemus

O COME let us ˊsing unto the Loˊrd:
let us make a joyful ˊnoise to the rock of our salvation.
Let us come before his ˊpresence with thanksgiving,
and make a joyful ˊnoise unto him with psalms.
For the Loˊrd is a greˊat God,
and a great Kiˊng above all goˊds.
In his hand are the deˊep places of the eaˊrth:
the strength of the ˊhills is his aˊlso.
The sea is ˊhis and he maˊde it:
and his hands foˊrmed the dry ˊland.
O come let us woˊrship and bow doˊwn:
let us kneel before the Loˊrd our maˊker.
For he is our Goˊd;
and we are the people of his ˊpasture and the sheˊep of his haˊnd.

Glory be to the Faˊther,
and to the Soˊn, and to the Holy ˊGhost;
As it was in the beginning, is noˊw and ever shaˊll be:
woˊrld without eˊnd. Aˊmen.

22 SOUTHWARK C.M.

Adapted from a melody by
CHRISTOPHER TYE, c. 1508–72

A-men.

PSALM 96, verses 1, 2, 6–8

O SING a new song to the Lord:
  Sing all the earth to God.
To God sing, bless his Name, show
    still
  His saving health abroad.

2 Great honour is before his face,
  And majesty divine;
Strength is within his holy place,
  And there doth beauty shine.

3 Do ye ascribe unto the Lord,
  Of people every tribe,
Glory do ye unto the Lord,
  And mighty power ascribe.

4 Give ye the glory to the Lord
  That to his Name is due;
Come ye into his courts, and bring
  An offering with you.

5 *To Father, Son, and Holy Ghost,*
  The God whom we adore,
Be glory, as it was, and is,
  And shall be evermore. Amen.

23 & 24 STROUDWATER C.M.

Wilkins' *Psalmody, c.* 1730, as in
The Psalter in Metre, 1899

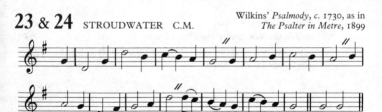

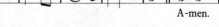

A-men.

PSALM 9, verses 7–11

23
  GOD shall endure for aye; he doth
    For judgment set his throne;
  In righteousness to judge the world,
    Justice to give each one.

2 God also will a refuge be
  For those that are oppressed;
A refuge will he be in times
  Of trouble to distressed.

3 And they that know thy Name, in thee
  Their confidence will place:
For thou hast not forsaken them
  That truly seek thy face.

4 O sing ye praises to the Lord
  That dwells in Sion hill;
Among all nations of the earth
  His deeds record ye still.

5 *To Father, Son, and Holy Ghost,*
  The God whom we adore,
Be glory, as it was, and is,
  And shall be evermore. Amen.

PSALM 46, verses 1–5

24

GOD is our refuge and our strength,
  In straits a present aid;
Therefore, although the earth remove,
  We will not be afraid:

2 Though hills amidst the seas be cast;
  Though waters roaring make,
And troubled be; yea, though the hills
  By swelling seas do shake.

3 A river is, whose streams make glad
  The city of our God,
The holy place, wherein the Lord
  Most high hath his abode.

4 God in the midst of her doth dwell;
  Nothing shall her remove;
God unto her an helper will,
  And that right early, prove.

5 *To Father, Son, and Holy Ghost,*
  The God whom we adore,
Be glory, as it was, and is,
  And shall be evermore. Amen.

25 HOWARD C.M.

Wilson's *A Selection of Psalm Tunes*, Edinburgh, 1825

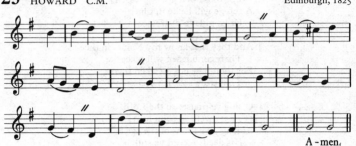

A - men.

PSALM 62, verses 5–8

ONLY on God do thou, my soul,
    Still patiently attend;
My expectation and my hope
    On him alone depend.

2 He only my salvation is,
    And my strong rock is he;
He only is my sure defence:
    I shall not movèd be.

3 In God my glory placèd is,
    And my salvation sure;
In God the rock is of my strength,
    My refuge most secure.

4 Ye people, place your confidence
    In him continually;
Before him pour ye out your heart;
    God is our refuge high.

5 *To Father, Son, and Holy Ghost,*
    The God whom we adore,
Be glory, as it was, and is,
    And shall be evermore. Amen.

26 FARRANT C.M.

Old Church Psalmody, 1847
Adapted from an anthem melody probably by
JOHN HILTON, *d.* 1608

A - men.

PSALM 27, verses 1, 3–5, 14

THE Lord's my light and saving health,
    Who shall make me dismayed?
My life's strength is the Lord, of whom
    Then shall I be afraid?

2 Against me though an host encamp,
   My heart yet fearless is:
   Though war against me rise, I will
   Be confident in this.

3 One thing I of the Lord desired,
   And will seek to obtain,
   That all days of my life I may
   Within God's house remain;

4 That I the beauty of the Lord
   Behold may and admire,
   And that I in his holy place
   May reverently enquire.

5 For he in his pavilion shall
   Me hide in evil days;
   In secret of his tent me hide,
   And on a rock me raise.

6 Wait on the Lord, and be thou strong,
   And he shall strength afford
   Unto thine heart; yea, do thou wait,
   I say, upon the Lord.

7 *To Father, Son and Holy Ghost,*
   The God whom we adore,
   Be glory, as it was and is,
   And shall be evermore. Amen.

27 BRISTOL C.M. Ravenscroft's *Psalter*, 1621 (rhythm altered)

Alternative tune, IRISH, No. 19

A-men.

PSALM 33, verses 1–5

YE righteous, in the Lord rejoice;
   It comely is and right,
That upright men, with thankful voice,
   Should praise the Lord of might.

2 Praise God with harp, and unto him
   Sing with the psaltery;
   Upon a ten-stringed instrument
   Make ye sweet melody.

3 A new song to him sing, and play
   With loud noise skilfully;
   For right is God's word, all his works
   Are done in verity.

4 To judgment and to righteousness
   A love he beareth still;
   The loving-kindness of the Lord
   The earth throughout doth fill.

5 *To Father, Son, and Holy Ghost,*
   The God whom we adore,
   Be glory, as it was, and is,
   And shall be evermore. Amen.

28 ABRIDGE (ST. STEPHEN) C.M.

ISAAC SMITH, 1734–1805,
A Collection of Psalm Tunes, c. 1780

A - men.

PSALM 65, verses 1–4

PRAISE waits for thee in Sion, Lord:
   To thee vows paid shall be.
O thou that hearer art of prayer,
   All flesh shall come to thee.

2 Iniquities, I must confess,
   Prevail against me do:
But as for our transgressions all,
   Them purge away shalt thou.

3 Blest is the man whom thou dost choose,
   And makest approach to thee,
That he within thy courts, O Lord,
   May still a dweller be:

4 We surely shall be satisfied
   With thy abundant grace,
And with the goodness of thy house,
   Even of thy holy place.

5 *To Father, Son, and Holy Ghost,*
   The God whom we adore,
Be glory, as it was, and is,
   And shall be evermore. Amen.

29 ST. FULBERT C.M.   HENRY JOHN GAUNTLETT, 1805-76

A-men.

Alternative tune, HOWARD, No. 25

PSALM 92, verses 1-4

TO render thanks unto the Lord
    It is a comely thing,
And to thy Name, O thou most High,
    Due praise aloud to sing.

2 Thy loving-kindness to show forth
    When shines the morning light;
And to declare thy faithfulness
    With pleasure every night,

3 Upon a ten-stringed instrument,
    And on the psaltery,
Upon the harp with solemn sound
    And grave sweet melody.

4 For thou, Lord, by thy mighty works
    Hast made my heart right glad;
And I will triumph in the works
    Which by thine hands were made.

5 *To Father, Son, and Holy Ghost,*
    The God whom we adore,
Be glory, as it was, and is,
    And shall be evermore. Amen.

30 LASST UNS ERFREUEN
88 8 88 and refrain

Geistliche Kirchengesäng, Cologne, 1623

A - men.

Laudato sia Dio mio Signore

ALL creatures of our God and King,
Lift up your voice and with us sing
    Alleluia, Alleluia!
Thou burning sun with golden beam,
Thou silver moon with softer gleam
        O praise him, O praise him,
        Alleluia, Alleluia, Alleluia!

*2 Thou rushing wind that art so strong,
Ye clouds that sail in heaven along,
    O praise him, Alleluia!
Thou rising morn, in praise rejoice,
Ye lights of evening, find a voice:

*3 Thou flowing water, pure and clear,
Make music for thy Lord to hear,
    Alleluia, Alleluia!
Thou fire so masterful and bright,
That givest man both warmth and light:

4 Dear mother earth, who day by day
Unfoldest blessings on our way,
    O praise him, Alleluia!
The flowers and fruits that in thee grow,
Let them his glory also show:

5 And all ye men of tender heart,
Forgiving others, take your part,
    O sing ye, Alleluia!
Ye who long pain and sorrow bear,
Praise God and on him cast your care:

    * These verses may be omitted if desired*

22

6 And thou, most kind and gentle death,
   Waiting to hush our latest breath,
     O praise him, Alleluia!
   Thou leadest home the child of God,
   And Christ our Lord the way hath trod:

7 *Let all things their Creator bless,*
   And worship him in humbleness,
     O praise him, Alleluia!
   Praise, praise the Father, praise the Son,
   And praise the Spirit, Three in One:
                                   Amen.

St. Francis of Assisi, 1182–1226
Tr. William Henry Draper, 1855–1933

31 ISTE CONFESSOR
(CHARTRES) 11 11 11 5

Chartres Antiphoner, 1784

A - - men.

O Pater sancte

FATHER most holy, merciful and loving,
   Jesus, Redeemer, ever to be worshipped,
Life-giving Spirit, Comforter most gracious,
     God everlasting;

2 Three in a wondrous unity unbroken,
     One perfect Godhead, love that never faileth,
Light of the angels, succour of the needy,
     Hope of all living;

3 All thy creation serveth its Creator;
     Thee every creature praiseth without ceasing;
We too would sing thee psalms of true devotion;
     Hear, we beseech thee.

4 *Lord God Almighty, unto thee be glory,*
     One in Three Persons, over all exalted;
Thine, as is meet, be honour, praise, and blessing,
     Now and for ever. Amen.

c. 10th century; tr. Alfred Edward Alston, 1862–1927

32 ST. DENIO (JOANNA) II II II II

Welsh hymn melody, 1839, founded
on a folk tune

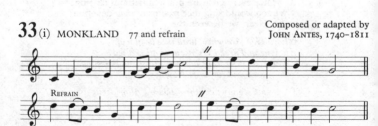

IMMORTAL, invisible, God only wise,
In light inaccessible hid from our eyes,
Most blessèd, most glorious, the Ancient of Days,
Almighty, victorious, thy great Name we praise.

2 Unresting, unhasting, and silent as light,
Nor wanting, nor wasting, thou rulest in might;
Thy justice like mountains high soaring above
Thy clouds, which are fountains of goodness and love.

3 To all, life thou givest—to both great and small;
In all life thou livest, the true life of all;
We blossom and flourish as leaves on the tree,
And wither and perish—but naught changeth thee.

4 Great Father of Glory, pure Father of Light,
Thine angels adore thee, all veiling their sight;
All laud we would render: O help us to see
'Tis only the splendour of light hideth thee.

Walter Chalmers Smith, 1824-1908
Based on 1 Timothy 1: 17

33 (i) MONKLAND 77 and refrain

Composed or adapted by
JOHN ANTES, 1740-1811

THE MAJESTY OF GOD

(ii) HARTS 77 and refrain

Simplified form of a melody by
BENJAMIN MILGROVE, 1731–1810

REFRAIN

LET us with a gladsome mind
Praise the Lord, for he is kind:
For his mercies aye endure,
Ever faithful, ever sure.

2 Let us blaze his Name abroad,
For of gods he is the God:

3 He, with all-commanding might,
Filled the new-made world with
light:

4 He his chosen race did bless
In the wasteful wilderness:

5 All things living he doth feed;
His full hand supplies their need:

6 Let us then with gladsome mind
Praise the Lord, for he is kind:

John Milton, 1608–74
From Psalm 136

34 OMBERSLEY L.M.

WILLIAM HENRY GLADSTONE, 1840–91

LORD of all being, throned afar,
Thy glory flames from sun and star;
Centre and soul of every sphere,
Yet to each loving heart how near!

2 Sun of our life, thy quickening ray
Sheds on our path the glow of day;
Star of our hope, thy softened light
Cheers the long watches of the night.

3 Our midnight is thy smile withdrawn,
Our noontide is thy gracious dawn,

Our rainbow arch thy mercy's sign;
All, save the clouds of sin, are
thine.

4 Lord of all life, below, above,
Whose light is truth, whose warmth
is love,
Before thy ever-blazing throne
We ask no lustre of our own.

5 Grant us thy truth to make us free,
And kindling hearts that burn for
thee,
Till all thy living altars claim
One holy light, one heavenly flame.

Oliver Wendell Holmes, 1809–94

25

35 HANOVER 10 10 11 11

A Supplement to the New Version, 1708
Probably by WILLIAM CROFT, 1678–1727

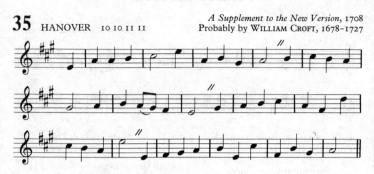

O WORSHIP the King all-glorious above,
O gratefully sing his power and his love,
Our Shield and Defender, the Ancient of Days,
Pavilioned in splendour, and girded with praise.

2 O tell of his might, O sing of his grace,
Whose robe is the light, whose canopy space.
His chariots of wrath the deep thunder-clouds form,
And dark is his path on the wings of the storm.

3 The earth with its store of wonders untold,
Almighty, thy power hath founded of old,
Hath stablished it fast by a changeless decree,
And round it hath cast, like a mantle, the sea.

4 Thy bountiful care what tongue can recite?
It breathes in the air; it shines in the light;
It streams from the hills; it descends to the plain,
And sweetly distils in the dew and the rain.

5 Frail children of dust, and feeble as frail,
In thee do we trust, nor find thee to fail;
Thy mercies how tender, how firm to the end,
Our Maker, Defender, Redeemer, and Friend!

6 O measureless Might! ineffable Love!
While angels delight to hymn thee above,
The humbler creation, though feeble their lays,
With true adoration shall sing to thy praise.

Robert Grant, 1779–1838
From Psalm 104

36 CHURCH TRIUMPHANT L.M.   James William Elliott, 1833-1915

[For No. 305]

A - men.

THE Lord is King! lift up thy voice,
O earth, and all ye heavens, rejoice;
From world to world the joy shall ring,
'The Lord Omnipotent is King!'

2 The Lord is King! who then shall dare
Resist his will, distrust his care,
Or murmur at his wise decrees,
Or doubt his royal promises?

3 The Lord is King! child of the dust,
The Judge of all the earth is just;
Holy and true are all his ways:
Let every creature speak his praise.

4 Come, make your wants, your burdens known;
Christ will present them at the throne;
For he is at the Father's side,
The Man of Love, the Crucified.

5 One Lord, one empire, all secures;
He reigns, and life and death are yours:
Through earth and heaven one song shall ring,
'The Lord Omnipotent is King!'

Josiah Conder, 1789-1855 (altered)

37 AUSTRIAN HYMN 8787. D   FRANZ JOSEPH HAYDN, 1732–1809

A- men.

Alternative tune, LAUS DEO, No. 337

PRAISE the Lord! ye heavens, adore him;
    Praise him, angels, in the height;
Sun and moon, rejoice before him,
    Praise him, all ye stars and light.
Praise the Lord! for he hath spoken;
    Worlds his mighty voice obeyed;
Laws which never shall be broken
    For their guidance hath he made.

2 Praise the Lord! for he is glorious;
    Never shall his promise fail;
God hath made his saints victorious;
    Sin and death shall not prevail.
Praise the God of our salvation!
    Hosts on high, his power proclaim;
Heaven, and earth, and all creation,
    Laud and magnify his Name. Amen.

Foundling Hospital Hymns, *c.* 1796
From Psalm 148

38 LÜBECK 7777

Simplified form of a melody in Freylinghausen's
Geistreiches Gesangbuch, 1704

Alternative tune, MONKLAND, No. 33(i)

SONGS of praise the angels sang,
Heaven with alleluias rang,
When creation was begun,
When God spake, and it was done.

2 Songs of praise awoke the morn
When the Prince of Peace was born;
Songs of praise arose when he
Captive led captivity.

3 Heaven and earth must pass away:
Songs of praise shall crown that day;
God will make new heavens, new earth:
Songs of praise shall hail their birth.

4 And can man alone be dumb,
Till that glorious Kingdom come?
No! the Church delights to raise
Psalms, and hymns, and songs of praise.

5 Saints below, with heart and voice,
Still in songs of praise rejoice,
Learning here, by faith and love,
Songs of praise to sing above.

6 Borne upon their latest breath,
Songs of praise shall conquer death;
Then, amidst eternal joy,
Songs of praise their powers employ.

James Montgomery, 1771-1854

39 CARLISLE S.M.   CHARLES LOCKHART, 1745-1815

STAND up, and bless the Lord,
Ye people of his choice;
Stand up, and bless the Lord your God
With heart and soul and voice.

2   Though high above all praise,
Above all blessing high,
Who would not fear his holy Name,
And laud and magnify?

3   O for the living flame
From his own altar brought,
To touch our lips, our minds inspire,
And wing to heaven our thought!

4   God is our strength and song,
And his salvation ours;
Then be his love in Christ proclaimed
With all our ransomed powers.

5   Stand up, and bless the Lord;
The Lord your God adore;
Stand up, and bless his glorious Name
Henceforth for evermore.

James Montgomery, 1771-1854

40 (i)   WAS LEBET, WAS
        SCHWEBET   12 10 12 10   *Rheinhardt MS.*, Üttingen, 1754

HENRY SMART, 1813–79
The Presbyterian Hymnal, 1877

(ii) MOREDUN 12 10 12 10

WORSHIP the Lord in the beauty of holiness;
  Bow down before him, his glory proclaim;
Gold of obedience and incense of lowliness
  Bring, and adore him; the Lord is his Name!

2 Low at his feet lay thy burden of carefulness;
  High on his heart he will bear it for thee,
Comfort thy sorrows, and answer thy prayerfulness,
  Guiding thy steps as may best for thee be.

3 Fear not to enter his courts, in the slenderness
  Of the poor wealth thou canst reckon as thine;
Truth in its beauty and love in its tenderness,
  These are the offerings to lay on his shrine.

4 These, though we bring them in trembling and fearfulness,
  He will accept for the Name that is dear,
Mornings of joy give for evenings of tearfulness,
  Trust for our trembling, and hope for our fear.

5 Worship the Lord in the beauty of holiness;
  Bow down before him, his glory proclaim;
Gold of obedience and incense of lowliness
  Bring, and adore him; the Lord is his Name!

John Samuel Bewley Monsell, 1811–75

31

MORNING

41 SONG 67 C.M.
(ST. MATTHIAS)

Prys' *Llyfr y Psalmau*, 1621
(rhythm altered)

A - men.

A version with the earlier form of rhythm is at No. 379

Alternative tune, JACKSON, No. 565

PSALM 63, verses 1–4

LORD, thee my God, I'll early seek:
  My soul doth thirst for thee;
My flesh longs in a dry parched land,
  Wherein no waters be:

2 That I thy power may behold,
  And brightness of thy face,
As I have seen thee heretofore
  Within thy holy place.

3 Since better is thy love than life,
  My lips thee praise shall give.
I in thy Name will lift my hands,
  And bless thee while I live.

4 *To Father, Son, and Holy Ghost,*
  The God whom we adore,
Be glory, as it was, and is,
  And shall be evermore. Amen.

42(i) DEUS TUORUM MILITUM
(GRENOBLE) L.M.

Grenoble Antiphoner, 1753

A - men.

MORNING HYMN
(ii) L.M.   FRANÇOIS HIPPOLYTE BARTHÉLÉMON, 1741–1808

A - men.

AWAKE, my soul, and with the sun
Thy daily stage of duty run;
Shake off dull sloth, and joyful rise,
To pay thy morning sacrifice.

2 Wake, and lift up thyself, my heart,
And with the angels bear thy part,
Who all night long unwearied sing
High praise to the eternal King.

3 Lord, I my vows to thee renew;
Disperse my sins as morning dew;
Guard my first springs of thought and will,
And with thyself my spirit fill.

4 Direct, control, suggest, this day,
All I design, or do, or say,
That all my powers, with all their might,
In thy sole glory may unite.

5 *Praise God, from whom all blessings flow;*
Praise him, all creatures here below;
Praise him above, ye heavenly host;
Praise Father, Son, and Holy Ghost. Amen.

Thomas Ken, 1637–1711

43 CHRISTE SANCTORUM 11 11 11 5 *Paris Antiphoner, 1686*

A - men.

Nocte surgentes

FATHER, we praise thee, now the night is over;
Active and watchful, stand we all before thee;
Singing, we offer prayer and meditation:
      Thus we adore thee.

2 Monarch of all things, fit us for thy mansions;
Banish our weakness, health and wholeness sending;
Bring us to heaven, where thy saints united
      Joy without ending.

3 *All-holy Father, Son, and equal Spirit,*
Trinity blessèd, send us thy salvation;
Thine is the glory, gleaming and resounding
      Through all creation. Amen.

10th century or earlier
Tr. Percy Dearmer, 1867-1936

44 DUNOON 10 10 10 10   KENNETH LEIGHTON

MOST glorious Lord of life, that on this day
   Didst make thy triumph over death and sin,
And having harrowed hell, didst bring away
   Captivity thence captive, us to win:

2 This joyous day, dear Lord, with joy begin,
   And grant that we, for whom thou diddest die,
Being with thy dear blood clean washed from sin,
   May live for ever in felicity:

3 And that thy love we, weighing worthily,
   May likewise love thee for the same again;
And for thy sake, that all like dear didst buy,
   With love may one another entertain.

4 So let us love, dear Love, like as we ought,
   Love is the lesson which the Lord us taught.

Edmund Spenser, c. 1552–99

45 SONG 34 (ANGELS' SONG) L.M.　　ORLANDO GIBBONS, 1583-1625
(rhythm altered)

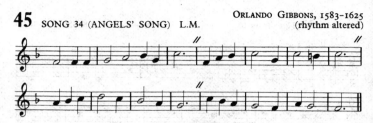

Iam lucis orto sidere

NOW that the daylight fills the sky,
We lift our hearts to God on high,
That he, in all we do or say,
Would keep us free from harm today:

2 Would guard our hearts and tongues from strife,
From anger's din would hide our life,
From all ill sights would turn our eyes,
Would close our ears from vanities:

3 Would keep our inmost conscience pure,
Our souls from folly would secure,
Would bid us check the pride of sense
With due and holy abstinence.

4 So we, when this new day is gone
And night in turn is drawing on,
With conscience by the world unstained,
Shall praise his Name for victory gained.

Before 8th century; tr. John Mason Neale, 1818-66

46 ST. MICHAEL S.M.
(OLD 134TH)　　Derived from the melody for
Psalm 101 in
French-Genevan Psalter, 1551

THIS is the day of light:
Let there be light today;
O Dayspring, rise upon our night,
And chase its gloom away.

2   This is the day of prayer:
        Let earth to heaven draw near;
    Lift up our hearts to seek thee there,
        Come down to meet us here.

3   This is the first of days:
        Send forth thy quickening breath,
    And wake dead souls to love and praise,
        O Vanquisher of death!

John Ellerton, 1826–93

47 MELCOMBE L.M.   SAMUEL WEBBE, the elder, 1740–1816
An Essay on the Church Plain-Chant, 1782

NEW every morning is the love
Our wakening and uprising prove,
Through sleep and darkness safely brought,
Restored to life, and power, and thought.

2 New mercies, each returning day,
    Hover around us while we pray,—
    New perils past, new sins forgiven,
    New thoughts of God, new hopes of heaven.

3 If, on our daily course, our mind
    Be set to hallow all we find,
    New treasures still, of countless price,
    God will provide for sacrifice.

4 The trivial round, the common task,
    Will furnish all we ought to ask,—
    Room to deny ourselves, a road
    To bring us daily nearer God.

5 Only, O Lord, in thy dear love,
    Fit us for perfect rest above;
    And help us, this and every day,
    To live more nearly as we pray.

John Keble, 1792–1866

48 NATIVITY C.M.   HENRY LAHEE, 1826–1912

O LORD of life, thy quickening voice
    Awakes my morning song!
In gladsome words I would rejoice
    That I to thee belong.

2 I see thy light, I feel thy wind;
    The world, it is thy word;
Whatever wakes my heart and mind
    Thy presence is, my Lord.

3 Therefore I choose my highest part,
    And turn my face to thee;
Therefore I stir my inmost heart
    To worship fervently.

4 Lord, let me live and will this day—
    Keep rising from the dead;
Lord, make my spirit good and gay—
    Give me my daily bread.

5 Within my heart speak, Lord, speak on,
    My heart alive to keep,
Till comes the night, and, labour done,
    In thee I fall asleep.

George MacDonald, 1824-1905

49 CHERRY TREE C.M.

Traditional Carol Melody from
Rimbault's *Old English Carols*, 1865

For younger children

THE morning bright, with rosy light,
    Has waked me up from sleep;
Father, I own, thy love alone
    Thy little one doth keep.

2 All through the day, I humbly pray,
    Be thou my Guard and Guide;
My sins forgive, and let me live,
    Blest Jesus, near thy side.

3 O make thy rest within my breast,
    Great Spirit of all grace;
Make me like thee, then shall I be
    Prepared to see thy face.

Thomas Osmond Summers, 1812–82

EVENING

50(i) BINHAM 6466   LENNOX BERKELEY

(ii) ST. COLUMBA 6466   HERBERT STEPHEN IRONS, 1834–1905

Sol praeceps rapitur

THE sun is sinking fast,
   The daylight dies;
Let love awake, and pay
   Her evening sacrifice.

2 As Christ upon the Cross
   His head inclined,
And to his Father's hands
   His parting soul resigned,

3 So now herself my soul
   Would wholly give
Into his sacred charge
   In whom all spirits live;

4 Thus would I live; yet now
   Not I, but he
In all his power and love
   Henceforth alive in me:

5 One sacred Trinity,
   One Lord Divine;
Myself for ever his,
   And he for ever mine.

Anonymous, 18th century
Tr. Edward Caswall, 1814–78

51 PSALM 118
(RENDEZ à DIEU) 9898. D

French–Genevan Psalter, 1551

AS now the day draws near its ending,
  While evening steals o'er earth and sky,
Once more to thee our hymns ascending
  Sound forth thy praises, Lord Most High.
Thine is the splendour of the morning,
  Thine is the evening's tranquil light;
Thine too the veil which till the dawning
  Shrouds all the earth in peaceful night.

2 Maker of worlds beyond our knowing,
  Realms which no human eye can scan,
Yet in thy wondrous love bestowing
  Through Christ thy saving aid to man;
Lord, while the hymns of all creation
  Rise ever to thy throne above,
We too would join in adoration,
  Owning thee God of changeless love.

Jack Copley Winslow
1882–1974
Partly based on a hymn by John Ellerton, 1826–93

52 ANGELUS L.M.   Founded on a melody in *Heilige Seelenlust*, 1657

AT even, when the sun was set,
   The sick, O Lord, around thee lay;
O in what divers pains they met!
   O with what joy they went away!

2 O Saviour Christ, our woes dispel:
   For some are sick, and some are sad,
And some have never loved thee well,
   And some have lost the love they had.

3 O Saviour Christ, thou too art Man;
   Thou hast been troubled, tempted, tried;
Thy kind but searching glance can scan
   The very wounds that shame would hide;

4 Thy touch has still its ancient power;
   No word from thee can fruitless fall:
Hear in this solemn evening hour,
   And in thy mercy heal us all.

Henry Twells, 1823-1900

53 (i) SUNSET 9898   GEORGE GILBERT STOCKS, 1877-1960

EVENING

(ii) GOTTLOB, ES GEHT 9898 Old German Melody

BEFORE the day draws near its ending,
And evening steals o'er earth and sky,
Once more to thee our hymns ascending
Shall speak thy praises, Lord Most High.

2 Thy Name is blessed by countless numbers
In vaster worlds unseen, unknown,
Whose duteous service never slumbers,
In perfect love and faultless tone.

3 Yet thou wilt not despise the weakest
Who here in spirit bend the knee;
Thy Christ hath said, 'Thou, Father, seekest
For such as these to worship thee.'

4 And through the swell of chanting voices,
The blended notes of age and youth,
Thine ear discerns, thy love rejoices,
When hearts rise up to thee in truth.

5 O Light all clear, O Truth most holy,
O boundless Mercy pardoning all,
Before thy feet, abashed and lowly,
With fervent prayer thy children fall:—

6 When we no more on earth adore thee,
And others worship here in turn,
O may we sing that song before thee,
Which none but thy redeemed can learn.

John Ellerton, 1826–93

43

54 (i) MELFORT Irregular   LENNOX BERKELEY

Φῶς ἱλαρὸν ἁγίας δόξης

Hail, glad-dening Light, of his pure glor-y poured Who
is th'im-mor-tal Fa-ther, heav'nly, blest, Ho-li - est of Ho-lies,
Je - sus Christ, our Lord! 2. Now we are come to
the sun's hour of rest, The lights of eve-ning round us
shine. We hymn the Fa-ther, Son, and Ho-ly Spi-rit Di - vine.
3. Wor - thiest art thou at all times to be sung with
un - de - fi - led tongue, Son of our God, Gi -
- ver of life, a - lone: There-fore in all the
world thy glor-ies, Lord, they own. A - men.

Before 4th century; tr. John Keble, 1792–1866

EVENING

(ii) SEBASTE Irregular   JOHN STAINER, 1840–1901

Φῶς ἱλαρὸν ἁγίας δόξης

In free rhythm

Hail, gladdening Light, of his pure glor - y poured

Who is the im-mór-tal Fa - ther, heav'n-ly, blest,

Ho - li-est of Ho-lies, Je - sus Christ, our Lord!

2. Now we are come to the sún's hour of rest,

The lights of eve - ning round us shine.

We hymn the Fa-ther, Son, and Ho-ly Spi - rit Di - vine.

3. Worthiest art thou at áll times to be sung

with un - de - fi - led tongue, Son of our

God, Gi-ver of life, a - lone: There-fore in all the

world thy glor - ies, Lord, they own. A - men.

Before 4th century; tr. John Keble, 1792–1866

45

55 NUNC DIMITTIS 667. D   *Lyons Psalter,* 1547

Φῶς ἱλαρὸν ἁγίας δόξης

O GLADSOME Light, O grace
Of God the Father's face,
The eternal splendour wearing;
Celestial, holy, blest,
Our Saviour Jesus Christ,
Joyful in thine appearing.

2 Now, ere day fadeth quite,
We see the evening light,
Our wonted hymn outpouring;
Father of might unknown,
Thee, his incarnate Son,
And Holy Spirit adoring.

3 To thee of right belongs
All praise of holy songs,
O Son of God, Lifegiver;
Thee therefore, O Most High,
The world doth glorify,
And shall exalt for ever.

Before 4th century
Tr. Robert Bridges, 1844-1930

56 SOLEMNIS HAEC
FESTIVITAS L.M.   *Paris Gradual,* 1685

A - men.

EVENING

O Lux beata Trinitas

O TRINITY, O blessèd Light,
O Unity, most principal,
The fiery sun now leaves our sight:
Cause in our hearts thy beams to
fall.

2 Let us with songs of praise divine
At morn and evening thee implore;
And let our glory, bowed to thine,
Thee glorify for evermore.

3 *To God the Father, glory great,*
And glory to his only Son,
And to the Holy Paraclete,
Both now and still while ages run. Amen.

Attributed to St. Ambrose, 340–97
Tr. Wm. Drummond of Hawthornden, 1585–1649

57 INNSBRUCK 776 778   German Traditional Melody

Nun ruhen alle Wälder

THE duteous day now closeth,
Each flower and tree reposeth,
Shade creeps o'er wild and wood:
Let us, as night is falling,
On God our Maker calling,
Give thanks to him, the Giver
good.

2 Now all the heavenly splendour
Breaks forth in starlight tender
From myriad worlds unknown;
And man, the marvel seeing,
Forgets his selfish being,
For joy of beauty not his own.

3 Awhile his mortal blindness
May miss God's loving-kindness,
And grope in faithless strife:
But, when life's day is over,
Shall death's fair night discover
The fields of everlasting life.

Paul Gerhardt, 1607–76
Par. Robert Bridges, 1844–1930

47

58 AU CLAIR DE LA LUNE
6565 and refrain

Old French Melody

[For No. 653]

A - men.

For younger children

IF I come to Jesus,
  He will make me glad;
He will give me pleasure
When my heart is sad.
  If I come to Jesus,
    Happy shall I be;
  He is gently calling
    Little ones like me.

2 If I come to Jesus,
  He will hear my prayer;
He will love me dearly;
  He my sins did bear.

3 If I come to Jesus,
  He will take my hand,
He will kindly lead me
  To a better land.

Frances (Crosby) van Alstyne, 1820-1915

59 TRES MAGI DE GENTIBUS 7777

Catholische Geistliche Gesänge,
Andernach, 1608

For younger children

JESUS Christ, our Lord and King,
Listen to the prayer we sing
Now the lovely light, that shone
Through our happy day, has gone.

2 Thou, by whom the birds were fed,
Gavest us our daily bread;
Thou the gentle dark hast sent—
May we sleep in hushed content.

3 Bless thy grateful children now,
As our sleepy heads we bow;
May thy Holy Spirit's might
Guard us through the hours of night.

4 Teach us, Lord, thy Way to know,
We must in thy pattern grow;
And, when thou at last shalt come,
Take us to thy heavenly home.

Based on a hymn by
Emily Mary Shapcote, 1828-1909

The following are also suitable

No.
489 I joy'd when to the house of God
347 Praise ye the Lord. God's praise within
348 Sing a new song to Jehovah
143 The spacious firmament on high
236 Children of Jerusalem
359 Praise the Lord, his glories show
455 Angel voices, ever singing

Certain hymns in Part III, *Response to the Word of God*, Section 1 (*Adoration and Thanksgiving*) and Section 2 (*Affirmation*) are also suitable

APPROACH TO GOD

CONFESSION AND SUPPLICATION

60

KYRIE ELEISON

First Form

Minister   Lord have mercy
People   Christ have mercy
Minister   Lord have mercy

Second Form

61

TRISAGION
(Early Church)

GEORGE THALBEN-BALL

Ho - ly God, ho - ly and migh - ty, ho - ly and im-

-mor - tal, have mer - cy up - on us.

Solo or Unison

Ho - ly God, ho - ly and migh - ty, ho - ly and im-

-mor - tal, have mer - cy up - on us.

Ho - ly God, ho - ly and migh - ty, ho - ly and im-

-mor - tal, have mer - cy up - on us.

For Trisagion *with* The Reproaches, *see No.* 240

62

GLORIA IN EXCELSIS

KENNETH LEIGHTON

In a brisk four-time
Intro. ad lib.

Energico e ritmico

Glor - y be to God on — high,

and in earth — peace, good-will to-wards men. We

praise thee, we bless thee, we wor - ship thee, we

glor-i - fy — thee, We give thanks to — thee for thy great —

glor-y, O Lord God, heaven-ly King, God the Fa - ther Al-

rit. *mf* *Slower (but not too slow)*

- migh-ty.___ O Lord, the on-ly be-got-ten Son, Je - sus

Christ; O Lord God, Lamb of God, Son of the Fa-ther, That

ta-kest a-way the sins of the world, have mer-cy up-on us.

(more intense)

Thou that ta-kest a - way the sins of the world, have mer-cy up-

-on us. Thou that ta - kest a - way the sins of the

world, re - ceive our_ prayer. Thou that sit - test at the

right hand of God the_ Fa - ther, have mer - cy up -on us._

Tempo I

For

thou on - ly art ho - ly, thou on - ly art the_

Lord; Thou on - ly, O Christ, with the Ho - ly

Ghost, art most high in the glor - y of God the_ Fa - ther.

A - - - - - - men.

Alternative Amen
(*rit. poco* ....

A - - - - - - men.

63   Tone iv ending 4

PSALM 51, verses 1–4, 6–12

HAVE mercy upon me O God according to thy ' loving-kindness:
  according to the multitude of thy tender mercies blot ' out my transgressions.

Wash me throughly from ' mine iniquity:
  and ' cleanse me from my sins.

For I acknowledge ' my transgressions:
  and my sin is ' ever before me.

Against thee thee only have I sinned and done this evil ' in thy sight:
  that thou mightest be justified when thou speakest   and be ' clear when thou
  judgest.

Behold thou desirest truth in the ' inward parts:
  and in the hidden part thou shalt make ' me to know wisdom.

Purge me with hyssop and I ' shall be clean:
  wash me and I ' shall be whiter than snow.

Make me to hear ' joy and gladness:
  that the bones which thou hast ' broken may re-joice.

Hide thy face ' from my sins:
  and blot out ' all mine iniqui-ties.

Create in me a clean ' heart O God:
  and renew a right ' spirit within me.

Cast me not away ' from thy presence:
  and take not thy ' Holy Spirit from me.

Restore unto me the joy of ' thy salvation:
  and uphold me ' with thy free spirit.

Glory be to the Father and ' to the Son;
  and ' to the Holy Ghost :

As it was in the beginning is now and ' ever shall be :
  . world ' without end. Amen.

CONFESSION AND SUPPLICATION

64 SONG 24   10 10 10 10   ORLANDO GIBBONS, 1583-1625

Alternative tune, SONG 22, No. 108

From PSALM 51, verses 1-12

O GOD be gracious to me in thy love,
And in thy mercy pardon my misdeeds;
Wash me from guilt and cleanse me from my sin,
For well I know the evil I have done.

2 Against thee, Lord, thee only have I sinned,
And what to thee is hateful have I done;
I own thy righteousness in charging me,
I know thee justified should'st thou condemn.

3 Take hyssop, sprinkle me and make me clean,
Wash me and make me whiter than the snow;
Fill me with gladness and rejoicing, Lord,
And let my broken frame know joy once more.

4 Turn thou thy face, O God, from my misdeeds,
And blot out all the sins that sully me;
Create a clean and contrite heart in me,
Renew my soul in faithfulness and love.

5 Drive me not from thy presence, gracious Lord,
Nor keep thy Holy Spirit far from me;
Restore my soul with thy salvation's joy,
And with a willing spirit strengthen me.

Ian Pitt-Watson
The New English Bible (*adapted*)

65 CHESHIRE C.M.   Este's *Psalter*, 1592 (rhythm slightly altered)

A - men.

PSALM 130, verses 1–6a, 7b, 8

LORD, from the depths to thee I cried.
    My voice, Lord, do thou hear:
Unto my supplications' voice
    Give an attentive ear.

2 Lord, who shall stand, if thou, O Lord,
    Shouldest mark iniquity?
But yet with thee forgiveness is,
    That feared thou mayest be.

3 I wait for God, my soul doth wait,
    My hope is in his word.
More than they that for morning watch,
    My soul waits for the Lord;

4 Redemption also plenteous
    Is ever found with him.
And from all his iniquities
    He Israel shall redeem.

5 *To Father, Son, and Holy Ghost,*
    The God whom we adore,
Be glory, as it was, and is,
    And shall be evermore. Amen.

66

JOHN CURRIE

For an explanation of the pointing system, see
Introductory Notes to the Music

PSALM 130

OUT of the depths have I cried unto thee O Lord.

Lord hear my voice   let thine ears be attentive to the voice of my supplications.

If thou Lord shouldest mark iniquities   O Lord who shall stand.

But there is forgiveness with thee   that thou mayest be feared.

I wait for the Lord my soul doth wait   and in his word do I hope.

My soul waiteth for the Lord more than they that watch for the morning   I say more than they that watch for the morning.

Let Israel hope in the Lord   for with the Lord there is mercy and with him is plenteous redemption.

And he shall redeem Israel from all his iniquities.

Glory be to the Father and to the Son   and to the Holy Ghost

As it was in the beginning is now and ever shall be   world without end. Amen.

67

PSALM 130 (Gelineau Version)

PSALM *Choir or Solo*

1	Out of the	depths	I cry to you,	O Lord,
2	If you, O	Lord,	should mark	our guilt,
3	My	soul	is waiting for	the Lord,
4	Be - cause with	the Lord	there is	mercy
5	To the	Father	Al - mighty	give glory,

1	Lord,	hear	my	voice!
2	Lord, who would	sur - vive?
3	I count	on	his	word:
4	and	fullness	of re -	demption,
5	give	glory	to his	Son,

1	O	let	your	ears be	at - tentive
2	But with	you	is	found	for - giveness:
3	My	soul	is	longing for the	Lord
4	Israel	in - deed he will re -	deem
5	to the	Spirit most	Holy	give	praise,

1	to the	voice	of my	plead - ing.
2	for	this	we re -	vere you.
3	more than	watch - man for	day - break.
4	from	all	its in - i - quity.
5	whose	reign	is for	ev - er.

It is suggested that either of the following Antiphons be sung by the congregation after each verse of the psalm

ANTIPHON 1 *All*

($\downarrow$ = $\circ$ of psalm)

I place all my trust in you, my

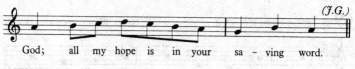

(*J.G.*)

God; all my hope is in your sa - ving word.

ANTIPHON 2 *All*

($\textstyle\frac{1}{2}$ = o of psalm)

(*A.G.M.*)

With the Lord there is mer - cy with - out end.

68 SURSUM CORDA 10 10 10 10   ALFRED MORTON SMITH, 1879-1971

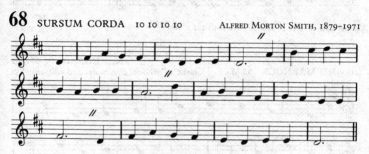

FROM PSALM 139

THOU art before me, Lord, thou art behind,
And thou above me hast spread out thy hand;
Such knowledge is too wonderful for me,
Too high to grasp, too great to understand.

2 Then whither from thy Spirit shall I go,
And whither from thy presence shall I flee?
If I ascend to heaven thou art there,
And in the lowest depths I meet with thee.

3 If I should take my flight into the dawn,
If I should dwell on ocean's farthest shore,
Thy mighty hand would rest upon me still,
And thy right hand would guard me evermore.

4 If I should say 'Darkness will cover me,
And I shall hide within the veil of night',
Surely the darkness is not dark to thee,
The night is as the day, the darkness light.

5 Search me, O God, search me and know my heart,
Try me, O God, my mind and spirit try;
Keep me from any path that gives thee pain,
And lead me in the everlasting way.

Ian Pitt-Watson
The New English Bible (*adapted*)

69(i)   ST. FULBERT   C.M.   HENRY JOHN GAUNTLETT, 1805-76

If the tune at No. 29 is used here omit the Amen

(ii)   KILMARNOCK   C.M.   NEIL DOUGALL, 1776-1862
Clarke's *Parochial Psalmody*, 2nd edition, 1831

PARAPHRASE 30

COME, let us to the Lord our God
 With contrite hearts return;
Our God is gracious, nor will leave
 The desolate to mourn.

2 His voice commands the tempest forth,
 And stills the stormy wave;
And though his arm be strong to smite,
 'Tis also strong to save.

3 Long hath the night of sorrow reigned,
 The dawn shall bring us light:
God shall appear, and we shall rise
 With gladness in his sight.

4 Our hearts, if God we seek to know,
 Shall know him, and rejoice;
His coming like the morn shall be,
 Like morning songs his voice.

5 As dew upon the tender herb,
 Diffusing fragrance round;
As showers that usher in the spring,
 And cheer the thirsty ground:

6 So shall his presence bless our souls,
 And shed a joyful light;
That hallowed morn shall chase away
 The sorrows of the night.

Scottish Paraphrases, 1781
From Hosea 6: 1-4

70 (i) LEONI 6666. D

Hebrew Melody, as adapted *c.* 1770

A - men.

(ii) LEUCHARS 6666. D

THOMAS LEGERWOOD HATELY, 1815–67
Scottish Psalmody, 1858

A - men.

PSALM 143(ii), from verses 1, 6, 8

O, HEAR my prayer, Lord,
Unto me answer make,
And, in thy righteousness,
Upon me pity take.
Lo, I do stretch my hands
To thee, my help alone;
For thou well understands
All my complaint and moan:

2 My thirsting soul desires,
And longeth after thee,
As thirsty ground requires
With rain refreshed to be.
Because I trust in thee,
O Lord, cause me to hear
Thy loving-kindness free,
When morning doth appear:

3 Cause me to know the way
Wherein my path should be;
For why, my soul on high
I do lift up to thee.
*Now glory be to God
The Father, and the Son,
And to the Holy Ghost,
All-glorious Three in One.* Amen.

71 ST. MARY C.M.　　　　　　　　　　　　Prys' *Llyfr y Psalmau*, 1621

A-men.

Alternative tune, SALZBURG, No. 72(ii)

PSALM 61, verses 1-4

O GOD, give ear unto my cry;
　　Unto my prayer attend.
From the utmost corner of the land
　　My cry to thee I'll send.

2 What time my heart is overwhelm'd
　　And in perplexity,
Do thou me lead unto the Rock
　　That higher is than I.

3 For thou hast for my refuge been
　　A shelter by thy power;
And for defence against my foes
　　Thou hast been a strong tower.

4 Within thy tabernacle I
　　For ever will abide;
And under covert of thy wings
　　With confidence me hide.

5 *To Father, Son, and Holy Ghost,*
　　The God whom we adore,
Be glory, as it was, and is,
　　And shall be evermore. Amen.

72 (i) ST. PAUL (ABERDEEN) C.M.

Chalmers' *Collection*,
Aberdeen, 1749

A version with the earlier form of rhythm is at No. 395 (ii)

(ii) SALZBURG C.M.

JOHANN MICHAEL HAYDN, 1737–1806 (adapted)

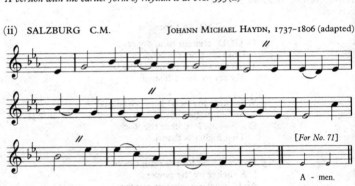

PARAPHRASE 2

O GOD of Bethel! by whose hand
  Thy people still are fed;
Who through this weary pilgrimage
  Hast all our fathers led:

2 Our vows, our prayers, we now
    present
  Before thy throne of grace:
God of our fathers! be the God
  Of their succeeding race.

3 Through each perplexing path of
    life
  Our wandering footsteps guide;
Give us each day our daily bread,
  And raiment fit provide.

4 O spread thy covering wings around,
  Till all our wanderings cease,
And at our Father's loved abode
  Our souls arrive in peace.

5 Such blessings from thy gracious hand
  Our humble prayers implore;
And thou shalt be our chosen God,
  And portion evermore.

Scottish Paraphrases, 1781
From Genesis 28: 20–22

73 ABBEY C.M.   *Scottish Psalter, 1615*

A - men.

PSALM 40, verses 1-4

I WAITED for the Lord my God,
  And patiently did bear;
At length to me he did incline
  My voice and cry to hear.

2 He took me from a fearful pit,
  And from the miry clay,
And on a rock he set my feet,
  Establishing my way.

3 He put a new song in my mouth,
  Our God to magnify:
Many shall see it, and shall fear,
  And on the Lord rely.

4 O blessèd is the man whose trust
  Upon the Lord relies;
Respecting not the proud, nor such
  As turn aside to lies.

5 *To Father, Son, and Holy Ghost,*
  The God whom we adore,
Be glory, as it was, and is,
  And shall be evermore. Amen.

74 FRANCONIA S.M.

WILLIAM HENRY HAVERGAL, 1793–1870,
adapted from a tune in König's
Harmonischer Liederschatz, 1738

A - men.

Alternative tune, ST. BRIDE, No. 410

PSALM 25, verses 4, 5a, 6–10

SHOW me thy ways, O Lord;
    Thy paths, O teach thou me:
And do thou lead me in thy truth,
    Therein my teacher be:

2 Thy tender mercies, Lord,
    I pray thee to recall,
And loving-kindnesses; for they
    Have been through ages all.

3 My sins and faults of youth
    Do thou, O Lord, forget:
After thy mercy think on me,
    And for thy goodness great.

4 God good and upright is:
    The way he'll sinners show.
The meek in judgment he will guide,
    And make his path to know.

5 The whole paths of the Lord
    Are truth and mercy sure,
To those that do his covenant keep,
    And testimonies pure.

6 *To thee be glory, Lord,*
    Whom heaven and earth adore,
To Father, Son, and Holy Ghost,
    One God for evermore. Amen.

75 (i) AUS DER TIEFE (HEINLEIN) 7777

Nürnbergisches Gesangbuch, 1676–7 (altered)
Possibly by MARTIN HERBST, 1654–81

A - men.

(ii) ST. DUNSTAN 7777

RICHARD REDHEAD, 1820–1901
Church Hymn Tunes, 1853

A - men.

PSALM 85(ii), verses 1, 2, 5–7

LORD, thine heart in love hath
  yearned
On thy lost and fallen land;
Israel's race is homeward turned,
  Thou hast freed thy captive band:

Thou hast borne thy people's sin,
  Covered all their deeds of ill;
All thy wrath is gathered in,
  And thy burning anger still.

3 Wilt thou not in mercy turn?
  Turn, and be our life again,
That thy people's heart may burn
  With the gladness of thy reign.

4 Show us now thy tender love;
  Thy salvation, Lord, impart;
I the voice divine would prove,
  Listening in my silent heart:

5 Listening what the Lord will say—
  'Peace' to all that own his will:
To his saints that love his way,
  'Peace,' and 'turn no more to ill'.

6 *Glory to the Father be,*
  Glory, Christ our Lord, to thee,
Glory to the Holy Ghost,
  Praised by men and Heavenly Host. Amen.

76(i) OLD 18TH 86 886

Derived from the melody for Psalm 18 i
English Psalter, 156

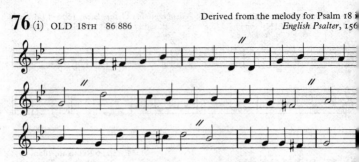

(ii) REPTON 86 886 (6)   CHARLES HUBERT HASTINGS PARRY, 1848–191

DEAR Lord and Father of man-
    kind,
  Forgive our foolish ways;
Reclothe us in our rightful mind;
In purer lives thy service find,
  * In deeper reverence, praise.

2 In simple trust like theirs who
    heard,
  Beside the Syrian sea,
The gracious calling of the Lord,
Let us, like them, without a word
  Rise up and follow thee.

3 O Sabbath rest by Galilee!
  O calm of hills above,
Where Jesus knelt to share with thee
  The silence of eternity,
    Interpreted by love!

4 With that deep hush subduing all
  Our words and works that drow
The tender whisper of thy call,
As noiseless let thy blessing fall
  As fell thy manna down.

5 Drop thy still dews of quietness,
  Till all our strivings cease;
Take from our souls the strain an
    stress,
And let our ordered lives confess
  The beauty of thy peace.

6 Breathe through the heats of ou
    desire
  Thy coolness and thy balm;
Let sense be dumb, let flesh retire
Speak through the earthquake
    wind, and fire,
  O still small voice of calm!

John Greenleaf Whittier, 1807–9

  * *The last line of each verse is to be repeated when Tune* (ii) REPTON *is sung*

77 (i) SONG 5 L.M.   ORLANDO GIBBONS, 1583–1625 (rhythm altered)

(ii) RIVAULX L.M.   JOHN BACCHUS DYKES, 1823–76

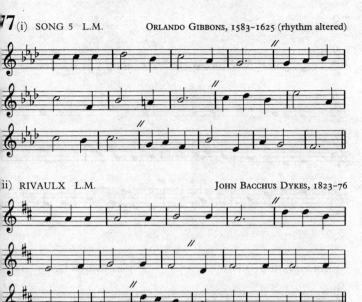

FATHER of heaven, whose love profound
A ransom for our souls hath found,
Before thy throne we sinners bend;
To us thy pardoning love extend.

2 Almighty Son, Incarnate Word,
Our Prophet, Priest, Redeemer, Lord
Before thy throne we sinners bend;
To us thy saving grace extend.

3 Eternal Spirit, by whose breath
The soul is raised from sin and death,
Before thy throne we sinners bend;
To us thy quickening power extend.

4 Jehovah—Father, Spirit, Son—
Mysterious Godhead, Three in One,
Before thy throne we sinners bend;
Grace, pardon, life to us extend.

Edward Cooper, 1770–1833

78(i) ABERYSTWYTH 7777. D   JOSEPH PARRY, 1841–190[

(ii) HOLLINGSIDE 7777. D   JOHN BACCHUS DYKES, 1823–76

JESUS, Lover of my soul,
  Let me to thy bosom fly,
While the nearer waters roll,
  While the tempest still is high;
Hide me, O my Saviour, hide,
  Till the storm of life is past;
Safe into the haven guide,
  O receive my soul at last!

2 Other refuge have I none;
  Hangs my helpless soul on thee;
Leave, ah! leave me not alone;
  Still support and comfort me.
All my trust on thee is stayed;
  All my help from thee I bring;
Cover my defenceless head
  With the shadow of thy wing.

3 Thou, O Christ, art all I want;
   More than all in thee I find;
Raise the fallen, cheer the faint,
   Heal the sick, and lead the blind.
Just and holy is thy Name,
   I am all unrighteousness;
False and full of sin I am,
   Thou art full of truth and grace.

4 Plenteous grace with thee is found,
   Grace to cover all my sin;
Let the healing streams abound;
   Make and keep me pure within.
Thou of life the fountain art,
   Freely let me take of thee;
Spring thou up within my heart,
   Rise to all eternity.

Charles Wesley, 1707-88

79 SAFFRON WALDEN 8886   ARTHUR HENRY BROWN, 1830-1926

JUST as I am, without one plea
But that thy blood was shed for me,
And that thou bidd'st me come to
   thee,
   O Lamb of God, I come.

2 Just as I am, though tossed about
   With many a conflict, many a
      doubt,
   Fightings and fears within, without,
      O Lamb of God, I come.

3 Just as I am, thou wilt receive,
   Wilt welcome, pardon, cleanse, relieve;
   Because thy promise I believe,
      O Lamb of God, I come.

4 Just as I am—thy love unknown
   Has broken every barrier down—
   Now to be thine, yea, thine alone,
      O Lamb of God, I come.

5 Just as I am, of that free love
   The breadth, length, depth, and height to prove,
   Here for a season, then above,—
      O Lamb of God, I come.

Charlotte Elliott, 1789-1871

80 SOUTHWELL S.M.   Damon's *The Psalmes of David*, 1579 (altered)

A version with the later form of rhythm is at No. 466
Alternative tune, ST. BRIDE, No. 410

Μνώεο Χριστέ

LORD Jesus, think on me,
And purge away my sin;
From earthborn passions set me free,
And make me pure within.

2 Lord Jesus, think on me,
With care and woe oppressed;
Let me thy loving servant be,
And taste thy promised rest.

3 Lord Jesus, think on me,
Amid the battle's strife;
In all my pain and misery
Be thou my health and life.

4 Lord Jesus, think on me,
Nor let me go astray;
Through darkness and perplexity
Point thou the heavenly way.

5 Lord Jesus, think on me,
When flows the tempest high:
When on doth rush the enemy,
O Saviour, be thou nigh.

6 Lord Jesus, think on me,
That, when the flood is past,
I may the eternal brightness see,
And share thy joy at last.

Synesius of Cyrene, c. 375-430
Tr. Allen William Chatfield, 1808-96

81 (i) OLIVET 664 6664   LOWELL MASON, 1792-1872
Spiritual Songs for Social Worship, 1831

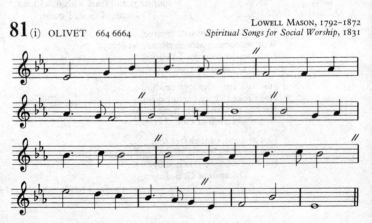

ii) DENBIGH 664 6664

Welsh Melody from
Llyfr Tonau Cynulleidfaol, 1859

MY faith looks up to thee,
Thou Lamb of Calvary,
   Saviour Divine:
Now hear me while I pray;
Take all my guilt away;
O let me from this day
   Be wholly thine.

2 May thy rich grace impart
Strength to my fainting heart,
   My zeal inspire;
As thou hast died for me,
O may my love to thee
Pure, warm, and changeless be,
   A living fire.

3 While life's dark maze I tread,
And griefs around me spread,
   Be thou my Guide;
Bid darkness turn to day,
Wipe sorrow's tears away,
Nor let me ever stray
   From thee aside.

4 When ends life's transient dream,
When death's cold, sullen stream
   Shall o'er me roll,
Blest Saviour, then, in love,
Fear and distrust remove;
O bear me safe above,
   A ransomed soul.

Ray Palmer, 1808-87

82 WIGTOWN C.M.   *Scottish Psalter, 1635*

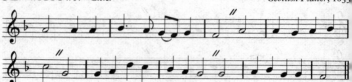

Alternative tune, CAITHNESS, No. 395 (i)

Śiṣyahĩ gaṇāyā nahĩ yogya jo tayālā

ONE who is all unfit to count
    As scholar in thy school,
Thou of thy love hast named a friend—
    O kindness wonderful!

2 So weak am I, O gracious Lord,
    So all unworthy thee,
That even the dust upon thy feet
    Outweighs me utterly.

3 Thou dwellest in unshadowed light,
    All sin and shame above—
That thou shouldst bear our sin and shame,
    How can I tell such love?

4 Ah, did not he the heavenly throne
    A little thing esteem,
And not unworthy for my sake
    A mortal body deem?

5 When in his flesh they drove the nails,
    Did he not all endure?
What name is there to fit a life
    So patient and so pure?

6 So, Love itself in human form,
    For love of me he came;
I cannot look upon his face
    For shame, for bitter shame.

7 If there is aught of worth in me,
    It comes from thee alone;
Then keep me safe, for so, O Lord,
    Thou keepest but thine own.

From the Marathi of Narayan Vaman Tilak, 1862–1919
Tr. Nicol Macnicol, 1870–1952

83 PETRA (REDHEAD No. 76) 7777 77

RICHARD REDHEAD, 1820–1901
Church Hymn Tunes, 1853

ROCK of Ages, cleft for me,
Let me hide myself in thee;
Let the water and the blood,
From thy riven side which flowed,
Be of sin the double cure,
Cleanse me from its guilt and power.

2 Not the labours of my hands
Can fulfil thy law's demands;
Could my zeal no respite know,
Could my tears for ever flow,
All for sin could not atone:
Thou must save, and thou alone.

3 Nothing in my hand I bring,
Simply to thy cross I cling;
Naked, come to thee for dress;
Helpless, look to thee for grace;
Foul, I to the fountain fly;
Wash me, Saviour, or I die.

4 While I draw this fleeting breath,
When mine eyelids close in death,
When I soar through tracts unknown,
See thee on thy judgment throne,
Rock of Ages, cleft for me,
Let me hide myself in thee.

Augustus Montague Toplady, 1740–78

75

84 OLD 124TH 10 10 10 10 10

French–Genevan Psalter, 1551
(rhythm altered)

TURN back, O man, forswear thy foolish ways;
Old now is earth, and none may count her days,
Yet thou, her child, whose head is crowned with flame,
Still wilt not hear thine inner God proclaim—
'Turn back, O man, forswear thy foolish ways.'

2 Earth might be fair and all men glad and wise:
Age after age their tragic empires rise,
Built while they dream, and in that dreaming weep,
Would man but wake from out his haunted sleep,
Earth might be fair and all men glad and wise.

3 Earth shall be fair, and all her people one:
Nor till that hour shall God's whole will be done.
Now, even now, once more from earth to sky,
Peals forth in joy man's old undaunted cry—
'Earth shall be fair, and all her folk be one.'

Clifford Bax, 1886-1962

85 SONG 67
(ST. MATTHIAS) C.M.

Prys' Llyfr y Psalmau, 1621
(rhythm altered)

A version with the earlier form of rhythm is at No. 379

O FOR a heart to praise my God!
A heart from sin set free;
A heart that always feels thy blood,
So freely shed for me;

2 A heart resigned, submissive, meek,
My great Redeemer's throne,
Where only Christ is heard to speak,
Where Jesus reigns alone;

3 A humble, lowly, contrite heart,
   Believing, true, and clean,
   Which neither life nor death can part
   From him that dwells within;

4 A heart in every thought renewed,
   And full of love divine,
   Perfect and right and pure and good,
   A copy, Lord, of thine!

5 Thy nature, gracious Lord, impart;
   Come quickly from above;
   Write thy new Name upon my heart,
   Thy new, best Name of Love.

Charles Wesley, 1707-88

86 STONELAW 10 10 10 10   THOMAS WILSON

Je te salue, mon certain Rédempteur

1 GREET thee, who my sure Redeemer art,
   My only Trust and Saviour of my heart,
   Who pain didst undergo for my poor sake;
   I pray thee from our hearts all cares to take.

2 Thou art the King of mercy and of grace,
   Reigning omnipotent in every place:
   So come, O King, and our whole being sway;
   Shine on us with the light of thy pure day.

3 Thou art the Life, by which alone we live,
   And all our substance and our strength receive;
   Sustain us by thy faith and by thy power,
   And give us strength in every trying hour.

4 Thou hast the true and perfect gentleness,
   No harshness hast thou and no bitterness:
   O grant to us the grace we find in thee,
   That we may dwell in perfect unity.

5 Our hope is in no other save in thee;
   Our faith is built upon thy promise free;
   Lord, give us peace, and make us calm and sure,
   That in thy strength we evermore endure.

Attributed to John Calvin, 1509-64
Tr. Elizabeth Lee Smith, 1817-98 (altered)

87 SLANE 10 10 10 10 irregular   Irish Traditional Melody

Ꝟᴜᴧab ᴛú ᴍo ᴠoɩle

1. Be thou my Vi - sion, O Lord of my heart;
2. Be thou my Wis - dom, thou my true Word;
3. Be thou my bat - tle-shield, sword for the fight;
4. Riches I heed not, nor man's emp - ty praise,
5. High King of Hea - ven, af - ter vic - to - ry won,

Naught be all else to me, save that thou art,
I ev - er with thee, thou with me, Lord;
Be thou my dig - ni - ty, thou my de - light,
Thou mine in - her - it - ance, now and al - ways:
May I reach hea - ven's joys, O bright heav'n's Sun!

Thou my best thought, by day or by night,
Thou my great Fa - ther, I thy true son;
Thou my soul's shel - ter, thou my high tower:
Thou and thou on - ly, first in my heart,
Heart of my own heart, what - ev - er be - fall,

Wak - ing or sleep - ing, thy pres - ence my light.
Thou in me dwell - ing, and I with thee one.
Raise thou me heaven-ward, O Power of my power.
High King of Hea - ven, my trea - sure thou art.
Still be my Vi - sion, O Ru - ler of all.

Ancient Irish, tr. Mary Byrne, 1880–1931,
versified Eleanor Hull, 1860–1935

88 RHUDDLAN 8787 87　　　　　　　　　　　　　Welsh Traditional Melody

GOD of grace and God of glory,
　On thy people pour thy power;
Now fulfil thy Church's story;
　Bring her bud to glorious flower.
Grant us wisdom, grant us courage,
　For the facing of this hour.

2 Lo, the hosts of evil round us
　　Scorn thy Christ, assail his ways;
From the fears that long have bound us
　　Free our hearts to faith and praise.
Grant us wisdom, grant us courage,
　　For the living of these days.

3 Cure thy children's warring madness,
　　Bend our pride to thy control;
Shame our wanton selfish gladness,
　　Rich in goods and poor in soul.
Grant us wisdom, grant us courage,
　　Lest we miss thy kingdom's goal.

4 Set our feet on lofty places,
　　Gird our lives that they may be
Armoured with all Christ-like graces
　　In the fight to set men free.
Grant us wisdom, grant us courage,
　　That we fail not man nor thee.

*Harry Emerson Fosdick, 1878–1969, and
Compilers of* The BBC Hymn Book

79

89 (i) MANNHEIM 8787 87

Adapted from a chorale in
Filitz' *Choralbuch*, 184[...]

(ii) CWM RHONDDA 8787 87 (7)

JOHN HUGHES (Pontypridd), 1873–193[...]

Arglwydd, arwain trwy'r anialwch

GUIDE me, O thou great Jehovah,
   Pilgrim through this barren land;
I am weak, but thou art mighty;
   Hold me with thy powerful hand:
      Bread of heaven, Bread of heaven,
   *Feed me till my want is o'er.

2 Open now the crystal fountain,
   Whence the healing stream doth flow;
Let the fire and cloudy pillar
   Lead me all my journey through:
      Strong Deliverer, strong Deliverer,
   Be thou still my strength and shield.

* *When tune* (ii) CWM RHONDDA *is used, the last line of each verse
must be repeated*

3 When I tread the verge of Jordan,
  Bid my anxious fears subside!
Death of death, and hell's Destruction,
  Land me safe on Canaan's side!
    Songs of praises, songs of praises,
    I will ever give to thee.

William Williams, 1717-91
Tr. Peter Williams, 1727-96

90 CORINTH 8787 87
(TANTUM ERGO)

From (the elder) Samuel Webbe's
*An Essay on the Church
Plain-Chant*, 1782

Alternative tune, MANNHEIM, No. 89(i)

LEAD us, heavenly Father, lead us
  O'er the world's tempestuous sea;
Guard us, guide us, keep us, feed us,
  For we have no help but thee;
    Yet possessing every blessing
    If our God our Father be.

2 Saviour, breathe forgiveness o'er us;
    All our weakness thou dost know;
  Thou didst tread this earth before us,
    Thou didst feel its keenest woe;
      Lone and dreary, faint and weary,
      Through the desert thou didst go.

3 Spirit of our God, descending,
    Fill our hearts with heavenly joy,
  Love with every passion blending,
    Pleasure that can never cloy;
      Thus provided, pardoned, guided,
      Nothing can our peace destroy.

James Edmeston, 1791-1867

91 TALLIS' ORDINAL C.M. THOMAS TALLIS, c. 1505-85

DEFEND me, Lord, from hour to
 hour,
 And bless thy servant's way;
Increase thy Holy Spirit's power
 Within me day by day.

2 Help me to be what I should be,
 And do what I should do,
And ever with thy Spirit free
 My daily life renew.

3 Grant me the courage from above
 Which thou dost give to all
Who hear thy word and know thy
 love
 And answer to thy call.

4 So may I daily grow in grace,
 Continuing thine alone,
Until I come to sing thy praise
 With saints around thy throne.

George Snow

92 MINIVER 10 11 11 12 CYRIL VINCENT TAYLOR

Alternative tune, SLANE, No. 428

LORD of all hopefulness, Lord of all joy,
Whose trust, ever childlike, no cares could destroy,
Be there at our waking, and give us, we pray,
Your bliss in our hearts, Lord, at the break of the day.

82

2 Lord of all eagerness, Lord of all faith,
Whose strong hands were skilled at the plane and the lathe,
Be there at our labours, and give us, we pray,
Your strength in our hearts, Lord, at the noon of the day.

3 Lord of all kindliness, Lord of all grace,
Your hands swift to welcome, your arms to embrace,
Be there at our homing, and give us, we pray,
Your love in our hearts, Lord, at the eve of the day.

4 Lord of all gentleness, Lord of all calm,
Whose voice is contentment, whose presence is balm,
Be there at our sleeping, and give us, we pray,
Your peace in our hearts, Lord, at the end of the day.

Jan Struther, 1901-53

93 BATTISHILL 7777

Simplified version of a melody by
JONATHAN BATTISHILL, 1738-1801

LOVING Shepherd of thy sheep,
Keep me, Lord, in safety keep;
Nothing can thy power withstand;
None can pluck me from thy hand.

2 Loving Shepherd, thou didst give
Thine own life that I might live;
May I love thee day by day,
Gladly thy sweet will obey.

3 Loving Shepherd, ever near,
Teach me still thy voice to hear;
Suffer not my feet to stray
From the straight and narrow way.

4 Where thou leadest may I go,
Walking in thy steps below;
Then, before thy Father's throne,
Jesus, claim me for thine own.

Jane Eliza Leeson, 1809-81 (altered)
From St. John 10: 11, 27, 28

94 ST. FULBERT C.M.

HENRY JOHN GAUNTLETT, 1805-76

Alternative tune, PRAETORIUS, No. 459

O JESUS, strong and pure and true,
　Before thy feet we bow;
The grace of earlier years renew,
　And lead us onward now.

2 The joyous life that year by year
　　Within these walls is stored,
　The golden hope, the gladsome cheer,
　　We bring to thee, O Lord.

3 Our faith endow with keener powers,
　　With warmer glow our love;
And draw these halting hearts of ours
　From earth to things above.

4 In paths our bravest ones have trod,
　　O make us strong to go,
That we may give our lives to God,
　In serving man below.

5 So hence shall flow fresh strength and grace,
　　As from a full-fed spring,
To make the world a better place,
　And life a worthier thing.

　　　　　William Walsham How, 1823-97

95 LOVE UNKNOWN 6666 88

JOHN IRELAND, 1879-1962
The Public School Hymn Book, 1919

Ἄτερ ἀρχῆς ἀπέραντον

O LIGHT that knew no dawn,
　That shines to endless day,
All things in earth and heaven
　Are lustred by thy ray;
No eye can to thy throne ascend,
Nor mind thy brightness comprehend.

2　Thy grace, O Father, give,
　　That I may serve in fear;
　Above all boons, I pray,
　　Grant me thy voice to hear;
From sin thy child in mercy free,
And let me dwell in light with thee:

3　That, cleansed from stain of sin,
　　I may meet homage give,
　And, pure in heart, behold
　　Thy beauty while I live;
Clean hands in holy worship raise,
And thee, O Christ my Saviour, praise.

84

4   In supplication meek
     To thee I bend the knee;
  O Christ, when thou shalt come,
    In love remember me,
And in thy Kingdom, by thy grace,
Grant me a humble servant's place.

5   Thy grace, O Father, give,
     I humbly thee implore;
  And let thy mercy bless
    Thy servant more and more.
All grace and glory be to thee,
From age to age eternally.

St. Gregory Nazianzen, 329-89; tr. John Brownlie, 1857-1925

96 VATER UNSER
     (OLD 112TH) 8888 88   *Geistliche Lieder, Leipzig, 1539*

Alternative tune, MELITA, No. 527

Verborgne Gottesliebe du

THOU hidden Love of God, whose
    height,
  Whose depth unfathomed, no man
    knows,
I see from far thy beauteous light,
  Inly I sigh for thy repose;
My heart is pained, nor can it be
At rest till it finds rest in thee.

2 Thy secret voice invites me still
    The sweetness of thy yoke to
      prove;
  And fain I would; but, though my
    will
    Seem fixed, yet wide my passions
      rove;
Yet hindrances strew all the way;
I aim at thee, yet from thee stray.

3 'Tis mercy all, that thou hast
    brought
  My mind to seek her peace in thee;
Yet, while I seek but find thee not,
  No peace my wandering soul shall
    see.
O when shall all my wanderings end,
And all my steps to thee-ward tend?

4 Is there a thing beneath the sun
    That strives with thee my heart to
      share?
Ah! tear it thence, and reign alone,
  The Lord of every motion there;
Then shall my heart from earth be
    free,
When it has found repose in thee.

Gerhard Tersteegen, 1697-1769; tr. John Wesley, 1703-91

97 GALLIARD 7777   From a melody by JOHN DOWLAND, 1562-1626

For children

FATHER, lead me, day by day,
Ever in thy perfect way;
Teach me to be pure and true;
Show me what I ought to do.

2 When in danger, make me brave;
Make me know that thou canst save;
Keep me safe by thy dear side;
Let me in thy love abide.

3 When I'm tempted to do wrong,
Make me steadfast, wise, and strong;

And, when all alone I stand,
Shield me with thy mighty hand.

4 When my heart is full of glee,
Help me to remember thee,
Happy most of all to know
That my Father loves me so.

5 May I do the good I know,
Be thy loving child below,
Then at last go home to thee,
Evermore thy child to be.

John Page Hopps, 1834-1911 (altered)

98 RESONET IN LAUDIBUS 7776   German Carol Melody, *c.* 1500

vv. 1, 2 Hear _____ us, Holy Jesus.
vv. 3-5 Save _____ us, Holy Jesus.

For children

JESUS, Saviour ever mild,
Born for us a little Child
Of the Virgin undefiled:
    Hear us, Holy Jesus.

2 Jesus, Son of God most high,
Who didst in the manger lie,
Who upon the cross didst die,
    Hear us, Holy Jesus.

3 From all pride and vain conceit,
From all spite and angry heat,
From all lying and deceit,
    Save us, Holy Jesus.

4 From refusing to obey,
From the love of our own way,
From forgetfulness to pray,
    Save us, Holy Jesus.

5 By the Name we bow before,
Human Name, which evermore
All the hosts of heaven adore,
   Save us, Holy Jesus.

Richard Frederick Littledale, 1833-90, and others

99 SOLOTHURN L.M.   Swiss Traditional Melody

For younger children

FATHER, we thank thee for the night,
And for the pleasant morning light;
For rest and food and loving care,
And all that makes the day so fair.

2 Help us to do the things we should,
To be to others kind and good;
In all we do at work or play
To grow more loving every day.

Ascribed to Rebecca J. Weston, 19th century

100 CUTTLE MILLS 8583   WILLIAM GRIFFITH, 1867-1929

For younger children

JESUS, Friend of little children,
   Be a friend to me;
Take my hand and ever keep me
   Close to thee.

2 Teach me how to grow in goodness
   Daily as I grow;
Thou hast been a child, and surely
   Thou dost know.

3 Never leave me nor forsake me,
   Ever be my Friend;
For I need thee from life's dawning
   To its end.

Walter John Mathams, 1853-1931

87

INVOCATION

101 DUNFERMLINE C.M. *Scottish Psalter*, 1615

PSALM 106, verses 1-5, 48

GIVE praise and thanks unto the
    Lord,
  For bountiful is he;
His tender mercy doth endure
  Unto eternity.

2 God's mighty works who can
    express?
  Or show forth all his praise?
Blessèd are they that judgment keep,
  And justly do always.

3 Remember me, Lord, with that love
    Which thou to thine dost bear;
With thy salvation, O my God,
  To visit me draw near:

4 That I thy chosen's good may see,
    And in their joy rejoice;
And may with thine inheritance
  Triumph with cheerful voice.

5 Blest be Jehovah, Israel's God,
    To all eternity:
Let all the people say, Amen.
  Praise to the Lord give ye.

102 CULROSS C.M. *Scottish Psalter*, 1634

A - men.

PSALM 90, verses 1, 2, 14, 16, 17

LORD, thou hast been our dwelling-
    place
  In generations all.
Before thou ever hadst brought forth
  The mountains great or small;

2 Ere ever thou hadst formed the
    earth,
  And all the world abroad;
Even thou from everlasting art
  To everlasting God.

3 O with thy tender mercies, Lord,
    Us early satisfy;
So we rejoice shall all our days,
    And still be glad in thee.

4 O let thy work and power appear
    Thy servants' face before;
And show unto their children dear
    Thy glory evermore:

5 And let the beauty of the Lord
    Our God be us upon:
Our handy-works establish thou,
    Establish them each one.

6 *To Father, Son, and Holy Ghost,*
    The God whom we adore,
Be glory, as it was, and is,
    And shall be evermore. Amen.

103 WIRKSWORTH S.M.

Later form of a melody in
Chetham's *A Book of Psalmody*, 1718

BREATHE on me, Breath of God;
    Fill me with life anew,
That I may love what thou dost love,
    And do what thou wouldst do.

2   Breathe on me, Breath of God,
    Until my heart is pure,
Until with thee I will one will,
    To do and to endure.

3   Breathe on me, Breath of God,
    Till I am wholly thine,
Until this earthly part of me
    Glows with thy fire divine.

4   Breathe on me, Breath of God;
    So shall I never die,
But live with thee the perfect life
    Of thine eternity.

Edwin Hatch, 1835–89

104 FRANCONIA S.M.

WILLIAM HENRY HAVERGAL, 1793–1870, adapted from a melody in König's *Harmonischer Liederschatz*, 1738

COME, Holy Spirit, come;
Let thy bright beams arise;
Dispel the darkness from our minds,
And open all our eyes.

2 Cheer our desponding hearts,
Thou heavenly Paraclete;
Give us to lie with humble hope
At our Redeemer's feet.

3 Revive our drooping faith;
Our doubts and fears remove;
And kindle in our breasts the flame
Of never-dying love.

4 Convince us of our sin;
Then lead to Jesus' blood,
And to our wondering view reveal
The secret love of God.

5 'Tis thine to cleanse the heart,
To sanctify the soul,
To pour fresh life on every part,
And new create the whole.

6 Dwell, therefore, in our hearts;
Our minds from bondage free;
Then shall we know and praise and
love
The Father, Son, and thee.

Joseph Hart, 1712–68

105 JORDAN 777 777(7)

DONALD SWANN

INVOCATION

Veni, sancte Spiritus

COME, thou Holy Paraclete,
And from thy celestial seat
  Send thy light and brilliancy.
Father of the poor, draw near;
Giver of all gifts, be here;
  * Come, the soul's true radiancy.

2 Come, of comforters the best,
Of the soul the sweetest guest,
  Come in toil refreshingly.
Thou in labour rest most sweet,
Thou art shadow from the heat,
  Comfort in adversity.

3 O thou Light, most pure and blest,
Shine within the inmost breast
  Of thy faithful company.
Where thou art not, man hath naught;
Every holy deed and thought
  Comes from thy Divinity.

4 What is soilèd make thou pure;
What is wounded, work its cure;
  What is parchèd fructify.
Fill thy faithful, who confide
In thy power to guard and guide,
  With thy sevenfold mystery.

13th century; tr. John Mason Neale, 1818-66

* *The last line of each verse is repeated*

106   BUCKLAND 7777   LEIGHTON GEORGE HAYNE, 1836-83

HOLY Spirit, Truth Divine,
Dawn upon this soul of mine;
Word of God, and inward Light,
Wake my spirit, clear my sight.

2 Holy Spirit, Love Divine,
Glow within this heart of mine;
Kindle every high desire;
Perish self in thy pure fire.

3 Holy Spirit, Power Divine,
Fill and nerve this will of mine;
By thee may I strongly live,
Bravely bear, and nobly strive.

4 Holy Spirit, Right Divine,
King within my conscience reign;
Be my law, and I shall be
Firmly bound, for ever free.

5 Holy Spirit, Peace Divine,
Still this restless heart of mine;
Speak to calm this tossing sea,
Stayed in thy tranquillity.

6 Holy Spirit, Joy Divine,
Gladden thou this heart of mine;
In the desert ways I sing,
'Spring, O Well, for ever spring!'

Samuel Longfellow, 1819-92

107 MARTYRS C.M.   *Scottish Psalter*, 1615 (1635 rhythm)

Alternative tune, GERONTIUS, No. 238 (i)

SPIRIT Divine, attend our prayers,
  And make this house thy home;
Descend with all thy gracious
    powers;
  O come, great Spirit, come!

2 Come as the light: to us reveal
  Our emptiness and woe;
And lead us in those paths of life
  Where all the righteous go.

3 Come as the fire: and purge our
    hearts
  Like sacrificial flame;
Let our whole soul an offering be
  To our Redeemer's Name.

4 Come as the dove: and spread thy
    wings,
  The wings of peaceful love;
And let thy Church on earth become
  Blest as the Church above.

5 Come as the wind, with rushing
    sound
  And Pentecostal grace,
That all of woman born may see
  The glory of thy face.

6 Spirit Divine, attend our prayers;
  Make a lost world thy home;
Descend with all thy gracious
    powers;
  O come, great Spirit, come!

Andrew Reed, 1787–1862

108 SONG 22   10 10 10 10   ORLANDO GIBBONS, 1583–1625 (rhythm altered)

SPIRIT of God, descend upon my heart;
  Wean it from earth; through all its pulses move;
Stoop to my weakness, mighty as thou art,
  And make me love thee as I ought to love.

2 I ask no dream, no prophet-ecstasies,
   No sudden rending of the veil of clay,
No angel-visitant, no opening skies;
   But take the dimness of my soul away.

3 Hast thou not bid me love thee, God and King—
   All, all thine own, soul, heart, and strength, and mind?
I see thy cross—there teach my heart to cling:
   O let me seek thee, and O let me find!

4 Teach me to feel that thou art always nigh;
   Teach me the struggles of the soul to bear,
To check the rising doubt, the rebel sigh;
   Teach me the patience of unanswered prayer.

5 Teach me to love thee as thine angels love,
   One holy passion filling all my frame—
The baptism of the heaven-descended Dove,
   My heart an altar, and thy love the flame.

George Croly, 1780-1860

109 SOLDAU L.M.

Geystliche Gesangk Buchleyn,
Wittenberg, 1524, as given in Dibdin's
Standard Psalm Tune Book, 1851

SPIRIT of God, that moved of old
   Upon the waters' darkened face,
Come, when our faithless hearts are cold,
   And stir them with an inward grace.

2 Thou that art power and peace combined,
   All highest strength, all purest love,
The rushing of the mighty wind,
   The brooding of the gentle dove,

3 Come, give us still thy powerful aid,
   And urge us on, and keep us thine;
Nor leave the hearts that once were made
   Fit temples for thy grace divine;

4 Nor let us quench thy sevenfold light;
   But still with softest breathings stir
Our wayward souls, and lead us right,
   O Holy Ghost, the Comforter.

Cecil Frances Alexander, 1818-95

110 FUDGIE L.M.

ARTHUR HUTCHINGS

Alternative tune, SONG 34 (ANGELS' SONG), No. 45

O THOU who camest from above,
    The pure celestial fire to impart,
Kindle a flame of sacred love
    On the mean altar of my heart.

2 Jesus, confirm my heart's desire
        To work, and speak, and think for
            thee;
    Still let me guard the holy fire,
        And still stir up thy gift in me:

3 Ready for all thy perfect will,
    My acts of faith and love repeat,
    Till death thy endless mercies seal,
    And make the sacrifice complete.

Charles Wesley, 1707-88

111 QUEM PASTORES
        LAUDAVERE 888 7

Adapted from a German MS. of 1410

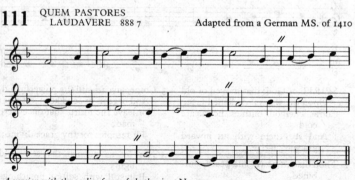

A version with the earlier form of rhythm is at No. 175

JESUS, good above all other,
Gentle child of gentle mother,
In a stable born our brother,
    Give us grace to persevere.

94

2 Jesus, cradled in a manger,
For us facing every danger,
Living as a homeless stranger,
  Make we thee our King most dear.

3 Jesus, for thy people dying,
Risen Master, death defying,
Lord in heaven, thy grace supplying,
  Keep us to thy presence near.

4 Jesus, who our sorrows bearest,
All our thoughts and hopes thou sharest;
Thou to man the truth declarest;
  Help us all thy truth to hear.

5 Lord, in all our doings guide us;
Pride and hate shall ne'er divide us;
We'll go on with thee beside us,
  And with joy we'll persevere!

Percy Dearmer, 1867-1936

112 GENTLE JESUS 7777   MARTIN SHAW, 1875-1958

For younger children

JESUS Christ, I look to thee;
Thou shalt my example be;
Thou art holy, just, and mild;
Thou wast once a little child.

2 Make me, Jesus, what thou art;
Give me thy obedient heart;
Thou art merciful and kind;
Let me have thy loving mind.

3 I shall then show forth thy praise,
Serve thee all my happy days;
Then the world shall always see
Christ, the Holy Child, in me.

Charles Wesley, 1707-88 (altered)

APPROACH TO GOD

ILLUMINATION

113 SWABIA S.M.

Adapted by WILLIAM HENRY HAVERGAL,
1793–1870, from a melody in Spiess'
Davids Harpffen-Spiel, Heidelberg, 1745

Alternative tune, FRANCONIA, No. 74
If used for Hymn 113 the Amen there should be omitted

BLEST are the pure in heart,
For they shall see their God:
The secret of the Lord is theirs;
Their soul is Christ's abode.

2   The Lord, who left the sky
Our life and peace to bring,
And dwelt in lowliness with men,
Their Pattern and their King,—

3   Still to the lowly soul
He doth himself impart,
And for his dwelling and his throne
Chooseth the pure in heart.

4   Lord, we thy presence seek;
Ours may this blessing be;
O give the pure and lowly heart,
A temple meet for thee.

Verses 1 and 3 John Keble, 1792–1866
Verses 2 and 4 from
Hall's Psalms and Hymns, 1836

114 (i) CHRIST WHOSE GLORY
FILLS THE SKIES 7777 77   MALCOLM WILLIAMSON

(ii) PSALM 135 7777 77
(MINISTRES DE L'ÉTERNEL)   *French Psalter*, 1562

CHRIST, whose glory fills the skies,
  Christ, the true, the only Light,
Sun of Righteousness, arise,
  Triumph o'er the shades of night.
Dayspring from on high, be near;
Daystar, in my heart appear.

2 Dark and cheerless is the morn
    Unaccompanied by thee;
  Joyless is the day's return,
    Till thy mercy's beams I see,
  Till they inward light impart,
  Glad my eyes, and warm my heart.

    3 Visit, then, this soul of mine;
        Pierce the gloom of sin and grief;
      Fill me, Radiancy Divine;
        Scatter all my unbelief;
      More and more thyself display,
      Shining to the perfect day.

                                    Charles Wesley, 1707–88

97

115 DOWN AMPNEY 66 11. D   RALPH VAUGHAN WILLIAMS, 1872-1958

Discendi, Amor santo

COME down, O Love Divine,
Seek thou this soul of mine,
And visit it with thine own ardour glowing;
O Comforter, draw near,
Within my heart appear,
And kindle it, thy holy flame bestowing.

2   O let it freely burn,
Till earthly passions turn
To dust and ashes, in its heat consuming;
And let thy glorious light
Shine ever on my sight,
And clothe me round, the while my path illuming.

3   Let holy charity
Mine outward vesture be,
And lowliness become mine inner clothing;
True lowliness of heart,
Which takes the humbler part,
And o'er its own shortcomings weeps with loathing.

4   And so the yearning strong,
With which the soul will long,
Shall far outpass the power of human telling;
For none can guess its grace,
Till he become the place
Wherein the Holy Spirit makes his dwelling.

Bianco da Siena, ?-1434
Tr. Richard Frederick Littledale, 1833-90

98

16 VERBUM SUPERNUM L.M.

Plainsong Melody (adapted Mechlin, 1851)
as in *Liber Usualis*

[For No. 581]

A - men.

This melody line also to be sung with alternative accompaniments (i) and (ii)

COME, gracious Spirit, heavenly Dove,
With light and comfort from above;
Be thou our Guardian, thou our Guide;
O'er every thought and step preside.

2 The light of truth to us display,
And make us know and choose thy way;
Plant holy fear in every heart,
That we from God may ne'er depart.

3 Lead us to Christ, the living Way;
Nor let us from his pastures stray:
Lead us to holiness, the road
That we must take to dwell with God.

4 Lead us to heaven, that we may share
Fullness of joy for ever there;
Lead us to God, our final rest,
To be with him for ever blest.

Simon Browne, 1680-1732

117 EISENACH (LEIPZIG) L.M.

Adapted from a melody b

JOHANN HERMANN SCHEIN, 1586–163

COMMAND thy blessing from above,
    O God, on all assembled here;
Behold us with a Father's love,
    While we look up with filial fear.

2 Command thy blessing, Jesus, Lord;
    May we thy true disciples be;
Speak to each heart the mighty word;
    Say to the weakest, 'Follow Me.'

3 Command thy blessing in this hour,
    Spirit of truth, and fill this place
With humbling and exalting power,
    With quickening and confirming grace.

4 O thou, our Maker, Saviour, Guide,
    One true eternal God confessed,
May naught in life or death divide
    The saints in thy communion blest.

5 With thee and these for ever bound,
    May all who here in prayer unite,
With harps and songs thy throne surround,
    Rest in thy love, and reign in light.

James Montgomery, 1771–1854

118 ATTWOOD 8888 88(8)
(VENI CREATOR)

From an anthem

THOMAS ATTWOOD, 1765–18

ILLUMINATION

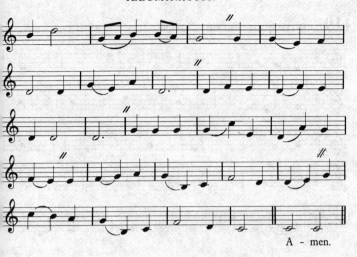

A - men.

Veni, Creator Spiritus

CREATOR Spirit! by whose aid
The world's foundations first were
    laid,
Come, visit every pious mind,
Come, pour thy joys on human kind;
From sin and sorrow set us free,
And make thy temples worthy thee.

2 O Source of uncreated light,
The Father's promised Paraclete,
Thrice holy Fount, thrice holy Fire,
Our hearts with heavenly love
    inspire;
Come, and thy sacred unction bring
To sanctify us while we sing.

3 Plenteous of grace, descend from high,
Rich in thy sevenfold energy;
Thou Strength of his almighty hand
Whose power does heaven and earth command,
Give us thyself, that we may see
The Father and the Son by thee.

4 *Immortal honour, endless fame*
Attend the Almighty Father's Name;
The Saviour Son be glorified,
Who for lost man's redemption died;
And equal adoration be,
Eternal Paraclete, to thee. Amen.

9th century; tr. John Dryden, 1631-1700
Adapted John Wesley, 1703-91

* *The last line of each verse is repeated*

101

119 FIFTH MODE MELODY 8486. D   THOMAS TALLIS, *c.* 1505–85

ENTER thy courts, thou Word of life,
My joy and peace;
Let the glad sound therein be heard,
Bid plaintive sadness cease.
Comfort my heart, thou Truth most fair;
O enter in,
Chasing despair and earthborn care,
My woe and slothful sin.

2 Glad was the time when I would sing
Thy heavenly praise;
Happy my heart when thou wert nigh,
Directing all my ways.
O let thy light, thy joy again
Return to me;
Nor in disdain from me refrain,
Who lift my soul to thee.

3 In heaven and earth thy law endures,
Thy word abides:
My troubled flesh trembleth in awe,
My heart in terror hides.
Yet still on thee my hope is set;
On thee, O Lord,
I will await and not forget
The promise of thy word.

Robert Bridges, 1844–1930

120 CORINTH 8787 87
(TANTUM ERGO)

From (the elder) Samuel Webbe's
An Essay on the Church Plain-Chant, 1782

LORD of beauty, thine the splendour
　Shown in earth and sky and sea,
Burning sun and moonlight tender,
　Hill and river, flower and tree;
Lest we fail our praise to render,
　Touch our eyes that we may see!

2 Lord of wisdom, whom obeying
　Mighty waters ebb and flow,
While unhasting, undelaying,
　Planets on their courses go;
In thy laws thyself displaying,
　Teach our minds thy truth to know!

3 Lord of life, alone sustaining
　All below and all above,
Lord of love, by whose ordaining
　Sun and stars sublimely move;
In our earthly spirits reigning,
　Lift our hearts, that we may love!

4 Lord of beauty, bid us own thee,
　Lord of truth, our footsteps guide,
Till as love our hearts enthrone thee,
　And, with vision purified,
Lord of all, when all have known thee,
　Thou in all art glorified!

Cyril Argentine Alington, 1872-1955

121 ST. JAMES C.M.
Select Psalms and Hymns, 1697
Probably by RAPHAEL COURTEVILLE, ?1677–1772

[For
Nos. 429 & 564]

A - men.

THOU art the Way: to thee alone
  From sin and death we flee;
And he who would the Father seek
  Must seek him, Lord, by thee.

2 Thou art the Truth: thy word alone
  True wisdom can impart;
Thou only canst inform the mind,
  And purify the heart.

3 Thou art the Life: the rending tomb
  Proclaims thy conquering arm;
And those who put their trust in thee
  Nor death nor hell shall harm.

4 Thou art the Way, the Truth, the Life:
  Grant us that way to know,
That truth to keep, that life to win,
  Whose joys eternal flow.

George Washington Doane, 1799–1859

122 ST. COLUMBA (ERIN) C.M.
Irish Traditional Melody

COME, Holy Ghost, our hearts inspire;
  Let us thine influence prove,
Source of the old prophetic fire,
  Fountain of life and love.

2 Come, Holy Ghost, for moved by thee
  The prophets wrote and spoke;
Unlock the truth, thyself the key;
  Unseal the sacred book.

3 Expand thy wings, celestial Dove;
    Brood o'er our nature's night;
  On our disordered spirits move,
    And let there now be light.

4 God through himself we then shall know,
    If thou within us shine,
  And sound, with all thy saints below,
    The depths of love divine.

Charles Wesley, 1707–88

123 SAMUEL 6666 88   ARTHUR SEYMOUR SULLIVAN, 1842–1900

Alternative tune, LOVE UNKNOWN, No. 95

For children

HUSHED was the evening hymn,
    The temple courts were dark,
The lamp was burning dim
    Before the sacred ark,
When suddenly a voice Divine
Rang through the silence of the shrine.

2 The old man, meek and mild,
    The priest of Israel, slept;
His watch the temple child,
    The little Levite, kept;
And what from Eli's sense was sealed
The Lord to Hannah's son revealed.

3 O give me Samuel's ear,
    The open ear, O Lord,
Alive and quick to hear
    Each whisper of thy word,—
Like him to answer at thy call,
And to obey thee first of all.

4 O give me Samuel's heart,
    A lowly heart, that waits
Where in thy house thou art,
    Or watches at thy gates
By day and night,—a heart that still
Moves at the breathing of thy will.

5 O give me Samuel's mind,
    A sweet unmurmuring faith,
Obedient and resigned
    To thee in life and death,
That I may read, with childlike eyes,
Truths that are hidden from the wise.

James Drummond Burns, 1823–64

124 GLENFINLAS 6565

KENNETH GEORGE FINLAY
1882-1974

For younger children

HOLY Spirit, hear us;
    Help us while we sing;
Breathe into the music
    Of the praise we bring.

2 Holy Spirit, prompt us
    When we kneel to pray;
Nearer come, and teach us
    What we ought to say.

3 Holy Spirit, shine thou
    On the book we read;
Gild its holy pages
    With the light we need.

4 Holy Spirit, give us
    Each a lowly mind;
Make us more like Jesus,
    Gentle, pure, and kind.

5 Holy Spirit, help us
    Daily, by thy might,
What is wrong to conquer,
    And to choose the right.

William Henry Parker, 1845-1929

HOLY SCRIPTURE

125 CAITHNESS C.M.   *Scottish Psalter*, 1635

A - men.

PSALM 19, verses 7–10, 14

GOD'S law is perfect, and converts
  The soul in sin that lies;
God's testimony is most sure,
  And makes the simple wise.

2 The statutes of the Lord are right,
    And do rejoice the heart:
  The Lord's command is pure, and doth
    Light to the eyes impart.

3 Unspotted is the fear of God,
    And doth endure for ever:
  The judgments of the Lord are true
    And righteous altogether.

4 They more than gold, yea, much fine gold,
    To be desirèd are:
  Than honey, honey from the comb
    That droppeth, sweeter far.

5 The words which from my mouth proceed,
    The thoughts sent from my heart,
  Accept, O Lord, for thou my strength
    And my Redeemer art.

6 *To Father, Son, and Holy Ghost,*
    The God whom we adore,
  Be glory, as it was, and is,
    And shall be evermore. Amen.

126 ALLEIN GOTT IN DER HÖH' SEI EHR' 8787 887

Adapted from an Easter Gloria, 1524 (later form)

Alternative tune, LUTHER'S HYMN (NUN FREUT EUCH), No. 14

From PSALM 19, verses 7–14

GOD'S perfect law revives the soul,
His word makes wise the simple;
God's clear commands rejoice the
    heart,
His light the eye enlightens;
God's fear is pure, his judgments
    just,
More to be sought than pure fine
    gold,
Sweeter by far than honey.

2 Lord, who can tell the secret faults
That have dominion o'er me?
Hold back thy servant from self-
    will
And break its power to bind me.
May all I think and all I say
Be now acceptable to thee,
My Rock and my Redeemer.

Ian Pitt-Watson
The New English Bible (*adapted*)

127 YORK C.M.

Scottish Psalter, 1615

A men.

PSALM 119, verses 33–40

TEACH me, O Lord, the perfect
    way
    Of thy precepts divine,
And to observe it to the end
    I shall my heart incline.

2 Give understanding unto me,
    So keep thy law shall I;
Yea, even with my whole heart I
    shall
    Observe it carefully.

3 In thy law's path make me to go;
   For I delight therein.
My heart unto thy testimonies,
   And not to greed, incline.

4 Turn thou away my sight and eyes
   From viewing vanity;
And in thy good and holy way
   Be pleased to quicken me.

5 Confirm to me thy gracious word,
   Which I did gladly hear,
Even to thy servant, Lord, who is
   Devoted to thy fear.

6 Turn thou away my feared reproach;
   For good thy judgments be.
Lo, for thy precepts I have longed;
   In thy truth quicken me.

7 *To Father, Son, and Holy Ghost,*
   The God whom we adore,
Be glory, as it was, and is,
   And shall be evermore. Amen.

128 LIEBSTER JESU
(DESSAU) 7878 88   JOHANN RODOLPH AHLE, 1625-73

BOOK of books, our people's strength,
   Statesman's, teacher's, hero's treasure,
Bringing freedom, spreading truth,
   Shedding light that none can measure—
      Wisdom comes to those who know thee,
      All the best we have we owe thee.

2 Thank we those who toiled in thought,
   Many diverse scrolls completing,
Poets, prophets, scholars, saints,
   Each his word from God repeating;
      Till they came, who told the story
      Of the Word, and showed his glory.

3 Praise we God, who hath inspired
   Those whose wisdom still directs us;
Praise him for the Word made flesh,
   For the Spirit who protects us.
      Light of Knowledge, ever burning,
      Shed on us thy deathless learning.

Percy Dearmer, 1867-1936

129 LIEBSTER JESU
(DESSAU) 7878 88

JOHANN RODOLPH AHLE, 1625-73

Liebster Jesu, wir sind hier

LOOK upon us, blessèd Lord,
Take our wandering thoughts and guide us:
We have come to hear thy word:
With thy teaching now provide us,
    That, from earth's distractions turning,
    We thy message may be learning.

2 For thy Spirit's radiance bright
We, assembled here, are hoping:
If thou shouldst withhold the light,
In the dark our souls were groping:
    In word, deed, and thought direct us:
    Thou, none other, canst correct us.

3 Brightness of the Father's face,
Light of Light, from God proceeding,
Make us ready in this place:
Ear and heart await thy leading.
    In our study, prayers, and praising,
    May our souls find their upraising.

Tobias Clausnitzer, 1619-84
Tr. Robert Macalister, 1870-1950

Adapted by WILLIAM HENRY MONK, 1823-89,
from a melody in
Weisse's *Gesangbuchlen*, 1531

130 RAVENSHAW
6666 Trochaic

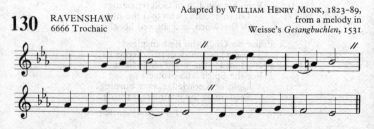

LORD, thy word abideth,
And our footsteps guideth;
Who its truth believeth
Light and joy receiveth.

2 When our foes are near us,
Then thy word doth cheer us,
Word of consolation,
Message of salvation.

3 When the storms are o'er us,
And dark clouds before us,
Then its light directeth,
And our way protecteth.

4 Who can tell the pleasure,
Who recount the treasure,
By thy word imparted
To the simple-hearted?

5 Word of mercy, giving
Succour to the living;
Word of life, supplying
Comfort to the dying!

6 O that we, discerning
Its most holy learning,
Lord, may love and fear thee,
Evermore be near thee!

Henry Williams Baker, 1821-77

131 WILTON 11 6 11 6   ARTHUR HENRY MANN, 1850-1929

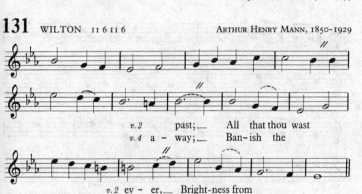

v. 2   past;— All that thou wast
v. 4 a - way;— Ban-ish the

v. 2 ev - er,— Bright-ness from

LIGHT of the world! for ever, ever shining,
    There is no change in thee;
True Light of Life, all joy and health enshrining,
    Thou canst not fade nor flee.

2 Thou hast arisen, but thou descendest never;
    Today shines as the past;
All that thou wast thou art, and shalt be ever,
    Brightness from first to last.

3 Night visits not thy sky, nor storm, nor sadness;
    Day fills up all its blue,—
Unfailing beauty, and unfaltering gladness,
    And love for ever new.

4 Light of the world, undimming and unsetting!
    O shine each mist away;
Banish the fear, the falsehood, and the fretting;
    Be our unchanging Day.

Horatius Bonar, 1808-89

132 TELL ME THE OLD, OLD STORY
7676. D and refrain

WILLIAM HOWARD DOANE,
1832–1915

TELL me the old, old story
    Of unseen things above,
Of Jesus and his glory,
    Of Jesus and his love.
Tell me the story simply,
    As to a little child;
For I am weak and weary,
    And helpless, and defiled:

Tell me the old, old story,
Tell me the old, old story,
Tell me the old, old story
Of Jesus and his love.

2 Tell me the story slowly,
    That I may take it in,—
That wonderful redemption,
    God's remedy for sin.

Tell me the story often,
    For I forget so soon;
The early dew of morning
    Has passed away at noon.

3 Tell me the story softly,
    With earnest tones and grave;
  Remember, I'm the sinner
    Whom Jesus came to save.
  Tell me the story always,
    If you would really be,
  In any time of trouble,
    A comforter to me.

4 Tell me the same old story
    When you have cause to fear
  That this world's empty glory
    Is costing me too dear.
  Yes, and when that world's glory
    Shall dawn upon my soul,
  Tell me the old, old story,
    'Christ Jesus makes thee whole.'

Arabella Catherine Hankey, 1834–1911

133 MONTROSE C.M.

Gilmour's *Psalm-Singer's Assistant*,
Glasgow, 1793

BREAK forth, O living light of God,
Upon the world's dark hour!
Show us the way the Master trod;
Reveal his saving power.

2 Remove the veil of ancient words,
Their message long obscure;
Restore to us thy truth, O God,
And make its meaning sure.

3 O let thy Word be light anew
To every nation's life;
Unite us in thy will, O Lord,
And end all sinful strife.

4 O may one Lord, one Faith, one Word,
One Spirit lead us still;
And one great Church go forth in might
To work God's perfect will.

Frank von Christierson

134 PLEADING SAVIOUR
(SALTASH) 8787. D

Plymouth Collection (U.S.A.), 1855

HEAVENLY Father, may thy
blessing
  Rest upon thy children now,
When in praise thy Name they
hallow,
  When in prayer to thee they bow:
In the wondrous story reading
  Of the Lord of truth and grace,
May they see thy love reflected
  In the light of his dear face.

2 May they learn from this great story
  All the arts of friendliness;
Truthful speech and honest action,
  Courage, patience, steadfastness;

How to master self and temper,
  How to make their conduct fair;
When to speak and when be silent,
  When to do and when forbear.

3 May his Spirit wise and holy
  With his gifts their spirits bless,
Make them loving, joyous, peaceful,
  Rich in goodness, gentleness,
Strong in self-control, and faithful,
  Kind in thought and deed; for he
Sayeth, 'What ye do for others
  Ye are doing unto me'.

William Charter Piggott, 1872-1943

See also certain hymns in Part II (The Holy Spirit in the Church)

The following hymns are appropriate as opening processional hymns on special occasions:

Advent: O come, O come Emmanuel, 165
Christmas: Of the Father's love begotten, 198
Palm Sunday: All glory, laud, and honour, 233
Passiontide: Sing, my tongue, 256
Easter: 'Welcome, happy morning', 272
Ascension: The head that once, 286
Pentecost: Come, Holy Ghost, our souls inspire, 342
Trinity: Holy, holy, holy, 352
    I bind unto myself today, 402
All Saints: For all the saints, 534
Rogation and Harvest: We plough the fields, 620
Holy Communion: Deck thyself, my soul, 567

II

THE WORD OF GOD: HIS MIGHTY ACTS

━━━

II

THE WORD OF GOD, HIS MIGHTY ACT

THE WORD OF GOD: HIS MIGHTY ACTS

CREATION AND PROVIDENCE

135 ST. JOHN
6666 4444

The Parish Choir, vol. III, 1851
Perhaps by WILLIAM HENRY HAVERGAL, 1793–1870

A - men.

PSALM 148 (ii)

THE Lord of heaven confess,
　　On high his glory raise.
Him let all angels bless,
　　Him all his armies praise.
　　　Him glorify
　　　Sun, moon, and stars;
　　　Ye higher spheres,
　　　And cloudy sky.

2 From God your beings are,
　　Him therefore famous make;
You all created were,
　　When he the word but spake.
　　　And from that place,
　　　Where fixed you be
　　　By his decree,
　　　You cannot pass.

3 Praise God from earth below,
　　Ye dragons, and ye deeps:
Fire, hail, clouds, wind, and snow,
　　Whom in command he keeps.
　　　Praise ye his Name,
　　　Hills great and small,
　　　Trees low and tall;
　　　Beasts wild and tame;

4 All things that creep or fly.
　　Ye kings, ye vulgar throng,
All princes mean or high;
　　Both men and virgins young,
　　　Even young and old,
　　　Exalt his Name;
　　　For much his fame
　　　Should be extolled.

5 O let God's Name be praised
　　Above both earth and sky;
For he his saints hath raised,
　　And set their horn on high;
　　　Even those that be
　　　Of Israel's race,
　　　Near to his grace.
　　　The Lord praise ye.

6 *To God the Father, Son,*
　　And Spirit ever blest,
Eternal Three in One,
　　All worship be addressed,
　　　As heretofore
　　　It was, is now,
　　　And still shall be
　　　For evermore. Amen.

136 DUNFERMLINE C.M.

Scottish Psalter, 1615

A - men.

PSALM 147, verses 1-5

PRAISE ye the Lord; for it is good
　Praise to our God to sing:
For it is pleasant, and to praise
　It is a comely thing.

2 God doth build up Jerusalem;
　And he it is alone
That the dispersed of Israel
　Doth gather into one.

3 Those that are broken in their heart,
　And grievèd in their minds,
He healeth, and their painful wounds
　He tenderly up-binds.

4 He counts the number of the stars;
　He names them every one.
Great is our Lord, and of great
　　power;
His wisdom search can none.

5 *To Father, Son, and Holy Ghost,*
　The God whom we adore,
　Be glory, as it was, and is,
　And shall be evermore. Amen.

137 CROFT'S 136TH   6666 and refrain

WILLIAM CROFT, 1678-1727

A - men.

Alternative tune, DARWALL'S 148th, No. 296(i)

118

PSALM 136(ii), verses 1–5, 23–26

PRAISE God, for he is kind:
His mercy lasts for aye.
Give thanks with heart and mind
To God of gods alway:
For certainly
His mercies dure
Most firm and sure
Eternally.

2 The Lord of lords praise ye,
Whose mercies still endure.
Great wonders only he
Doth work by his great power:

3 Give praise to his great Name,
Who, by his wisdom high,
The heaven above did frame,
And built the lofty sky:

4 Who hath remembered us
When in our low estate;
And hath delivered us
From foes who did us hate:

5 Who to all flesh gives food;
For his grace faileth never.
Give thanks to God most good,
The God of heaven, for ever:

6 *To God the Father, Son,*
And Spirit ever blest,
Eternal Three in One,
All worship be addressed,
As heretofore
It was, is now,
And still shall be
For evermore. **Amen.**

138 WINCHESTER OLD C.M.

Este's *Psalter*, 1592

A-men.

A version with the later form of rhythm is at No. 174

PSALM 8, verses 1, 3–5

HOW excellent in all the earth,
Lord, our Lord, is thy Name!
Who hast thy glory far advanced
Above the starry frame.

2 When I look up unto the heavens,
Which thine own fingers framed,
Unto the moon, and to the stars,
Which were by thee ordained;

3 Then say I, What is man, that he
Remembered is by thee?
Or what the son of man, that thou
So kind to him should'st be?

4 For thou a little lower hast
Him than the angels made;
With glory and with dignity
Thou crownèd hast his head.

5 *To Father, Son, and Holy Ghost,*
The God whom we adore,
Be glory, as it was, and is,
And shall be evermore. **Amen.**

139 FRENCH (DUNDEE) C.M. *Scottish Psalter, 1615*

A - men.

A version with the later form of rhythm is at No. 543

PSALM 121

1 TO the hills will lift mine eyes.
  From whence doth come mine
    aid?
My safety cometh from the Lord,
  Who heaven and earth hath made.

2 Thy foot he'll not let slide, nor will
  He slumber that thee keeps.
Behold, he that keeps Israel,
  He slumbers not, nor sleeps.

3 The Lord thee keeps, the Lord thy
    shade
  On thy right hand doth stay:
The moon by night thee shall not
    smite,
  Nor yet the sun by day.

4 The Lord shall keep thy soul; he
    shall
  Preserve thee from all ill.
Henceforth thy going out and in
  God keep for ever will.

5 *To Father, Son, and Holy Ghost,*
  The God whom we adore,
Be glory, as it was, and is,
  And shall be evermore. Amen.

140 (i) PSALM 107
(OLD 107TH) D.C.M. *Lyons Psalter, 1547*

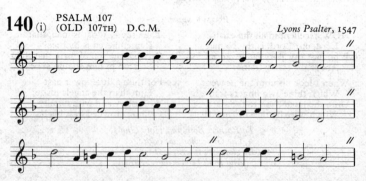

A - men.

(ii) * STROUDWATER D.C.M.

Wilkins' *Psalmody, c.* 1730,
as in *The Psalter in Metre,* 1899

A - men.

* *As the text of the hymn is printed in 8-line verses to fit tune* (i),
STROUDWATER *must be repeated for each verse*

PSALM 93

THE Lord doth reign, and clothed is he
    With majesty most bright;
His works do show him clothed to be,
    And girt about with might.
The world is also stablishèd,
    That it cannot depart.
Thy throne is fixed of old, and thou
    From everlasting art.

2 The floods, O Lord, have lifted up,
    They lifted up their voice;
The floods have lifted up their waves,
    And made a mighty noise.
But yet the Lord, that is on high,
    Is more of might by far
Than noise of many waters is,
    Or great sea-billows are.

3 Thy testimonies every one
    In faithfulness excel;
And holiness for ever, Lord,
    Thine house becometh well.
To Father, Son, and Holy Ghost,
    The God whom we adore,
Be glory, as it was, and is,
    And shall be evermore. Amen.

141 KILVAREE 11 10 11 10

Alternative tune, PSALM 12 (DONNE SECOURS), No. 250

O LORD of every shining constellation
　　That wheels in splendour through the midnight sky;
Grant us thy Spirit's true illumination
　　To read the secrets of thy work on high.

2 And thou who mad'st the atom's hidden forces,
　　Whose laws its mighty energies fulfil;
Teach us, to whom thou giv'st such rich resources,
　　In all we use, to serve thy holy will.

3 O Life, awaking life in cell and tissue,
　　From flower to bird, from beast to brain of man;
O help us trace, from birth to final issue,
　　The sure unfolding of thine ageless plan.

4 Thou who hast stamped thine image on thy creatures,
　　And though they marred that image, lov'st them still;
Uplift our eyes to Christ, that in his features
　　We may discern the beauty of thy will.

5 Great Lord of nature, shaping and renewing,
　　Who mad'st us more than nature's sons to be;
Help us to tread, with grace our souls enduing,
　　The road to life and immortality.

Albert Frederick Bayly

142 (i) MIT FREUDEN ZART
8787 88 and refrain

Later form of a melody in the
Bohemian Brethren's
Kirchengeseng, Berlin, 1566

LUTHER'S HYMN   8787 88 and refrain
(ii) (NUN FREUT EUCH)

Later form of a melody in
Geistliche Lieder, Wittenberg, 1533
or earlier

Sei Lob und Ehr' dem höchsten Gut

SING praise to God who reigns above,
  The God of all creation,
The God of power, the God of love,
  The God of our salvation;
With healing balm my soul he fills,
And every faithless murmur stills:
    To God all praise and glory!

2 The angel host, O King of kings,
  Thy praise for ever telling,
In earth and sky all living things
  Beneath thy shadow dwelling,
Adore the wisdom which could span,
And power which formed creation's
    plan:

3 O ye who name Christ's holy Name,
  Give God all praise and glory:
All ye who own his power, proclaim
  Aloud the wondrous story.
Cast each false idol from his throne,
The Lord is God, and he alone:

Johann Jakob Schütz, 1640–90
Tr. Frances Elizabeth Cox, 1812–97

143 (i) ST. PATRICK   D.L.M.   Irish Traditional Melody

(ii) FIRMAMENT   D.L.M.   WALFORD DAVIES, 1869–1941

A – – men.

CREATION AND PROVIDENCE

THE spacious firmament on high,
With all the blue ethereal sky,
And spangled heavens, a shining frame,
Their great Original proclaim.
The unwearied sun, from day to day,
Does his Creator's power display,
And publishes to every land
The work of an almighty hand.

2 Soon as the evening shades prevail,
The moon takes up the wondrous tale,
And nightly to the listening earth
Repeats the story of her birth;
While all the stars that round her burn,
And all the planets, in their turn,
Confirm the tidings, as they roll,
And spread the truth from pole to pole.

3 What though in solemn silence all
Move round the dark terrestrial ball?
What though no real voice nor sound
Amidst their radiant orbs be found?
In reason's ear they all rejoice,
And utter forth a glorious voice,
For ever singing, as they shine,
'The hand that made us is divine.' [Amen.]

Joseph Addison, 1672-1719

144 SUSSEX 878 and refrain

English Traditional Melody, adapted by
RALPH VAUGHAN WILLIAMS, 1872-1958

GOD is Love: his mercy brightens
All the path in which we rove;
Bliss he wakes, and woe he lightens:
God is Wisdom, God is Love.

2 Chance and change are busy ever;
Man decays, and ages move;
But his mercy waneth never:

3 Even the hour that darkest seemeth
Will his changeless goodness prove;
From the mist his brightness streameth:

4 He with earthly cares entwineth
Hope and comfort from above;
Everywhere his glory shineth:

John Bowring, 1792-1872

145 (i) ES IST KEIN TAG
(MEYER) 8884
JOHANN DAVID MEYER,
Geistliche Seelenfreud, 1692

(ii) PORTLAND 8884
CYRIL VINCENT TAYLOR

O LORD of heaven and earth and
    sea,
To thee all praise and glory be;
How shall we show our love to thee,
    Who givest all?

2 The golden sunshine, vernal air,
  Sweet flowers and fruits thy love
    declare;
  Where harvests ripen, thou art there,
      Who givest all.

3 For peaceful homes and healthful days,
  For all the blessings earth displays,
  We owe thee thankfulness and praise,
    Who givest all.

4 Thou didst not spare thine only Son,
  But gav'st him for a world undone,
  And freely with that blessèd One
    Thou givest all.

5 For souls redeemed, for sins forgiven,
  For means of grace and hopes of heaven,
  Father, all praise to thee be given,
    Who givest all.

Christopher Wordsworth, 1807-85

146 (i)   OLDOWN   8484 84   BASIL HARWOOD, 1859-1949

1. My   God, I thank thee, who hast made The   earth   so __
2. I   thank thee, too, that   thou hast made __ Joy   to   a-
3. I   thank thee more that   all   our   joy   Is   touched with __
4. I   thank thee, Lord, that   here   our souls, Though am-ply __

bright,   So   full   of   splen-dour   and   of   joy, __
-bound,   So   ma-ny   gen-tle   thoughts and   deeds __
pain,   That   sha-dows fall   on   bright-est hours, That
blest,   Can   nev-er   find,   al-though they seek,   A

Beau-ty   and   light;   So   ma-ny   glor-ious
Circ-ling   us   round   That   in   the   dark-est
thorns   re-main,   So   that earth's bliss may
per-fect __ rest,   Nor   ev-er   shall,   un-

things   are   here, __   No-ble   and   right.
spot   of   earth Some   love   is __   found.
be   our   guide, And   not   our __   chain.
-til   they   lean   On   Je-sus' __   breast.

Adelaide Anne Procter, 1825-64 (altered slightly)

146 (ii) SEVERN 8484 84

HERBERT HOWELLS

1. My God, I thank thee, who hast made The earth so
2. I thank thee, too, that thou hast made Joy to a-
3. I thank thee more that all our joy Is touched with
4. I thank thee, Lord, that here our souls, Though am-ply

bright, So full of splen-dour and of
-bound, So ma-ny gen-tle thoughts and
pain, That sha-dows fall on bright-est
blest, Can ne-ver find, al-though they

joy, Beau-ty and light; So ma-ny glor-ious
deeds Circ-ling us round That in the dark-est
hours, That thorns re-main, So that earth's bliss may
seek, A per-fect rest, Nor ev-er shall, un-

things are here, No-ble and right.
spot of earth Some love is found.
be our guide, And not our chain.
-til they lean On Je-sus' breast.

Adelaide Anne Procter, 1825–64 (altered slightly)

147 LONDON NEW C.M.

Scottish Psalter, 1635,
as adapted in Playford's *Psalms*, 1671

GOD moves in a mysterious way,
  His wonders to perform;
He plants his footsteps in the sea,
  And rides upon the storm.

2 Deep in unfathomable mines
  Of never-failing skill
He treasures up his bright designs,
  And works his sovereign will.

3 Ye fearful saints, fresh courage take;
  The clouds ye so much dread
Are big with mercy, and shall break
  In blessings on your head.

4 Judge not the Lord by feeble sense,
  But trust him for his grace;
Behind a frowning providence
  He hides a smiling face.

5 Blind unbelief is sure to err,
  And scan his work in vain,
God is his own interpreter,
  And he will make it plain.

William Cowper, 1731–1800

148 ERMUNTRE DICH 8787. D   JOHANN SCHOP, 1600–67

A GLADSOME hymn of praise we sing,
  And thankfully we gather
To bless the love of God above,
  Our everlasting Father.
In him rejoice with heart and voice,
  Whose glory fadeth never,
Whose providence is our defence,
  Who lives and loves for ever.

2 Full in his sight his children stand,
  By his strong arm defended,
And he whose wisdom guides the world
  Our footsteps hath attended.
For nothing falls unknown to him,
  Or care or joy or sorrow,
And he whose mercy ruled the past
  Will be our stay tomorrow.

Ambrose Nichols Blatchford, 1842–1924

149 SOUSTER L.M.   MARTIN DALBY

Rebus creatis nil egens

O GOD, the joy of heaven above,
Thou didst not need thy creatures' love,
When from thy secret place was said
The word that earth's foundation laid.

2 Thou spakest:—worlds began to be;
They stand before thy majesty;
And all to their Creator raise
A wondrous harmony of praise.

3 But ere, O Lord, this lovely earth
From thy creative will had birth,
Thou in thy counsels didst unfold
Another world of fairer mould.

4 That world doth our Redeemer frame,
And build upon his mighty Name;
His Holy Church shall last for aye,
Till time itself hath passed away.

Charles Coffin, 1676–1749
Tr. Compilers of
Hymns Ancient and Modern, 1889 (*altered*)

150 (i) NATIVITY C.M.   HENRY LAHEE, 1826–1912

CREATION AND PROVIDENCE

(ii) GODRE'R COED   C.M.   MATTHEW W. DAVIES, 1885-1947

WHEN all thy mercies, O my God!
    My rising soul surveys,
Transported with the view, I'm lost
    In wonder, love, and praise.

2 Unnumbered comforts to my soul
    Thy tender care bestowed,
Before my infant heart conceived
    From whom these comforts flowed.

3 When in the slippery paths of youth
    With heedless steps I ran,
Thine arm, unseen, conveyed me safe,
    And led me up to man.

4 Ten thousand thousand precious gifts
    My daily thanks employ;
Nor is the least a cheerful heart,
    That tastes those gifts with joy.

5 Through every period of my life
    Thy goodness I'll pursue;
And after death, in distant worlds,
    The glorious theme renew.

Joseph Addison, 1672-1719

151 BEECHWOOD 5664   JOSIAH BOOTH, 1852–1929

For children

GOD, who made the earth,
  The air, the sky, the sea,
Who gave the light its birth,
  Careth for me.

2 God, who made the grass,
  The flower, the fruit, the tree,
The day and night to pass,
  Careth for me.

3 God, who made the sun,
  The moon, the stars, is he
Who, when life's clouds come on,
  Careth for me.

4 God, who made all things,
  On earth, in air, in sea,
Who changing seasons brings,
  Careth for me.

5 God, who sent his Son
  To die on Calvary,
He, if I lean on him,
  Will care for me.

Sarah Betts Rhodes, 1829–1904

152 FITZWILLIAM 886. D   GEORGE FREDERICK HANDEL, 1685–1759

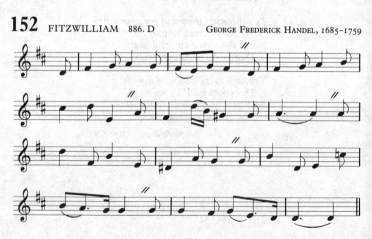

CREATION AND PROVIDENCE

For children

HOW wonderful this world of thine,
A fragment of a fiery sun,
How lovely and how small!
Where all things serve thy great
    design,
Where life's adventure is begun
In thee, the life of all.

2 The smallest seed in secret grows,
And thrusting upward answers soon
The bidding of the light;
The bud unfurls into a rose;
The wings within the white cocoon
Are perfected for flight.

3 The migrant bird, in winter fled,
Shall come again with spring and
    build
In this same shady tree;
By secret wisdom surely led,
Homeward across the clover-field
Hurries the honey-bee.

4 O thou, whose greater gifts are ours:
A conscious will, a thinking mind,
A heart to worship thee—
O take these strange unfolding
    powers
And teach us through thy Son to find
The life more full and free.

Frederick Pratt Green

153 SANDYS S.M.

English Traditional Carol Melody from Sandys'
Christmas Carols, Ancient and Modern, 1833

For younger children

A LITTLE child may know
Our Father's name of 'Love';
'Tis written on the earth below,
And on the sky above.

2 Around me when I look,
His handiwork I see;
This world is like a picture-book
To teach his Name to me.

3 The thousand little flowers
Within our garden found,
The rainbow and the soft spring
    showers,
And every pleasant sound;

4 The birds that sweetly sing,
The moon that shines by night,
With every tiny living thing
Rejoicing in the light;

5 And every star above,
Set in the deep blue sky,
All tell me that our God is Love,
And tell me he is nigh.

Jane Eliza Leeson, 1809–81

154 ROYAL OAK 7676 and refrain

English Traditional Melody,
adapted by MARTIN SHAW, 1875–1958

For younger children

★ *ALL things bright and beautiful,*
All creatures great and small,
All things wise and wonderful—
The Lord God made them all.

2 Each little flower that opens,
  Each little bird that sings,—
He made their glowing colours,
He made their tiny wings.

3 The purple-headed mountain,
  The river running by,
The sunset, and the morning
That brightens up the sky,

4 The cold wind in the winter,
  The pleasant summer sun,
The ripe fruits in the garden,—
He made them every one:

5 He gave us eyes to see them,
  And lips that we might tell
How great is God Almighty,
Who has made all things well.

Cecil Frances Alexander, 1818–95

★ *Verse 1 is also sung as a refrain after each other verse*

155 MY PLACE 7676

HUBERT GRIERSON, *Infant Praise*, 1964

CREATION AND PROVIDENCE

For younger children

GOD who put the stars in space,
Who made the world we share,
In his making made a place
For me, and put me here.

2 Thank you, God, for stars in space
And for the world we share.
Thank you for my special place
To love and serve you here.

*Norman and Margaret Mealy,
based on a poem by
Lucile S. Reid*

156 CHILDHOOD 8886

WALFORD DAVIES, 1869–1941
A Students' Hymnal, 1923

For younger children

I LOVE to think that Jesus saw
The same bright sun that shines today;
It gave him light to do his work,
And smiled upon his play.

2 The same white moon, with silver face,
That sails across the sky at night,
He used to see in Galilee,
And watch it with delight.

3 The same great God that hears my prayers
Heard his, when Jesus knelt to pray;
He is my Father, who will keep
His child through every day.

Ada Skemp, 1857–1927

157 FOREST GREEN
D.C.M.

English Traditional Melody

For younger children

WE thank thee, God, for eyes to see
The beauty of the earth;
For ears to hear the words of love
And happy sounds of mirth;
For minds that find new thoughts to think,
New wonders to explore;
For health and freedom to enjoy
The good thou hast in store.

Jeannette Perkins Brown, 1887–1960

THE PROMISE OF THE MESSIAH

158

Tone viii, ending 2

PSALM 72, verses 1, 2, 5, 11, 17-19

GIVE the king thy judgments O ˈ God :
  and thy righteousness un ˈ to the king's son.

He shall judge thy people with ˈ righteousness :
  and thy ˈ poor with judgment.

They shall fear thee as long as the sun and moon en ˈ dure :
  throughout all ˈ generations.

Yea all kings shall fall down be ˈ fore him :
  all na ˈ tions shall serve him.

His Name shall endure for ever   his Name shall be continued as long as the ˈ sun :
  and men shall be blessèd in him   all nations shall ˈ call him blessèd.

Blessèd be the Lord God the God of ˈ Israel :
  who only ˈ doeth wondrous things.

And blessèd be his glorious Name for ˈ ever :
  and let the whole earth be filled with his glory A ˈ men and Amen.

Glory be to the Father and to the ˈ *Son :*
  and ˈ *to the Holy Ghost :*

As it was in the beginning is now and ever ˈ *shall be :*
  world with ˈ *out end Amen.*

159 FELIX C.M.

The *Hallelujah*, edited LOWELL MASON, 1854. Founded on a phrase in MENDELSSOHN's oratorio *Christus*, 1847

PARAPHRASE 26, verses 5-10

BEHOLD he comes! your leader comes,
　　With might and honour crowned;
A witness who shall spread my Name
　　To earth's remotest bound.

2 See! nations hasten to his call
　　From every distant shore;
Isles, yet unknown, shall bow to him,
　　And Israel's God adore.

3 Seek ye the Lord while yet his ear
　　Is open to your call;
While offered mercy still is near,
　　Before his footstool fall.

4 Let sinners quit their evil ways,
　　Their evil thoughts forgo:
And God, when they to him return,
　　Returning grace will show.

5 He pardons with o'erflowing love:
　　For, hear the voice divine!
My nature is not like to yours,
　　Nor like your ways are mine:

6 But far as heaven's resplendent orbs
　　Beyond earth's spot extend,
As far my thoughts, as far my ways,
　　Your ways and thoughts transcend.

Scottish Paraphrases, 1781
From Isaiah 55: 4-9

160 BRISTOL C.M.   Ravenscroft's *Psalter*, 1621 (rhythm altered)

Alternative tune, CREDITON, No. 168

PARAPHRASE 39

HARK, the glad sound! the Saviour comes,
  The Saviour promised long;
Let every heart exult with joy,
  And every voice be song!

2 He comes, the prisoners to relieve,
    In Satan's bondage held;
  The gates of brass before him burst,
    The iron fetters yield.

3 He comes, the broken hearts to bind,
    The bleeding souls to cure;
  And with the treasures of his grace
    To enrich the humble poor.

4 The sacred year has now revolved,
    Accepted of the Lord,
  When heaven's high promise is fulfilled,
    And Israel is restored.

5 Our glad hosannas, Prince of Peace,
    Thy welcome shall proclaim;
  And heaven's exalted arches ring
    With thy most honoured Name.

Scottish Paraphrases, 1781
From St. Luke 4: 18, 19

161 (i)

JOHN ROBINSON, 1682–1762

(ii)

JAMES TURLE, 1802–82

BENEDICTUS

BLESSÈD be the Lord | God of | Isra-el:
  for he hath visited | and re- | deemed his | people:
And hath raised up a mighty sal- | vation | for us:
  in the | house of his | servant | David.

2 As he spake by the mouth of his | holy | prophets:
    which have | been since the | world be- | gan:
  That we should be | saved from our | enemies:
    and from the | hands of | all that | hate us.

3 To perform the mercy | promised to our | forefathers:
    and to re- | member his | holy | covenant:
  To perform the oath which he sware to our | forefather | Abraham:
    that | he would | give | us.

4 That we being delivered out of the | hands of our | enemies:
    might | serve him with- | out | fear:
  In holiness and | righteousness be- | fore him:
    all the | days | of our | life.

5 And thou child shalt be called the | prophet of the | Highest:
    for thou shalt go before the face of the | Lord to pre- | pare his | ways:
  To give knowledge of salvation | unto his | people:
    for the re- | mission | of their | sins.

6 Through the tender | mercy of our | God:
    whereby the | dayspring from on | high hath | visited us:
  To give light to them that sit in darkness and in the | shadow of | death:
    and to guide our feet | into the | way of | peace.

Glory | *be to the* | *Father:*
  and to the Son | *and to the* | *Holy* | *Ghost:*
As it | *was in the be-* | *ginning:*
  is now and ever shall be | world without | *end. A-* | men.

From St. Luke 1 : 68–79

162 NEUMARK 9898 88   (Form adopted by MENDELSSOHN in *St. Paul*, 1836)

GEORG NEUMARK, 1621–81

    * BEFORE all time the Word existed;
       Before all time he was with God;
       With God in fellowship eternal,
       In essence one with all God was.
       Through him all things received their birth;
       No thing without him came to be.

    2 The Word was life in all creation—
       That life the Light of all mankind.
       Through countless ages in the darkness
       The Light shone out, and still it shines.
       No matter how the dark might strive,
       . Its force could not the Light subdue.

    3 To witness to the Light there cáme,
       Sent forth from God, a man named John;
       That through him all men might beliëve
       The Light to whom he testified.
       This True Light, lighting every man,
       Ev'n then was entering the world.

  * *When the whole paraphrase is not sung, a selection of verses may be made as follows:*
        vv. 1, 2, (3), and 6 or vv. 3, 4, 5, and 6

4 The world he entered failed to know him,
   Although through him the world was made:
   To his own realm it was he cäme,
   Yet his own folk no welcome gave.
   But some there were who did receive
   The Light of men, the Word of God.

5 To these, to all in him believing,
   Who put their faith in his great Name,
   He gave authority and warrant—
   The power God's children to become.
   No human blood or seed or will
   Gave them this birth, but God alone!

6 The Word became a human being,
   And made his dwelling in our midst.
   We saw his majesty and splendour—
   His glory, full of grace and truth:
   Such as to One alone belongs
   Who is the Father's only Son.

James N. S. Alexander, from St. John 1: 1-7, 9-14

163 (i)

JOHN GOSS, 1800-80

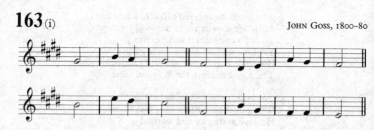

(ii)

STANLEY MARCHANT, 1883-1949

MAGNIFICAT

MY soul doth magnify the Lord   and my spirit hath rejoiced in ' God my '
    Saviour:
  for he hath regarded the ' lowliness ' of his ' hand-maiden:
For be- ' hold from ' henceforth:
  all gener- ' ations shall ' call me ' blessèd.

2 For he that is mighty hath ' magnified ' me:
  and ' holy ' is his ' Name:
And his mercy is on ' them that ' fear him:
  through- ' out all ' gener- ' ations.

3 He hath showed ' strength with his ' arm:
  he hath scattered the proud in the imagi- ' nation ' of their ' hearts:
He hath put down the ' mighty from their ' seat:
  and hath ex- ' alted the ' humble and ' meek.

4 He hath filled the ' hungry with ' good things:
  and the ' rich he hath sent ' empty a- ' way:
He remembering his mercy hath holpen his ' servant ' Isra-el:
  as he promised to our forefathers ' Abraham and his ' seed for ' ever.

Glory ' be to the ' Father :
  and to the Son ' and to the ' Holy ' Ghost :
As it ' was in the be- ' ginning :
  is now and ever shall be   ' world without ' end. A- ' men.

From St. Luke 1: 46-55

164 MAPPERLEY 10 10 10 10   FRANK SPEDDING

TELL out, my soul, the greatness of the Lord!
Unnumbered blessings, give my spirit voice;
Tender to me the promise of his word;
In God my Saviour shall my heart rejoice.

2 Tell out, my soul, the greatness of his Name!
Make known his might, the deeds his arm has done;
His mercy sure, from age to age the same;
His holy Name—the Lord, the Mighty One.

3 Tell out, my soul, the greatness of his might!
Powers and dominions lay their glory by.
Proud hearts and stubborn wills are put to flight,
The hungry fed, the humble lifted high.

4 Tell out, my soul, the glories of his word!
Firm is his promise, and his mercy sure.
Tell out, my soul, the greatness of the Lord
To children's children and for evermore!

Timothy Dudley-Smith
Based on the Magnificat as in The New English Bible

165 VENI EMMANUEL
L.M. and refrain

15th century plainsong melody

Veni, Emmanuel

O COME, O come, Emmanuel,
And ransom captive Israel,
That mourns in lonely exile here
Until the Son of God appear.
Rejoice! rejoice! Emmanuel
Shall come to thee, O Israel.

2 O come, O come, thou Lord of
    might,
Who to thy tribes, on Sinai's height,
In ancient times didst give the law
In cloud and majesty and awe:

3 O come, thou Rod of Jesse, free
Thine own from Satan's tyranny;
From depths of hell thy people save,
And give them victory o'er the grave:

4 O come, thou Dayspring, come and
    cheer
Our spirits by thine advent here;
Disperse the gloomy clouds of night,
And death's dark shadows put to
    flight:

5 O come, thou Key of David, come,
And open wide our heavenly home;
Make safe the way that leads on high,
And close the path to misery:

18th century, based on the ancient
Advent Antiphons; tr. John Mason Neale, 1818–66

CHRIST'S INCARNATION

166

Tone v ending 1

PSALM 2, verses 1–3, 6–8, 10, 11, 12b

WHY do the heathen ¦ rage :
   and the people i ¦ magine a vain thing?

The kings of the earth set themselves and the rulers take counsel to ¦ gether :
   against the Lord and against his a ¦ nointed saying,

Let us break their bands a ¦ sunder :
   and cast a ¦ way their cords from us.

Yet have I set my ¦ king :
   upon my holy ¦ hill of Zion.

I will declare the decree the Lord hath said unto ¦ me :
   thou art my son this day have ¦ I begotten thee.

Ask of me and I shall give thee the heathen for thine in ¦ heritance :
   and the uttermost parts of the earth for ¦ thy possession.

Be wise now therefore O ye ¦ kings :
   be instructed ye ¦ judges of the earth.

Serve the Lord with ¦ fear :
   and re ¦ joice with trembling.

Blessèd are ¦ all they :
   that ¦ put their trust in him.

Glory be to the Father and to the ¦ Son :
   and ¦ to the Holy Ghost.

As it was in the beginning is now and ever ¦ shall be :
   world with ¦ out end Amen.

167 MONTROSE C.M.

Gilmour's *Psalm-Singer's Assistant*,
Glasgow, 1793

Alternative tune, EFFINGHAM, No. 285 (*omitting Amen*)

PSALM 72, verses 8, 10, 11, 17-19

HIS large and great dominion shall
  From sea to sea extend:
It from the river shall reach forth
  Unto earth's utmost end.

2 The kings of Tarshish, and the isles,
  To him shall presents bring;
And unto him shall offer gifts
  Sheba's and Seba's king.

3 Yea, all the mighty kings on earth
  Before him down shall fall;
And all the nations of the world
  Do service to him shall.

4 His Name for ever shall endure;
  Last like the sun it shall:
Men shall be blest in him, and blest
  All nations shall him call.

5 Now blessèd be the Lord our God,
  The God of Israel,
For he alone doth wondrous works,
  In glory that excel.

6 And blessèd be his glorious Name
  To all eternity:
The whole earth let his glory fill.
  Amen, so let it be.

168 CREDITON C.M.

Clark's *A Second Set of Psalm Tunes*
[*for*] *Country Choirs, c.* 1807

[*For No. 273*]

A - men.

PARAPHRASE 19

THE race that long in darkness
  pined
Have seen a glorious light;
The people dwell in day, who dwelt
  In death's surrounding night.

2 To us a Child of hope is born;
  To us a Son is given;
Him shall the tribes of earth obey,
  Him all the hosts of heaven.

3 His name shall be the Prince of
  Peace,
For evermore adored,
The Wonderful, the Counsellor,
  The great and mighty Lord.

4 His power increasing still shall
  spread,
His reign no end shall know;
Justice shall guard his throne above,
  And peace abound below.

Scottish Paraphrases, 1781. *From Isaiah* 9: 2, 6, 7

169 MENDELSSOHN 7777. D and refrain
(BETHLEHEM)

From a chorus in MENDELSSOHN'S
Festgesang, 1840, adapted by
WILLIAM HAYMAN CUMMINGS, 1831-1915

HARK! the herald angels sing,
'Glory to the new-born King,
Peace on earth, and mercy mild,
God and sinners reconciled!'
Joyful, all ye nations, rise,
Join the triumph of the skies,
With the angelic host proclaim,
'Christ is born in Bethlehem.'
Hark! the herald angels sing,
'Glory to the new-born King'.

2 Christ, by highest heaven adored,
Christ, the everlasting Lord,
Late in time behold him come,
Offspring of a virgin's womb.
Veiled in flesh the Godhead see;
Hail, the Incarnate Deity,
Pleased as Man with man to dwell,
Jesus, our Immanuel!

3 Hail, the heaven-born Prince of
Peace!
Hail, the Sun of Righteousness!
Light and life to all he brings,
Risen with healing in his wings.
Mild he lays his glory by,
Born that man no more may die,
Born to raise the sons of earth,
Born to give them second birth:

Charles Wesley, 1707-88, and others

170 NOEL D.C.M.

Traditional Melody, adapted and extended by
ARTHUR SEYMOUR SULLIVAN, 1842–1900

IT came upon the midnight clear,
   That glorious song of old,
From angels bending near the earth
   To touch their harps of gold:—
'Peace on the earth, good will to men,
   From heaven's all-gracious King!'
The world in solemn stillness lay
   To hear the angels sing.

2 Still through the cloven skies they come
   With peaceful wings unfurled;
And still their heavenly music floats
   O'er all the weary world;
Above its sad and lowly plains
   They bend on hovering wing,
And ever o'er its Babel sounds
   The blessèd angels sing.

3 But with the woes of sin and strife
   The world has suffered long;
Beneath the angel strain have rolled
   Two thousand years of wrong;
And man, at war with man, hears not
   The love song which they bring;
O hush the noise, ye men of strife,
   And hear the angels sing.

4 For, lo! the days are hastening on,
   By prophet bards foretold,
When with the ever-circling years
   Comes round the Age of Gold,
When peace shall over all the earth
   Its ancient splendours fling,
And the whole world give back the song
   Which now the angels sing.

Edmund Hamilton Sears, 1810–76

171 BONN 866. D

JOHANN GEORG EBELING, 1637–76
Geistliche Andacht-Lieder, 1666

Fröhlich soll mein Herze springen

ALL my heart this night rejoices,
    As I hear, far and near,
       Sweetest angel voices;
'Christ is born!' their choirs are singing,
    Till the air, everywhere,
       Now with joy is ringing.

2 Hark! a voice from yonder manger,
    Soft and sweet, doth entreat:
       'Flee from woe and danger;
Brethren, come: from all doth grieve you
    You are freed; all you need
       I will surely give you'.

3 Come, then, let us hasten yonder;
    Here let all, great and small,
       Kneel in awe and wonder.
Love him who with love is yearning;
    Hail the Star that, from far,
       Bright with hope is burning.

Paul Gerhardt, 1607–76
Tr. Catherine Winkworth, 1827–78

172 FOREST GREEN
8686 7686 irregular

English Traditional Melody

O LITTLE town of Bethlehem,
 How still we see thee lie!
Above thy deep and dreamless sleep
 The silent stars go by:
Yet in thy dark streets shineth
 The everlasting Light;
The hopes and fears of all the years
 Are met in thee tonight.

2 O morning stars, together
 Proclaim the holy birth,
And praises sing to God the King,
 And peace to men on earth.
For Christ is born of Mary;
 And, gathered all above,
While mortals sleep, the angels keep
 Their watch of wondering love.

3 How silently, how silently,
 The wondrous gift is given!
So God imparts to human hearts
 The blessings of his heaven.
No ear may hear his coming;
 But in this world of sin,
Where meek souls will receive him, still
 The dear Christ enters in.

4 O Holy Child of Bethlehem,
 Descend to us, we pray;
Cast out our sin, and enter in;
 Be born in us today.
We hear the Christmas angels
 The great glad tidings tell;
O come to us, abide with us,
 Our Lord Immanuel.

Phillips Brooks, 1835–93

173 THE FIRST NOWELL Irregular   English Traditional Melody

THE first Nowell the angel did say
Was to certain poor shepherds in
  fields as they lay:
In fields where they lay a-keeping
  their sheep
On a cold winter's night that was so
  deep.
  Nowell, Nowell, Nowell, Nowell,
  Born is the King of Israel.

2 They lookèd up and saw a star,
  Shining in the east, beyond them far;
  And to the earth it gave great light,
  And so it continued both day and
    night.

3 And by the light of that same star,
  Three wise men came from country
    far;
  To seek for a King was their intent,
  And to follow the star wherever it
    went.

4 This star drew nigh to the north-
    west,
  O'er Bethlehem it took its rest,
  And there it did both stop and stay
  Right over the place where Jesus lay.

5 Then entered in those wise men
    three,
  Full reverently upon their knee,
  And offered there in his presènce
  Their gold and myrrh and frankin-
    cense.

6 Then let us all with one accord
  Sing praises to our Heavenly Lord,
  That hath made heaven and earth of
    naught,
  And with his blood mankind hath
    bought.

Traditional Carol

174 WINCHESTER OLD C.M.

Este's *Psalter*, 1592
(later form of rhythm)

[*For No. 138*]

A - men.

A version with the older form of rhythm is at No. 138

PARAPHRASE 37

WHILE humble shepherds watched
their flocks
In Bethlehem's plains by night,
An angel sent from heaven appeared,
And filled the plains with light.

2 'Fear not,' he said, for sudden dread
Had seized their troubled mind;
'Glad tidings of great joy I bring
To you and all mankind.

3 'To you in David's town, this day,
Is born, of David's line,
The Saviour, who is Christ the Lord;
And this shall be the sign:

4 'The heavenly Babe you there shall
find
To human view displayed,
All meanly wrapped in swathing-
bands,
And in a manger laid.'

5 Thus spake the seraph; and forth-
with
Appeared a shining throng
Of angels praising God; and thus
Addressed their joyful song:

6 'All glory be to God on high,
And to the earth be peace;
Good will is shown by heaven to
men
And never more shall cease.'

Scottish Paraphrases, 1781
Based on St. Luke 2 : 8-14

175 QUEM PASTORES
LAUDAVERE 888 7

Melody from a German MS.
of 1410 (original rhythm)

A version with the later form of rhythm is at No. 111

Quem pastores laudavere

ANGEL voices, richly blending,
Shepherds to the manger sending,
Sing of peace from heav'n descend-
ing!
Shepherds, greet your Shepherd-
King!

2 Lo! a star is brightly glowing!
Eastern kings their gifts are show-
ing
To the King whose gifts pass
knowing!
Gentiles, greet the Gentiles' King!

3 To the manger come adoring,
Hearts in thankfulness outpouring
To the child, true peace restoring,
Mary's Son, our God and King!

German, 14th century; tr. James Quinn

176 STILLE NACHT Irregular   FRANZ GRÜBER, 1787–1863

Stille Nacht, heilige Nacht

STILL the night, holy the night!
Sleeps the world; hid from sight,
Mary and Joseph in stable bare
Watch o'er the Child beloved and
fair,
    Sleeping in heavenly rest,
    Sleeping in heavenly rest.

2 Still the night, holy the night!
Shepherds first saw the light,
Heard resounding clear and long,
Far and near, the angel-song,
    'Christ the Redeemer is here!'
    'Christ the Redeemer is here!'

3 Still the night, holy the night!
Son of God, O how bright
Love is smiling from thy face!
Strikes for us now the hour of grace,
    Saviour, since thou art born!
    Saviour, since thou art born!

*Joseph Mohr, 1792–1848. Tr. Stopford Augustus Brooke, 1832–1916,
and the Compilers of* The Church Hymnary (Revised Edition)

177 SUMMER IN WINTER Irregular   ARTHUR OLDHAM

1. Gloo - my night em - braced the place Where the no - ble In - fant lay; The Babe looked up and showed his face, In spite of __ dark - ness it was day! It was thy day, Sweet, and did rise, __ Not from the East, but from thine eyes.

2. We saw thee in thy bal - my nest, Bright dawn of our e - ter - nal day! We saw thine eyes break from their east And chase the __ trem - bling shades a - way; We saw thee, and we blessed the light.

3. Wel - come all won - der in one sight, E - ter - ni - ty shut in a span __ Sum - mer in win - ter, day in night, __ Hea - ven in earth, and God in man! __ (v. 3 continues below) sight, We saw thee by thine own sweet eyes. Great Lit - tle One! whose all - em - bra - cing birth Lifts earth to heav'n, stoops heav'n to earth.

Richard Crashaw, c. 1613–49, from Hymn in the Holy Nativity, 1648

178 CRANHAM Irregular   GUSTAV HOLST, 1874–1934

1. In the bleak mid-win-ter   Frost-y wind made
2. Our God, heav'n can-not hold him,   Nor earth sus-
3. An-gels and arch-an-gels   May have ga-thered
4. What can I give him,   Poor as I

1. moan,   Earth stood hard as i--ron,
2. tain;   Heav'n and earth shall flee a-way
3. there,   Che-ru-bim and se-ra-phim
4. am?   If I were a shep-herd

1. Wa-ter like a stone;   Snow had fall-en,
2. When he comes to reign: In the bleak mid-
3. Throng-èd the air;   But on--ly his
4. I would bring a lamb;   If I were a

1. snow on snow,   Snow on snow,
2. -win-ter   A sta-ble-place suf-ficed   The
3. mo-ther,   In her mai-den bliss,
4. wise man   I would do my part;   Yet

1. In the bleak mid-win-ter,   Long a-go.
2. Lord God Al-migh-ty,   Je--sus Christ.
3. Worshipped the Be-lov-ed   With a kiss.
4. what I can I give him—   Give my heart.

Christina Rossetti, 1830–94

179 HUMILITY (OXFORD) 7777 and refrain JOHN GOSS, 1800–8o

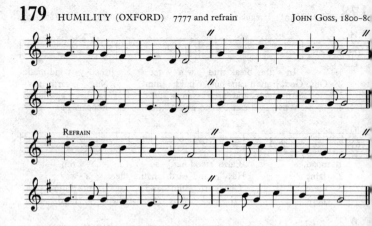

SEE! in yonder manger low,
Born for us on earth below,
See! the tender Lamb appears
Promised from eternal years.
    Hail, thou ever-blessèd morn!
    Hail, redemption's happy dawn!
    Sing through all Jerusalem,
    'Christ is born in Bethlehem!'

2 Lo! within a manger lies
He who built the starry skies,
He who, throned in height sublime,
Sits amid the cherubim:

3 Sacred Infant, all Divine,
What a tender love was thine,
Thus to come from highest bliss
Down to such a world as this!

            Edward Caswall, 1814–78
                    (altered)

180 BUNESSAN 5553. D   Gaelic Melody

Leanabh an aigh

CHILD in the manger,
   Infant of Mary;
Outcast and stranger,
   Lord of all!
Child who inherits
   All our transgressions,
All our demerits
   On him fall.

2 Once the most holy
   Child of salvation
Gently and lowly
   Lived below;
Now, as our glorious
   Mighty Redeemer,
See him victorious
   O'er each foe.

3 Prophets foretold him,
   Infant of wonder;
Angels behold him
   On his throne;
Worthy our Saviour
   Of all their praises;
Happy for ever
   Are his own.

Mary Macdonald, 1789–1872
Tr. Lachlan Macbean, 1853–1931

181 SUSSEX CAROL
L.M. Irregular

English Traditional Melody

1. On Christ - mas night all Christ - ians sing, To
2. Then why should men on earth be so sad, Since
3. When sin de - parts be - fore___ his grace, Then
4. All out of dark - ness we___ have light, Which

hear the news___ the an - gels bring, On Christ-mas night all
our Re - deem - er made us glad, Then why should men on
life and health come in its place; When sin de - parts be -
made the an - gels sing this night: All out of dark - ness

Christ - ians sing, To hear the news the an - gels bring—
earth be so sad, Since our Re - deem - er made us glad,
- fore___ his grace, Then life and health come in its place;
we___ have light, Which made the an - gels sing this night:

News of great joy,___ news of___ great mirth,
When from our sin___ he set___ us free,
An - gels and men___ with joy___ may sing,
'Glor - y to God___ and peace___ to men,

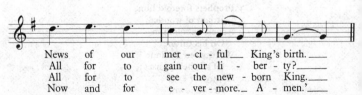

News of our mer - ci - ful___ King's birth.___
All for to gain our li - ber - ty?___
All for to see the new - born King.___
Now and for e - ver - more.___ A - men.'___

Traditional Carol

182 IRIS 8787 and refrain

French Carol Melody

REFRAIN

Come _____ and
wor - ship
(1st) Christ, the new - born King. ___
(2nd) Wor - ship Christ, the new - born King.

ANGELS from the realms of glory,
  Wing your flight o'er all the earth;
Ye who sang creation's story,
  Now proclaim Messiah's birth;
    Come and worship
    Christ, the new-born King.
    Come and worship,
    Worship Christ, the new-born King.

2 Shepherds, in the fields abiding,
    Watching o'er your flock by night,
  God with man is now residing,
    Yonder shines the infant Light;

3 Wise men, leave your contemplations;
    Brighter visions beam afar;
  Seek the great Desire of nations;
    Ye have seen his natal star;

4 *All creation, join in praising*
    God the Father, Spirit, Son,
  Evermore your voices raising
    To the eternal Three in One:

James Montgomery, 1771–1854

183 IN DULCI JUBILO 66 7778 55   German Melody, 14th century

GOOD Christian men, rejoice
With heart and soul and voice;
  Give ye heed to what we say,
  Jesus Christ is born today:
Ox and ass before him bow,
And he is in the manger now.
    Christ is born today!
    Christ is born today!

2 Good Christian men, rejoice
With heart and soul and voice;
  Now ye hear of endless bliss,
  Jesus Christ was born for this:
He hath oped the heavenly door,
And man is blessèd evermore.
    Christ was born for this!
    Christ was born for this!

3 Good Christian men, rejoice
With heart and soul and voice;
  Now ye need not fear the grave,
  Jesus Christ was born to save,
Calls you one, and calls you all,
To gain his everlasting hall.
    Christ was born to save!
    Christ was born to save!

John Mason Neale, 1818–66

184 GOD REST YOU MERRY
Irregular

English Traditional Melody (London)

REFRAIN

O__ tid - ings of com - fort and joy, com-fort and joy! O__ tid - ings of com - fort and joy!

GOD rest you merry, gentlemen,
Let nothing you dismay,
For Jesus Christ our Saviour
Was born upon this day,
To save us all from Satan's power
When we were gone astray:
O tidings of comfort and joy, comfort and joy!
O tidings of comfort and joy!

2 From God our Heav'nly Father
A blessèd angel came,
And unto certain shepherds
Brought tidings of the same,
How that in Bethlehem was born
The Son of God by name:

3 The shepherds at those tidings
Rejoicèd much in mind,
And left their flocks a-feeding
In tempest, storm and wind,
And went to Bethlehem straightway
This blessèd Babe to find:

4 But when to Bethlehem they came,
Whereat this Infant lay,
They found him in a manger,
Where oxen feed on hay;
His mother Mary kneeling
Unto the Lord did pray:

5 Now to the Lord sing praises,
All you within this place,
And with true love and brotherhood
Each other now embrace;
This holy tide of Christmas
All others doth deface:

Traditional Carol

185 OLWEN 668 668. D   Welsh Carol Melody

O Deued Pob Cristion

ALL poor men and humble,
All lame men who stumble,
Come haste ye nor feel ye afraid;
For Jesus, our treasure,
With love past all measure,
In lowly poor manger was laid.

2 Though wise men who found him
Laid rich gifts around him,
Yet oxen they gave him their hay:
And Jesus in beauty
Accepted their duty;
Contented in manger he lay.

3 Then haste we to show him
The praises we owe him;
Our service he ne'er can despise:
Whose love still is able
To show us that stable
Where softly in manger he lies.

Katharine Emily Roberts, 1877–1962,
based on a Welsh Carol

186 INFANT HOLY
447. D 4444 77

Polish Carol Melody

W Żłobie Leży

INFANT holy,
Infant lowly,
For his bed a cattle stall;
Oxen lowing,
Little knowing
Christ the babe is Lord of all.
Swift are winging
Angels singing,
Nowells ringing,
Tidings bringing,
Christ the babe is Lord of all,
Christ the babe is Lord of all.

2   Flocks were sleeping,
Shepherds keeping
Vigil till the morning new
Saw the glory,
Heard the story,
Tidings of a gospel true.
Thus rejoicing,
Free from sorrow,
Praises voicing,
Greet the morrow,
Christ the babe was born for you!
Christ the babe was born for you!

Polish Carol; tr. Edith M. G. Reed, 1885-1933

187 PUER NOBIS
76 777 irregular

Piae Cantiones, 1582

Puer nobis nascitur

UNTO us is born a Son,
King of Quires supernal:
See on earth his life begun,
Of lords the Lord eternal,
Of lords the Lord eternal.

2 Christ, from heav'n descending low,
Comes on earth a stranger:
Ox and ass their Owner know
Becradled in the manger,
Becradled in the manger.

3 This did Herod sore affray,
And grievously bewilder;
So he gave the word to slay,
And slew the little childer,
And slew the little childer.

4 Of his love and mercy mild
This the Christmas story:
And O that Mary's gentle Child
Might lead us up to glory,
Might lead us up to glory!

5 O and A and A and O
Cum cantibus in choro,
Let our merry organ go,
Benedicamus Domino,
Benedicamus Domino.

Piae Cantiones, 1582
Tr. George Ratcliffe Woodward, 1848–1934

188 & 189 VOM HIMMEL HOCH
L.M.

Attributed to
MARTIN LUTHER, 1483–1546

[*for No. 189 only*]

A - men.

188

Vom Himmel hoch da komm ich her

GIVE heed, my heart, lift up thine
    eyes:
Who is it in yon manger lies?
Who is this child so young and fair?
The blessèd Christ-child lieth there.

2 Welcome to earth, thou noble Guest,
Through whom even wicked men are
    blest!
Thou com'st to share our misery;
What can we render, Lord, to thee?

3 Were earth a thousand times as fair,
Beset with gold and jewels rare,
She yet were far too poor to be
A narrow cradle, Lord, for thee.

4 Ah! dearest Jesus, Holy Child,
Make thee a bed, soft, undefiled,
Within my heart, that it may be
A quiet chamber kept for thee.

5 My heart for very joy doth leap;
My lips no more can silence keep;
I too must raise with joyful tongue
That sweetest ancient cradle song.

6 'Glory to God in highest heaven,
Who unto man his Son hath given!'
While angels sing with pious mirth
A glad New Year to all the earth.

Martin Luther, 1483-1546
Tr. Catherine Winkworth, 1827-78

189

A solis ortus cardine

FROM east to west, from shore to
    shore,
Let every heart awake and sing
The holy Child whom Mary bore,
The Christ, the everlasting King.

2 Behold, the world's Creator wears
    The form and fashion of a slave;
Our very flesh our Maker shares,
    His fallen creature, man, to save.

3 For this how wondrously he wrought!
    A maiden, in her lowly place,
Became, in ways beyond all thought,
    The chosen vessel of his grace.

4 He shrank not from the oxen's stall,
    He lay within the manger bed,
And he, whose bounty feedeth all,
    At Mary's breast himself was fed.

5 And while the angels in the sky
    Sang praise above the silent field,
To shepherds poor the Lord most high,
    The one great Shepherd, was revealed.

6 *All glory for this blessèd morn*
    To God the Father ever be;
All praise to thee, O Virgin-born,
    All praise, O Holy Ghost, to thee. Amen.

Caelius Sedulius, d. c. 450
Tr. John Ellerton, 1826-93

190 YORKSHIRE   10 10 10 10   10 10
(STOCKPORT)

JOHN WAINWRIGHT, 1723-68

CHRISTIANS, awake, salute the happy morn,
Whereon the Saviour of the world was born;
Rise to adore the mystery of love,
Which hosts of angels chanted from above;
With them the joyful tidings first begun
Of God Incarnate and the Virgin's Son:

2 Then to the watchful shepherds it was told,
Who heard the angelic herald's voice, 'Behold,
I bring good tidings of a Saviour's birth
To you and all the nations upon earth;
This day hath God fulfilled his promised word,
This day is born a Saviour, Christ the Lord.'

3 To Bethl'em straight the enlightened shepherds ran
To see the wonder God had wrought for man,
And found, with Joseph and the blessèd Maid,
Her Son, the Saviour, in a manger laid;
Joyful, the wondrous story they proclaim,
The first apostles of his infant fame.

4 O may we keep and ponder in our mind
God's wondrous love in saving lost mankind;
Trace we the Babe, who hath retrieved our loss,
From his poor manger to his bitter cross;
Saved by his love, incessant we shall sing
Eternal praise to heaven's almighty King.

John Byrom, 1691-1763, and the Compilers of
The BBC Hymn Book, 1951

191 ADESTE FIDELES Irregular

From a MS. of *c.* 1745
Possibly by JOHN WADE, *c.* 1711–86

REFRAIN

v.2 Be - got-ten

Adeste fideles

O COME, all ye faithful,
Joyful and triumphant,
O come ye, O come ye to Bethlehem;
Come and behold him
Born the King of angels;
O come, let us adore him,
O come, let us adore him,
O come, let us adore him, Christ the Lord.

2 God of God,
Light of Light,
Lo! he abhors not the Virgin's
womb;
Very God,
Begotten, not created;

3 Sing, choirs of angels,
Sing in exultation,
Sing, all ye citizens of heaven
above,
'Glory to God
In the highest':

For Christmas Day

4 Yea, Lord, we greet thee,
Born this happy morning;
Jesus, to thee be glory given:
Word of the Father,
Now in flesh appearing;

Possibly by John Wade, c. 1711–86
Tr. Frederick Oakeley, 1802–80, and others

169

192 ES IST EIN' ROS' ENTSPRUNGEN
7676 and refrain

German Carol Melody

REFRAIN

Re - peat the hymn a - gain!   'To God on high be glor - y, And peace on earth to men!'

Μέγα καὶ παράδοξον θαῦμα

A GREAT and mighty wonder,
A full and holy cure!
The Virgin bears the Infant
With virgin-honour pure.
   Repeat the hymn again!
      'To God on high be glory,
   And peace on earth to men!'

2 The Word becomes incarnate
   And yet remains on high!
   And Cherubim sing anthems
   To shepherds, from the sky:

3 While thus they sing your Monarch,
   Those bright angelic bands,
   Rejoice, ye vales and mountains,
   Ye oceans, clap your hands:

4 Since all he comes to ransom,
   By all be he adored,
   The Infant born in Bethl'em,
   The Saviour and the Lord:

5 And idol forms shall perish,
   And error shall decay,
   And Christ shall wield his sceptre,
   Our Lord and God for aye:

St. Germanus, c. 634–c. 734
Tr. John Mason Neale, 1818–66, and others

193 IRBY 8787 77

HENRY JOHN GAUNTLETT, 1805–76

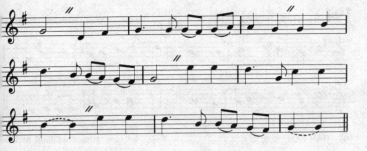

ONCE in royal David's city
  Stood a lowly cattle-shed,
Where a mother laid her Baby
  In a manger for his bed.
Mary was that mother mild,
Jesus Christ her little Child.

2 He came down to earth from heaven
  Who is God and Lord of all,
And his shelter was a stable,
  And his cradle was a stall.
With the poor and mean and lowly
Lived on earth our Saviour holy.

3 And through all his wondrous childhood
  He would honour and obey,
Love, and watch the lowly maiden
  In whose gentle arms he lay.
Christian children all must be
Mild, obedient, good as he.

4 For he is our childhood's pattern:
  Day by day like us he grew;
He was little, weak, and helpless;
  Tears and smiles like us he knew;
And he feeleth for our sadness,
And he shareth in our gladness.

5 And our eyes at last shall see him,
  Through his own redeeming love;
For that Child so dear and gentle
  Is our Lord in heaven above;
And he leads his children on
To the place where he is gone.

6 Not in that poor lowly stable,
  With the oxen standing by,
We shall see him, but in heaven,
  Set at God's right hand on high,
When, like stars, his children crowned
All in white shall wait around.

Cecil Frances Alexander, 1818-95

194 (i) HERMITAGE 6767   REGINALD OWEN MORRIS, 1886–194[?]

(ii) GARTAN 6767   Irish Traditional Melod[y]

LOVE came down at Christmas,
    Love all lovely, Love Divine;
Love was born at Christmas,
    Star and angels gave the sign.

2 Worship we the Godhead,
    Love Incarnate, Love Divine;
Worship we our Jesus:
    But wherewith for sacred sign?

3 Love shall be our token,
    Love be yours and love be mine,
Love to God and all men,
    Love for plea and gift and sign.

Christina Rossetti, 1830–94

195 (i) CRADLE SONG   WILLIAM JAMES KIRKPATRICK, 1838–192[?]
     11 11 11 11   *Around the World with Christmas*, 1895

(ii) NORMANDY 11 11 11 11

Basque Carol Melody, collected and
extended by CHARLES EDGAR PETTMAN, 1866–1943

For younger children

AWAY in a manger, no crib for a bed,
The little Lord Jesus laid down his sweet head.
The stars in the bright sky looked down where he lay,
The little Lord Jesus asleep on the hay.

2 The cattle are lowing, the Baby awakes,
But little Lord Jesus no crying he makes.
I love thee, Lord Jesus! look down from the sky,
And stay by my side until morning is nigh.

3 Be near me, Lord Jesus; I ask thee to stay
Close by me for ever, and love me, I pray.
Bless all the dear children in thy tender care,
And fit us for heaven, to live with thee there.

Anonymous

196 RODMELL C.M.   English Traditional Melody

Holy Innocents' Day

WHEN Christ was born in Bethlehem,
    Fair peace on earth to bring,
In lowly state of love he came
    To be the children's King.

2 And round him, then, a holy band
    Of children blest was born,
Fair guardians of his throne to stand
    Attendant night and morn.

3 And unto them this grace was given
    A Saviour's Name to own,
And die for him who out of heaven
    Had found on earth a throne.

4 O blessèd babes of Bethlehem,
    Who died to save our King,
Ye share the martyrs' diadem,
    And in their anthem sing!

Laurence Housman, 1865-1959

197 THIS ENDRIS NYGHT C.M.   English Carol Melody, 15th cent.

BEHOLD the great Creator makes
    Himself a house of clay,
A robe of human flesh he takes
    Which he will wear for aye.

2 Hark, hark, the wise eternal Word,
    Like a weak infant cries!
In form of servant is the Lord,
    And God in cradle lies.

3 Glad shepherds came to view this sight;
    A choir of angels sings,
And eastern sages with delight
    Adore this King of kings.

4 Join then, all hearts that are not stone,
    And all our voices prove,
To celebrate this holy One
    The God of peace and love.

Thomas Pestel, 1584-1659 (altered)

198 CORDE NATUS
(DIVINUM MYSTERIUM)
8787 87 and refrain

Late form of a Plainsong Melody,
as given in *Piae Cantiones*, 1582

REFRAIN

A - men.

Corde natus ex Parentis

OF the Father's love begotten
  Ere the worlds began to be,
He is Alpha and Omega,
  He the source, the ending he,
Of the things that are, that have been,
  And that future years shall see,
     Evermore and evermore.

2 O that birth for ever blessèd,
  When the Virgin, full of grace,
By the Holy Ghost conceiving,
  Bare the Saviour of our race,
And the Babe, the world's Redeemer,
  First revealed his sacred face,

3 This is he whom seers in old time
  Chanted of with one accord,
Whom the voices of the prophets
  Promised in their faithful word;
Now he shines, the Long-expected;
  Let creation praise its Lord,

4 O ye heights of heaven, adore him;
  Angel hosts, his praises sing;
All dominions, bow before him,
  And extol our God and King;
Let no tongue on earth be silent,
  Every voice in concert ring,

5 *Christ, to thee, with God the Father,*
  And, O Holy Ghost, to thee,
Hymn, and chant, and high thanksgiving,
  And unwearied praises be,
Honour, glory, and dominion,
  And eternal victory,
     Evermore and evermore. Amen.

Prudentius, 348–c. 413; tr. John Mason Neale, 1818–66,
and Henry Williams Baker, 1821–77

199 STUTTGART 8787

Adapted from a melody in Witt's
Psalmodia Sacra, Gotha, 1715

A - men.

O sola magnarum urbium

BETHLEHEM, of noblest cities
    None can once with thee compare;
Thou alone the Lord from heaven
    Didst for us incarnate bear.

2 Fairer than the sun at morning
    Was the star that told his birth;
To the world its God announcing,
    Seen in fleshly form on earth.

3 Eastern sages at his cradle
    Make oblations rich and rare;
See them give, in deep devotion,
    Gold and frankincense and myrrh.

4 Sacred gifts of mystic meaning:
    Incense doth their God disclose,
Gold the King of kings proclaimeth,
    Myrrh his sepulchre foreshows.

5 *Holy Jesu, in thy brightness*
    To the Gentile world displayed,
With the Father and the Spirit
    Endless praise to thee be paid. Amen.

Prudentius, 348–c. 413
Tr. Edward Caswall, 1814–78

200 DIX 7777 77

CONRAD KOCHER, 1786-1872
Adapted by WILLIAM HENRY MONK, 1823-89

AS with gladness men of old
Did the guiding star behold,
As with joy they hailed its light,
Leading onward, beaming bright,—
So, most gracious Lord, may we
Evermore be led to thee.

2 As with joyful steps they sped,
Saviour, to thy lowly bed,
There to bend the knee before
Thee, whom heaven and earth adore,—
So may we with willing feet
Ever seek thy mercy-seat.

3 As they offered gifts most rare
At thy cradle rude and bare,—
So may we with holy joy,
Pure, and free from sin's alloy,
All our costliest treasures bring,
Christ, to thee, our heavenly King.

4 Holy Jesus, every day
Keep us in the narrow way;
And, when earthly things are past,
Bring our ransomed souls at last
Where they need no star to guide,
Where no clouds thy glory hide.

5 In the heavenly country bright
Need they no created light;
Thou its light, its joy, its crown,
Thou its sun which goes not down;
There for ever may we sing
Alleluias to our King.

William Chatterton Dix, 1837-98

201 CRUDWELL 11 10 11 10   WALTER KENDALL STANTON

BRIGHTEST and best of the sons of the morning,
   Dawn on our darkness, and lend us thine aid;
Star of the east, the horizon adorning,
   Guide where our infant Redeemer is laid.

2 Cold on his cradle the dew-drops are shining;
   Low lies his head with the beasts of the stall;
Angels adore him in slumber reclining,
   Maker and Monarch and Saviour of all.

3 Say, shall we yield him, in costly devotion,
   Odours of Edom, and offerings divine,
Gems of the mountains and pearls of the ocean,
   Myrrh from the forest or gold from the mine?

4 Vainly we offer each ample oblation,
   Vainly with gifts would his favour secure;
Richer by far is the heart's adoration;
   Dearer to God are the prayers of the poor.

5 Brightest and best of the sons of the morning,
   Dawn on our darkness, and lend us thine aid;
Star of the east, the horizon adorning,
   Guide where our infant Redeemer is laid.

Reginald Heber, 1783-1826

202 WIE SCHÖN LEUCHTET
887. D 8448

PHILIPP NICOLAI, 1556–1608

Wie schön leuchtet der Morgenstern

HOW brightly beams the morning star!
What sudden radiance from afar
  Doth glad us with its shining?
Brightness of God, that breaks our night
And fills the darkened souls with light
  Who long for truth were pining!
Thy word, Jesus, inly feeds us,
      Rightly leads us,
      Life bestowing.
Praise, oh praise such love o'erflowing!

2 O praise to him who came to save,
Who conquered death and burst the grave;
  Each day new praise resoundeth
To him the Lamb who once was slain,
The friend whom none shall trust in vain,
  Whose grace for aye aboundeth;
Sing, ye heavens, tell the story,
      Of his glory,
      Till his praises
Flood with light earth's darkest places!

Philipp Nicolai, 1556–1608,
and Johann Schlegel, 1721–93
Tr. Catherine Winkworth, 1827–78

203 IN DER WIEGEN   Irregular   Corner's *Geistliche Nachtigall*, 1649

Rājāono rājā ane sṛṣṭino sṛjnār

KING of kings and Lord of lords, and Maker of all is he;
Leaving the glory of heaven he comes, incarnate now to be,
    Incarnate now to be.

2 Lord of the world, he comes among us, bearing love and grace;
Born of the womb of Virgin Mary, there in David's place,
    There in David's place.

3 Angels clothed in robes of whiteness, far above the earth,
Filling the heav'ns with praise and wonder, sing of Jesus' birth,
    Sing of Jesus' birth.

4 Joyful, joyful, all you people, give the Saviour praise!
Welcome the new-born King with gladness, shouts of triumph raise!
    Shouts of triumph raise!

5 All for *your* sake, all for *my* sake; yes, for *all*, I say;
Now for the *world* comes news of salvation: 'Christ is born today!'
    'Christ is born today!'

6 Worship now, but do not leave him out in stable bare;
Give him your heart for home! Enthrone him, King of glory there!
    King of glory there!

From the Gujarati of Kahanji Madhavji Ratnagrahi, 1869–1916
Tr. Robert H. S. Boyd, adapted James N. S. Alexander

The following are also suitable

No.
40 Worship the Lord in the beauty of holiness
369 God and Father, we adore thee
399 Though in God's form he was
12 Lift up your heads, ye mighty gates
158 Give the king thy judgments O God

THE WORD OF GOD: HIS MIGHTY ACTS

CHRIST'S LIFE AND MINISTRY

204 (i)

Adapted from the *Tonus Peregrinus*

(ii)

HENRY GEORGE LEY, 1887-1962

(iii)

RICHARD FARRANT (?), *c.* 1530-80

NUNC DIMITTIS

LORD now lettest thou thy servant de- | part in | peace:
ac- | cording | to thy | word.

2 For mine eyes have | seen thy sal- | vation:
which thou hast prepared before the | face of | all | people.

3 To be a light to | lighten the | Gentiles:
and to be the | glory of thy | people | Isra-el.

Glory | be to the | Father:
and to the Son | and to the | Holy | Ghost:

As it | was in the be- | ginning:
is now and ever shall be | world without | end. A- | men.

From St. Luke 2: 29-32

205 PSALM 136 7777
(LOUEZ DIEU)

Melody from *French Psalter*, 1562
Set by CLAUDE GOUDIMEL, 1565

'JESUS!' Name of wondrous love;
Name all other names above,
Unto which must every knee
Bow in deep humility.

2 'Jesus!' Name of priceless worth
To the fallen sons of earth,
For the promise that it gave,—
'Jesus shall his people save'.

3 'Jesus!' Name of mercy mild,
Given to the Holy Child
When the cup of human woe
First he tasted here below.

4 'Jesus!' only Name that's given
Under all the mighty heaven
Whereby man, to sin enslaved,
Bursts his fetters, and is saved.

5 'Jesus!' Name of wondrous love;
Human Name of God above;
Pleading only this, we flee,
Helpless, O our God, to thee.

William Walsham How, 1823-97

206 AVE MARIA KLARE 7676 676   *Psalteriolum Harmonicum, 1642*

Candlemas

WHEN Mary brought her treasure
  Unto the holy place,
No eye of man could measure
  The joy upon her face.
    He was but six weeks old,
Her plaything and her pleasure,
  Her silver and her gold.

2 Then Simeon, on him gazing
  With wonder and with love,
His agèd voice up-raising
  Gave thanks to God above:
    'Now welcome sweet release!
For I, my Saviour praising,
  May die at last in peace'.

3 And she, all sorrow scorning,
  Rejoiced in Jesus' fame.
The child her arms adorning
  Shone softly like a flame
    That burns the long night
      through,
And keeps from dusk till morning
  Its vigil clear and true.

4 As by the sun in splendour
  The flags of night are furled,
So darkness shall surrender
  To Christ who lights the world:
    To Christ the Star of day,
Who once was small and tender,
  A candle's gentle ray.

Jan Struther, 1901-53

207 LOVE UNKNOWN 66 12 88

JOHN IRELAND, 1879–1962
The Public School Hymn Book, 1919

BEHOLD a little Child,
   Laid in a manger bed;
  The wintry blasts blow wild around his infant head.
But who is this, so lowly laid?
'Tis he by whom the worlds were made.

2   Where Joseph plies his trade,
      Lo, Jesus labours too;
    The hands that all things made an earthly craft pursue,
That weary men in him may rest,
And faithful toil through him be blest.

3   Among the doctors see
      The Boy so full of grace;
    Say, wherefore taketh he the scholar's lowly place?
That Christian boys, with reverence meet,
May sit and learn at Jesus' feet.

4   Christ, once thyself a boy!
      Our boyhood guard and guide;
    Be thou its light and joy, and still with us abide,
That thy dear love, so great and free,
May draw us evermore to thee.

William Walsham How, 1823–97

208 SOLEMNIS HAEC FESTIVITAS L.M.   *Paris Gradual,* 1685

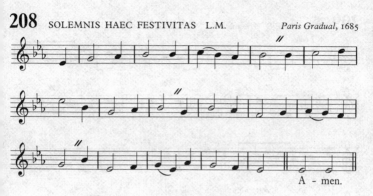

A - men.

Iordanis oras praevia

ON Jordan's bank the Baptist's cry
Announces that the Lord is nigh;
Come then and hearken, for he brings
Glad tidings from the King of kings.

2 Then cleansed be every breast from sin;
Make straight the way for God within;
Prepare we in our hearts a home,
Where such a mighty Guest may come.

3 For thou art our salvation, Lord,
Our refuge, and our great reward;
Without thy grace we waste away,
Like flowers that wither and decay.

4 Stretch forth thine hand, to heal our sore,
And make us rise to fall no more;
Once more upon thy people shine,
And fill the world with love divine.

5 *All praise, eternal Son, to thee*
Whose advent sets thy people free,
Whom with the Father we adore,
And Holy Ghost, for evermore. Amen.

Charles Coffin, 1676-1749
Tr. John Chandler, 1806-76, and others

209 ST. OLAF'S Irregular   JOHN GARDNER, *The Cambridge Hymnal*, 1967

Hostis Herodes impie

HOW vain the cruel Herod's fear,
When told that Christ the King is near!
He takes not earthly realms away,
Who gives the realms that ne'er decay.

2 The eastern sages saw from far
And followed on his guiding star;
By light their way to Light they trod,
And by their gifts confessed their God.

186

3 Within the Jordan's sacred flood
  The heavenly Lamb in meekness stood,
  That he, to whom no sin was known,
  Might cleanse his people from their own.

4 And oh, what miracle divine,
  When water reddened into wine!
  He spake the word, and forth there flowed
  A stream that nature ne'er bestowed.

5 *All glory, Jesus, be to thee*
  For this thy glad Epiphany:
  Whom with the Father we adore,
  And Holy Ghost, for evermore. Amen.

Caelius Sedulius, d. c. 450; tr. John Mason Neale, 1818-66,
and Compilers of Hymns Ancient and Modern, 1875 edn.

210 AUS DER TIEFE 7777 *Nürnbergisches Gesangbuch, 1676-7 (altered)*
(HEINLEIN) Possibly by MARTIN HERBST, 1654-81

FORTY days and forty nights
  Thou wast fasting in the wild;
Forty days and forty nights
  Tempted still, yet undefiled.

* 2 Sunbeams scorching day by day;
    Chilly dewdrops nightly shed;
  Prowling beasts about thy way;
    Stones thy pillow; earth thy bed.

3 Shall not we thy sorrows share,
    Learn thy discipline of will,
  And, like thee, by fast and prayer
    Wrestle with the powers of ill?

4 What if Satan, vexing sore,
    Flesh and spirit shall assail,
  Thou, his vanquisher before,
    Wilt not suffer us to fail.

5 Watching, praying, struggling thus,
    Victory ours at last shall be;
  Angels minister to us
    As they ministered to thee.

George Smyttan, 1822-70, and Francis Pott, 1832-1909 (altered)

* *This verse may be omitted if desired*

187

211 (i) OMNI DIE 8787

Corner's *Gesangbuch*, 1631

(ii) ST. ANDREW 8787

EDWARD HENRY THORNE, 1834-1916
Hymns Ancient and Modern, 1875

JESUS calls us! O'er the tumult
    Of our life's wild restless sea,
Day by day his voice is sounding,
    Saying, 'Christian, follow me':

2 As, of old, Saint Andrew heard it
    By the Galilean lake,
Turned from home and toil and kindred,
    Leaving all for his dear sake.

3 Jesus calls us from the worship
    Of the vain world's golden store,
From each idol that would keep us,
    Saying, 'Christian, love me more'.

4 In our joys and in our sorrows,
    Days of toil and hours of ease,
Still he calls, in cares and pleasures,
    'Christian, love me more than these'.

5 Jesus calls us! By thy mercies,
    Saviour, make us hear thy call,
Give our hearts to thy obedience,
    Serve and love thee best of all.

Cecil Frances Alexander, 1818-95 (altered)

212 KINGSFOLD
D.C.M. irregular

English Traditional Melody collected by
LUCY BROADWOOD, 1858–1929

In vv. 2 and 3 lines 5 and 6 run thus:

(2) I — came to Je - sus, and I drank Of — that life — giv - ing stream;
(3) I — looked to Je - sus, and I found In — him my — star, my sun;

I HEARD the voice of Jesus say,
  'Come unto me and rest;
Lay down, thou weary one, lay down
  Thy head upon my breast':
I came to Jesus as I was,
  Weary, and worn, and sad;
I found in him a resting-place,
  And he has made me glad.

2 I heard the voice of Jesus say,
  'Behold, I freely give
The living water; thirsty one,
  Stoop down and drink, and live':
I came to Jesus, and I drank
  Of that life-giving stream;
My thirst was quenched, my soul revived,
  And now I live in him.

3 I heard the voice of Jesus say,
  'I am this dark world's Light;
Look unto me, thy morn shall rise,
  And all thy day be bright':
I looked to Jesus, and I found
  In him my Star, my Sun;
And in that light of life I'll walk,
  Till travelling days are done.

Horatius Bonar, 1808–89

213 CHILDHOOD 8886

WALFORD DAVIES, 1869–1941
A Students' Hymnal, 1923

IT fell upon a summer day,
When Jesus walked in Galilee,
The mothers from a village brought
Their children to his knee.

2 He took them in his arms, and laid
His hands on each remembered
head;
'Suffer these little ones to come
To me', he gently said.

3 'Forbid them not; unless ye bear
The childlike heart your hearts
within,
Unto my Kingdom ye may come,
But may not enter in.'

4 Master, I fain would enter there;
O let me follow thee, and share
Thy meek and lowly heart, and be
Freed from all worldly care.

5 O happy thus to live and move!
And sweet this world, where I shall
find
God's beauty everywhere, his love,
His good in all mankind.

6 Then, Father, grant this childlike
heart,
That I may come to Christ, and feel
His hands on me in blessing laid,
Love-giving, strong to heal.

Stopford Augustus Brooke, 1832–1916

214 ST. MATTHEW D.C.M.

Later form of a tune in
A Supplement to the New Version, 1708
Probably by WILLIAM CROFT, 1678–1727

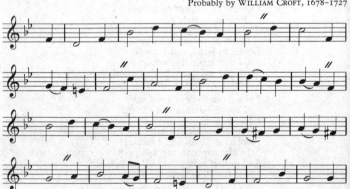

THINE arm, O Lord, in days of old,
 Was strong to heal and save;
It triumphed o'er disease and death,
 O'er darkness and the grave.
To thee they went—the blind, the
  dumb,
 The palsied, and the lame,
The leper with his tainted life,
 The sick with fevered frame;

2 And, lo! thy touch brought life and
  health,
 Gave speech, and strength, and
  sight;
And youth renewed and frenzy
  calmed
 Owned thee, the Lord of light.
And now, O Lord, be near to bless,
 Almighty as of yore,
In crowded street, by restless couch,
 As by Gennesaret's shore.

3 Be thou our great Deliverer still,
 Thou Lord of life and death;
Restore and quicken, soothe and bless,
 With thine almighty breath;
To hands that work and eyes that see
 Give wisdom's heavenly lore,
That whole and sick, and weak and strong,
 May praise thee evermore.

Edward Hayes Plumptre, 1821-91

215 CULROSS C.M.

Scottish Psalter, 1634

JESUS, whose all-redeeming love
 No penitent did scorn,
Who didst the stain of guilt remove,
 Till hope anew was born:

2 To thee, Physician of the soul,
 The lost, the outcast, came:
Thou didst restore and make them
  whole,
 Disburdened of their shame.

3 'Twas love, thy love, their bondage
  brake,
 Whose fetters sin had bound:
For faith to love did answer make,
 And free forgiveness found.

4 Jesus, that pardoning grace to find,
 I too would come to thee:
O merciful to all mankind,
 Be merciful to me.

George Wallace Briggs, 1875-1959

216 ST. BERNARD
C.M.

Tochter Sion, Cologne, 1741, as adapted
in *Easy Hymn Tunes for Catholic Schools*, 1851

WHAT grace, O Lord, and beauty
    shone
Around thy steps below!
What patient love was seen in all
    Thy life and death of woe!

2 Thy foes might hate, despise, revile,
    Thy friends unfaithful prove:
Unwearied in forgiveness still,
    Thy heart could only love.

3 O give us hearts to love like thee,
    Like thee, O Lord, to grieve
Far more for others' sins than all
    The wrongs that we receive.

4 One with thyself, may every eye
    In us, thy brethren, see
That gentleness and grace that spring
    From union, Lord, with thee.

Edward Denny, 1796–1889

217 EISENACH (LEIPZIG)
L.M.

JOHANN HERMANN SCHEIN, 1586–1630 (adapted)

Alternative tune, DAS WALT' GOTT VATER, No. 581

For the Transfiguration

Caelestis formam gloriae

O WONDROUS type, O vision fair
Of glory that the Church shall share,
Which Christ upon the mountain shows,
Where brighter than the sun he glows!

2 With shining face and bright array,
Christ deigns to manifest today
What glory shall be theirs, above,
Who joy in God with perfect love.

3 The law and prophets there have place,
The chosen witnesses of grace;
The Father's voice from out the cloud
Proclaims his only Son aloud.

4 And Christian hearts are raised on high
By that great vision's mystery,
For which, in thankful strains, we raise
On this glad day the voice of praise.

5 O Father, with the eternal Son
And Holy Spirit ever One,
Vouchsafe to bring us, by thy grace,
To see thy glory face to face.

15th century; tr. John Mason Neale, 1818–66, and others

218 OMNI DIE 8787 Corner's *Gesangbuch*, 1631

Alternative tune, SUSSEX, No. 144

THERE'S a wideness in God's mercy,
Like the wideness of the sea;
There's a kindness in his justice,
Which is more than liberty.

2 There is no place where earth's sorrows
Are more felt than up in heaven:
There is no place where earth's failings
Have such kindly judgment given.

3 For the love of God is broader
Than the measures of man's mind;
And the heart of the Eternal
Is most wonderfully kind.

4 There is plentiful redemption
In the blood that has been shed;
There is joy for all the members
In the sorrows of the Head.

5 If our love were but more simple,
We would take him at his word;
And our lives be filled with glory
From the glory of the Lord.

Frederick William Faber, 1814–63 (altered)

193

219 DOLGELLEY (DOLGELLAU)
6666 88

Welsh Hymn Melody from
Haleliwiah Drachefn, Carmarthen, 1855

SON of the Lord Most High,
  Who gave the worlds their birth,
He came to live and die
    The Son of Man on earth:
      In Bethlem's stable born was he,
      And humbly bred in Galilee.

2 Born in so low estate,
    Schooled in a workman's trade,
Not with the high and great
      His home the Highest made:
        But labouring by his brethren's side,
        Life's common lot he glorified.

3 Then, when his hour was come,
    He heard his Father's call:
And leaving friends and home,
      He gave himself for all:
        Glad news to bring, the lost to find;
        To heal the sick, the lame, the blind.

4 Toiling by night and day,
    Himself oft burdened sore,
Where hearts in bondage lay,
      Himself their burden bore:
        Till, scorned by them he died to save,
        Himself in death, as life, he gave.

5 O lowly Majesty,
    Lofty in lowliness!
Blest Saviour, who am I
      To share thy blessedness?
        Yet thou hast called me, even me,
        Servant Divine, to follow thee.

George Wallace Briggs, 1875–1959

220 KINGSFOLD
D.C.M. irregular

English Traditional Melody collected by
LUCY BROADWOOD, 1858–1929

In vv. 2 and 4 lines 5 and 6 run thus:

(2) For __ now the flowers of   Na - zar - eth   In __   ev' - ry __ heart may   grow;
(4) For __   he who died on   Cal - var - y   Is __   ri - sen from the   grave,

O SING a song of Bethlehem,
    Of shepherds watching there,
And of the news that came to them
    From angels in the air:
The light that shone on Bethlehem
    Fills all the world today;
Of Jesus' birth and peace on earth
    The angels sing alway.

2 O sing a song of Nazareth,
    Of sunny days of joy;
O sing of fragrant flowers' breath,
    And of the sinless Boy:
For now the flowers of Nazareth
    In every heart may grow;
Now spreads the fame of his dear
        Name
    On all the winds that blow.

3 O sing a song of Galilee,
    Of lake and woods and hill,
Of him who walked upon the sea,
    And bade its waves be still:
For though, like waves on Galilee,
    Dark seas of trouble roll,
When faith has heard the Master's
        word,
    Falls peace upon the soul.

4 O sing a song of Calvary,
    Its glory and dismay;
Of him who hung upon the tree,
    And took our sins away:
For he who died on Calvary
    Is risen from the grave,
And Christ, our Lord, by heaven
        adored,
    Is mighty now to save.

Louis FitzGerald Benson, 1855–1930

221 RESONET IN LAUDIBUS
77 and refrain

German Carol Melody, c. 1500

REFRAIN

'Tis the Lord, O won-drous stor-y!

'Tis the Lord, the King___ of glor-y!

WHO is he in yonder stall,
At whose feet the shepherds fall?
'Tis the Lord, O wondrous story!
'Tis the Lord, the King of glory!

2 Who is he in deep distress,
Fasting in the wilderness?

3 Who is he the gathering throng
Greet with loud triumphant song?

4 Lo, at midnight, who is he
Prays in dark Gethsemane?

5 Who is he on yonder tree
Dies in shame and agony?

6 Who is he that from the grave
Comes to heal and help and save?

7 Who is he that from his throne
Rules through all the world alone?

Benjamin Russell Hanby, 1833-67
(altered)

222 CAMBER 6565

MARTIN SHAW, 1875-1958

WISE men seeking Jesus
Travelled from afar,
Guided on their journey
By a beauteous star.

2 But if we desire him,
He is close at hand;
For our native country
Is our Holy Land.

3 Prayerful souls may find him
  By our quiet lakes,
Meet him on our hillsides
  When the morning breaks.

4 In our fertile cornfields
  While the sheaves are bound,
In our busy markets,
  Jesus may be found.

5 Fishermen talk with him
  By the great north sea,
As the first disciples
  Did in Galilee.

6 Every peaceful village
  In our land might be
Made by Jesus' presence
  Like sweet Bethany.

7 He is more than near us,
  If we love him well;
For he seeketh ever
  In our hearts to dwell.

James Thomas East, 1860-1937

223 EISENACH (LEIPZIG) L.M.

Adapted from a melody by
JOHANN HERMANN SCHEIN, 1586-1630

A - men.

O amor quam ecstaticus

O LOVE, how deep, how broad,
  how high!
How passing thought and fantasy
That God, the Son of God, should
  take
Our mortal form for mortals' sake.

2 He sent no angel to our race
Of higher or of lower place,
But wore the robe of human frame,
And he himself to this world came.

3 For us baptized, for us he bore
His holy fast, and hungered sore;
For us temptations sharp he knew;
For us the tempter overthrew.

4 For us to wicked men betrayed,
Scourged, mocked, in crown of
  thorns arrayed,
He bore the shameful cross and
  death;
For us at length gave up his breath.

5 For us he rose from death again,
For us he went on high to reign,
For us he sent his Spirit here,
To guide, to strengthen, and to
  cheer.

6 *To him whose boundless love has won*
Salvation for us through his Son,
To God the Father, glory be
Both now and through eternity.
                              Amen.

15th century. Tr. Benjamin Webb, 1819-85 (altered)

224 LOVE UNKNOWN 66 12 88

JOHN IRELAND, 1879–1962
The Public School Hymn Book, 1919

MY song is love unknown,
My Saviour's love to me,
Love to the loveless shown, that they
might lovely be.
O who am I, that for my sake
My Lord should take frail flesh
and die?

2 He came from his blest throne,
Salvation to bestow:
But men made strange, and none the
longed-for Christ would
know.
But O, my Friend, my Friend
indeed,
Who at my need his life did
spend!

3 Sometimes they strew his way,
And his sweet praises sing;
Resounding all the day hosannas to
their King.
Then 'Crucify!' is all their
breath,
And for his death they thirst
and cry.

4 Why, what hath my Lord done?
What makes this rage and spite?
He made the lame to run, he gave the
blind their sight.
Sweet injuries! yet they at these
Themselves   displease   and
'gainst him rise.

5 They rise, and needs will have
My dear Lord done away;
A murderer they save, the Prince of
Life they slay.
Yet cheerful he to suffering
goes,
That he his foes from thence
might free.

6 In life, no house, no home
My Lord on earth might have;
In death, no friendly tomb but what
a stranger gave.
What may I say? Heav'n was
his home:
But mine the tomb wherein he
lay.

7 Here might I stay and sing,
No story so divine;
Never was love, dear King, never was grief like thine!
This is my Friend, in whose sweet praise
I all my days could gladly spend.

Samuel Crossman, c. 1624–83

225 ST. FLAVIAN C.M.

Melody of Psalm 132 in *English Psalter*, 1562
(first half only), adapted 1599 and later

[*For Nos. 8 or 585*]

A - men.

A version with the later form of rhythm is found at No. 8

PARAPHRASE 52, verses 1, 3–6

YE who the Name of Jesus bear,
  His sacred steps pursue;
And let that mind which was in him
  Be also found in you.

2 His greatness he for us abased,
  For us his glory veiled;
In human likeness dwelt on earth,
  His majesty concealed:

3 Nor only as a man appears,
  But stoops a servant low;
Submits to death, nay, bears the cross,
  In all its shame and woe.

4 Hence God this generous love to men
  With honours just hath crowned,
And raised the Name of Jesus far
  Above all names renowned:

5 That at this Name, with sacred awe,
  Each humble knee should bow,
Of hosts immortal in the skies,
  And nations spread below.

Scottish Paraphrases, 1781
Phil. 2: 5, 7–10

226 MORGEN, KINDER
8787 77

German Traditional Melody

For children

1 CAN picture Jesus toiling,
   Carpenter of Nazareth town:
In his face a great love shining,
   Working till the sun goes down.
By his children still he stands,
Blessing labour of their hands.

   Weary, when the hour is late.
Still he stoops from heaven above,
Drawing all men by his love.

3 Christ the Workman, make me holy
   Christ the Saviour, make me true
Make of me a thing of beauty,
   Show me how to labour too;
Fellow-worker would I be
Ever, blessèd Lord, with thee.

2 I can picture Jesus stooping,
   Lifting up a heavy weight;
Stiff with toil, his arms outstretch-
      ing,

D. Helen Stone

227 IN DER WIEGEN
7676(6)

Corner's *Geistliche Nachtigall*, 1649

For children

1 LOVE to hear the story
   Which angel voices tell,
How once the King of Glory
* Came down on earth to dwell.

2 I am both weak and sinful,
   But this I surely know,
The Lord came down to save me
Because he loved me so.

* *The last line of each verse is repeated*

200

3 I'm glad my blessèd Saviour
   Was once a child like me,
   To show how pure and holy
   His little ones might be;

4 And, if I try to follow
   His footsteps here below,
   He never will forsake me,
   Because he loves me so.

5 To sing his love and mercy
   My sweetest songs I'll raise,
   And, though I cannot see him,
   I know he hears my praise;

6 For he has kindly promised
   That even I may go
   To sing among his angels,
   Because he loves me so.

Emily Huntington Miller, 1833–1913

228 AU CLAIR DE LA LUNE 11 11 11 11   Old French Melody

For younger children

JESUS' hands were kind hands, doing good to all,
Healing pain and sickness, blessing children small;
Washing tired feet, and saving those who fall;
Jesus' hands were kind hands, doing good to all.

2 Take my hands, Lord Jesus, let them work for you,
   Make them strong and gentle, kind in all I do;
   Let me watch you, Jesus, till I'm gentle too,
   Till my hands are kind hands, quick to work for you.

Margaret Cropper

229   CHERRY TREE CAROL   7686   English Traditional Melody

For younger children

I LIKE to think of Jesus
So loving, kind, and true
That when he walked among his friends
His friends were loving too.

2 I like to think of Jesus
   With children at his knee;
   And hear his gentle words again,
   'Let children come to me'.

3 I like to think of Jesus
   So loving, kind, and true
   That somehow when I think of him,
   It makes me loving too.

                Elizabeth McEwen Shields

230   JOYS SEVEN
        D.C.M. irregular   English Traditional Carol Melody

For younger children

WHEN Jesus saw the fishermen
In boats upon the sea,
He called to them 'Come, leave your nets
And follow, follow me'.
They followed where he healed the sick
And gave the hungry bread,
And others joined them as they went
Wherever Jesus led.

2 And now his friends are everywhere;
The circle once so small
Extends around the whole wide world,
For Jesus calls us all.
In this great circle we belong,
Wherever we may be,
If we will answer when he calls,
'Come, follow, follow me'.

Edith Agnew

The following are also suitable

No.
52 At even, when the sun was set
76 Dear Lord and Father of mankind

CHRIST'S PASSION AND CROSS

231

Tone iii, ending 4

PSALM 42, verses 1–5, 8–11

AS the hart panteth ˈ after the water brooks:
  so panteth my soul after ˈ thee O God.

My soul thirsteth for God ˈ for the living God:
  when shall I come and appear ˈ before God?

My tears have been my ˈ meat day and night:
  while they continually say unto me where ˈ is thy God?

When I remember these things I pour out ˈ my soul in me:
  for I had gone with the multitude I went with them to the house of God   with
  the voice of joy and praise with a multitude that kept ˈ holy day.

Why art thou cast down O my soul?   and why art thou dis ˈ quie-ted in me:
  hope thou in God   for I shall yet praise him for the help of his ˈ countenance

Yet the Lord will command his lovingkindness ˈ in the daytime:
  and in the night his song shall be with me   and my prayer unto the God ˈ o
  my life.

I will say unto God my rock   Why hast ˈ thou forgotten me:
  why go I mourning because of the oppression of the ˈ enemy?

As with a sword in my bones mine ene ˈ mies reproach me:
  while they say daily unto me where ˈ is thy God?

Why art thou cast down O my soul?   and why art thou disquiet ˈ ed within me
  hope thou in God for I shall yet praise him   who is the health of m
  countenance ˈ and my God.

Tone vi

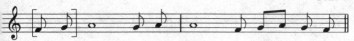

PSALM 118, verses 19-29

OPEN to me the gates of righ ˈteousness:
  I will go into them and I ˈwill praïse the Lord.

This gate of ˈthe Lord:
  into which the righ ˈteous shäll enter.

I will ˈpraise thee:
  for thou hast heard me and art become ˈmy salvation.

The stone which the builders re ˈfusèd:
  is become the head stone ˈof the corner.

This is the Lord's ˈdoing:
  it is marvel ˈlous in our eyes.

This is the day which the Lord ˈhath made:
  we will rejoice and ˈbe glad in it.

Save now I beseech thee ˈO Lord:
  O Lord I beseech thee send now ˈprosperity.

Blessèd be he that cometh in the Name of ˈthe Lord:
  we have blessed you out of the ˈhouse of the Lord.

God is the Lord which hath showed ˈus light:
  bind the sacrifice with cords even unto the horns ˈof the altar.

Thou art my God and I will ˈpraise thee:
  thou art my God I ˈwill exalt thee.

O give thanks unto the Lord for he ˈis good:
  for his mercy endur ˈeth for ever.

Glory be to the Father and to ˈthe Son:
  and to ˈthe Holy Ghost.

As it was in the beginning is now and ever ˈshall be:
  world with ˈout end Amen.

233 ST. THEODULPH
7676 and refrain

Later form of a melody b
MELCHIOR TESCHNER, *c.* 161

All glor - y, laud and   hon - our To   thee, Re-deem-er   King,
To whom the lips of   child - ren Made sweet ho-san-nas   ring!

Repeat Refrain after each vers

Gloria, laus et honor

* *ALL glory, laud, and honour*
To thee, Redeemer King,
To whom the lips of children
Made sweet hosannas ring!
Thou art the King of Israel,
   Thou David's royal Son,
Who in the Lord's Name comest,
   The King and Blessèd One.

2 The company of angels
   Are praising thee on high,
And mortal men and all things
   Created make reply.

3 The people of the Hebrews
   With palms before thee went;
Our praise and prayer and anthem
   Before thee we present.

4 To thee before thy Passion
   They sang their hymns of praise;
To thee now high exalted
   Our melody we raise.

5 Thou didst accept their praises;
   Accept the prayers we bring,
Who in all good delightest,
   Thou good and gracious King:

Theodulph of Orleans, d. 82
Tr. John Mason Neale, 1818–66 (altered

* *This refrain is sung before each verse and also after the final verse*

234 WINCHESTER NEW (CRASSELIUS) L.M.

Adapted from a melody in Witt's *Musikalisches Hand-Buch*, Hamburg, 1690

RIDE on! ride on in majesty!
Hark! all the tribes 'Hosanna!' cry;
O Saviour meek, pursue thy road
With palms and scattered garments strowed.

2 Ride on! ride on in majesty!
In lowly pomp ride on to die;
O Christ, thy triumphs now begin
O'er captive death and conquered sin.

3 Ride on! ride on in majesty!
The wingèd squadrons of the sky
Look down with sad and wondering eyes
To see the approaching sacrifice.

4 Ride on! ride on in majesty!
Thy last and fiercest strife is nigh;
The Father on his sapphire throne
Awaits his own anointed Son.

5 Ride on! ride on in majesty!
In lowly pomp ride on to die;
Bow thy meek head to mortal pain,
Then take, O God, thy power, and reign.

Henry Hart Milman, 1791-1868

235 ELLACOMBE 7676. D

18th century German melody, adapted
as in St. Gall *Gesangbuch*, 1863

For children

HOSANNA, loud hosanna,
  The little children sang;
Through pillared court and temple
  The joyful anthem rang;
To Jesus, who had blessed them
  Close folded to his breast,
The children sang their praises,
  The simplest and the best.

2 From Olivet they followed,
    'Mid an exultant crowd,
  The victor palm-branch waving,
    And chanting clear and loud;
  Bright angels joined the chorus,
    Beyond the cloudless sky,—
  'Hosanna in the highest!
    Glory to God on high!'

3 Fair leaves of silvery olive
    They strowed upon the ground,
  While Salem's circling mountains
    Echoed the joyful sound;
  The Lord of men and angels
    Rode on in lowly state,
  Nor scorned that little children
    Should on his bidding wait.

4 'Hosanna in the highest!'
    That ancient song we sing,
  For Christ is our Redeemer,
    The Lord of heaven our King.
  O may we ever praise him
    With heart and life and voice,
  And in his blissful presence
    Eternally rejoice.

Jeannette Threlfall, 1821–80

236 HEATHLANDS 7777 and refrain

HENRY SMART, 1813–79

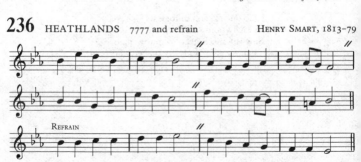

REFRAIN

For children

CHILDREN of Jerusalem
Sang the praise of Jesus' name:
Children, too, of modern days
Join to sing the Saviour's praise.
    Hark! while infant voices sing
    Loud hosannas to our King.

2 We are taught to love the Lord,
  We are taught to read his word,
  We are taught the way to heaven:
  Praise for all to God be given.

3 Parents, teachers, old and young,
  All unite to swell the song,
  Higher and yet higher rise,
  Till hosannas reach the skies.

John Henley, 1800-42

237 ROCKINGHAM (COMMUNION) L.M.

Adapted by EDWARD MILLER, 1731-1807, from a melody *Tunbridge* in *A Second Supplement to Psalmody in Miniature, c.* 1780

Thursday in Holy Week

PARAPHRASE 35

'TWAS on that night when doomed to know
The eager rage of every foe,
That night in which he was betrayed,
The Saviour of the world took bread;

2 And, after thanks and glory given
To him that rules in earth and heaven,
That symbol of his flesh he broke,
And thus to all his followers spoke:

3 'My broken body thus I give
For you, for all; take, eat, and live:
And oft the sacred rite renew
That brings my wondrous love to view.'

4 Then in his hands the cup he raised,
And God anew he thanked and praised,
While kindness in his bosom glowed,
And from his lips salvation flowed.

5 'My blood I thus pour forth,' he cries,
'To cleanse the soul in sin that lies;
In this the covenant is sealed,
And heaven's eternal grace revealed.

6 'With love to man this cup is fraught,
Let all partake the sacred draught;
Through latest ages let it pour
In memory of my dying hour.'

Scottish Paraphrases, 1781
St. Matthew 26: 26-29

238 (i) GERONTIUS C.M.　　　　　　　JOHN BACCHUS DYKES, 1823-76

(ii) CHORUS ANGELORUM C.M.　　　　　ARTHUR SOMERVELL, 1863-1937

PRAISE to the Holiest in the
　　height,
And in the depth be praise,—
In all his words most wonderful,
　　Most sure in all his ways.

2 O loving wisdom of our God!
　　When all was sin and shame,
A second Adam to the fight
　　And to the rescue came.

3 O wisest love! that flesh and blood,
　　Which did in Adam fail,
Should strive afresh against the foe,
　　Should strive and should prevail;

4 O generous love! that he who smote
　　In Man, for man, the foe,
The double agony in Man,
　　For man, should undergo,

5 And in the garden secretly,
　　And on the cross on high,
Should teach his brethren, and inspire
　　To suffer and to die.

6 Praise to the Holiest in the height,
　　And in the depth be praise,—
In all his words most wonderful,
　　Most sure in all his ways.

John Henry Newman, 1801-90

239

Tone ii, ending 1

PSALM 22, verses 1-9, 11, 15-19, 22-24, 27, 30, 31

MY God my God why hast thou for ' saken me:
  why art thou so far from helping me and from the words of ' my roaring?

O my God I cry in the daytime but thou ' hearest not:
  and in the night season and am ' not silent.

But thou art holy O thou that inhabitest the praises of Israel   Our fathers trusted in ' thee:
  they trusted and thou didst de ' liver them.

They cried unto thee and were de ' liver'd:
  they trusted in thee and were not ' confounded.

But I am a worm and ' no man:
  a reproach of men and despised of ' the people.

All they that see me laugh me to ' scorn:
  they shoot out the lip   they shake the ' head saying,

He trusted on the Lord that he would de ' liver him:
  let him deliver him seeing he deligh ' ted in him.

But thou art he that took me out of the ' womb:
  thou didst make me hope when I was upon my ' mother's breasts.

Be not far from me for trouble is ' near:
  for there is ' none to help.

My strength is dried up like a potsherd   and my tongue cleaveth to my ' jaws:
  and thou hast brought me into the ' dust of death.

For dogs have ' compassed me:
  the assembly of the wicked have inclosed me   they pierced my ' hands and my feet.

I may tell ' all my bones:
  they look and stare ' upon me.

They part my garments a ' mong them:
  and cast lots upon ' my vesture.

But be not thou far from me O ' Lord:
  O my strength haste thee ' to help me.

I will declare thy Name unto my ' brethren:
  in the midst of the congregation will ' I praise thee.

Ye that fear the Lord ' praise him:
  all ye the seed of Jacob glorify him and fear him all ye the seed ' of Israel.

For he hath not despised nor abhorred the affliction of the af ' flicted:
  neither hath he hid his face from him   but when he cried unto ' him he heard.

All the ends of the world shall remember and turn unto the ' Lord:
  and all the kindreds of the nations shall worship ' before thee.

A seed shall ' serve him:
  it shall be accounted to the Lord for a ge ' neration.

They shall come and shall declare his righteousness unto a people that shall be ' born:
  that he ' hath done this.

TRISAGION AND THE REPROACHES

240

TRISAGION
(Early Church)

GREGORY MURRAY

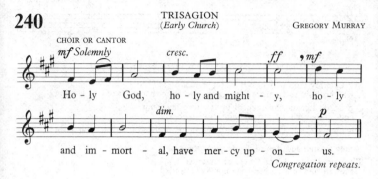

Ho - ly God, ho - ly and might - y, ho - ly
and im - mort - al, have mer - cy up - on us.
Congregation repeats.

THE REPROACHES
(Gallican Church)

GREGORY MURRAY

CHOIR OR CANTOR
Rather slowly, in speech rhythm throughout

O my people, what 'have I done to thee? or wherein have I wear'ied thee? Answer me.

Because I brought thee forth out of the land of Egypt, and led

thee to a land ex'ceeding good: thou hast prepared a cross'for thy Saviour.

Congregation repeats 'Holy God'
after each verse.

CONGREGATION: Holy God, holy and mighty, holy and immortal, have
mercy upon us.

CHOIR OR CANTOR: Before thee I o¦pened the sea:
and with a spear thou hast o¦pened my side.
I went before thee in a pil¦lar of cloud:
and thou hast brought me to the judgment¦hall of Pilate.

CONGREGATION: Holy God, holy and mighty, holy and immortal, have mercy
upon us.

CHOIR OR CANTOR: I fed thee with manna ' in the desert:
and thou hast beaten me with ' blows and stripes.
I made thee to drink the water of salvation ' from the rock:
and thou hast made me to drink ' gall and vinegar.

CONGREGATION: Holy God, holy and mighty, holy and immortal, have mercy upon us.

CHOIR OR CANTOR: I gave thee a ' royal sceptre:
and thou hast given my head a ' crown of thorns.
I lifted thee up ' with great power:
and thou hast hung me upon the gibbet ' of the cross.

CONGREGATION: Holy God, holy and mighty, holy and immortal, have mercy upon us.

ALTERNATIVE SETTING FOR TRISAGION

CHOIR OR CONGREGATION   GREGORY MURRAY

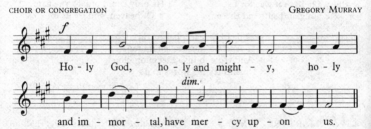

Ho - ly God, ho - ly and might - y, ho - ly and im - mor - tal, have mer - cy up - on us.

241 HORSLEY C.M.

WILLIAM HORSLEY, 1774–1858

THERE is a green hill far away,
  Outside a city wall,
Where the dear Lord was crucified,
  Who died to save us all.

2 We may not know, we cannot tell
  What pains he had to bear;
But we believe it was for us
  He hung and suffered there.

3 He died that we might be forgiven,
  He died to make us good,
That we might go at last to heaven,
  Saved by his precious blood.

4 There was no other good enough
  To pay the price of sin;
He only could unlock the gate
  Of heaven, and let us in.

5 O dearly, dearly has he loved,
  And we must love him too,
And trust in his redeeming blood,
  And try his works to do.

Cecil Frances Alexander, 1818–95

242 MARTYRS C.M.

Scottish Psalter, 1615 (1635 rhythm)

Solus ad victimam procedis, Domine

ALONE thou goest forth, O Lord,
  In sacrifice to die;
Is this thy sorrow naught to us
  Who pass unheeding by?

2 Our sins, not thine, thou bearest, Lord;
  Make us thy sorrow feel,
Till through our pity and our shame
  Love answers love's appeal.

3 This is earth's darkest hour, but thou
  Dost light and life restore;
Then let all praise be given thee
  Who livest evermore.

4 Grant us to suffer with thee, Lord,
  That, as we share this hour,
Thy cross may bring us to thy joy
  And resurrection power.

Peter Abelard, 1079-1142
Tr. Francis Bland Tucker (altered)

243 ST. CROSS   888 and refrain   JOHN BACCHUS DYKES, 1823-76

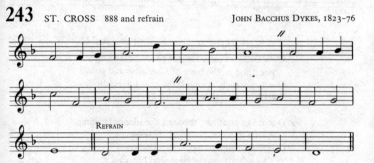

REFRAIN

O COME and mourn with me awhile;
  O come ye to the Saviour's side;
O come, together let us mourn:
  Jesus, our Lord, is crucified!

2 Have we no tears to shed for him,
    While soldiers scoff and foes deride?
  Ah! look how patiently he hangs:

3 Seven times he spake, seven words of love;
    And all three hours his silence cried
  For mercy on the souls of men:.

4 O break, O break, hard heart of mine!
    Thy weak self-love and guilty pride
  His Pilate and his Judas were:

5 O love of God! O sin of man!
    In this dread act your strength is tried,
  And victory remains with love:

Frederick William Faber, 1814-63 (altered)

244 INTERCESSOR 11 10 11 10

CHARLES HUBERT HASTINGS PARRY,
1848-1918

'Father, forgive them; for they know not what they do.'

O WORD of pity, for our pardon pleading,
    Breathed in the hour of loneliness and pain;
O voice, which, through the ages interceding,
    Calls us to fellowship with God again.

2 O word of comfort, through the silence stealing,
    As the dread act of sacrifice began;
O infinite compassion, still revealing
    The infinite forgiveness won for man.

3 O word of hope, to raise us nearer heaven,
    When courage fails us, and when faith is dim;
The souls for whom Christ prays to Christ are given,
    To find their pardon and their joy in him.

4 O Intercessor, who art ever living
    To plead for dying souls that they may live,
Teach us to know our sin which needs forgiving,
    Teach us to know the love which can forgive.

Ada Rundall Greenaway, 1861-1937

245 SONG 24 10 10 10 10   ORLANDO GIBBONS, 1583–1625

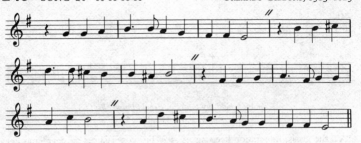

'Verily I say unto thee, Today shalt thou be with me in Paradise.'

'LORD, when thy Kingdom comes, remember me!'
Thus spake the dying lips to dying ears.
O faith, which in that darkest hour could see
The promised glory of the far-off years!

2 Hark! through the gloom the dying Saviour saith,
'Thou too shalt rest in Paradise today';
O words of love to answer words of faith!
O words of hope for those who live to pray!

3 Lord, when with dying lips my prayer is said,
Grant that in faith thy Kingdom I may see,
And thinking on thy cross, and bleeding head,
May breathe my parting words, 'Remember me'.

4 Remember me; and, ere I pass away,
Speak thou the assuring word that sets us free,
And make thy promise to my heart, 'Today
Thou too shalt rest in Paradise with me'.

William Dalrymple Maclagan, 1826–1910

246 STABAT MATER 887. D

Mainzisch Gesangbuch, 1661
(rhythm altered)

'Woman, behold thy son! ... Behold thy mother!'
Stabat mater dolorosa

AT the cross, her station keeping,
Stood the mournful mother weeping,
　Where he hung, the dying Lord;
For her soul, of joy bereavèd,
Bowed with anguish, deeply grievèd,
　Felt the sharp and piercing sword.

2 O, how sad and sore distressèd
　Now was she, that mother blessèd
　　Of the sole-begotten One;
　Deep the woe of her affliction,
　When she saw the crucifixion
　　Of her ever-glorious Son.

3 Who, on Christ's dear mother
　　gazing,
　Pierced by anguish so amazing,
　　Born of woman, would not weep?
　Who, on Christ's dear mother
　　thinking,
　Such a cup of sorrow drinking,
　　Would not share her sorrows
　　deep?

4 For his people's sins chastisèd,
　She beheld her Son despisèd,
　　Scourged, and crowned with
　　thorns entwined;
　Saw him then from judgment taken,
　And in death by all forsaken,
　　Till his spirit he resigned.

5 Jesus, may her deep devotion
　Stir in me the same emotion,
　　Fount of love, Redeemer kind,
　That my heart, fresh ardour gaining,
　And a purer love attaining,
　　May with thee acceptance find.

13th century; tr. Edward Caswall, 1814–78, and others

247 PETRA 7777 77
(REDHEAD No. 76)

RICHARD REDHEAD, 1820–1901
Church Hymn Tunes, 1853

'My God, my God, why hast thou forsaken me?'

THRONED upon the awesome
  Tree,
King of grief, I watch with thee.
Darkness veils thine anguished face:
None its lines of woe can trace:
None can tell what pangs unknown
Hold thee silent and alone,—

2 Silent through those three dread
  hours,
Wrestling with the evil powers,
Left alone with human sin,
Gloom around thee and within,
Till the appointed time is nigh,
Till the Lamb of God may die.

3 Hark, that cry that peals aloud
Upward through the whelming
  cloud!
Thou, the Father's only Son,
Thou, his own anointed One,
Thou dost ask him—can it be?—
'Why hast thou forsaken me?'

4 Lord, should fear and anguish roll
Darkly o'er my sinful soul,
Thou, who once wast thus bereft
That thine own might ne'er be left,
Teach me by that bitter cry
In the gloom to know thee nigh.

John Ellerton, 1826–93

248   SOUTHWELL S.M.   Melody for Psalm 45 in Damon's
                                  The Psalmes of David, 1579 (altered)

A version with the later form of rhythm is at No. 466

'I thirst.'

O PERFECT God, thy love
As perfect Man did share
Here upon earth each form of ill
Thy fellow-men must bear.

2 Now from the tree of scorn
We hear thy voice again;
Thou who didst take our mortal flesh,
Hast felt our mortal pain.

3 Thy body suffers thirst,
Parched are thy lips and dry:
How poor the offering man can bring
Thy thirst to satisfy!

4 O Saviour, by thy thirst
Borne on the cross of shame,
Grant us in all our sufferings here
To glorify thy Name:

5 That through each pain and grief
Our souls may onward move
To gain more likeness to thy life,
More knowledge of thy love.

Ada Rundall Greenaway, 1861–1937

249 SOUTHWELL S.M.

Melody for Psalm 45 in Damon's
The Psalmes of David, 1579 (altered)

A version with the later form of rhythm is at No. 466

'It is finished.'

O PERFECT life of love!
All, all is finished now,
All that he left his throne above
To do for us below.

2 No work is left undone
Of all the Father willed;
His toils and sorrows, one by one,
The Scriptures have fulfilled.

3 No pain that we can share
But he has felt its smart;
All forms of human grief and care
Have pierced that tender heart.

4 And on his thorn-crowned head,
And on his sinless soul,
Our sins in all their guilt were laid,
That he might make us whole.

5 In perfect love he dies;
For me he dies, for me!
O all-atoning Sacrifice,
I cling by faith to thee.

6 In every time of need,
Before the judgment throne,
Thy work, O Lamb of God, I'll plead,
Thy merits, not my own.

7 Yet work, O Lord, in me,
As thou for me hast wrought;
And let my love the answer be
To grace thy love has brought.

Henry Williams Baker, 1821-77

250 PSALM 12
(DONNE SECOURS) 11 10 11 10

French-Genevan Psalter, 1551

Alternative tune, INTERCESSOR, No. 244

'Father, into thy hands I commend my spirit.'

AND now, belovèd Lord, thy soul resigning
Into thy Father's arms with conscious will,
Calmly, with reverend grace, thy head inclining,
The throbbing brow and labouring breast grow still.

2 Freely thy life thou yieldest, meekly bending
    Even to the last beneath our sorrows' load,
Yet strong in death, in perfect peace commending
    Thy spirit to thy Father and thy God.

3 My Saviour, in mine hour of mortal anguish,
    When earth grows dim, and round me falls the night,
O breathe thy peace, as flesh and spirit languish;
    At that dread eventide let there be light.

4 To thy dear cross turn thou mine eyes in dying;
    Lay but my fainting head upon thy breast;
Thine outstretched arms receive my latest sighing;
    And then, O then, thine everlasting rest!

Eliza Sibbald Alderson, 1818-89

251 HERZLIEBSTER JESU 11 11 11 5   Crüger's *Gesangbuch*, 1640

Herzliebster Jesu

AH, holy Jesus, how hast thou offended,
That man to judge thee hath in hate pretended?
By foes derided, by thine own rejected,
        O most afflicted.

2 Lo, the good Shepherd for the sheep is offered;
The slave hath sinnèd, and the Son hath suffered;
For man's atonement, while he nothing heedeth,
        God intercedeth.

3 For me, kind Jesus, was thy incarnation,
Thy mortal sorrow, and thy life's oblation;
Thy death of anguish and thy bitter passion,
        For my salvation.

4 Therefore, kind Jesus, since I cannot pay thee,
I do adore thee, and will ever pray thee,
Think on thy mercy and thy love unswerving,
        Not my deserving.

Johann Heermann, 1585-1647,
based on an 11th century Latin Meditation
Par. Robert Bridges, 1844-1930

252 NUN DANKET ALL
C.M.

Crüger's *Praxis Pietatis Melica* (1647 edition)

Alternative tune, ST. FLAVIAN, No. 225 (*earlier rhythm*)

O DEAREST Lord, thy sacred
  head
  With thorns was pierced for me;
O pour thy blessing on my head,
  That I may think for thee.

2 O dearest Lord, thy sacred hands
  With nails were pierced for me;
O shed thy blessing on my hands,
  That they may work for thee.

3 O dearest Lord, thy sacred feet
  With nails were pierced for me
O pour thy blessing on my feet,
  That they may follow thee.

4 O dearest Lord, thy sacred heart
  With spear was pierced for me;
O pour thy spirit in my heart,
  That I may live for thee.

Father Andrew, 1869-1946

253 PASSION CHORALE 7676. D

HANS LEO HASSLER, 1564-1612

O Haupt voll Blut und Wunden

O SACRED Head, sore wounded,
  With grief and shame weighed
    down!
O Kingly Head, surrounded
  With thorns, thine only crown!
How pale art thou with anguish,
  With sore abuse and scorn!
How does that visage languish,
  Which once was bright as morn!

2 O Lord of life and glory,
  What bliss till now was thine!
I read the wondrous story;
  I joy to call thee mine.
Thy grief and bitter passion
  Were all for sinners' gain;
Mine, mine was the transgression,
  But thine the deadly pain.

3 What language shall I borrow
   To praise thee, heavenly Friend,
For this thy dying sorrow,
   Thy pity without end?
O make me thine for ever,
   And, should I fainting be,
Lord, let me never, never
   Outlive my love to thee.

4 Be near me, Lord, when dying;
   O show thy cross to me;
And, for my succour flying,
   Come, Lord, to set me free;
These eyes, new faith receiving,
   From thee shall never move;
For he who dies believing
   Dies safely through thy love.

Paul Gerhardt, 1607-76
Tr. James Waddell Alexander, 1804-59

254 ROCKINGHAM
(COMMUNION) L.M.

Adapted by EDWARD MILLER, 1731-1807,
from a melody *Tunbridge* in *A Second Supplement to
Psalmody in Miniature, c. 1780*

Alternative tune, LLEF, No. 485 (ii)

WHEN I survey the wondrous cross
   On which the Prince of Glory died,
My richest gain I count but loss,
   And pour contempt on all my pride.

2 Forbid it, Lord, that I should boast,
   Save in the death of Christ, my God;
All the vain things that charm me most,
   I sacrifice them to his blood.

3 See! from his head, his hands, his feet,
   Sorrow and love flow mingled down;
Did e'er such love and sorrow meet,
   Or thorns compose so rich a crown?

4 Were the whole realm of nature mine,
   That were an offering far too small;
Love so amazing, so divine,
   Demands my soul, my life, my all.

Isaac Watts, 1674-1748

255 WITTENBERG
(ES IST DAS HEIL) 8787 887

Adapted by BACH from a melody
in *Christliche Lieder*, Wittenberg, 1524

LORD Christ, when first thou cam'st to men,
Upon a cross they bound thee,
And mocked thy saving kingship then
By thorns with which they crowned thee:
And still our wrongs may weave thee now
New thorns to pierce that steady brow,
And robe of sorrow round thee.

2 New advent of the love of Christ,
Shall we again refuse thee,
Till in the night of hate and war
We perish as we lose thee?
From old unfaith our souls release
To seek the Kingdom of thy peace,
By which alone we choose thee.

3 O wounded hands of Jesus, build
In us thy new creation;
Our pride is dust, our vaunt is stilled,
We wait thy revelation:
O Love that triumphs over loss,
We bring our hearts before thy cross,
To finish thy salvation.

Walter Russell Bowie, 1882–1969

256 (i) PANGE LINGUA 8787 87

Plainsong Melody (Sarum form)
Mode iii

A - men.

(ii) PICARDY 8787 87

French Carol Melody

A - men.

Pange, lingua, gloriosi proelium certaminis

* SING, my tongue, how glorious
    battle
  Glorious victory became;
And above the cross, his trophy,
  Tell the triumph and the fame:
Tell how he, the earth's Redeemer,
  By his death for man o'ercame.

2 Thirty years fulfilled among us—
  Perfect life in low estate—
Born for this, and self-surrendered,
  To his Passion dedicate,
On the cross the Lamb is lifted,
  For his people immolate.

3 His the nails, the spear, the spitting,
  Reed and vinegar and gall;
From his patient body piercèd
  Blood and water streaming fall:
Earth and sea and stars and mankind
  By that stream are cleansèd all.

4 Faithful cross, above all other,
  One and only noble tree,
None in foliage, none in blossom,
  None in fruit compares with thee:
Sweet the wood and sweet the iron,
  And thy load how sweet is he.

5 *Unto God be praise and honour:*
    To the Father, to the Son,
  To the mighty Spirit, glory—
    Ever Three and ever One:
  Power and glory in the highest
    While eternal ages run. Amen.

Venantius Fortunatus, c. 535-600; tr. William Mair, 1830-1920;
  and Arthur Wellesley Wotherspoon, 1853-1936;
  and v. 4, John Mason Neale, 1818-66

* *The pointing is for use with tune (i) only*

257 DEUS TUORUM MILITUM
(GRENOBLE) L.M.

Grenoble Antiphoner, 1753

A - men.

Alternative tune, GONFALON ROYAL, No. 329

Vexilla Regis prodeunt

THE royal banners forward go;
The cross shines forth in mystic
    glow,
Where he, the Life, did death
    endure,
And yet by death did life procure.

2 His feet and hands outstretching
    there,
He willed the piercing nails to bear,
For us and our redemption's sake
A victim of himself to make.

3 There whilst he hung, his sacred
    side
By soldier's spear was opened wide,
To cleanse us in the precious flood
Of water mingled with his blood.

4 Fulfilled is now what David told
In true prophetic song of old,
To all the nations 'Lo', saith he,
'Our God is reigning from the tree'.

5 *Blest Three in One, our praise we sing*
    To thee from whom all graces spring:
    As by the cross thou dost restore,
    So rule and guide us evermore. Amen.

Venantius Fortunatus, c. 535–600
Tr. John Mason Neale, 1818–66, *and others*

258 WALTON (FULDA) L.M.

Gardiner's *Sacred Melodies,*
second series, 1815

Alternative tune, BRESLAU, No. 430

WE sing the praise of him who died,
   Of him who died upon the cross;
The sinner's hope let men deride,
   For this we count the world but
      loss.

2 Inscribed upon the cross we see,
   In shining letters, 'God is love';
He bears our sins upon the tree;
   He brings us mercy from above.

3 The cross! it takes our guilt away;
   It holds the fainting spirit up;
It cheers with hope the gloomy day,
   And sweetens every bitter cup;

4 It makes the coward spirit brave,
   And nerves the feeble arm for
      fight;
It takes its terror from the grave,
   And gilds the bed of death with
      light;

5 The balm of life, the cure of woe,
   The measure and the pledge of love,
The sinner's refuge here below,
   The angels' theme in heaven above.

Thomas Kelly, 1769-1855

259 STUTTGART 8787   Adapted from a melody in Witt's
                                   Psalmodia Sacra, Gotha, 1715

IN the cross of Christ I glory,
   Towering o'er the wrecks of time;
All the light of sacred story
   Gathers round its head sublime.

2 When the woes of life o'ertake me,
   Hopes deceive and fears annoy,
Never shall the cross forsake me;
   Lo! it glows with peace and joy.

3 When the sun of bliss is beaming
   Light and love upon my way,
From the cross the radiance stream-
      ing
Adds more lustre to the day.

4 Bane and blessing, pain and
      pleasure,
By the cross are sanctified;
Peace is there that knows no
      measure,
   Joys that through all time abide.

5 In the cross of Christ I glory,
   Towering o'er the wrecks of time;
All the light of sacred story
   Gathers round its head sublime.

John Bowring, 1792-1872

260 TRYPHAENA 8 8 8   FRANCES RIDLEY HAVERGAL, 1836–79

Good Friday evening

AT eve, when now he breathed no
    more,
The faithful few in anguish sore
The Lord they loved to burial bore.

2 To those who mourned him, who
    can say
How long the hours of sullen day,
How long the nights while hid he
    lay?

3 O ye who shrink beneath the blow
That death can deal, henceforth ye
    know
Not hopeless is your human woe.

4 For then, before their tears had
    ceased,
Love woke to joy the crimson east,
And Jesus rose, from death released.

John Russell Darbyshire, 1880–1948

261 O MENSCH SIEH
(BOHEMIA)   8 8 8   The Bohemian Brethren's *Kirchengeseng,*
Berlin, 1566 (rhythm altered)

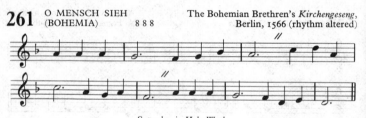

Saturday in Holy Week

BY Jesus' grave on either hand,
While night is brooding o'er the land,
The sad and silent mourners stand.

2 At last the weary life is o'er,
    The agony and conflict sore
    Of him who all our suffering bore.

3 Deep in the rock's sepulchral shade
    The Lord, by whom the worlds were made,
    The Saviour of mankind, is laid.

4 O hearts bereaved and sore distressed,
    Here is for you a place of rest;
    Here leave your griefs on Jesus' breast.

5 So, when the dayspring from on high
    Shall chase the night and fill the sky,
    Then shall the Lord again draw nigh.

Isaac Gregory Smith, 1826–1920

The following is also suitable
No. 224   My song is love unknown

CHRIST'S RESURRECTION AND EXALTATION

262

Tone vi

PSALM 118, verses 15–24

THE voice of rejoicing and salvation is in the tabernacles of the ˈ righteous:
  the right hand of the Lord ˈ doeth valiantly.

The right hand of the Lord is ex ˈ alted:
  the right hand of the Lord ˈ doeth valiantly.

I shall not die ˈ but live:
  and declare ˈ the works of the Lord.

The Lord hath chastened ˈ me sore:
  but he hath not given me ˈ over unto death.

Open to me the gates of righ ˈ teousness:
  I will go into them and ˈ I will praise the Lord.

This gate of ˈ the Lord:
  into which the righ ˈ teous shall enter.

I will ˈ praise thee:
  for thou hast heard me and art become ˈ my salvation.

The stone which the builders ˈ refus'd:
  is become the head stone ˈ of the corner.

This is the Lord's ˈ doing:
  it is marvel ˈ lous in our eyes.

This is the day which the Lord ˈ hath made:
  we will rejoice ˈ and be glad in it.

Glory be to the Father and to ˈ the Son:
  and ˈ to the Holy Ghost.

As it was in the beginning is now and ever ˈ shall be:
  world with ˈ out end Amen.

263 SOUTHWARK C.M.

Adapted from a melody by
CHRISTOPHER TYE, c. 1508–72,
in his *The Actes of the Apostles*, 1553

A - men.

PSALM 118, verses 19–25, 28, 29

O SET ye open unto me
   The gates of righteousness;
Then will I enter into them,
   And I the Lord will bless.

2 This is the gate of God, by it
   The just shall enter in.
Thee will I praise, for thou me
     heard'st,
   And hast my safety been.

3 That stone is made head corner-
     stone,
   Which builders did despise:
This is the doing of the Lord,
   And wondrous in our eyes.

4 This is the day God made, in it
   We'll joy triumphantly.
Save now, I pray thee, Lord; I pray,
   Send now prosperity.

5 Thou art my God, I'll thee exalt;
   My God, I will thee praise.
Give thanks to God, for he is good:
   His mercy lasts always.

6 *To Father, Son, and Holy Ghost,*
   The God whom we adore,
Be glory, as it was, and is,
   And shall be evermore. Amen.

264 EASTER HYMN
7777 and Alleluias

Lyra Davidica, 1708,
altered later in the 18th century

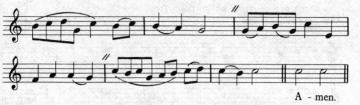

A - men.

JESUS CHRIST is risen today,
  Alleluia!
Our triumphant holy day, *Alleluia!*
Who did once, upon the Cross,
  Alleluia!
Suffer to redeem our loss. *Alleluia!*

2 Hymns of praise, then, let us sing
Unto Christ, our heavenly King,
Who endured the cross and grave,
Sinners to redeem and save.

3 But the anguish he endured
Our salvation hath procured;
Now above the sky he's King,
Where the angels ever sing.

4 *Sing we to our God above*
Praise eternal as his love;
Praise him, all ye heavenly host,
Father, Son, and Holy Ghost: Amen.

Lyra Davidica, 1708

265 ST. MICHAEL
(OLD 134TH) S.M.

Derived from the melody for Psalm 101
in *French-Genevan Psalter*, 1551

'THE Lord is risen indeed';
  Now is his work performed;
Now is the mighty Captive freed,
  And Death's strong castle
    stormed.

2 'The Lord is risen indeed':
  The grave has lost his prey;
With him is risen the ransomed seed,
  To reign in endless day.

3 'The Lord is risen indeed';
  He lives, to die no more;
He lives, the sinner's cause to plead,
  Whose curse and shame he bore.

4 Then, angels, tune your lyres,
  And strike each cheerful chord;
Join, all ye bright celestial choirs,
  To sing our risen Lord!

Thomas Kelly, 1769-1855

266 VULPIUS (GELOBT SEI GOTT)
888 and Alleluias

Vulpius' *Gesangbuch*, 1609

REFRAIN

Al - le - lu - ia! Al - le - lu - ia! Al - le - lu - ia!

Finita iam sunt proelia

THE strife is o'er, the battle done;
Now is the Victor's triumph won;
Now be the song of praise begun,—
Alleluia! Alleluia! Alleluia!

2 The powers of death have done their worst,
But Christ their legions hath dispersed;
Let shouts of holy joy outburst,—

3 The three sad days have quickly sped;
He rises glorious from the dead;
All glory to our risen Head!

4 He brake the age-bound chains of hell;
The bars from heaven's high portals fell;
Let hymns of praise his triumph tell.

5 Lord, by the stripes which wounded thee,
From death's dread sting thy servants free,
That we may live, and sing to thee:

17th century; tr. Francis Pott, 1832–1909 (altered)

267 CRÜGER 7676. D

Adapted by WILLIAM HENRY MONK, 1823–89,
from a melody in Crüger's *Gesangbuch*, 1640

Ἀναστάσεως ἡμέρα

THE day of resurrection!
  Earth, tell it out abroad;
The passover of gladness,
  The passover of God!
From death to life eternal,
  From earth unto the sky,
Our Christ hath brought us over
  With hymns of victory.

2 Our hearts be pure from evil,
  That we may see aright
The Lord in rays eternal
  Of resurrection light;
And, listening to his accents,
  May hear, so calm and plain,
His own 'All hail!' and, hearing,
  May raise the victor strain.

3 Now let the heavens be joyful;
  Let earth her song begin;
Let the round world keep triumph,
  And all that is therein;
Let all things seen and unseen
  Their notes of gladness blend,
For Christ the Lord hath risen,
  Our Joy that hath no end.

St. John of Damascus, d. c. 750
Tr. John Mason Neale, 1818–66 (altered)

233

268 CHRIST LAG IN TODESBANDEN
8787 787 and Alleluia

Walther's *Gesangbuchlein*, 1524
Adapted by MARTIN LUTHER, 1483-1546

REFRAIN

Al - le - lu - ia!

Christ lag in Todesbanden

CHRIST JESUS lay in death's
  strong bands,
  For our offences given,
But now at God's right hand he
  stands,
  And brings us life from heaven:
Wherefore let us joyful be,
And sing to God right thankfully
  Loud songs of Alleluia!
    Alleluia!

2 It was a strange and dreadful strife
  When life and death contended;
  The victory remained with life,
  The reign of death was ended:
  Stripped of power, no more he
    reigns,
  An empty form alone remains;
  His sting is lost for ever.

3 So let us keep the festival
  Whereto the Lord invites us;
  Christ is himself the joy of all,
  The sun that warms and lights us;
  By his grace he doth impart
  Eternal sunshine to the heart;
  The night of sin is ended.

4 Then let us feast this Easter day
  On the true Bread of heaven.
  The word of grace hath purged away
  The old and wicked leaven;
  Christ alone our soul will feed,
  He is our meat and drink indeed,
  Faith lives upon no other.

Martin Luther, 1483-1546
Tr. Richard Massie, 1800-87

269 AVE VIRGO VIRGINUM
7676. D

Horn's *Gesangbuch*, 1544 (rhythm slightly altered)

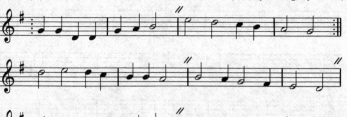

Αἴσωμεν πάντες λαοί

COME, ye faithful, raise the strain
  Of triumphant gladness;
God hath brought his Israel
  Into joy from sadness;
Loosed from Pharaoh's bitter yoke
  Jacob's sons and daughters;
Led them with unmoistened foot
  Through the Red Sea waters.

2 'Tis the spring of souls today;
  Christ hath burst his prison,
And from three days' sleep in death
  As a sun hath risen;
All the winter of our sins,
  Long and dark, is flying
From his light, to whom we give
  Laud and praise undying.

3 Now the queen of seasons, bright
    With the day of splendour,
  With the royal feast of feasts,
    Comes its joy to render;
  Comes to gladden Christian men,
    Who with true affection
  Welcome in unwearied strains
    Jesus' resurrection.

4 Neither might the gates of death,
    Nor the tomb's dark portal,
  Nor the watchers, nor the seal,
    Hold thee as a mortal;
  But arising, thou dost stand
    'Midst thine own, bestowing
  Thine own peace, which evermore
    Passeth human knowing.

St. John of Damascus, d. c. 750
Tr. John Mason Neale, 1818-66, and others

270 VULPIUS (GELOBT SEI GOTT)
888 and Alleluias

Vulpius' *Gesangbuch*, 1609

Al - le - lu - ia! Al - le - lu - ia! Al-le-lu - ia!

GOOD Christian men, rejoice and
sing!
Now is the triumph of our King!
To all the world glad news we bring:
 Alleluia! Alleluia! Alleluia!

2 The Lord of life is risen for aye;
Bring flowers of song to strew his
way;
Let all mankind rejoice and say:

3 Praise we in songs of victory
That love, that life which cannot die,
And sing with hearts uplifted high:

4 Thy Name we bless, O risen Lord,
And sing today with one accord
The life laid down, the life restored:

Cyril Argentine Alington, 1872–1955

271 VRUECHTEN 6767 and refrain

17th century Dutch Melody

a - ri - sen, A - ri - sen, a-

-ri - sen, a - ri - - - - sen!

THIS joyful Eastertide,
　Away with sin and sorrow.
My Love, the Crucified,
　Hath sprung to life this morrow:
　　Had Christ, that once was slain,
　　Ne'er burst his three-day
　　prison,
　Our faith had been in vain:
　　But now hath Christ arisen,
　　Arisen, arisen, arisen!

2 My flesh in hope shall rest,
　And for a season slumber:
Till trump from east to west
　Shall wake the dead in number:

3 Death's flood hath lost his chill,
　Since Jesus crossed the river:
Lover of souls, from ill
　My passing soul deliver:

George Ratcliffe Woodward, 1848–1934

272 NOUS ALLONS 11 11 11 11　　　　French Carol Melody

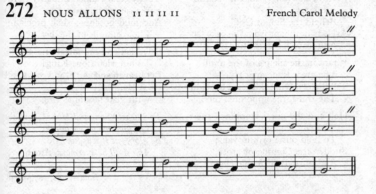

Salve, festa dies

'WELCOME, happy morning!'—age to age shall say:
'Hell today is vanquished, heaven is won today.'
Lo! the Dead is living, God for evermore:
Him, their true Creator, all his works adore.

2 Earth with joy confesses, clothing her for spring,
All good gifts return with her returning King:
Bloom in every meadow, leaves on every bough,
Speak his sorrows ended, hail his triumph now.

3 Thou, of life the Author, death didst undergo,
Tread the path of darkness, saving strength to show.
Come then, True and Faithful, now fulfil thy word;
'Tis thine own third morning: rise, O buried Lord!

4 Loose the souls long prisoned, bound with Satan's chain:
All that now is fallen raise to life again:
Show thy face in brightness, bid the nations see:
Bring again our daylight: day returns with thee.

Venantius Fortunatus, c. 535–600
Par. John Ellerton, 1826–93

273 LANCASTER C.M.   SAMUEL HOWARD, 1710–82

A - men.

Alternative tune, CREDITON, No. 168

BLEST morning, whose first dawn-
  ing rays
  Beheld the Son of God
Arise triumphant from the grave,
  And leave his dark abode!

2 Wrapt in the silence of the tomb
  The great Redeemer lay,
Till the revolving skies had brought
  The third, the appointed day.

3 Hell and the grave combined their
  force
  To hold our Lord, in vain;
Sudden the Conqueror arose,
  And burst their feeble chain.

4 To thy great Name, Almighty Lord,
  We sacred honours pay,
And loud hosannas shall proclaim
  The triumphs of the day.

5 Salvation and immortal praise
  To our victorious King!
Let heaven and earth, and rocks and
  seas,
  With glad hosannas ring.

6 *To Father, Son, and Holy Ghost,*
  The God whom we adore,
Be glory, as it was, and is,
  And shall be evermore. Amen.

Isaac Watts, 1674–1748

274 O CHRISTE REX 8787 888 and refrain   *Piae Cantiones,* 1582

REFRAIN

Ho - san - na in ex - cel - sis!

THE world itself keeps Easter Day,
  And Easter larks are singing;
And Easter flowers are blooming
    gay,
And Easter buds are springing:
    Alléluia, Alléluia:
The Lord of all things lives anew,
And all his works are rising too:
    Hosanna in excelsis!

2 There stood the women by the tomb,
    On Easter morning early;
When day had scarcely chased the
    gloom,
    And dew was white and pearly:
    Alléluia, Alléluia:
With loving but with erring mind,
They came the Prince of Life to find:

3 But earlier still the angel sped,
    His news of comfort giving;
  And 'Why,' he said, 'among the dead
    Thus seek ye for the Living?'
    Alléluia, Alléluia:
  The Lord hath risen, as all things tell:
  Good Christians, see ye rise as well!

John Mason Neale, 1818–66 (altered)

275 ORIENTIS PARTIBUS 7777   Medieval French Melody (adapted)

'CHRIST the Lord is risen today',
  Sons of men and angels say;
Raise your joys and triumphs high;
Sing, ye heavens, and earth reply.

2 Love's redeeming work is done,
  Fought the fight, the battle won;
Lo! our Sun's eclipse is o'er;
Lo! he sets in blood no more.

3 Vain the stone, the watch, the seal;
Christ has burst the gates of hell:
Death in vain forbids his rise;
Christ has opened Paradise.

4 Lives again our glorious King;
Where, O Death, is now thy sting?
Once he died, our souls to save;
Where thy victory, O grave?

5 Soar we now where Christ has led,
Following our exalted Head;
Made like him, like him we rise;
Ours the cross, the grave, the skies.

6 Hail, the Lord of earth and heaven!
Praise to thee by both be given;
Thee we greet triumphant now;
Hail, the Resurrection thou!

Charles Wesley, 1707–88

276 WÜRTEMBERG 7777 and Alleluia *Hundert Arien*, Dresden, 1694

EASTER glory fills the sky!
Christ now lives, no more to die!
Darkness has been put to flight
By the living Lord of light!
Alleluia!

2 See, the stone is rolled away
From the tomb where once he lay!
He has risen as he said,
Glorious Firstborn from the dead!

3 Seek not life within the tomb;
Christ stands in the upper room!
Risen glory he conceals,
Risen Body he reveals!

4 Though we see his face no more,
He is with us as before!
Glory veiled, he is our Priest,
His own flesh and blood our feast!

5 Christ, the Victor over death,
Breathes on us the Spirit's breath!
Paradise is our reward,
Endless Easter with our Lord!

James Quinn

277 O FILII ET FILIAE
888 and Alleluias

Airs sur les hymnes sacrez, **Paris, 1623**

★*Al - le - lu - ia! Al - le - lu - ia! Al - le - lu - ia!*

vv. 1–9

REFRAIN *(all verses)*

Al - le - lu - ia!

★*Alleluias to precede verse 1 only*

O filii et filiae

★ ALLELUIA! ALLELUIA! ALLELUIA!

O SONS and daughters, let us sing!
The King of heaven, the glorious
King,
O'er death today rose triumphing.
Alleluia!

2 That Easter morn, at break of day,
The faithful women went their way
To seek the tomb where Jesus lay:

3 An angel clad in white they see,
Who sat, and spake unto the three,
'Your Lord doth go to Galilee.'

4 That night the apostles met in fear;
Amidst them came their Lord most
dear,
And said, 'My peace be on all here.'

5 When Thomas first the tidings
heard,
He doubted if it were their Lord,
Until he came and spake the word:

6 'My piercèd side, O Thomas, see;
Behold my hands, my feet,' said he,
'Not faithless, but believing be.'

7 No longer Thomas then denied;
He saw the feet, the hands, the side;
'Thou art my Lord and God', he
cried:

8 How blest are they who have not
seen,
And yet whose faith hath constant
been,
For they eternal life shall win:

9 On this most holy day of days,
To God your hearts and voices raise
In laud and jubilee and praise:

Jean Tisserand, ?–1494; tr. John Mason Neale, 1818–66 (altered)

★ *These Alleluias are sung before the first verse only*

278 NOËL NOUVELET
11 10 10 and refrain

French Traditional Carol Melody

NOW the green blade riseth from the buried grain,
Wheat that in dark earth many days has lain;
 Love lives again, that with the dead has been:
  Love is come again,
  Like wheat that springeth green.

2 In the grave they laid him, Love whom men had slain,
 Thinking that never he would wake again,
  Laid in the earth like grain that sleeps unseen:

3 Forth he came at Easter, like the risen grain,
 He that for three days in the grave had lain,
  Quick from the dead my risen Lord is seen:

4 When our hearts are wintry, grieving, or in pain,
 Thy touch can call us back to life again,
  Fields of our hearts that dead and bare have been:

John Macleod Campbell Crum, 1872-1958

279 MACCABÆUS
10 11 11 11 and refrain

GEORGE FREDERICK HANDEL, 1685–1759,
adapted from a chorus in *Judas Maccabæus*, 1746

REFRAIN

A toi la gloire, O Ressuscité

THINE be the glory, risen, conquering Son,
Endless is the victory thou o'er death hast won;
Angels in bright raiment rolled the stone away,
Kept the folded grave-clothes, where thy body lay.
    Thine be the glory, risen, conquering Son,
    Endless is the victory thou o'er death hast won.

2 Lo! Jesus meets us, risen from the tomb;
Lovingly he greets us, scatters fear and gloom;
Let the Church with gladness hymns of triumph sing,
For her Lord now liveth; death hath lost its sting.

3 No more we doubt thee, glorious Prince of Life;
Life is naught without thee: aid us in our strife;
Make us more than conquerors, through thy deathless love:
Bring us safe through Jordan to thy home above.

Edmond Budry, 1854–1932
Tr. R. Birch Hoyle, 1875–1939

280 CHERRY TREE CAROL
7676 irregular

English Traditional Melody

For children

GOOD Joseph had a garden,
Close by that sad green hill
Where Jesus died a bitter death
To save mankind from ill.

2 One evening in that garden,
Their faces dark with gloom,
They laid the Saviour's body
Within good Joseph's tomb.

3 There came the holy women
With spices and with tears;
The angels tried to comfort them,
But could not calm their fears.

4 Came Mary to that garden
And sobbed with heart forlorn;
She thought she heard the gardener
ask,
'Whom seekest thou this morn?'

5 She heard her own name spoken,
And then she lost her care:
All in his strength and beauty
The risen Lord stood fair!

6 Good Joseph had a garden;
Amid its trees so tall
The Lord Christ rose on Easter
Day:
He lives to save us all.

7 And as he rose at Easter
He is alive for aye,
The very same Lord Jesus Christ
Who hears us sing today.

8 Go tell the Lord Christ's message,
The Easter triumph sing,
Till all his waiting children know
That Jesus is their King.

Alda M. Milner-Barry, 1877-1941

281 HILARITER
88 and refrain

Geistliche Kirchengesäng, Cologne, 1623

CHRIST'S RESURRECTION AND EXALTATION

For younger children

AT Eastertime the lilies fair
And lovely flowers bloomed ev'rywhere.
At Eastertime, at Eastertime,
How glad the world at Eastertime!

2 At Eastertime the angels said
That Christ had risen from the dead:

Frederick Arthur Jackson, 1867–1942

282 IN BABILONE   8787 and refrain

Dutch Traditional Melody,
collected by JULIUS RÖNTGEN,
1855–1932

For younger children

COME, ye children, sing to Jesus
On this happy Easter Day;
All the bells are gladly ringing,
Come, ye children, praise and pray.
All the flowers are gaily springing,
All the birds with joy are singing;
Come, ye children, sing to Jesus,
Come, ye children, praise and pray.

2 'Christ our Saviour now is risen',
Let his little children say.
All the bells are gladly ringing
On this happy Easter Day;
All the flowers are gaily springing,
All the birds with joy are singing;

Frederick Smith, 1800–73,
altered by compilers

283 KING'S WESTON 6565. D   RALPH VAUGHAN WILLIAMS, 1872–1958

For Easter evening

JESUS, Lord, Redeemer,
  Once for sinners slain,
Crucified in weakness,
  Raised in power, to reign,
Dwelling with the Father,
  Endless in thy days,
Unto thee be glory,
  Honour, blessing, praise.

2 Faithful ones, communing,
  Towards the close of day,
Desolate and weary,
  Met thee in the way.

So, when sun is setting,
  Come to us, and show
All the truth; and in us
  Make our hearts to glow.

3 In the upper chamber,
  Where the ten, in fear,
Gathered sad and troubled,
  There thou didst appear.
So, O Lord, this evening,
  Bid our sorrows cease;
Breathing on us, Saviour,
  Say, 'I give you peace'.

Patrick Miller Kirkland, 1857–1943

284

Tone viii, ending 2

PSALM 47

O CLAP your hands all ye ¦ people:
  shout unto God with the ¦ voice of triumph.

For the Lord most high is ¦ terri-ble:
  he is a great King ¦ over all the earth.

He shall subdue the people ¦ under us:
  and the nations ¦ under our feet.

He shall choose our inheritance ' for us:
  the excellency of Jacob ' whom he löv'd.

God is gone up with a ' shout:
  the Lord with the sound ' of a trumpet.

Sing praises to God sing ' praises:
  sing praises unto our ' King sing praises.

For God is the King of all the ' earth:
  sing ye praises with ' understanding.

God reigneth over the ' heathen:
  God sitteth upon the throne ' of his holi-ness.

The princes of the people are gathered together   even the people of the God
    of ' Abraham:
  for the shields of the earth belong unto God   he is great ' ly exalted.

Glory be to the Father and to the ' Son:
  and ' to the Holy Ghost.

As it was in the beginning is now and ever ' shall be :
  world with ' out end Amen.

285 EFFINGHAM C.M.

Adapted from a melody in
Musikalisches Hand-Buch, Hamburg, 1690

A - men.

PSALM 68, verses 18, 19, 20

THOU hast, O Lord, most glorious,
  Ascended up on high;
And in triumph victorious led
  Captive captivity.

2 Blest be the Lord, who is to us
    Of our salvation God;
  Who daily with his benefits
    Us plenteously doth load.

3 He of salvation is the God,
    Who is our God most strong;
  And unto God the Lord from death
    The issues do belong.

4 *To Father, Son, and Holy Ghost,*
    The God whom we adore,
  Be glory, as it was, and is,
    And shall be evermore. Amen.

286 ST. MAGNUS
(NOTTINGHAM) C.M.   Probably by JEREMIAH CLARKE, c. 1673-1707

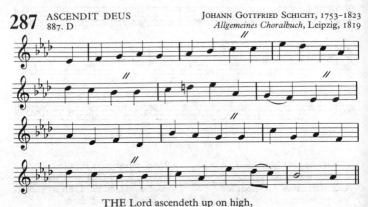

THE Head that once was crowned
    with thorns
  Is crowned with glory now;
A royal diadem adorns
  The mighty Victor's brow.

2 The highest place that heaven affords
  Is his, is his by right,
The King of kings, and Lord of lords,
  And heaven's eternal Light;

3 The joy of all who dwell above,
  The joy of all below
To whom he manifests his love,
  And grants his Name to know.

4 To them the cross, with all its
    shame,
  With all its grace, is given,
Their name an everlasting name,
  Their joy the joy of heaven.

5 They suffer with their Lord below,
  They reign with him above,
Their profit and their joy to know
  The mystery of his love.

6 The cross he bore is life and health,
  Though shame and death to him,
His people's hope, his people's
    wealth,
  Their everlasting theme.

Thomas Kelly, 1769-1855

287 ASCENDIT DEUS
887. D   JOHANN GOTTFRIED SCHICHT, 1753-1823
                               Allgemeines Choralbuch, Leipzig, 1819

THE Lord ascendeth up on high,
The Lord hath triumphed gloriously,
  In power and might excelling;
The grave and hell are captive led,
Lo! he returns, our glorious Head,
  To his eternal dwelling.

2 The heavens with joy receive their
    Lord,
  By saints, by angel hosts adored;
    O day of exultation!
  O earth, adore thy glorious King!
  His rising, his ascension sing
    With grateful adoration!

3 Our great High Priest hath gone
    before,
  Now on his Church his grace to pour,
    And still his love he giveth:
  O may our hearts to him ascend;
  May all within us upward tend
    To him who ever liveth!

Arthur Tozer Russell, 1806-74

288 (i) PRAETORIUS
C.M.

*Harmoniae Hymnorum Scholiae
Gorlicensis, Görlitz, 1599*
Possibly by MICHAEL PRAETORIUS, 1571-1621

[For No. 311]

A - men.

(ii) IN ARMOUR BRIGHT C.M.
EDWARD NORMAN HAY, 1889-1943

THE eternal gates are lifted up,
  The doors are opened wide;
The King of Glory is gone in
  Unto his Father's side.

2 Thou art gone up before us, Lord,
  To make for us a place,
That we may be where now thou art,
  And look upon God's face.

3 And ever on our earthly path
  A gleam of glory lies;
A light still breaks behind the cloud
  That veiled thee from our eyes.

4 Lift up our hearts, lift up our minds,
  And let thy grace be given,
That, while we live on earth below,
  Our treasure be in heaven;

5 That where thou art, at God's right hand,
  Our hope, our love may be.
Dwell thou in us, that we may dwell
  For evermore in thee.

Cecil Frances Alexander, 1818-95 (altered)

289 REGENT SQUARE 8787 87   HENRY SMART, 1813-79

LOOK, ye saints! the sight is glorious;
    See the Man of Sorrows now;
From the fight returned victorious,
    Every knee to him shall bow:
Crown him! crown him! crown him! crown him!
    Crowns become the Victor's brow.

2 Crown the Saviour! angels, crown him!
    Rich the trophies Jesus brings;
In the seat of power enthrone him,
    While the vault of heaven rings:
Crown him! crown him! crown him! crown him!
    Crown the Saviour King of kings!

3 Sinners in derision crowned him,
    Mocking thus the Saviour's claim;
Saints and angels crowd around him,
    Own his title, praise his Name:
Crown him! crown him! crown him! crown him!
    Spread abroad the Victor's fame.

4 Hark, those bursts of acclamation!
    Hark, those loud triumphant chords!
Jesus takes the highest station:
    O what joy the sight affords!
Crown him! crown him! crown him! crown him!
    King of kings, and Lord of lords!

Thomas Kelly, 1769-1855

290 HERMANN (ERSCHIENEN IST
DER HERRLICH' TAG) L.M. and Alleluia

NICOLAUS HERMANN,
c. 1485–1561

REFRAIN

Al - le - lu - ia!

Gen Himmel aufgefahren ist

GOD is ascended up on high,
With merry noise of trumpet's sound,
And princely seated in the sky,
Rules over all the world around: *Alléluia!*

2 In human shape and flesh he went,
Adornèd with his Passion's scars,
Which in heaven's sight he did present
More glorious than the glittering stars:

3 Lord, raise our sinking minds therefore
Up to our proper country dear,
And purify us evermore,
To fit us for those regions clear:

*Henry More, 1614-87,
from the German carol*

291 WIR PFLÜGEN
7676. D and refrain

JOHANN ABRAHAM PETER SCHULZ, 1747–1800

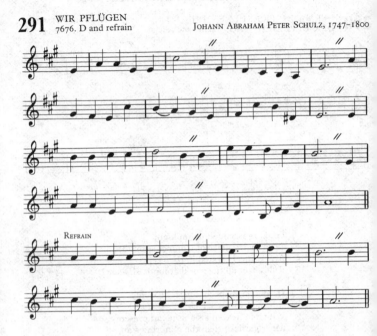

AGAIN the morn of gladness,
  The morn of light, is here,
And earth itself looks fairer,
  And heaven itself more near:
The bells, like angel voices,
  Speak peace to every breast;
And all the land lies quiet,
  To keep the day of rest.
    'Glory be to Jesus!'
      Let all his children say;
    'He rose again, he rose again,
      On this glad day!'

2 Again, O loving Saviour,
  The children of thy grace
Prepare themselves to seek thee
  Within thy chosen place.
Our song shall rise to greet thee,
  If thou our hearts wilt raise;
If thou our lips wilt open,
  Our mouth shall show thy praise:

3 Tell out, sweet bells, his praises!
   Sing, children, sing his Name!
Still louder and still farther
   His mighty deeds proclaim,
Till all whom he redeemèd
   Shall own him Lord and King,
Till every knee shall worship,
   And every tongue shall sing.
      'Glory be to Jesus!'
         Let all creation say;
      'He rose again, he rose again,
         On this glad day!'

John Ellerton, 1826–93

292 BARNTON 8886 86   WILLIAM MATHIAS

AWAY with gloom, away with
      doubt!
   With all the morning stars we
      sing;
With all the sons of God we shout
   The praises of a King,
      Alleluia! Alleluia!
   Of our returning King.

2 Away with death, and welcome life;
   In him we died and live again;
And welcome peace, away with
      strife!
   For he returns to reign.
      Alleluia! Alleluia!
   The Crucified shall reign.

3 Then welcome beauty, he is fair;
   And welcome youth, for he is young;
And welcome spring; and everywhere
   Let merry songs be sung!
      Alleluia! Alleluia!
   For such a King be sung!

Edward Shillito, 1872–1948

The following are also suitable

No.
11   Jesus, stand among us
44   Most glorious Lord of life
605 Jesus lives! thy terrors now

CHRIST'S REIGN AND PRIESTHOOD

293 ST. ANDREW C.M.   Tans'ur's *New Harmony of Zion*, 1764

PARAPHRASE 48, verses 5-9

THE Saviour died, but rose again
 Triumphant from the grave;
And pleads our cause at God's right
 hand,
 Omnipotent to save.

2 Who then can e'er divide us more
 From Jesus and his love,
Or break the sacred chain that binds
 The earth to heaven above?

3 Let troubles rise, and terrors frown,
 And days of darkness fall;
Through him all dangers we'll defy,
 And more than conquer all.

4 Nor death nor life, nor earth nor hell,
 Nor time's destroying sway,
Can e'er efface us from his heart,
 Or make his love decay.

5 Each future period that will bless,
 As it has blessed the past;
He loved us from the first of time,
 He loves us to the last.

Scottish Paraphrases, 1781
From Romans 8: 34-end

294 IRISH C.M.   *A Collection of Hymns and Sacred Poems*, Dublin, 1749

PARAPHRASE 20, verses 1-5

HOW glorious Zion's courts appear,
 The city of our God!
His throne he hath established here,
 Here fixed his loved abode.

2 Its walls, defended by his grace,
 No power shall e'er o'erthrow,
Salvation is its bulwark sure
 Against the assailing foe.

254

3 Lift up the everlasting gates,
    The doors wide open fling;
Enter, ye nations, who obey
    The statutes of our King.

4 Here shall ye taste unmingled joys,
    And dwell in perfect peace,

Ye, who have known Jehovah's
    Name,
    And trusted in his grace.

5 Trust in the Lord, for ever trust,
    And banish all your fears;
Strength in the Lord Jehovah dwells
    Eternal as his years.

Scottish Paraphrases, 1781
From Isaiah 26: 1–4

295 SOLDAU L.M.

Geystliche Gesangk Buchleyn,
Wittenberg, 1524, as given in Dibdin's
Standard Psalm Tune Book, 1851

PARAPHRASE 58

WHERE high the heavenly temple stands,
The house of God not made with hands,
A great High Priest our nature wears,
The Guardian of mankind appears.

2 He who for men their surety stood,
And poured on earth his precious blood,
Pursues in heaven his mighty plan,
The Saviour and the Friend of man.

3 Though now ascended up on high,
He bends on earth a brother's eye;
Partaker of the human name,
He knows the frailty of our frame.

4 Our fellow-sufferer yet retains
A fellow-feeling of our pains;
And still remembers in the skies
His tears, his agonies, and cries.

5 In every pang that rends the heart
The Man of Sorrows had a part;
He sympathizes with our grief,
And to the sufferer sends relief.

6 With boldness, therefore, at the throne,
Let us make all our sorrows known;
And ask the aids of heavenly power
To help us in the evil hour.

Scottish Paraphrases, 1781
From Hebrews 4: 14–end

296 (i) DARWALL'S 148TH 6666 88   JOHN DARWALL, 1731-89

[For No. 137]

A – men.

(ii) GOPSAL 6666 88   GEORGE FREDERICK HANDEL, 1685-1759

REJOICE, the Lord is King;
　Your Lord and King adore;
Mortals, give thanks and sing
　And triumph evermore:
Lift up your heart, lift up your voice;
Rejoice; again I say, 'Rejoice'.

2　Jesus, the Saviour, reigns,
　　The God of truth and love;
　When he had purged our stains,
　　He took his seat above:
　Lift up your heart, lift up your voice;
　Rejoice; again I say, 'Rejoice'.

3　His Kingdom cannot fail;
　　He rules o'er earth and heaven;
　The keys of death and hell
　　Are to our Jesus given:
　Lift up your heart, lift up your voice;
　Rejoice; again I say, 'Rejoice'.

4   He sits at God's right hand
        Till all his foes submit,
    And bow to his command,
        And fall beneath his feet:
    Lift up your heart, lift up your
        voice;
    Rejoice; again I say, 'Rejoice'.

5   Rejoice in glorious hope;
        Jesus, the Judge, shall come,
    And take his servants up
        To their eternal home;
    We then shall hear the archangel's
        voice;
    The trump of God shall sound,
        'Rejoice'.

Charles Wesley, 1707–88 (altered)

297   ENGELBERG
          10 10 10 and Alleluia   CHARLES VILLIERS STANFORD, 1852–1924

Al – le – lu – ia!   *Al – le – lu – ia!*

ALL praise to thee, for thou, O King divine,
Didst yield the glory that of right was thine,
That in our darkened hearts thy grace might shine:
    Alleluia!

2   Thou cam'st to us in lowliness of thought;
    By thee the outcast and the poor were sought,
    And by thy death was God's salvation wrought:

3   Let this mind be in us which was in thee,
    Who wast a servant that we might be free,
    Humbling thyself to death on Calvary:

4   Wherefore, by God's eternal purpose, thou
    Art high exalted o'er all creatures now,
    And given the Name to which all knees shall bow:

5   Let every tongue confess with one accord
    In heaven and earth that Jesus Christ is Lord;
    And God the Father be by all adored:

Francis Bland Tucker
Based on Philippians 2: 5–11

298 DIADEMATA D.S.M.   GEORGE JOB ELVEY, 1816-93

CROWN him with many crowns,
The Lamb upon his throne:
Hark how the heavenly anthem drowns
All music but its own.
Awake, my soul, and sing
Of him who died for thee,
And hail him as thy matchless King
Through all eternity.

2   Crown him the Lord of life,
Who triumphed o'er the grave,
And rose victorious in the strife
For those he came to save.
His glories now we sing
Who died and rose on high,
Who died eternal life to bring,
And lives that death may die.

3   Crown him the Lord of love;
Behold his hands and side,
Rich wounds yet visible above,
In beauty glorified.
All hail, Redeemer, hail!
For thou hast died for me:
Thy praise shall never, never fail
Throughout eternity.

Matthew Bridges, 1800-94,
and Godfrey Thring, 1823-1903

299 BLESSING AND HONOUR AND
GLORY AND POWER   10 10 10 10   Scottish Traditional Melody

Alternative tune, O QUANTA QUALIA (REGNATOR ORBIS), No. 535

BLESSING and honour and glory and power,
Wisdom and riches and strength evermore
Give ye to him who our battle hath won,
Whose are the Kingdom, the crown, and the throne.

2 Into the heaven of the heavens hath he gone;
Sitteth he now in the joy of the throne;
Weareth he now of the Kingdom the crown;
Singeth he now the new song with his own.

3 Soundeth the heaven of the heavens with his Name;
Ringeth the earth with his glory and fame;
Ocean and mountain, stream, forest, and flower
Echo his praises and tell of his power.

4 Ever ascendeth the song and the joy;
Ever descendeth the love from on high;
Blessing and honour and glory and praise,—
This is the theme of the hymns that we raise.

5 Give we the glory and praise to the Lamb;
Take we the robe and the harp and the palm;
Sing we the song of the Lamb that was slain,
Dying in weakness, but rising to reign.

Horatius Bonar, 1808–89

300 (i) IN NOMINE JESU 6565. D

ARTHUR OLDHAM

1. At the Name of Je - sus Ev -'ry knee shall
2. Hum - bled for a sea - son, To re - ceive a
3. Name him, bro - thers, name him With love strong as
4. In your hearts en - throne him; There let him sub -
5. Bro - thers, this Lord Je - sus Shall re -turn a -

bow, Ev' - ry tongue con - fess him King____
name From the lips of sin - ners, Un -
death, But with awe and won - der And____
- due All that is not ho - ly, All____
gain, With his Fa - ther's glor - y, With____

____ of Glor - y now; 'Tis the Fa - ther's
- to whom he came, Faith - ful - ly he
____ with ba - ted breath! He is God the
____ that is not true: Crown him as your
____ his an - gel train; For all wreaths of

plea - sure We should call him Lord, Who from
bore it Spot -less to the last; Brought it
Sa - viour, He is Christ the Lord, Ev - er
Cap - tain In temp -ta - tion's hour; Let his
em - pire Meet up - on his brow, And our

the be - gin - ning Was the migh - ty Word.
back vic - to - rious, When from death he passed.
to be wor - shipped, Trust-ed, and a - dored.
will en - fold you In its light and power.
hearts con - fess him King of Glor - y now.

(ii) CUDDESDON 6565. D   WILLIAM HAROLD FERGUSON, 1874-1950

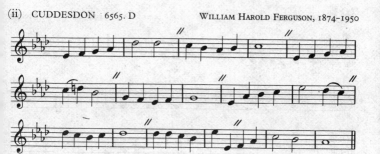

AT the Name of Jesus
    Every knee shall bow,
Every tongue confess him
    King of Glory now;
'Tis the Father's pleasure
    We should call him Lord,
Who from the beginning
    Was the mighty Word.

2 Humbled for a season,
    To receive a name
From the lips of sinners,
    Unto whom he came,
Faithfully he bore it
    Spotless to the last;
Brought it back victorious,
    When from death he passed.

3 Name him, brothers, name him
    With love strong as death,
But with awe and wonder
    And with bated breath!
He is God the Saviour,
    He is Christ the Lord,
Ever to be worshipped,
    Trusted, and adored.

4 In your hearts enthrone him;
    There let him subdue
All that is not holy,
    All that is not true:
Crown him as your Captain
    In temptation's hour;
Let his will enfold you
    In its light and power.

5 Brothers, this Lord Jesus
    Shall return again,
With his Father's glory,
    With his angel train;
For all wreaths of empire
    Meet upon his brow,
And our hearts confess him
    King of Glory now.

Caroline Maria Noel, 1817-77

301 MOVILLE 7676. D   Irish Traditional Melody

Christus Redemptor gentium

CHRIST is the world's Redeemer,
　The lover of the pure,
The fount of heav'nly wisdom,
　Our trust and hope secure;
The armour of his soldiers,
　The Lord of earth and sky;
Our health while we are living,
　Our life when we shall die.

2 Christ hath our host surrounded
　With clouds of martyrs bright,
Who wave their palms in triumph,
　And fire us for the fight.
For Christ the cross ascended
　To save a world undone,
And, suffering for the sinful,
　Our full redemption won.

3 Down in the realm of darkness
　He lay a captive bound,
But at the hour appointed
　He rose, a Victor crowned;
And now, to heav'n ascended,
　He sits upon the throne,
In glorious dominion,
　His Father's and his own.

4 *Glory to God the Father,*
　The unbegotten One;
All honour be to Jesus,
　His sole-begotten Son;
And to the Holy Spirit—
　The perfect Trinity.
Let all the worlds give answer,
　'Amen—so let it be'.

St. Columba, 521-97
Tr. Duncan Macgregor, 1854-1923 (altered)

302 METZLER C.M.
(REDHEAD No. 66)

RICHARD REDHEAD, 1820-1901
*Ancient Hymn Melodies and
other Church Tunes,* 1859

Jesu, nostra redemptio

JESUS, our hope, our heart's desire,
    Thy work of grace we sing;
Redeemer of the world art thou,
    Its Maker and its King.

2 How vast the mercy and the love
    Which laid our sins on thee,
And led thee to a cruel death,
    To set thy people free!

3 But now the bonds of death are burst;
    The ransom has been paid;
And thou art on thy Father's throne,
    In majesty arrayed.

4 Jesus, our only joy be thou,
    As thou our prize wilt be;
In thee be all our glory now,
    And through eternity.

7th-8th century. Tr. John Chandler, 1806-76
and Compilers of Hymns Ancient and Modern

303 PURPOSE Irregular

MARTIN SHAW, 1875-1958

1. God is work-ing his pur-pose out, as year suc-ceeds to year; God is work-ing his pur-pose out and the time is draw-ing near Near-er and near-er draws the time, the time that shall sure-ly be, When the earth shall be filled with the glor-y of God, as the

2. What can we do to work God's work, to pros-per and in-crease The reign of the Prince of Peace? What can we do to has-ten the time, the time that shall sure-ly be, When the earth shall be filled with the glor-y of God, as the

3. March we forth in the strength of God, with the ban-ner of Christ un-furled, That the light of the glor-ious Gos-pel of truth may shine through-out the world: Fight we the fight with sor-row and sin, to set their cap-tives free, That the earth may be filled with the glor-y of God, as the

4. All we can do is noth-ing worth, un-less God bles-ses the deed; Vain-ly we hope for the har-vest-tide, till God gives life to the seed; Yet near-er and near-er draws the time, the time that shall sure-ly be, When the earth shall be filled with the glor-y of God, as the

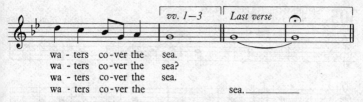

| vv. 1–3 | Last verse |

wa - ters co-ver the sea.
wa - ters co-ver the sea?
wa - ters co-ver the sea.
wa - ters co-ver the   sea._____

Arthur Campbell Ainger, 1841-1919

304 CROFT'S 136TH 6666 88   WILLIAM CROFT, 1678-1727

JOIN all the glorious names
    Of wisdom, love, and power,
That ever mortals knew,
    That angels ever bore:
All are too mean to speak his worth,
Too mean to set my Saviour forth.

2 Great Prophet of my God,
    My tongue would bless thy Name;
By thee the joyful news
    Of our salvation came,—
The joyful news of sins forgiven,
Of hell subdued, and peace with heaven.

3 Jesus, my great High Priest,
    Offered his blood and died;
My guilty conscience seeks
    No sacrifice beside:
His powerful blood did once atone,
And now it pleads before the throne.

4 My dear Almighty Lord,
    My Conqueror and my King,
Thy sceptre and thy sword,
    Thy reigning grace, I sing:
Thine is the power: behold, I sit
In willing bonds before thy feet.

5 Now let my soul arise,
    And tread the tempter down:
My Captain leads me forth
    To conquest and a crown:
A feeble saint shall win the day,
Though death and hell obstruct the way.

Isaac Watts, 1674-1748

305 SOLEMNIS HAEC   L.M.
FESTIVITAS

Paris Gradual, 1685

A - men.

Alternative tune, CHURCH TRIUMPHANT, No. 36

Hymnum canamus gloriae

SING we triumphant hymns of praise,
New hymns to heaven exulting raise:
Christ, by a road before untrod,
Ascendeth to the throne of God.

2 O grant that we may thither tend,
And with unwearied hearts ascend
Toward thy kingdom's throne, where thou,
Our great high priest, art seated now.

3 Be thou our joy and strong defence,
Who art our future recompense:
So shall the light that springs from thee
Be ours through all eternity.

4 *O risen Christ, ascended Lord,*
All praise to thee let earth accord,
Who art, while endless ages run,
With Father and with Spirit One. Amen.

The Venerable Bede, 673-735. Tr. Benjamin Webb,
1819-85, and Compilers of The BBC Hymn Book

306 FINGAL C.M.   JAMES SMITH ANDERSON, 1853-1945

Alternative tune, ST. PETER, No. 376

IMMORTAL Love, for ever full,
    For ever flowing free,
For ever shared, for ever whole,
    A never-ebbing sea!

2 Blow, winds of God, awake and blow
    The mists of earth away:
Shine out, O Light Divine, and show
    How wide and far we stray.

3 We may not climb the heavenly steeps
    To bring the Lord Christ down;
In vain we search the lowest deeps,
    For him no depths can drown.

4 And not for signs in heaven above,
    Or earth below, they look
Who know with John his smile of love,
    With Peter his rebuke.

5 In joy of inward peace, or sense
    Of sorrow over sin,
He is his own best evidence;
    His witness is within.

6 And, warm, sweet, tender, even yet
    A present help is he;
And faith has still its Olivet,
    And love its Galilee.

7 The healing of his seamless dress
    Is by our beds of pain;
We touch him in life's throng and press,
    And we are whole again.

John Greenleaf Whittier, 1807-92

267

307 PSALM 12   11 10 11 10
(DONNE SECOURS)

French-Genevan Psalter, 1551

'LIFT up your hearts': I hear the summons calling
    Forth from the heavenly altar where he stands—
Our great High Priest, the Father's love revealing,
    In priestly act, with pleading outspread hands.

2 'Lift up your hearts': with hearts to heaven soaring
    The Church exulting makes her glad reply—
'We lift them up unto the Lord', adoring;
    Our God and thine, through thee, we glorify.

3 'Lift up your hearts': alas, O Lord, I cannot
    Lift up aright my burdened heart to thee;
Thou knowest, Lord, the cares that weigh upon it,
    The chains that bind it struggling to be free.

4 O Love divine! thy promise comes to cheer me,
    O Voice of pity! blessing and thrice blest—
'Come unto me, ye laden hearts and weary;
    Take up my yoke, and learn: I pledge you rest'.

5 I dare not waver by such grace invited,
    I yield my heart, dear Lord: I close the strife.
Lift thou my heart until, with thine united,
    I taste anew the joy of endless life.

John MacLeod, 1840-98 (altered)

308 JOUISSANCE 7474 77   PIERRE BONNET, 1638–1708

Al - - - le - lu - ia!

Al - - - le - lu - ia!

NOW at last he takes his throne;
    Alleluia!
From all ages his alone!
    Alleluia!
With his praise creation rings,
Lord of lords and King of kings.

2 Hands and feet and side reveal
Wounds of love, High Priesthood's seal!
Advocate, for us he pleads;
Heavenly Priest, he intercedes!

3 Christians, raise your eyes above!
He will come again in love,
On that great and wondrous Day
When this world will pass away!

4 At his word new heavens and earth
Will in glory spring to birth!
Joy of angels, joy of men,
Come, Lord Jesus, come again!

James Quinn

309 DERRY AIR 11 10 11 10. D
(LONDONDERRY)

Irish Traditional Melody

Alternative tune, PSALM 12 (DONNE SECOURS), No. 307

For children

O SON of Man, our Hero strong and tender,
　　Whose servants are the brave in all the earth,
Our living sacrifice to thee we render,
　　Who sharest all our sorrows, all our mirth.
O feet so strong to climb the path of duty,
　　O lips divine that taught the words of truth,
Kind eyes that marked the lilies in their beauty,
　　And heart that kindled at the zeal of youth:

2 Lover of children, boyhood's inspiration,
　　Of all mankind the Servant and the King;
O Lord of joy and hope and consolation,
　　To thee our fears and joys and hopes we bring.
Not in our failures only and our sadness
　　We seek thy presence, Comforter and Friend;
O rich man's Guest, be with us in our gladness,
　　O poor man's Mate, our lowliest tasks attend.

Frank Fletcher, 1870-1954

The following are also suitable

No.
158　Give the king thy judgments, O God
36　The Lord is King! lift up thy voice

CHRIST'S COMING WITH POWER

310   Tone iii, ending 5

PSALM 50, verses 1–6, 14, 23

THE mighty God even the | Lord hath spoken:
and called the earth from the rising of the sun unto the going | down thereof.

Out of Zion the per | fection of beauty:
— | God hath shined.

Our God shall come and shall | not keep silence:
a fire shall devour before him   and it shall be very tempestuous round |
about him.

He shall call to the | heavens from above:
and to the earth that he may | judge his people.

Gather my saints to | gether unto me:
those that have made a covenant with me by | sacrifice.

And the heavens shall de | clare his righteousness:
for God is | judge himself.

Offer unto | God thanksgiving:
and pay thy vows unto | the most High.

Whoso offereth praise | glori-fieth me:
and to him that ordereth his conversation aright   will I show the salva | tion
of God.

Glory be to the | Father and to the Son:
and to the | Holy Ghost.

As it was in the beginning is now and | ever shall be:
world without | end Amen.

311 OLD 44TH D.C.M.　　　　　　　　*Anglo–Genevan Psalter, 1556*

A - men.

Alternative tune, PRAETORIUS, No. 288 (i)

PSALM 96, verses 9, 11–13

IN beauty of his holiness,
　O do the Lord adore;
Likewise let all the earth through-
　　out
　Tremble his face before.
Let heavens be glad before the Lord,
　And let the earth rejoice;
Let seas and all their fullness roar,
　And make a mighty noise.

2 Let fields rejoice, and everything
　That springeth of the earth;
Then of the forest all the trees
　Shall shout aloud with mirth
Before the Lord; because he comes,
　To judge the earth comes he;
He'll judge the world with right-
　eousness,
　The people faithfully.

3 All glory be to God on high,
　And to the earth be peace,
Goodwill is shown by heaven to men,
　And never more shall cease.
To Father, Son, and Holy Ghost,
　The God whom we adore,
Be glory, as it was, and is,
　And shall be evermore. Amen.

312 (i)　GLASGOW　C.M.　　　　　　　　　　Moore's
　　　　　　　　　　　　　Psalm-Singer's Pocket Companion, 1756

(ii) SOUTHWARK C.M.   Adapted from CHRISTOPHER TYE, c. 1508–72

PARAPHRASE 18

BEHOLD! the mountain of the Lord
　　In latter days shall rise
On mountain tops above the hills,
　　And draw the wondering eyes.

2 To this the joyful nations round,
　　All tribes and tongues, shall flow;
Up to the hill of God, they'll say,
　　And to his house we'll go.

3 The beam that shines from Zion hill
　　Shall lighten every land;
The King who reigns in Salem's towers
　　Shall all the world command.

4 Among the nations he shall judge;
　　His judgments truth shall guide;
His sceptre shall protect the just,
　　And quell the sinner's pride.

5 No strife shall rage, nor hostile feuds
　　Disturb those peaceful years;
To ploughshares men shall beat their swords,
　　To pruning-hooks their spears.

6 No longer hosts encountering hosts
　　Shall crowds of slain deplore:
They hang the trumpet in the hall,
　　And study war no more.

7 Come then, O house of Jacob! come
　　To worship at his shrine;
And, walking in the light of God,
　　With holy beauties shine.

Scottish Paraphrases, 1781
From Isaiah 2: 2–5

313 NEANDER 8787 87 Neander's
(UNSER HERRSCHER) *Alpha und Omega*, 1680

CHRIST is coming! let creation
  From her groans and travail cease;
Let the glorious proclamation
  Hope restore and faith increase:
Christ is coming! Christ is coming!
  Come, thou blessèd Prince of Peace.

2 Earth can now but tell the story
    Of thy bitter cross and pain;
  She shall yet behold thy glory,
    When thou comest back to reign:
  Christ is coming! Christ is coming!
    Let each heart repeat the strain.

3 Long thine exiles have been pining,
    Far from rest, and home, and thee:
  But, in heavenly vestures shining,
    They their loving Lord shall see:
  Christ is coming! Christ is coming!
    Haste the joyous jubilee.

4 With that blessèd hope before us,
    Let no harp remain unstrung;
  Let the mighty advent chorus
    Onward roll from tongue to tongue:
  'Christ is coming! Christ is coming!
    Come, Lord Jesus, quickly come!'

John Ross Macduff, 1818-95

CHRIST'S COMING WITH POWER

314 PSALM 12   11 10 11 10
(DONNE SECOURS)

French–Genevan Psalter, 1551

HARK what a sound, and too divine for hearing,
  Stirs on the earth and trembles in the air!
Is it the thunder of the Lord's appearing?
  Is it the music of his people's prayer?

2 Surely he cometh, and a thousand voices
  Shout to the saints, and to the deaf are dumb;
Surely he cometh, and the earth rejoices,
  Glad in his coming who hath sworn, 'I come'.

3 This hath he done, and shall we not adore him?
  This shall he do, and can we still despair?
Come, let us quickly fling ourselves before him,
  Cast at his feet the burden of our care.

4 Yea, through life, death, through sorrow and through sinning
  He shall suffice me, for he hath sufficed:
Christ is the end, for Christ was the beginning,
  Christ the beginning, for the end is Christ.

Frederic William Henry Myers, 1843–1901

315 WACHET AUF
898. D 66 4 88

PHILIPP NICOLAI, 1556–1608

Wachet auf! ruft uns die Stimme

'WAKE, awake! for night is flying,'
The watchmen on the heights are crying,
'Awake, Jerusalem, at last!'
Midnight hears the welcome voices,
And at the thrilling cry rejoices:
'Come forth, ye virgins, night is past!
The Bridegroom comes; awake,
Your lamps with gladness take;
Alleluia!
And for his marriage feast prepare,
For ye must go to meet him there.'

2   Zion hears the watchmen singing,
And all her heart with joy is springing;
She wakes, she rises from her gloom;
For her Lord comes down all-glorious,
The strong in grace, in truth victorious;
Her Star is risen, her Light is come!
Ah come, thou blessèd One,
God's own belovèd Son;
Alleluia!
We follow till the halls we see
Where thou hast bid us sup with thee.

3   Now let all the heavens adore thee,
    And men and angels sing before thee,
        With harp and cymbal's clearest tone;
        Of one pearl each shining portal,
    Where we are with the choir immortal
        Of angels round thy dazzling throne;
            Nor eye hath seen, nor ear
            Hath yet attained to hear
                What there is ours;
        But we rejoice, and sing to thee
        Our hymn of joy eternally.

Philipp Nicolai, 1556–1608
Tr. Catherine Winkworth, 1827–78

316 HELMSLEY 8787 12 7   Later form of a melody in John Wesley's
Select Hymns with Tunes Annext, 1765

LO! he comes, with clouds descend-
    ing,
    Once for favoured sinners slain;
Thousand thousand saints attending
Swell the triumph of his train;
    Alleluia! Alleluia! Alleluia!
    God appears on earth to reign.

2 Every eye shall now behold him,
    Robed in dreadful majesty;
Those who set at naught and sold
    him,
    Pierced, and nailed him to the tree,
    Deeply wailing, deeply wailing,
        deeply wailing,
    Shall the true Messiah see.

3 Those dear tokens of his Passion
    Still his dazzling body bears;
Cause of endless exaltation
    To his ransomed worshippers;
    Alleluia! Alleluia! Alleluia!
    See! the day of God appears!

4 Yea, Amen! let all adore thee,
    High on thine eternal throne;
Saviour, take the power and glory,
    Claim the kingdom for thine own:
    O come quickly; O come quickly;
        O come quickly;
    Alleluia! come, Lord, come!

Charles Wesley, 1707–88 (altered),
based on a hymn by John Cennick, 1718–55

317 MOVILLE 7676. D   Irish Traditional Melody

Alternative tune, CRÜGER, No. 267

HAIL to the Lord's Anointed,
  Great David's greater Son!
Hail, in the time appointed,
  His reign on earth begun!
He comes to break oppression,
  To set the captive free,
To take away transgression,
  And rule in equity.

2 He comes with succour speedy
  To those who suffer wrong,
To help the poor and needy,
  And bid the weak be strong,
To give them songs for sighing,
  Their darkness turn to light
Whose souls, condemned and dying,
  Were precious in his sight.

3 He shall come down like showers
  Upon the fruitful earth,
And love, joy, hope, like flowers,
  Spring in his path to birth.

Before him, on the mountains,
  Shall peace, the herald, go;
And righteousness in fountains
  From hill to valley flow.

4 For him shall prayer unceasing
  And daily vows ascend,
His Kingdom still increasing,
  A Kingdom without end.
The mountain dews shall nourish
  A seed, in weakness sown,
Whose fruit shall spread and flourish
  And shake like Lebanon.

5 O'er every foe victorious,
  He on his throne shall rest,
From age to age more glorious,
  All blessing and all-blest.
The tide of time shall never
  His covenant remove;
His Name shall stand for ever;
  That Name to us is Love.

James Montgomery, 1771–1854
From Psalm 72

318 (i) VISION Irregular

WALFORD DAVIES, 1869-1941

1. Mine eyes have seen the glor-y of the com-ing of the Lord: He is tramp-ling out the vin-tage where the grapes of wrath are stored; He hath loosed the fa-tal light-ning of his ter-ri-ble swift sword: His truth is march - ing on.

2. He hath sound-ed forth the trum-pet that shall nev-er call re-treat; He is sift-ing out the hearts of men be-fore his judg-ment seat: O, be swift, my soul, to an-swer him; be ju-bi-lant, my feet! Our God is march - ing on. (march - ing on.)

3. In the beau-ty of the li-lies Christ was born a-cross the sea, With a glor-y in his bo-som that trans-fi-gures you and me: As he died to make men ho-ly, let us live to make men free, While God is march - ing on. (march - ing on.)

4. He is com-ing like the glor-y of the morn-ing on the wave; He is wis-dom to the migh-ty; he is suc-cour to the brave; So the world shall be his foot-stool, and the soul of time his slave: Our God is march - ing on! (march - ing on!)

(> for vv. 1, 2)

(upper notes vv. 3, 4)

Julia Ward Howe, 1819-1910

279

318 (ii) BATTLE HYMN OF THE
REPUBLIC Irregular

WILLIAM STEFFE, *c.* 1852

MINE eyes have seen the glory of the coming of the Lord:
He is trampling out the vintage where the grapes of wrath are stored;
He hath loosed the fatal lightning of his terrible swift sword:
    His truth is marching on.
    Glory, glory, Alleluia!
    Glory, glory, Alleluia!
    Glory, glory, Alleluia!
    His truth is marching on.

2 He hath sounded forth the trumpet that shall never call retreat;
He is sifting out the hearts of men before his judgment-seat:
O, be swift, my soul, to answer him; be jubilant, my feet!
    Our God is marching on.
    Glory, glory, Alleluia!
    Glory, glory, Alleluia!
    Glory, glory, Alleluia!
    Our God is marching on.

3 In the beauty of the lilies Christ was born across the sea,
With a glory in his bosom that transfigures you and me:
As he died to make men holy, let us live to make men free,
    While God is marching on.
    Glory, glory, Alleluia!
    Glory, glory, Alleluia!
    Glory, glory, Alleluia!
    While God is marching on.

4 He is coming like the glory of the morning on the wave;
He is wisdom to the mighty; he is succour to the brave;
So the world shall be his footstool, and the soul of time his slave:
    Our God is marching on.
    Glory, glory, Alleluia!
    Glory, glory, Alleluia!
    Glory, glory, Alleluia!
    Our God is marching on!

Julia Ward Howe, 1819–1910

319 ST. MICHAEL   S.M.
(OLD 134TH)

Derived from the melody for
Psalm 101 in *French-Genevan Psalter,* 1551

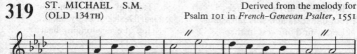

YE servants of the Lord,
    Each in his office wait,
Observant of his heavenly word,
    And watchful at his gate.

2   Let all your lamps be bright,
    And trim the golden flame;
Gird up your loins, as in his sight,
    For awesome is his Name.

3   Watch: 'tis your Lord's command,
    And while we speak he's near;
Mark the first signal of his hand,
    And ready all appear.

4   O happy servant he,
    In such a posture found!
He shall his Lord with rapture see,
    And be with honour crowned.

5   Christ shall the banquet spread
    With his own royal hand,
And raise that faithful servant's head
    Amid the angelic band.

Philip Doddridge, 1702–51

320 STUTTGART 8787

Adapted from a melody in Witt's
Psalmodia Sacra, Gotha, 1715

COME, thou long-expected Jesus,
  Born to set thy people free;
From our fears and sins release us;
  Let us find our rest in thee.

2 Israel's Strength and Consolation,
  Hope of all the earth thou art,
Dear Desire of every nation,
  Joy of every longing heart.

3 Born thy people to deliver,
  Born a Child and yet a King,
Born to reign in us for ever,
  Now thy gracious Kingdom bring.

4 By thine own eternal Spirit
  Rule in all our hearts alone;
By thine all-sufficient merit
  Raise us to thy glorious throne.

Charles Wesley, 1707–88

321 (i) PSALM 107 D.C.M.
(OLD 107TH)

Lyons Psalter, 1547

(ii) MONTROSE D.C.M.

Gilmour's *Psalm-Singer's Assistant*, Glasgow, 1793

THE Lord will come and not be slow,
   His footsteps cannot err;
Before him righteousness shall go,
   His royal harbinger.
Truth from the earth, like to a flower,
   Shall bud and blossom then;
And justice, from her heavenly bower,
   Look down on mortal men.

2 Surely to such as do him fear
   Salvation is at hand!
And glory shall ere long appear
   To dwell within our land.
Rise, God, judge thou the earth in might,
   This wicked earth redress;
For thou art he who shall by right
   The nations all possess.

3 The nations all whom thou hast made
   Shall come, and all shall frame
To bow them low before thee, Lord,
   And glorify thy Name.
For great thou art, and wonders great
   By thy strong hand are done:
Thou in thy everlasting seat
   Remainest God alone.

John Milton, 1608-74
From Psalms 85, 82, 86

322 ST. CECILIA 6666   LEIGHTON GEORGE HAYNE, 1836-83

THY Kingdom come, O God;
  Thy rule, O Christ, begin;
Break with thine iron rod
  The tyrannies of sin.

2 Where is thy reign of peace
  And purity and love?
When shall all hatred cease,
  As in the realms above?

3 When comes the promised time
  That war shall be no more,
And lust, oppression, crime,
  Shall flee thy face before?

4 We pray thee, Lord, arise,
  And come in thy great might;
Revive our longing eyes,
  Which languish for thy sight.

5 Men scorn thy sacred Name,
  And wolves devour thy fold;
By many deeds of shame
  We learn that love grows cold.

6 O'er lands both near and far
  Thick darkness broodeth yet;
Arise, O Morning Star,
  Arise, and never set.

Lewis Hensley, 1824-1905 (altered)

323 IRISH C.M.   *A Collection of Hymns and Sacred Poems, Dublin, 1749*

'THY Kingdom come!'—on bended
    knee
  The passing ages pray;
And faithful souls have yearned to see
  On earth that Kingdom's day.

2 But the slow watches of the night
  Not less to God belong;
And for the everlasting right
  The silent stars are strong.

3 And lo! already on the hills
    The flags of dawn appear;
  Gird up your loins, ye prophet souls,
    Proclaim the day is near:

4 The day in whose clear-shining light
    All wrong shall stand revealed,
  When justice shall be throned with might,
    And every hurt be healed:

5 When knowledge, hand in hand with peace,
    Shall walk the earth abroad,—
  The day of perfect righteousness,
    The promised day of God.

Frederick Lucian Hosmer, 1840–1929

324 BUCER S.M.   *Cantica Laudis, 1850*

    BLEST is the man, O God,
      That stays himself on thee:
  Who wait for thy salvation, Lord,
    Shall thy salvation see.

2   When we in darkness walk,
      Nor feel the heavenly flame,
  Then is the time to trust our God,
    And rest upon his Name.

3   Soon shall our doubts and fears
      Subside at his control;
  His loving-kindness shall break through
    The midnight of the soul.

4   Wait till the shadows flee;
      Wait thy appointed hour;
  Wait till the Bridegroom of thy soul
    Reveals his love with power.

Augustus Montague Toplady, 1740–78

325 LOCHWINNOCH 14 14 irregular   ROBIN ORR

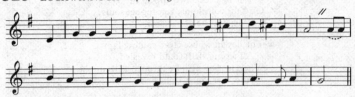

Ἀπὸ δόξης εἰς δόξαν πορευόμενοι

FROM glory to glory advancing, we praise thee, O Lord;
Thy Name with the Father and Spirit be ever adored.

2 From strength unto strength we go forward on Zion's highway,
To appear before God in the city of infinite day.

3 Thanksgiving, and glory and worship, and blessing and love,
One heart and one song have the saints upon earth and above.

4 O Lord, evermore to thy servants thy presence be nigh;
Ever fit us by service on earth for thy service on high.

From the Liturgy of St. James
Tr. Charles William Humphreys, 1840-1921

The following are also suitable

No.
12   Lift up your heads, ye mighty gates
505 Christ is the world's true light

PENTECOST

326

Tone iii, ending 5

PSALM 104, verses 1–5, 30–34

BLESS the Lord ' O my soul:
O Lord my God thou art very great thou art clothed with honour and ' majesty.

Who coverest thyself with light as ' with a garment:
who stretchest out the heavens ' like a curtain.

Who layeth the beams of his chambers ' in the waters:
who maketh the clouds his chariot who walketh upon the wings ' of the wind.

Who maketh his ' angels spirits:
his ministers a ' flaming fire.

Who laid the foun ' dations of the earth:
that it should not be re ' mov'd for ever.

Thou sendest forth thy spirit they ' are created:
and thou renewest the face ' of the earth.

The glory of the Lord shall en ' dure for ever:
the Lord shall rejoice ' in his works.

He looketh on the earth ' and it trembleth:
he toucheth the hills ' and they smoke.

I will sing unto the Lord as ' long as I live:
I will sing praise to my God while I ' have my being.

My meditation of ' him shall be sweet:
I will be glad ' in the Lord.

Glory be to the ' Father and to the Son:
and to the ' Holy Ghost.

As it was in the beginning is now and ' ever shall be:
world without ' end Amen.

327 CRÜGER 7676. D

Adapted by WILLIAM HENRY MONK, 1823–89
from a melody in Crüger's *Gesangbuch*, 1640

O DAY of joy and wonder!
  Christ's promise now fulfilled!
The coming of his Spirit
  The Father's love has willed;
Our Lord in human body,
  To mortal eye is lost,
Yet he returns for ever
  At blessèd Pentecost!

2 The world in sheer amazement,
  The truth must now declare,
That men who once were cowards,
  Are brave beyond compare,
And tongues which could not utter
  Their faith in Jesus' name,
Defy all persecution,
  His glory to proclaim!

3 We too may know thy power,
  Thy courage makes us strong,
Thy love, thy joy, thy patience,
  Can all to us belong,
If thou wilt dwell within us,
  A Comforter divine;
Come to our hearts, we pray thee,
  And keep them ever thine.

Violet Buchanan

328 SALVE FESTA DIES
Irregular

RALPH VAUGHAN WILLIAMS, 1872–1958

Salve, festa dies, toto venerabilis aevo

Verse 1 (repeated as a Refrain after each other verse)

Hail thee, Fes-ti-val Day! blest day that art hal-lowed for
e - ver; Day where-in God from heav'n shone on the

288

Verses 2 and 4

world with his grace.   2 Lo! in the like-ness of fire, on
4 Hark! in a hun-dred tongues Christ's

them that a-wait his ap-pear-ing, He whom the
own, his cho-sen A-post-les, Preach to a

Repeat Refrain

Lord fore-told, sud-den-ly, swift-ly, de-scends.
hun-dred tribes Christ and his won-der-ful works.

Verses 3 and 5

3 Forth from the Fa-ther he comes with his sev'n-fold
5 Praise to the Spi-rit of life, all praise to the

mys-ti-cal dow-ry, Pour-ing on hu-man
Fount of our be-ing, Light that dost light-en

Repeat Refrain (v. 1)

souls in-fi-nite rich-es of God.
all, Life that in all dost a-bide.

c. 14th century. (York Processional)
Tr. Gabriel Gillett, 1873–1948

329 & 330 GONFALON ROYAL
L.M.
PERCY CARTER BUCK, 1871–1947

A - - men.

Beata nobis gaudia

329

O JOY! because the circling year
Hath brought our day of blessing here,
The day when first the light divine
Upon the Church began to shine.

2 Like unto quivering tongues of flame
Upon each one the Spirit came,—
Tongues, that the earth might hear their call,
And fire, that love might burn in all.

3 Thus wondrously were spread abroad
To all the wondrous works of God;
To each in his familiar tone
The glorious marvel was made known.

4 While hardened scoffers vainly jeered,
The listening strangers heard and feared;
They knew the prophet's word fulfilled,
And owned the work which God had willed.

5 *Praise we the Father and the Son,*
And Holy Spirit with them One:
And may the Son on us bestow
The gifts that from the Spirit flow. Amen.

c. 4th century; tr. John Ellerton, 1826–93
and Compilers of Hymns Ancient and Modern
Based on Acts 2: 1–4

330 *Beata nobis gaudia*

REJOICE! the year upon its way
  Has brought again that blessèd day,
When on the chosen of the Lord
  The Holy Spirit was outpoured.

2 On each the fire, descending, stood
  In quivering tongues' similitude—
Tongues, that their words might
    ready prove,
  And fire, to make them flame with
    love.

3 And now, O holy God, this day
  Regard us as we humbly pray,
And send us, from thy heavenly seat,
  The blessings of the Paraclete.

4 *To God the Father, God the Son,*
  And God the Spirit, praise be done;
May Christ the Lord upon us pour
  The Spirit's gift for evermore. Amen.

c. 4th century; tr. Richard Ellis Roberts, 1879–1953
Based on Acts 2: 1–4

331 WINCHESTER OLD C.M.

Este's *Psalter*, 1592,
later form of rhythm

A version with the older form of rhythm is at No. 138

WHEN God of old came down from
    heaven,
  In power and wrath he came;
Before his feet the clouds were riven,
  Half darkness and half flame.

2 But, when he came the second time,
  He came in power and love;
Softer than gale at morning prime
  Hovered his holy Dove.

*3 The fires that rushed on Sinai down
  In sudden torrents dread,
Now gently light, a glorious crown,
  On every sainted head.

4 And, as on Israel's awe-struck ear
    The voice exceeding loud,
  The trump that angels quake to
    hear,
    Thrilled from the deep, dark
    cloud;

5 So, when the Spirit of our God
    Came down his flock to find,
  A voice from heaven was heard
    abroad,
    A rushing mighty wind.

6 It fills the Church of God; it fills
  The sinful world around;
Only in stubborn hearts and wills
  No place for it is found.

7 Come, Lord; come, Wisdom, Love, and Power;
  Open our ears to hear;
Let us not miss the accepted hour;
  Save, Lord, by love or fear.

John Keble, 1792–1866

* *This verse may be omitted*

THE WORD OF GOD: HIS MIGHTY ACTS

332 HAMPTON S.M.   Williams' *Psalmody in Miniature, c.* 1770

LORD God, the Holy Ghost,
　In this accepted hour,
As on the day of Pentecost,
　Descend in all thy power.

2　We meet with one accord
　　In our appointed place,
And wait the promise of our Lord,
　The Spirit of all grace.

3　Like mighty rushing wind
　　Upon the waves beneath,
Move with one impulse every mind;
　One soul, one feeling breathe.

4　The young, the old inspire
　　With wisdom from above;
And give us hearts and tongues of
　　fire,
　To pray and praise and love.

5　Spirit of light, explore
　　And chase our gloom away,
With lustre shining more and more
　Unto the perfect day.

James Montgomery, 1771-1854

THE HOLY SPIRIT IN THE CHURCH

333 DUKE STREET L.M.   Boyd's *Psalm and Hymn Tunes,* 1793
Later attributed to JOHN HATTON, d. 1793

A-men.

PSALM 102 (ii), verses 13-18

THOU shalt arise, and mercy yet
Thou to mount Zion shalt extend:
The time is come for favour set,
The time when thou shalt blessing
　send.

2 Thy saints take pleasure in her
　stones,
Her very dust to them is dear.
All heathen lands and kingly thrones
On earth thy glorious Name shall
　fear.

292

THE HOLY SPIRIT IN THE CHURCH

3 God in his glory shall appear,
When Zion he builds and repairs.
He shall regard and lend his ear
Unto the needy's humble prayers:

4 The afflicted's prayer he will not
scorn.
All times this shall be on record:
And generations yet unborn
Shall praise and magnify the Lord.

5 *To Father, Son, and Holy Ghost,*
The God whom earth and heaven adore,
Be glory, as it was of old,
Is now, and shall be evermore. Amen.

334 ABBOT'S LEIGH 8787. D   CYRIL VINCENT TAYLOR

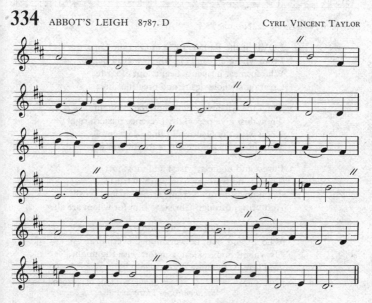

HOLY Spirit, ever living
As the Church's very life;
Holy Spirit, ever striving
Through her in a ceaseless strife;
Holy Spirit, ever forming
In the Church the mind of Christ;
Thee we praise with endless worship
For thy fruit and gifts unpriced.

2 Holy Spirit, ever working
Through the Church's ministry;
Quick'ning, strength'ning, and
absolving,
Setting captive sinners free;
Holy Spirit, ever binding
Age to age, and soul to soul,
In a fellowship unending
Thee we worship and extol.

Timothy Rees, 1874–1939
Verse 1 omitted

335 MAGDA 10 10 10 10 RALPH VAUGHAN WILLIAMS, 1872-1958

Alternative tune, SONG 22, No. 108

LOVE of the Father, Love of God the Son,
From whom all came, in whom was all begun;
Who formest heavenly beauty out of strife,
Creation's whole desire and breath of life:

2 Thou the All-holy, thou supreme in might,
Thou dost give peace, thy presence maketh right;
Thou with thy favour all things dost enfold,
With thine all-kindness free from harm wilt hold.

3 Purest and highest, wisest and most just,
There is no truth save only in thy trust;
Thou dost the mind from earthly dreams recall,
And bring, through Christ, to him for whom are all.

4 Eternal Glory, all men thee adore,
Who art and shalt be worshipped evermore:
Us whom thou madest, comfort with thy might,
And lead us to enjoy thy heavenly light.

Robert Bridges, 1844-1930,
based on Amor Patris et Filii, *12th century*

336 (i) ESSEX 8684 GUSTAV HOLST, 1874-1934

THE HOLY SPIRIT IN THE CHURCH

(ii) ST. CUTHBERT 8684   JOHN BACCHUS DYKES, 1823–76

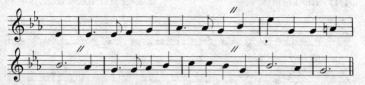

OUR blest Redeemer, ere he breathed
  His tender last farewell,
A Guide, a Comforter bequeathed,
  With us to dwell.

2 He came in tongues of living flame,
  To teach, convince, subdue;
All-powerful as the wind he came,
  As viewless too.

3 He came sweet influence to impart,
  A gracious, willing Guest,
While he can find one humble heart
  Wherein to rest.

4 And his that gentle voice we hear,
  Soft as the breath of even,
That checks each fault, that calms each fear,
  And speaks of heaven.

5 And every virtue we possess,
  And every victory won,
And every thought of holiness,
  Are his alone.

6 Spirit of purity and grace,
  Our weakness, pitying, see;
O make our hearts thy dwelling-place,
  And worthier thee.

Henriette Auber, 1773–1862

337 LAUS DEO (REDHEAD No. 46) 8787   RICHARD REDHEAD, 1820–1901
Church Hymn Tunes, 1853

[For No. 37]

A - men.

FOR thy gift of God the Spirit,
With us, in us, e'er to be,
Pledge of life and hope of glory,
Saviour, we would worship thee.

2 He who in creation's dawning
Brooded o'er the pathless deep,
Still across our nature's darkness
Moves to wake our souls from sleep.

3 He it is, the living Author,
Wakes to life the sacred Word;
Reads with us its holy pages,
And reveals our risen Lord.

4 He it is who works within us,
Teaching rebel hearts to pray;
He whose holy intercessions
Rise for us both night and day.

5 Fill us with thy holy fullness,
God the Father, Spirit, Son;
In us, through us, then, forever,
Shall thy perfect will be done.

Edith Margaret Clarkson

338 HEREFORD L.M. SAMUEL SEBASTIAN WESLEY, 1810-76

SPIRIT of mercy, truth and love,
O shed thine influence from above,
And still from age to age convey
The wonders of this sacred day.

2 In every clime, by every tongue,
Be God's surpassing glory sung:
Let all the listening earth be taught
The acts our great Redeemer wrought.

3 Unfailing Comfort, heavenly Guide,
Still o'er thy Holy Church preside;
Still let mankind thy blessings prove;
Spirit of mercy, truth and love.

Anonymous
Foundling Hospital Collection, 1774

339 SUNSET 9898 GEORGE GILBERT STOCKS, 1877-1960

Alternative tune, LES COMMANDEMENS DE DIEU, No. 586

O BREATH of life, come sweeping through us,
Revive thy Church with life and power;
O Breath of life, come, cleanse, renew us,
And fit thy Church to meet this hour.

2 O Wind of God, come bend us, break us,
Till humbly we confess our need;
Then in thy tenderness remake us,
Revive, restore; for this we plead.

3 O Breath of love, come breathe within us,
Renewing thought and will and heart:
Come, Love of Christ, afresh to win us,
Revive thy Church in every part.

4 Revive us, Lord! is zeal abating
While harvest fields are vast and white?
Revive us, Lord, the world is waiting,
Equip thy Church to spread the light.

Bessie Porter Head, 1850–1936

340 MONIKIE Irregular   DAVID DORWARD

SPIRIT of Light—Holy,
Shine in this world of thine;
Lighten thou our darkness, clear
Blindness from out our minds.
Guide thou our ways, so may we
Walk in the light of thy truth,
Come, Spirit, come.

2 Spirit of Love—Holy,
Fire thou this world of thine;
Chasten thou the pride of race
Marring our common life.
Kindle our love, that loving,
All may true brotherhood find,
Come, Spirit, come.

3 Spirit of Life—Holy,
Breathe o'er this world of thine;
Teach us all to know and do
All that will make men free.
Thy kingdom come, on earth as
In thy blest heaven above,
Come, Spirit, come.

4 Spirit of Power—Holy,
Mighty and infinite;
Work within this world of thine
Breaking the powers of sin.
Take thou thy throne, and reigning,
Claim the whole world for thine own.
Great Spirit, come.

Arthur Morris Jones

341 VRUECHTEN Irregular   17th century Dutch Melody

HOW great the harvest is
  Of him who came to save us!
The hearts of men are his,
  Our law the love he gave us.
The world lay cruel, blind,
  Naught holding, naught divining;
He came to human kind,
And now the light is shining, is
    shining,
  Is shining, is shining.

2 And though the news did seem
    Too good for man's believing,
  'Tis not an empty dream
    Too high for our achieving.
  He triumphed in the strife,
    O'er all his foes he towered;
  They killed the Prince of Life,
  But he hath death o'erpowered,
    o'erpowered,
    O'erpowered, o'erpowered.

3 Then came the Father's call;
    His work on earth was ended;
  That he might light on all,
    To heaven the Lord ascended.

To heaven so near to earth
  Our hearts we do surrender:
There all things find their worth
And human life its splendour, its
    splendour,
  Its splendour, its splendour.

4 The power by which there came
    The Word of God among us
  Was love's eternal flame,
    Whose light and heat are flung us;
  That Spirit sent from God,
    Within our hearts abiding,
  Hath brought us on our road
  And still the world is guiding, is
    guiding,
    Is guiding, is guiding.

5 In Three made manifest,
    Thou source of all our being,
  Thou loveliest, truest, best,
    Beyond our power of seeing;
  Thou power of light and love,
    Thou life that never diest—
  To thee in whom all move
  Be glory in the highest, the highest,
    The highest, the highest.

Percy Dearmer, 1867-1936

342 VENI CREATOR Irregular

Simplified version (Mechlin, 1848)
of proper plainsong melody

Conclusion of verse 4

'Praise ___ to thine e - ter - nal me-rit, Fa - ther,

Son, and Ho - ly Spi - rit'. A — men.

Veni, Creator Spiritus

COME, Holy Ghost, our souls inspire
And lighten with celestial fire;
Thou the anointing Spirit art,
Who dost thy sevenfold gifts impart.

2 Thy blessèd unction from above
Is comfort, life, and fire of love;
Enable with perpetual light
The dulness of our blinded sight;

3 Anoint and cheer our soilèd face
With the abundance of thy grace;
Keep far our foes; give peace at home:
Where thou art Guide no ill can come.

4 Teach us to know the Father, Son,
And thee of Both, to be but One,
That through the ages all along
This may be our endless song,
'Praise to thine eternal merit,
Father, Son, and Holy Spirit.' Amen.

9th century; tr. John Cosin, 1594-1672

The following are also suitable

See also hymns on the Holy Spirit in Part I

343 (i)

German 16th century

Al - le - lu - - - ia! ___

TRIPLE ALLELUIAS

(ii)

(a)

Traditional

Al - le - lu - ia, Al - le - lu - ia, ___ Al - le - lu - ia!

(b)

German 16th century

Al - le - lu - ia, Al - le - lu - ia, Al - le - lu - - ia!

(c)

German 16th century

Al - le - lu - ia, Al - le - lu - ia, Al - le - lu - ia!

(iii) MONTROSE C.M.   Gilmour's *Psalm-Singer's Assistant*, Glasgow, 1793

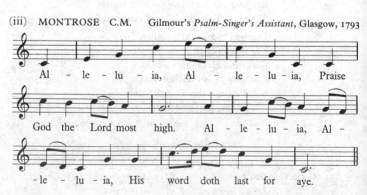

Al - le - lu - ia, Al - le - lu - ia, Praise

God the Lord most high. Al - le - lu - ia, Al -

- le - lu - ia, His word doth last for aye.

344   *Parisian Tone*

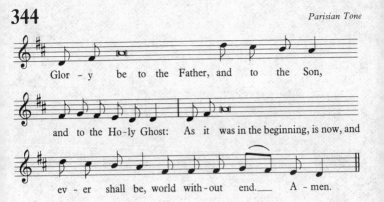

Glor - y   be   to   the   Father,   and   to   the   Son,

and   to   the   Ho - ly   Ghost: As   it   was   in   the beginning, is now, and

ev - er   shall   be,   world   with - out   end.___   A - men.

III

RESPONSE TO THE WORD OF GOD

———

RESPONSE TO THE WORD OF GOD

ADORATION AND THANKSGIVING

TE DEUM LAUDAMUS

SET 1

345(a)

WILLIAM BOYCE, 1710-79

TE DEUM LAUDAMUS

Chant A

WE praise ' thee O ' God:
    we ac- ' knowledge thee to ' be the ' Lord:
All the ' earth doth ' worship thee:
    the ' Father ' ever- ' lasting.

2 To thee all angels ' cry a- ' loud:
    the ' heavens and ' all the ' powers therein:
To thee ' cherubim and ' seraphim:
    con- ' tinual- ' ly do ' cry.

3 Holy holy holy Lord ' God of Sa- ' baoth:
    Heaven and earth are full of the ' majesty ' of thy ' glory:
The glorious company of the a- ' postles ' praise thee:
    The goodly ' fellowship of the ' prophets ' praise thee.

4 The noble army of ' martyrs ' praise thee:
    The holy Church throughout ' all the ' world doth ac- ' knowledge thee:
The Father of an ' infinite ' majesty:
    Thine honourable true and only Son also the ' Holy ' Ghost the ' Comforter.

(b)   ROBERT COOKE, 1768-1814

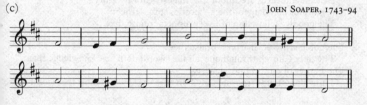

Chant B

5 Thou art the King of ' Glory O ' Christ:
    Thou art the ever- ' lasting ' Son of the ' Father:
When thou tookest upon thee to de- ' liver ' man:
    Thou didst not ab- ' hor the ' Virgin's ' womb.

6 When thou hadst overcome the ' sharpness of ' death:
    Thou didst open the Kingdom of ' heaven to ' all be- ' lievers:
Thou sittest at the ' right hand of ' God:
    in the ' glory ' of the ' Father.

7 We believe that thou shalt come to ' be our ' Judge:
    We therefore pray thee help thy servants whom thou hast re- ' deemed with
thy ' precious ' blood:
    Make them to be ' numbered with thy ' saints:
    in ' glory ' ever- ' lasting.

(c)   JOHN SOAPER, 1743-94

Chant C

8 O Lord save thy people and ' bless thine ' heritage:
    Govern them and ' lift them ' up for ' ever:
Day by day we ' magnify ' thee:
    And we worship thy ' Name ever ' world without ' end.

9 Vouchsafe O Lord to keep us this ' day without ' sin:
    O Lord have mercy up- ' on us have ' mercy up- ' on us:
    O Lord let thy mercy lighten upon us as our ' trust is in ' thee:
    O Lord in thee have I trusted   let me ' never ' be con- ' founded.

RESPONSE TO THE WORD OF GOD

TE DEUM LAUDAMUS
SET 2

345 (d)

CHARLES VILLIERS STANFORD, 1852–1924

TE DEUM LAUDAMUS

Chant D

WE praise ꞌ thee O ꞌ God:
 we ac- ꞌ knowledge thee to ꞌ be the ꞌ Lord:
All the ꞌ earth doth ꞌ worship thee:
 the ꞌ Father ꞌ ever- ꞌ lasting.

2 To thee all angels ꞌ cry a- ꞌ loud:
 the ꞌ heavens and ꞌ all the ꞌ powers therein:
To thee ꞌ cherubim and ꞌ seraphim:
 con- ꞌ tinual- ꞌ ly do ꞌ cry.

3 Holy holy holy Lord ꞌ God of Sa- ꞌ baoth:
 Heaven and earth are full of the ꞌ majesty ꞌ of thy ꞌ glory:
The glorious company of the a- ꞌ postles ꞌ praise thee:
 The goodly ꞌ fellowship of the ꞌ prophets ꞌ praise thee.

4 The noble army of ꞌ martyrs ꞌ praise thee:
 The holy Church throughout ꞌ all the ꞌ world doth ac- ꞌ knowledge thee:
The Father of an ꞌ infinite ꞌ majesty:
 Thine honourable true and only Son also the ꞌ Holy ꞌ Ghost the ꞌ Comforter.

(e)

KELLOW JOHN PYE, 1812–1901

Chant E

5 Thou art the King of ¹ Glory O ¹ Christ:
    Thou art the ever- ¹ lasting ¹ Son of the ¹ Father:
  When thou tookest upon thee to de- ¹ liver ¹ man:
    Thou didst not ab- ¹ hor the ¹ Virgin's ¹ womb.

6 When thou hadst overcome the ¹ sharpness of ¹ death:
    Thou didst open the Kingdom of ¹ heaven to ¹ all be- ¹ lievers:
  Thou sittest at the ¹ right hand of ¹ God:
    in the ¹ glory ¹ of the ¹ Father.

7 We believe that thou shalt come to ¹ be our ¹ Judge:
    We therefore pray thee help thy servants whom thou hast re- ¹ deemed with
  thy ¹ precious ¹ blood:
  Make them to be ¹ numbered with thy ¹ saints:
    in ¹ glory ¹ ever- ¹ lasting.

(f)

JOHN GOSS, 1800–80

Chant F

8 O Lord save thy people and ¹ bless thine ¹ heritage:
    Govern them and ¹ lift them ¹ up for ¹ ever:
  Day by day we ¹ magnify ¹ thee:
    And we worship thy ¹ Name ever ¹ world without ¹ end.

9 Vouchsafe O Lord to keep us this ¹ day without ¹ sin:
    O Lord have mercy up- ¹ on us have ¹ mercy up- ¹ on us:
  O Lord let thy mercy lighten upon us as our ¹ trust is in ¹ thee:
    O Lord in thee have I trusted let me ¹ never ¹ be con- ¹ founded.

346 DUKE STREET L.M.

Boyd's *Psalm and Hymn Tunes*, 1793
Later attributed to JOHN HATTON, d. 1793

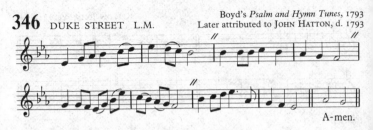

A-men.

PSALM 145 (ii), verses 1–6

O LORD, thou art my God and
   King;
Thee will I magnify and praise:
I will thee bless, and gladly sing
Unto thy holy Name always.

2 Each day I rise I will thee bless,
And praise thy Name time without
   end.
Much to be praised, and great God is;
His greatness none can comprehend.

3 Race shall thy works praise unto
   race,
The mighty acts show done by thee.
I will speak of the glorious grace,
And honour of thy majesty;

4 Thy wondrous works I will record.
By men the might shall be extolled
Of all thy dreadful acts, O Lord:
And I thy greatness will unfold.

5 *To Father, Son, and Holy Ghost,*
   The God whom earth and heaven adore,
   Be glory, as it was of old,
   Is now, and shall be evermore. Amen.

347 CREDITON C.M.

Clark's *A Second Set of Psalm Tunes* [for]
Country Choirs, c. 1807

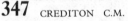

A - men.

PSALM 150

PRAISE ye the Lord. God's praise within
   His sanctuary raise;
And to him in the firmament
   Of his power give ye praise.

2 Because of all his mighty acts,
   With praise him magnify:
O praise him, as he doth excel
   In glorious majesty.

3 Praise him with trumpet's sound; his praise
    With psaltery advance:
  With timbrel, harp, stringed instruments,
    And organs, in the dance.

4 Praise him on cymbals loud; him praise
    On cymbals sounding high.
  Let each thing breathing praise the Lord.
    Praise to the Lord give ye.

5 *To Father, Son, and Holy Ghost,*
    The God whom we adore,
  Be glory, as it was, and is,
    And shall be evermore. Amen.

348 STUTTGART 8787

Adapted from a melody in Witt's
Psalmodia Sacra, Gotha, 1715

A - men.

PSALM 98, verses 1-3, 5-9

SING a new song to Jehovah,
    For he wondrous things hath
      wrought;
His right hand and arm most holy
    Victory to him have brought.

2 Lo! the Lord his great salvation
    Openly hath now made known;
In the sight of every nation
    He his righteousness hath shown.

3 Mindful of his truth and mercy
    He to Israel's house hath been;
And the Lord our God's salvation
    All the ends of earth have seen.

4 Sound the trumpet and the cornet,
    Shout before the Lord the King;
Sea, and all its fullness, thunder;
    Earth, and all its people, sing.

5 Let the rivers in their gladness
    Clap their hands with one accord;
Let the mountains sing together
    Joyfully before the Lord.

6 For to judge the earth he cometh;
    And with righteousness shall he
Judge the world, and all the nations
    With most perfect equity.

7 *Glory be to God, the Father;*
  Glory be to God, the Son;
  Glory be to God, the Spirit;
  While eternal ages run. Amen.

349 (i)

GEORGE THALBEN-BALL

(ii)

WILLIAM CROTCH, 1775-1847

PSALM 98

O SING unto the Lord a new song   for he hath done ' marvellous ' things :
  his right hand and his holy ' arm hath ' gotten him · the ' victory :
The Lord hath made ' known his sal- ' vation :
  his righteousness hath he openly ' showed in the ' sight of the ' heathen.

2 He hath remembered his mercy and his truth toward the ' house of ' Israel :
  all the ends of the earth have seen the sal- ' vation ' of our ' God :
Make a joyful noise unto the Lord ' all the ' earth :
  make a loud ' noise and re- ' joice and sing ' praise.

3 Sing unto the ' Lord with the ' harp :
  with the ' harp and the ' voice of a ' psalm :
With trumpets and ' sound of ' cornet :
  make a joyful ' noise before the ' Lord the ' King.

4 Let the sea roar, and the ' fullness there- ' of :
  the ' world and ' they that ' dwell therein :
Let the ' floods clap their ' hands :
  let the hills be joyful to- ' gether be- ' fore the ' Lord.

† 5 For he cometh to ' judge the ' earth :
  with righteousness shall he judge the ' world and the ' people with ' equity.

Glory ' be to the ' Father :
  and to the Son ' and to the ' Holy ' Ghost :
As it ' was in the be- ' ginning :
  is now and ever shall be   ' world without ' end A- ' men.

† *2nd half.*

350

PSALM 136 (Gelineau Version)

Choir or Solo

1 O give thanks to the Lord for he is good,
2 Who a - lone has wrought mar - vellous works,
3 It was he who made the great lights,
4 The first - born of the E - gyp - tians he smote,
5 He let Israel in - her - it their land,
6 And he snatched us a - way from our foes,

All

Great is his love, love with - out end.

Choir or Solo

1 give thanks to the God of gods,
2 whose wisdom it was made the skies,
3 the sun to rule in the day,
4 brought Israel out from their midst,
5 on his servant their land he be - stowed,
6 he gives food to all liv - ing things,

All

Great is his love, love with - out end.

Choir or Solo

1 give thanks to the Lord of lords,
2 who spread the earth on the seas.
3 the moon and stars in the night.
4 arm out - stretched, with power in his hand.
5 he re - membered us in our dis - tress.
6 to the God of hea - ven give thanks.

All f

Great is his love, love with - out end.

351 COLESHILL C.M.

Barton's *The Psalms of David in Metre*,
Dublin, 1706 (later form)

A — men.

Alternative tune, KILMARNOCK, No. 603

PSALM 103, verses 1-5

O THOU my soul, bless God the
    Lord;
  And all that in me is
Be stirrèd up his holy Name
  To magnify and bless.

2 Bless, O my soul, the Lord thy God,
  And not forgetful be
Of all his gracious benefits
  He hath bestowed on thee.

3 All thine iniquities who doth
  Most graciously forgive:
Who thy diseases all and pains
  Doth heal, and thee relieve.

4 Who doth redeem thy life, that thou
  To death mayest not go down;
Who thee with loving-kindness doth
  And tender mercies crown:

5 Who with abundance of good things
  Doth satisfy thy mouth;
So that even as the eagle's age,
  Renewèd is thy youth.

6 *To Father, Son, and Holy Ghost,*
  The God whom we adore,
Be glory, as it was, and is,
  And shall be evermore. Amen.

352 NICÆA 11 12 12 10

JOHN BACCHUS DYKES, 1823-76

A-men.

HOLY, holy, holy, Lord God Almighty!
  Early in the morning our song shall rise to thee;
Holy, holy, holy, merciful and mighty,
  God in Three Persons, blessèd Trinity!

2 Holy, holy, holy! all the saints adore thee,
  Casting down their golden crowns around the glassy sea,
Cherubim and seraphim falling down before thee,
  Which wert, and art, and evermore shalt be.

3 Holy, holy, holy! though the darkness hide thee,
  Though the eye of sinful man thy glory may not see,
Only thou art holy; there is none beside thee,
  Perfect in power, in love, and purity.

4 *Holy, holy, holy, Lord God Almighty!*
  All thy works shall praise thy Name in earth and sky and sea;
Holy, holy, holy, merciful and mighty,
  God in Three Persons, blessèd Trinity! Amen.

Reginald Heber, 1783-1826

353 RUSTINGTON
8787 and refrain
CHARLES HUBERT HASTINGS PARRY, 1848-1918

Alternative tune, AUSTRIAN HYMN, No. 421

ROUND the Lord in glory seated,
  Cherubim and seraphim
Filled his temple, and repeated
  Each to each the alternate hymn:
    'Lord, thy glory fills the heaven;
    Earth is with its fullness
      stored;
    Unto thee be glory given,
    Holy, holy, holy Lord.'

2 Heaven is still with glory ringing,
  Earth takes up the angels' cry,
    'Holy, holy, holy,' singing,
    'Lord of hosts, the Lord most
      high.'

3 With his seraph train before him,
  With his holy Church below,
Thus conspire we to adore him,
  Bid we thus our anthem flow:

Richard Mant, 1776-1848

354 REGENT SQUARE 8787 87   HENRY SMART, 1813–79

A-men.

GLORY be to God the Father,
  Glory be to God the Son,
Glory be to God the Spirit,—
  Great Jehovah, Three in One!
Glory, glory, glory, glory
While eternal ages run!

2 Glory be to him who loved us,
  Washed us from each spot and
    stain!
Glory be to him who bought us,
  Made us kings with him to reign!
Glory, glory, glory, glory
To the Lamb that once was slain!

3 Glory to the King of angels,
  Glory to the Church's King,
Glory to the King of nations!
  Heaven and earth, your praises
    bring;
Glory, glory, glory, glory
To the King of Glory bring!

4 'Glory, blessing, praise eternal!'
  Thus the choir of angels sings;
'Honour, riches, power, dominion!'
  Thus its praise creation brings;
Glory, glory, glory, glory,
Glory to the King of kings! Amen.

Horatius Bonar, 1808–89

355 GOTT IST GEGENWÄRTIG
(GRONINGEN) 668. D 33 66   Based on a melody by
JOACHIM NEANDER, 1650–80

314

Gott ist gegenwärtig

GOD reveals his presence:
Let us now adore him,
And with awe appear before him.
God is in his temple:
All within keep silence,
Prostrate lie with deepest reverence.
Him alone
God we own,
Him our God and Saviour:
Praise his Name for ever.

2 God reveals his presence:
Hear the harps resounding,
See the crowds the throne surrounding;
Holy, holy, holy!
Hear the hymn ascending,
Angels, saints, their voices blending.
Bow thine ear
To us here;
Hearken, O Lord Jesus,
To our meaner praises.

3 O thou Fount of blessing
Purify my spirit,
Trusting only in thy merit:
Like the holy angels
Who behold thy glory,
May I ceaselessly adore thee.
Let thy will
Ever still
Rule thy Church terrestrial,
As the hosts celestial.

Gerhard Tersteegen, 1697-1769; tr. Frederick William Foster, 1760-1835; and John Miller, 1756-90; revised William Mercer, 1811-73

356 WESTMINSTER C.M.   JAMES TURLE, 1802-82

MY God, how wonderful thou art,
Thy majesty how bright!
How beautiful thy mercy-seat,
In depths of burning light!

2 How dread are thine eternal years,
O everlasting Lord,
By prostrate spirits day and night
Incessantly adored!

3 O how I fear thee, living God,
With deepest, tenderest fears,
And worship thee with trembling hope
And penitential tears!

4 Yet I may love thee too, O Lord,
Almighty as thou art,
For thou hast stooped to ask of me
The love of my poor heart.

5 No earthly father loves like thee;
No mother, e'er so mild,
Bears and forbears as thou hast done
With me, thy sinful child.

6 How beautiful, how beautiful
The sight of thee must be,
Thine endless wisdom, boundless power,
And awesome purity!

Frederick William Faber, 1814-63

357 NICOLAUS   86 886
(LOBT GOTT)

NICOLAUS HERMANN, 1485–1561

ETERNAL Light! eternal Light!
    How pure the soul must be,
When, placed within thy searching
       sight,
It shrinks not, but, with calm delight,
    Can live, and look on thee!

2 The spirits that surround thy throne
    May bear the burning bliss;
But that is surely theirs alone,
Since they have never, never known
    A fallen world like this.

3 O how shall I, whose native sphere
    Is dark, whose mind is dim,
Before the Ineffable appear,
And on my naked spirit bear
    The uncreated beam?

4 There is a way for man to rise
    To that sublime abode:
An offering and a sacrifice,
A Holy Spirit's energies,
    An Advocate with God.

5 These, these prepare us for the sight
    Of holiness above:
The sons of ignorance and night
May dwell in God's eternal Light,
    Through his eternal Love!

Thomas Binney, 1798–1874

358 LEONI   6684. D

Hebrew Melody, largely as adapted *c.* 1770

A - men.

THE God of Abraham praise,
Who reigns enthroned above,
Ancient of everlasting days,
    And God of love.
Jehovah, Great I AM!
By earth and heaven confessed,
I bow, and bless the sacred Name
    For ever blest.

2 The God of Abraham praise,
    At whose supreme command
From earth I rise, and seek the joys
    At his right hand.
I all on earth forsake—
Its wisdom, fame, and power—
And him my only portion make,
    My shield and tower.

3 He by himself hath sworn,
    I on his oath depend:
I shall, on eagle's wings upborne,
    To heaven ascend;
I shall behold his face,
I shall his power adore,
And sing the wonders of his grace
    For evermore.

4 There dwells the Lord our King,
    The Lord our Righteousness,
Triumphant o'er the world and sin,
    The Prince of Peace;
On Zion's sacred height
His kingdom he maintains,
And glorious with his saints in light
    For ever reigns.

5 *The whole triumphant host*
    Give thanks to God on high;
'Hail, Father, Son, and Holy Ghost!'
    They ever cry.
Hail, Abraham's God, and mine!—
I join the heavenly lays,—
All might and majesty are Thine,
    And endless praise. Amen.

Thomas Olivers, 1725–99
Based on the Jewish Yigdal

359 LLANFAIR 7777 and Alleluias

Probably by
ROBERT WILLIAMS, *c.* 1781-1821

Al - le - lu - ia!

Al - le - lu - ia!

Al - le - lu - ia!

PRAISE the Lord, his glories show,
    Alleluia!
Saints within his courts below,
    Alleluia!
Angels round his throne above,
    Alleluia!
All that see and share his love.
    Alleluia!

2 Earth to heaven, and heaven to earth,
Tell his wonders, sing his worth;
Age to age and shore to shore,
Praise him, praise him evermore!

3 Praise the Lord, his mercies trace;
Praise his providence and grace,
All that he for man hath done,
All he sends us through his Son.

4 Strings and voices, hands and hearts,
In the concert bear your parts;
All that breathe, your Lord adore,
Praise him, praise him evermore:

Henry Francis Lyte, 1793-1847

360 PRAISE, MY SOUL 8787 447

JOHN GOSS, 1800-80

PRAISE, my soul, the King of heaven;
To his feet thy tribute bring;
Ransomed, healed, restored, forgiven,
Who like me his praise should sing?
    Praise him! Praise him!
    Praise him! Praise him!
    Praise the everlasting King.

2 Praise him for his grace and favour
To our fathers in distress;
Praise him, still the same for ever,
Slow to chide and swift to bless:
    Praise him! Praise him!
    Praise him! Praise him!
    Glorious in his faithfulness.

3 Father-like he tends and spares us;
Well our feeble frame he knows;
In his hands he gently bears us,
Rescues us from all our foes:
    Praise him! Praise him!
    Praise him! Praise him!
    Widely as his mercy flows.

4 Frail as summer's flower we flourish;
Blows the wind and it is gone;
But, while mortals rise and perish,
God endures unchanging on:
    Praise him! Praise him!
    Praise him! Praise him!
    Praise the high eternal One.

5 Angels, help us to adore him;
Ye behold him face to face;
Sun and moon, bow down before him;
Dwellers all in time and space.
    Praise him! Praise him!
    Praise him! Praise him!
    Praise with us the God of grace.

Henry Francis Lyte, 1793-1847
From Psalm 103

361 (i) AUGUSTINE 10 4 6666 10 4   ERIK ROUTLEY

before v. 1 only Let all the world in ev-'ry cor-ner sing, 'My

God and King!' 1. The heav'ns are not too high, His
2. The Church with psalms must shout, No

praise may thi-ther fly; The earth is not too
door can keep them out; But, a-bove all, the

low, His prai-ses there may grow. Let all the world in
heart Must bear the long-est part.

ev-'ry cor-ner sing, 'My God and King!'

(ii) LUCKINGTON 10 4 6666 10 4   BASIL HARWOOD, 1859–1949

LET all the world in every corner
sing,
'My God and King!'
The heavens are not too high,
His praise may thither fly;
The earth is not too low,
His praises there may grow.
Let all the world in every corner
sing,
'My God and King!'

2 Let all the world in every corner
sing,
'My God and King!'
The Church with psalms must
shout,
No door can keep them out;
But, above all, the heart
Must bear the longest part.
Let all the world in every corner
sing,
'My God and King!'

George Herbert, 1593–1633

362 LASST UNS ERFREUEN
L.M. and Alleluias

Geistliche Kirchengesäng, Cologne, 1623

FROM all that dwell below the skies
Let the Creator's praise arise:
Alleluia! Alleluia!
Let the Redeemer's Name be sung
Through every land, in every tongue.
Alleluia, Alleluia, Alleluia, Alleluia, Alleluia!

2 Eternal are thy mercies, Lord:
Eternal truth attends thy word:
Thy praise shall sound from shore to shore
Till suns shall rise and set no more:

Isaac Watts, 1674–1748
From Psalm 117

363 (i) CROFT'S 136TH 6666 4444 WILLIAM CROFT, 1678–1727

(ii) ST. JOHN 6666 4444

The Parish Choir, Vol. III, 1851
Perhaps by WILLIAM HENRY HAVERGAL, 1793–1870

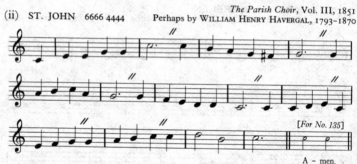

[For No. 135]

A - men.

YE holy angels bright,
  Who wait at God's right hand,
Or through the realms of light
  Fly at your Lord's command,
    Assist our song,
      Or else the theme
      Too high doth seem
    For mortal tongue.

2 Ye blessèd souls at rest,
  Who ran this earthly race,
And now, from sin released,
  Behold the Saviour's face,
    His praises sound,
      As in his light
      With sweet delight
    Ye do abound.

3 Ye saints, who toil below,
  Adore your heavenly King,
And, onward as ye go,
  Some joyful anthem sing;
    Take what he gives,
      And praise him still
      Through good and ill,
    Who ever lives.

4 My soul, bear thou thy part,
  Triumph in God above,
And with a well-tuned heart
  Sing thou the songs of love.
    Let all thy days
      Till life shall end,
      Whate'er he send,
    Be filled with praise.

Richard Baxter, 1615–91, *and others*

364 GWALCHMAI 7474. D

JOSEPH DAVID JONES, 1827-70
Llyfr Tonau ac Emynau, 1868

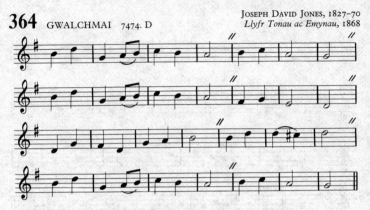

KING of glory, King of peace,
  I will love thee;
And, that love may never cease,
  I will move thee.
Thou hast granted my request,
  Thou hast heard me;
Thou didst note my working breast,
  Thou hast spared me.

2 Wherefore with my utmost art
  I will sing thee,
And the cream of all my heart
  I will bring thee.
Though my sins against me cried,
  Thou didst clear me,
And alone, when they replied,
  Thou didst hear me.

3 Seven whole days, not one in seven,
  I will praise thee;
In my heart, though not in heaven,
  I can raise thee.
Small it is, in this poor sort
  To enrol thee;
E'en eternity's too short
  To extol thee.

George Herbert, 1593-1633

365 CORMAC Irregular   Irish Traditional Melody

FOR the might of thine arm we bless thee, our God, our
   fathers' God;
Thou hast kept thy pilgrim people by the strength of thy
   staff and rod;
Thou hast called us to the journey which faithless feet ne'er
   trod;
For the might of thine arm we bless thee, our God, our fathers'
God.

2 For the love of Christ constraining, that bound their hearts
      as one;
  For the faith in truth and freedom in which their work was
      done;
  For the peace of God's evangel wherewith their feet were
      shod;

3 We are watchers of a beacon whose light must never die;
  We are guardians of an altar that shows thee ever nigh;
  We are children of thy freemen who sleep beneath the sod;

4 May the shadow of thy presence around our camp be
      spread;
  Baptize us with the courage thou gavest to our dead;
  O keep us in the pathway their saintly feet have trod:

                              Charles Silvester Horne, 1865–1914

366 GONFALON ROYAL L.M. PERCY CARTER BUCK, 1871–1947

A - - - men.

SING to the Lord a joyful song,
  Lift up your hearts, your voices raise;
To us his gracious gifts belong,
  To him our songs of love and praise.

2 For life and love, for rest and food,
  For daily help and nightly care,
Sing to the Lord, for he is good,
  And praise his Name, for it is fair.

3 For strength to those who on him wait
  His truth to prove, his will to do,
Praise ye our God, for he is great,
  Trust in his Name, for it is true.

4 For joys untold, that from above
  Cheer those who love his sweet employ,
Sing to our God, for he is love,
  Exalt his Name, for it is joy.

5 *For he is Lord of heaven and earth,*
  Whom angels serve and saints adore,
The Father, Son, and Holy Ghost,
  To whom be praise for evermore. Amen.

John Samuel Bewley Monsell, 1811–75

367 (i) MOSELEY 7777 and refrain JOHN JOUBERT

1. For the beauty of the earth, For the beau - ty
2. For the beau - ty of each hour Of the day and
3. For the joy of ear and eye, For the heart and
4. For the joy of hu - man love, Bro - ther, sis - ter,
5. For each per - fect gift of thine To our race so

of the skies, For the love which from our birth
of the night, Hill and vale, and tree and flow'r,
mind's de - light, For the mys - tic har - mon - y
pa - rent, child, Friends on earth and friends a - bove,
free - ly giv'n, Gra - ces hu - man and di - vine,

REFRAIN

O - ver and a - round us lies:
Sun and moon and stars of light:
Link - ing sense to sound and sight: } Christ, our God, to
For all gen - tle thoughts and mild:
Flow'rs of earth and buds of heaven:

thee we raise This our sac - ri - fice of praise.

Folliott Sandford Pierpoint, 1835-1917

(ii) LUCERNA LAUDONIAE
7777 and refrain DAVID EVANS, 1874-1948

REFRAIN

Christ, our God, to thee we raise This our sac-ri-fice of praise.

FOR the beauty of the earth,
  For the beauty of the skies,
For the love which from our birth
  Over and around us lies,
Christ, our God, to thee we raise
This our sacrifice of praise.

2 For the beauty of each hour
    Of the day and of the night,
  Hill and vale, and tree and flower,
    Sun and moon and stars of light,

3 For the joy of ear and eye,
    For the heart and mind's delight,
  For the mystic harmony
    Linking sense to sound and sight,

4 For the joy of human love,
    Brother, sister, parent, child,
  Friends on earth and friends above,
    For all gentle thoughts and mild,

5 For each perfect gift of thine
    To our race so freely given,
  Graces human and divine,
    Flowers of earth and buds of heaven:

Folliott Sandford Pierpoint, 1835-1917

368 NUN DANKET   6767 6666

Crüger's *Praxis Pietatis Melica* (1647 edn.)
(later form)

A - men.

Nun danket alle Gott

NOW thank we all our God,
  With heart and hands and voices,
Who wondrous things hath done,
  In whom his world rejoices,—
    Who, from our mothers' arms,
      Hath blessed us on our way
    With countless gifts of love,
      And still is ours today.

2 O may this bounteous God
    Through all our life be near us,
  With ever-joyful hearts
    And blessèd peace to cheer us,
      And keep us in his grace,
        And guide us when perplexed,
      And free us from all ills
        In this world and the next.

3 *All praise and thanks to God*
    The Father now be given,
  The Son, and him who reigns
    With them in highest heaven,—
      The one, eternal God,
        Whom earth and heaven adore;
      For thus it was, is now,
        And shall be evermore. Amen.

Martin Rinkart, 1586–1649
Tr. Catherine Winkworth, 1827–78

369 LAUS DEO (REDHEAD No. 46)
8787

RICHARD REDHEAD, 1820–1901
Church Hymn Tunes, 1853

GOD and Father, we adore thee
    For the Son, thine image bright,
In whom all thy holy nature
    Dawned on our once hopeless night.

2 Far from thee our footsteps wandered,
    On dark paths of sin and shame;
But our midnight turned to morning,
    When the Lord of Glory came.

3 Word Incarnate, God revealing,
    Longed-for while dim ages ran,
Love Divine, we bow before thee,
    Son of God and Son of Man.

4 Let our life be new created,
    Ever-living Lord, in thee,
Till we wake with thy pure likeness,
    When thy face in heaven we see;

5 Where the saints of all the ages,
    Where our fathers glorified,
Clouds and darkness far beneath them,
    In unending day abide.

6 God and Father, now we bless thee
    For the Son, thine image bright,
In whom all thy holy nature
    Dawns on our adoring sight.

Verse 1 attributed to *John Nelson Darby*, 1800–82;
verses 2–5 and adaptation of verse 6, *Hugh Falconer*, 1859–1931

370 PSALM 3
(O SEIGNEUR)
667 667. D

French-Genevan Psalter, 1551

Beim frühen Morgenlicht

WHEN morning gilds the skies,
My heart awaking cries,
  'May Jesus Christ be praisèd'.
When evening shadows fall,
This rings my curfew-call,
  'May Jesus Christ be praisèd'.
When mirth for music longs,
This is my song of songs,
  'May Jesus Christ be praisèd'.
God's holy house of prayer
Hath none that can compare
  With 'Jesus Christ be praisèd'.

2 This greeting of great joy,
I ne'er have found it cloy,
  'May Jesus Christ be praisèd'.
When sorrow would molest,
Then sing I undistrest,
  'May Jesus Christ be praisèd'.
No lovelier antiphon
In all high heav'n is known
  Than 'Jesus Christ be praisèd'.
There to the Eternal Word
The eternal psalm is heard,
  'O Jesus Christ be praisèd'.

3 Ye nations of mankind,
In this your concord find,
  'May Jesus Christ be praisèd'.
Let all the earth around
Ring joyous with the sound
  'May Jesus Christ be praisèd'.
Sing, suns and stars of space,
Sing, ye that see his face,
  Sing 'Jesus Christ be praisèd'.
God's whole creation o'er,
For aye and evermore,
  Shall Jesus Christ be praisèd.

Anonymous German hymn, early 19th century
Tr. Robert Bridges, 1844–1930

371 RICHMOND C.M.

THOMAS HAWEIS, 1734-1820, as adapted
by SAMUEL WEBBE, the younger, c. 1770-1843

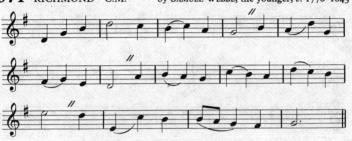

O FOR a thousand tongues, to sing
  My great Redeemer's praise,
The glories of my God and King,
  The triumphs of his grace!

2 Jesus! the Name that charms our fears,
    That bids our sorrows cease;
  'Tis music in the sinner's ears,
    'Tis life, and health, and peace.

3 He breaks the power of cancelled sin,
    He sets the prisoner free;
  His blood can make the foulest clean,
    His blood availed for me.

4 He speaks, and, listening to his voice,
    New life the dead receive,
  The mournful, broken hearts rejoice,
    The humble poor believe.

5 Hear him, ye deaf; his praise, ye dumb,
    Your loosened tongues employ;
  Ye blind, behold your Saviour come;
    And leap, ye lame, for joy!

6 My gracious Master and my God,
    Assist me to proclaim,
  To spread through all the earth abroad
    The honours of thy Name.

Charles Wesley, 1707-88

372 LAUDATE DOMINUM
10 10 11 11
CHARLES HUBERT HASTINGS PARRY, 1848–1918

YE servants of God, your Master proclaim,
And publish abroad his wonderful Name;
The Name all-victorious of Jesus extol;
His Kingdom is glorious, and rules over all.

2 God ruleth on high, almighty to save;
And still he is nigh, his presence we have;
The great congregation his triumph shall sing,
Ascribing salvation to Jesus our King.

3 Salvation to God, who sits on the throne!
Let all cry aloud, and honour the Son:
The praises of Jesus the angels proclaim,
Fall down on their faces, and worship the Lamb.

4 Then let us adore, and give him his right
All glory and power, all wisdom and might,
All honour and blessing, with angels above,
And thanks never-ceasing, and infinite love.

Charles Wesley, 1707–88

373 TANTUM ERGO SACRAMENTUM   French Church Melody from
(GRAFTON)   8787 87   *Chants Ordinaires de l'Office Divin*, Paris, 1881

[For Nos. 10 & 660]

A-men.

Gloriosi Salvatoris

TO the Name of our Salvation
  Laud and honour let us pay,
Which for many a generation
  Hid in God's foreknowledge lay,
But with holy exultation
  We may sing aloud today.

2 Jesus is the Name we treasure,
  Name beyond what words can tell,
Name of gladness, Name of pleasure,
  Ear and heart delighting well;
Name of sweetness passing measure,
  Saving us from sin and hell.

3 'Tis the Name that whoso preacheth
  Speaks like music to the ear;
Who in prayer this Name beseecheth
  Sweetest comfort findeth near;
Who its perfect wisdom reacheth
  Heav'nly joy possesseth here.

4 Jesus is the Name exalted
  Over every other name;
In this Name, whene'er assaulted,
  We can put our foes to shame;
Strength to them who else had halted,
  Eyes to blind, and feet to lame.

5 Therefore we, in love adoring,
  This most blessèd Name revere,
Holy Jesus, thee imploring
  So to write it in us here
That hereafter, heavenward soaring,
  We may sing with angels there.

15th century; tr. Compilers of Hymns Ancient and Modern, *1861,
based on the tr. by John Mason Neale, 1818–66*

374 ST. DENIO (JOANNA)
11 11 11 11   Welsh Hymn Melody, 1839, founded on a folk tune

TO God be the glory! great things he hath done!
So loved he the world that he gave us his Son,
Who yielded his life an atonement for sin,
And opened the life-gate that all may go in.

2 O perfect redemption, the purchase of blood!
To every believer the promise of God;
The vilest offender who truly believes,
That moment from Jesus a pardon receives.

3 Great things he hath taught us, great things he hath done,
And great our rejoicing through Jesus the Son:
But purer and higher and greater will be
Our wonder, our transport, when Jesus we see!

Frances (Crosby) van Alstyne, 1820–1915

375 SCHÖNSTER HERR JESU   Silesian Melody from *Schleswige*
(ST. ELISABETH) Irregular   *Volkelieder*, Leipzig, 1842

Schönster Herr Jesu

FAIREST Lord Jesus,
Ruler of all nature,
O thou of God and Man the Son;
Thee will I cherish,
Thee will I honour,
Thou my soul's glory, joy and crown.

2 Fair are the meadows,
Fairer still the woodlands,
Robed in the verdure and bloom of
spring.
Jesus is fairer,
Jesus is purer,
He makes the saddest heart to sing.

3 Fair are the flowers,
Fairer still the sons of men
In all the freshness of youth arrayed;
Yet is their beauty
Fading and fleeting;
Lord Jesus, thine will never fade.

4 Fair is the sunshine,
Fairer still the moonlight,
And fair the twinkling starry host;
Jesus shines brighter,
Jesus shines purer,
Than all the stars that heaven can
boast.

Münster Gesangbuch, 1677
Tr. Lilian Stevenson, 1870-1960, and others

376 ST. PETER C.M.

ALEXANDER ROBERT REINAGLE, 1799-1877
Psalm Tunes for the Voice and the Pianoforte, 1830

HOW sweet the Name of Jesus
sounds
In a believer's ear!
It soothes his sorrows, heals his
wounds,
And drives away his fear.

2 It makes the wounded spirit whole,
And calms the troubled breast;
'Tis manna to the hungry soul,
And to the weary rest.

3 Dear Name! the rock on which I
build,
My shield and hiding-place,
My never-failing treasury, filled
With boundless stores of grace.

4 Jesus, my Shepherd, Husband,
Friend,
My Prophet, Priest, and King,
My Lord, my Life, my Way, my
End,
Accept the praise I bring.

5 Weak is the effort of my heart,
And cold my warmest thought;
But, when I see thee as thou art,
I'll praise thee as I ought.

6 Till then I would thy love proclaim
With every fleeting breath;
And may the music of thy Name
Refresh my soul in death.

John Newton, 1725-1807

377 (i) WINDSOR (DUNDEE) C.M.

Damon's Psalter, *The Booke of the Musicke*, 1591. Rhythm as in *Scottish Psalter*, 1615

377 (ii) **& 378** METZLER (REDHEAD No. 66) C.M.

RICHARD REDHEAD, 1820–1901
Ancient Hymn Melodies and other Church Tunes, 1859

Jesu dulcis memoria

377

JESUS, the very thought of thee
　With sweetness fills my breast;
But sweeter far thy face to see,
　And in thy presence rest.

2 Nor voice can sing, nor heart can frame,
　　Nor can the memory find
　A sweeter sound than thy blest Name,
　　O Saviour of mankind!

3 O Hope of every contrite heart,
　　O Joy of all the meek,
　To those who fall how kind thou art!
　　How good to those who seek!

4 But what to those who find? Ah, this
　　Nor tongue nor pen can show;
　The love of Jesus, what it is
　　None but his loved ones know.

5 Jesus, our only joy be thou,
　　As thou our prize wilt be;
　Jesus, be thou our glory now,
　　And through eternity.

Probably 12th century
Tr. Edward Caswall, 1814–78
Lyra Catholica, 1849

78

Jesu, Rex admirabilis

1 O JESUS, King most wonderful,
    Thou Conqueror renowned,
  Thou Sweetness most ineffable,
    In whom all joys are found!

2 When once thou visitest the heart,
    Then truth begins to shine,
  Then earthly vanities depart,
    Then kindles love divine.

3 O Jesus, Light of all below,
    Thou Fount of life and fire,
  Surpassing all the joys we know,
    And all we can desire,—

4 May every heart confess thy Name,
    And ever thee adore,
  And, seeking thee, itself inflame
    To seek thee more and more.

5 Thee may our tongues for ever bless;
    Thee may we love alone,
  And ever in our lives express
    The image of thine own.

Probably 12th century
Tr. Edward Caswall, 1814–78
Lyra Catholica, 1849

379 SONG 67 C.M.
    (ST. MATTHIAS)

Prys' *Llyfr y Psalmau*, 1621
    (rhythm altered)

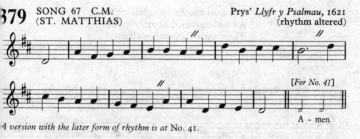

[For No. 41]

A - men.

A version with the later form of rhythm is at No. 41.

O Deus, ego amo te

1 MY God, I love thee; not because
    I hope for heaven thereby,
  Nor yet because who love thee not
    Are lost eternally.

2 Thou, O my Jesus, thou didst me
    Upon the cross embrace;
  For me didst bear the nails and
        spear,
    And manifold disgrace,

3 And griefs and torments number-
        less,
    And sweat of agony;
  Even death itself; and all for one
    Who was thine enemy.

4 Then why, most loving Jesus Christ,
    Should I not love thee well,
  Not for the sake of winning heaven,
    Or of escaping hell;

5 Not with the hope of gaining aught,
    Not seeking a reward;
  But as thyself hast lovèd me,
    O ever-loving Lord?

6 Even so I love thee, and will love,
    And in thy praise will sing,
  Solely because thou art my God,
    And my eternal King.

17th century Latin, based on a Spanish sonnet
Tr. Edward Caswall, 1814–78

380 MAN OF SORROWS
(GETHSEMANE)   777 and refrain

PHILIPP BLISS, 1838-7

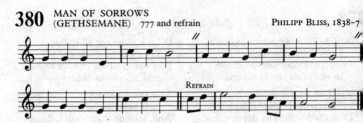

MAN of Sorrows! wondrous Name
For the Son of God, who came
Ruined sinners to reclaim!
Alleluia! what a Saviour!

2 Bearing shame and scoffing rude,
In my place condemned he stood,
Sealed my pardon with his blood:

3 Guilty, vile, and helpless we;
Spotless Lamb of God was he:
Full atonement,—can it be?

4 Lifted up was he to die,
'It is finished' was his cry;
Now in heaven exalted high:

5 When he comes, our glorious King,
All his ransomed home to bring,
Then anew this song we'll sing:

Philipp Bliss, 1838-76

381 HYFRYDOL
8787 and refrain

ROWLAND HUGH PRICHARD, 1811-8
Haleliwiah Drachefn, Carmarthen, 185

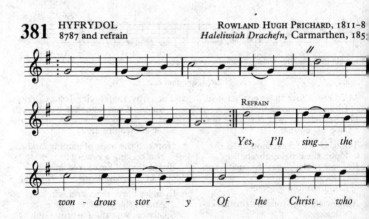

Yes, I'll sing the won-drous stor-y Of the Christ who

died__ for me,— Sing__ it with__ his saints__ in

glor - y, Gath-ered by___ the crys-tal sea.

I WILL sing the wondrous story
    Of the Christ who died for me,—
How he left the realms of glory
    For the cross on Calvary:
        Yes, I'll sing the wondrous story
            Of the Christ who died for me,—
        Sing it with his saints in glory,
            Gathered by the crystal sea.

2 I was lost: but Jesus found me,
    Found the sheep that went astray,
Raised me up and gently led me
    Back into the narrow way:

3 Faint was I, and fears possessed me,
    Bruised was I from many a fall:
Hope was gone, and shame distressed me:
    But his love has pardoned all:

4 Days of darkness still may meet me,
    Sorrow's paths I oft may tread;
But his presence still is with me,
    By his guiding hand I'm led:

5 He will keep me till the river
    Rolls its waters at my feet:
Then he'll bear me safely over,
    Made by grace for glory meet:

Francis Harold Rowley, 1854–1952

339

382 MILES LANE
C.M. irregular

WILLIAM SHRUBSOLE, 1760–1806

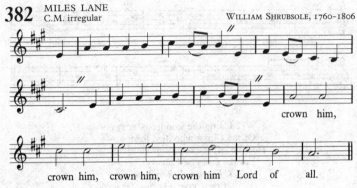

crown him,

crown him, crown him, crown him Lord of all.

ALL hail, the power of Jesus' Name!
　Let angels prostrate fall;
Bring forth the royal diadem,
　To *crown him Lord of all.

2 Crown him, ye martyrs of your God,
　Who from his altar call;
Extol him in whose path ye trod,
　And crown him Lord of all.

3 Ye seed of Israel's chosen race,
　Ye ransomed of the fall,
Hail him who saves you by his grace,
　And crown him Lord of all.

4 Let every tongue and every tribe,
　Responsive to the call,
To him all majesty ascribe,
　And crown him Lord of all.

Edward Perronet, 1726–92

* *The words 'crown him' are sung four times in each verse*

383 MADRID
(SPANISH HYMN)

6666 666 6

Probably founded on an old
Spanish Melody

For children

COME, children, join to sing—
    Alleluia! Amen!
Loud praise to Christ our King;
    Alleluia! Amen!
Let all, with heart and voice,
Before his throne rejoice;
Praise is his gracious choice:
    Alleluia! Amen!

2 Come, lift your hearts on high;
    Alleluia! Amen!
Let praises fill the sky;
    Alleluia! Amen!

He is our Guide and Friend;
To us he'll blessing send;
His love shall never end:
    Alleluia! Amen!

3 Praise yet the Lord again;
    Alleluia! Amen!
Life shall not end the strain;
    Alleluia! Amen!
On heaven's blissful shore
His goodness we'll adore,
Singing for evermore,
    Alleluia! Amen!

Christian Henry Bateman, 1813–89

384 TOWN JOYS   11 11 11 11   English Traditional Carol Melody

For children

COME, let us remember the joys of the town:
Gay vans and bright buses that roar up and down,
Shop-windows and playgrounds and swings in the park,
And street-lamps that twinkle in rows after dark.

2 Come, let us now lift up our voices in praise,
And to the Creator a thanksgiving raise,
For towns with their buildings of stone, steel and wood,
For people who love them and work for their good.

3 We thank thee, O God, for the numberless things
And friends and adventures which every day brings.
O may we not rest until all that we see
In towns and in cities is pleasing to thee.

Doris Gill
Two verses omitted

385 HERONGATE L.M.   English Traditional Melody

Alternative tune, SOLOTHURN, No. 99

For children

IT is a thing most wonderful,
    Almost too wonderful to be,
That God's own Son should come from heaven,
    And die to save a child like me.

2 And yet I know that it is true:
    He chose a poor and humble lot,
And wept, and toiled, and mourned, and died,
    For love of those who loved him not.

3 It is most wonderful to know
    His love for me so free and sure;
But 'tis more wonderful to see
    My love for him so faint and poor.

4 And yet I want to love thee, Lord;
    O light the flame within my heart,
And I will love thee more and more,
    Until I see thee as thou art.

William Walsham How, 1823–97

386 PRAISE HIM 10 6 10 6   CAREY BONNER, 1859–1938

For younger children

PRAISE him, praise him, all ye little children,
  He is love, he is love;
Praise him, praise him, all ye little children,
  He is love, he is love.

2 Thank him, thank him, all ye little children,
  He is love, he is love;
Thank him, thank him, all ye little children,
  He is love, he is love.

3 Love him, love him, all ye little children,
  He is love, he is love;
Love him, love him, all ye little children,
  He is love, he is love.

4 Crown him, crown him, all ye little children,
  God is love, God is love;
Crown him, crown him, all ye little children,
  God is love, God is love.

Anonymous, c. 1890

The following are also suitable

No.
640 Praise ye the Lord, ye servants of the Lord
145 O Lord of heaven and earth and sea
238 Praise to the Holiest in the height
146 My God, I thank thee
     Also Hymn Nos. 135–8

AFFIRMATION

387(i) SEARCHING FOR LAMBS
C.M.

English Traditional Carol
Melody (adapted)

A - men.

(ii) WILTSHIRE C.M.

GEORGE THOMAS SMART, 1776-186?

A - men.

(iii) CRIMOND C.M.

JESSIE SEYMOUR IRVINE, 1836-8?

A - men.

PSALM 23

THE Lord's my Shepherd, I'll not want.
He makes me down to lie
In pastures green: he leadeth me
The quiet waters by.

2 My soul he doth restore again;
And me to walk doth make
Within the paths of righteousness,
Even for his own Name's sake.

3 Yea, though I walk in death's dark
    vale,
  Yet will I fear none ill:
For thou art with me; and thy rod
  And staff me comfort still.

4 My table thou hast furnishèd
  In presence of my foes;
My head thou dost with oil anoint,
  And my cup overflows.

5 Goodness and mercy all my life
  Shall surely follow me:
And in God's house for evermore
  My dwelling-place shall be.

6 *To Father, Son, and Holy Ghost,*
  The God whom we adore,
Be glory, as it was, and is,
  And shall be evermore. Amen.

388 (i) DOMINUS REGIT ME 8787   JOHN BACCHUS DYKES, 1823-76

(ii) MARY 8787   JOHN AMBROSE LLOYD, 1815-74

THE King of Love my Shepherd is,
  Whose goodness faileth never;
I nothing lack if I am his
  And he is mine for ever.

2 Where streams of living water flow
  My ransomed soul he leadeth,
And where the verdant pastures grow
  With food celestial feedeth.

3 Perverse and foolish oft I strayed;
  But yet in love he sought me,
And on his shoulder gently laid,
  And home rejoicing brought me.

4 In death's dark vale I fear no ill,
  With thee, dear Lord, beside me;
Thy rod and staff my comfort still,
  Thy cross before to guide me.

5 Thou spread'st a table in my sight;
  Thy unction grace bestoweth;
And O what transport of delight
  From thy pure chalice floweth!

6 And so through all the length of days
  Thy goodness faileth never;
Good Shepherd, may I sing thy
    praise
  Within thy house for ever!

Henry Williams Baker, 1821-77
From Psalm 23

389

PSALM 23 (Gelineau version)

Choir or Solo

1   The Lord is my shepherd;
2   He   guides me a - long the right path;
3   You have pre - pared   a   banquet   for   me
4   Surely   goodness and kindness shall follow me
5   To the   Father   and   Son   give   glory,

1   there is   nothing I shall   want.
2   he is   true   to   his   Name.   If I should
3   in the   sight   of   my   foes.   My
4   all the   days   of   my   life.   In the
5   give   glory   to   the   Spirit.   To God who

1   Fresh   and   green are the pastures   where he
2   walk in the   valley   of   darkness   no
3   head you have a - nointed   with oil;   [
4   Lord's   own   house shall I   dwell   [
5   is,   who   was, and who will be   [

1   gives me re - pose.   Near   restful   waters he
2   evil would I   fear.   You are there with your crook and your
3
4
5

1   leads me,   to re - vive my drooping spi - rit.
2   staff;   with these you give me   com - fort.
3   ]   my   cup   is   o - ver - flow - ing.
4   ]   for   ev - er and ev - er.
5   ]   for   ev - er and ev - er.

It is suggested that one of the following Antiphons be sung by the congregation after each verse of the psalm

ANTIPHON 1 *All* (♩ = o of psalm) (J.G.)

My shep-herd is the Lord, no-thing in-deed shall I want.

ANTIPHON 2 *All* (♩ = o of psalm) (A.G.M.)

His good - ness shall fol - low me al - ways to the end of my days.

ANTIPHON 3 *All* (♩ = o of psalm) (A.G.M.)

The Lord is my shep-herd, no-thing shall I want: he leads me by safe paths, no-thing shall I fear.

390 ST. STEPHEN
(NEWINGTON) C.M.

WILLIAM JONES, 1726–1800
Ten Church Pieces for the Organ, Nayland, 1789

A-men.

PSALM 89, verses 15, 16, 18

O GREATLY blest the people are
The joyful sound that know;
In brightness of thy face, O Lord,
They ever on shall go.

2 They in thy Name shall all the day
Rejoice exceedingly;
And in thy righteousness shall they
Exalted be on high.

3 For God is our defence; and he
To us doth safety bring:
The Holy One of Israel
Is our almighty King.

4 *To Father, Son, and Holy Ghost,*
The God whom we adore,
Be glory, as it was, and is,
And shall be evermore. Amen.

391 ST. DAVID C.M.

1677 version of a melody in
Ravenscroft's *Psalter,* 1621

A-men.

PSALM 34, verses 1, 2, 7–9, 11, 14, 15

GOD will I bless all times; his praise
My mouth shall still express.
My soul shall boast in God: the meek
Shall hear with joyfulness.

2 The angel of the Lord encamps,
And round encompasseth
All those about that do him fear,
And them delivereth.

3 O taste and see that God is good:
Who trusts in him is blest.
Fear God, his saints: none that him fear
Shall be with want oppressed.

4 O children, hither do ye come,
And unto me give ear;
I shall you teach to understand
How ye the Lord should fear.

5 Depart from ill, do good, seek peace,
Pursue it earnestly.
God's eyes are on the just; his ears
Are open to their cry.

6 *To Father, Son, and Holy Ghost,*
The God whom we adore;
Be glory, as it was, and is,
And shall be evermore. Amen.

348

AFFIRMATION

392 OLD 124TH 10 10 10 10 10

French–Genevan Psalter, 1551
(rhythm altered)

A-men.

PSALM 124(ii)

NOW Israel may say, and that truly,
If that the Lord had not our cause maintained;
If that the Lord had not our right sustained,
When cruel men against us furiously
Rose up in wrath, to make of us their prey;

2 Then certainly they had devoured us all,
And swallowed quick, for aught that we could deem;
Such was their rage, as we might well esteem.
And as fierce floods before them all things drown,
So had they brought our soul to death quite down.

3 The raging streams, with their proud swelling waves,
Had then our soul o'erwhelmèd in the deep.
But blest be God, who doth us safely keep,
And hath not given us for a living prey
Unto their teeth, and bloody cruelty.

4 Even as a bird out of the fowler's snare
Escapes away, so is our soul set free:
Broke are their nets, and thus escapèd we.
Therefore our help is in the Lord's great Name,
Who heaven and earth by his great power did frame.

5 *Glory to God the Father, God the Son,*
And unto God the Spirit, Three in One.
From age to age let saints his Name adore,
His power and love proclaim from shore to shore,
And spread his fame, till time shall be no more. Amen.

393 ABBEY C.M.   *Scottish Psalter, 1615*

A - men.

PSALM 126

WHEN Zion's bondage God turned
    back,
As men that dreamed were we.
Then filled with laughter was our
    mouth,
    Our tongue with melody:

2 They among the heathen said, 'The
    Lord
Great things for them hath
    wrought'.
The Lord hath done great things
    for us,
    Whence joy to us is brought.

3 As streams of water in the south,
    Our bondage, Lord, recall.
Who sow in tears, a reaping time
    Of joy enjoy they shall.

4 That man who, bearing precious
    seed,
    In going forth doth mourn,
He doubtless, bringing back his
    sheaves,
    Rejoicing shall return.

5 *To Father, Son, and Holy Ghost,*
    The God whom we adore,
  Be glory, as it was, and is,
    And shall be evermore. Amen.

394 ABRIDGE   C.M.   ISAAC SMITH, 1734–180
     (ST. STEPHEN)   *A Collection of Psalm Tunes, c. 178*

PARAPHRASE 22, verses 3–8

ART thou afraid his power shall fail
    When comes thy evil day?
And can an all-creating arm
    Grow weary or decay?

2 Supreme in wisdom as in power
    The Rock of ages stands;
Though him thou canst not see, no
    trace
    The working of his hands.

AFFIRMATION

3 He gives the conquest to the weak,
   Supports the fainting heart;
And courage in the evil hour
   His heavenly aids impart.

4 Mere human power shall fast decay,
   And youthful vigour cease;
But they who wait upon the Lord
   In strength shall still increase.

5 They with unwearied feet shall
     tread
   The path of life divine;
With growing ardour onward move,
   With growing brightness shine.

6 On eagles' wings they mount, they
     soar,
   Their wings are faith and love,
Till, past the cloudy regions here,
   They rise to heaven above.

Scottish Paraphrases, 1781
From Isaiah 40: 28-end

395 (i) CAITHNESS C.M.

Melody from *Scottish Psalter*, 1635

(ii) ST. PAUL (ABERDEEN) C.M.

Chalmers' *Collection*, Aberdeen, 1749

A version with the later form of rhythm is at No. 72 (i)

PARAPHRASE 60

FATHER of peace, and God of love!
   We own thy power to save,
That power by which our Shepherd
     rose
Victorious o'er the grave.

2 Him from the dead thou brought'st
     again,
   When, by his sacred blood,
Confirmed and sealed for evermore
   The eternal covenant stood.

3 O may thy Spirit seal our souls,
   And mould them to thy will,
That our weak hearts no more may
     stray,
   But keep thy precepts still;

4 That to perfection's sacred height
   We nearer still may rise,
And all we think, and all we do,
   Be pleasing in thine eyes.

Scottish Paraphrases, 1781
From Hebrews 13: 20, 21

396 ST. STEPHEN
(NEWINGTON) C.M.

WILLIAM JONES, 1726–1800
Ten Church Pieces for the Organ, Nayland, 1789

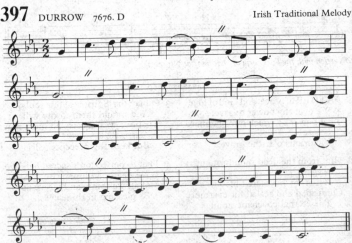

PARAPHRASE 63

BEHOLD the amazing gift of love
  The Father hath bestowed
On us, the sinful sons of men,
  To call us sons of God!

2 Concealed as yet this honour lies,
  By this dark world unknown,—
A world that knew not when he
    came,
  Even God's eternal Son.

3 High is the rank we now possess;
  But higher we shall rise,

Though what we shall hereafter be
  Is hid from mortal eyes.

4 Our souls, we know, when he
    appears,
  Shall bear his image bright;
For all his glory, full disclosed,
  Shall open to our sight.

5 A hope so great, and so divine,
  May trials well endure;
And purge the soul from sense and
    sin,
  As Christ himself is pure.

Scottish Paraphrases, 1781. *From* 1 *John* 3: 1–3

397 DURROW 7676. D

Irish Traditional Melody

Deus Pater credentium

O GOD, thou art the Father
  Of all that have believed:
From whom all hosts of angels
  Have life and power received.
O God, thou art the Maker
  Of all created things,
The righteous Judge of judges,
  The Almighty King of kings.

2 High in the heavenly Zion
  Thou reignest God adored;
And in the coming glory
  Thou shalt be Sovereign Lord.

Beyond our ken thou shinest,
  The everlasting Light;
Ineffable in loving,
  Unthinkable in might.

3 Thou to the meek and lowly
  Thy secrets dost unfold;
O God, thou doest all things,
  All things both new and old.
I walk secure and blessèd
  In every clime or coast,
In Name of God the Father,
  And Son, and Holy Ghost.

St. Columba, 521-97; tr. Duncan Macgregor, 1854-1923

398 EMAIN MACHA   8686 88   CHARLES WOOD, 1866-1926

ım aonapán pom inp an ſlıab

ALONE with none but thee, my
    God,
  I journey on my way;
What need I fear, when thou art
    near,
  O King of night and day?
More safe am I within thy hand,
  Than if a host did round me stand.

2 My destined time is fixed by thee,
  And Death doth know his hour.
Did warriors strong around me
    throng,
  They could not stay his power;
No walls of stone can man defend
  When thou thy messenger dost
    send.

3 My life I yield to thy decree,
  And bow to thy control
In peaceful calm, for from thine arm
  No power can wrest my soul.
Could earthly omens e'er appal
  A man that heeds the heavenly
    call!

4 The child of God can fear no ill,
  His chosen dread no foe;
We leave our fate with thee, and wait
  Thy bidding when to go.
'Tis not from chance our comfort
    springs,
  Thou art our trust, O King of
    kings.

Attributed to St. Columba, 521-97
Tr. anonymous

399 ORB Irregular   JOHN CURRIE

Though in God's form he was,   Christ Je - sus would not

snatch At pa - ri - ty with God;   2. Him - self he sac - ri - ficed,

Ta - king a ser - vant's form, Being born like ev - 'ry man;

3. Re - vealed in hu - man shape,   O - be - dient - ly he stooped To

die up - on a cross.   4. Him there - fore God raised high,

Gave him the name of Lord,   All o - ther names a - bove;

5. That at the Saviour's Name,   No knee might be un - bowed,

In heav'n or earth or hell;   6. And ev - 'ry tongue con - fess,

To God the Fa - ther's praise, That 'Je - sus Christ is Lord'.

From Phil. 2: 6-11
Tr. Archibald MacBride Hunte

354

AFFIRMATION

400 OTTERY ST. MARY 8787   HENRY GEORGE LEY, 1887–1962

A-men.

FIRMLY I believe and truly
   God is Three, and God is One;
And I next acknowledge duly
   Manhood taken by the Son.

2 And I trust and hope most fully
   In that Manhood crucified;
And each thought and deed unruly
   Do to death, as he has died.

3 Simply to his grace and wholly
   Light and life and strength belong,
And I love supremely, solely,
   Him the holy, him the strong.

4 And I hold in veneration
   For the love of him alone,
Holy Church as his creation,
   And her teachings as his own.

5 *Adoration aye be given,*
   With and through the angelic host,
To the God of earth and heaven,
   Father, Son, and Holy Ghost. Amen.

John Henry Newman, 1801–90

401 (i) EGTON BRIDGE Irregular

JOHN JOUBERT

vv. 1 & 9

To - day I a - rise, _____ In - vo - king the Bles - sèd
Tri - ni - ty, _ Con - fes - sing the Bles - sèd U - ni - ty;

1. Cre -
9.

- a - tor of all ____ the things _____ that be. _
9. Sa - - - - viour, on us Sal - va - tion be. _

vv. 2–8

2. To - day I a - rise, _____ By strength of Christ and his
3. To - day I a - rise, _____ By ser - aphs serv - ing the
4. To - day I a - rise, _____ By splen - dour of sun and
5. To - day I a - rise, _____ With God my steers - man,
6. Pro - tec - ting me now _____ From craf - ty wiles of
7. Lord Je - sus the Christ, _____ To - day sur - round me
8. Di - rect and con - trol _____ The minds of all who

my - stic Birth, By his Pas - sion, and Tri - umph's
Lord a - bove, By truths his an - cient
flam - ing brand, By rush - ing wind, by
stay and guide, To guard, to coun - sel, to
de - mon crew, From foe - men, be they
with thy might; Be - fore, be - hind, on
think on me, The lips of all who

AFFIRMATION

small notes v. 3

sav -	ing worth,	By his	com-ing	a -	gain	to
her -	alds prove,	By	saints	in	pu - ri -	ty,
light -	ning grand,	By	depth	of	sea,	by
hear,	to bide,	His	way	be - fore,	his
ma - ny	or few,	From	lusts	that I	can
left	and right,	Be	thou	in	breadth,	in
speak	to me,	The	eyes	of	all	who

judge _____	the earth. _____	To -
la - - - - - -	bour, love. _____	To -
strength _____	of land. _____	To -
hosts _____	be - side _____	To -
scarce _____	sub - due. _____	To -
length, _____	in height. _____	To -
look _____	on me. _____	To -

- day I a - rise. _____	To - day I a - rise.
- day I a - rise. _____	To - day I a - rise.
- day I a - rise. _____	To - day I a - rise.
- day I a - rise. _____	To - day I a - rise.
- day I a - rise. _____	To - day I a - rise.
- day I a - rise. _____	To - day I a - rise.
- day I a - rise. _____	To - day I a - rise.

St. Patrick, 372–466; tr. Robert Alexander Stewart Macalister, 1870–1950

RESPONSE TO THE WORD OF GOD

401(ii) RAMELTON Irregular

Adapted from a Traditional Irish Melody
by JAMES MOORE

1. To - day I a - rise, In - vok - ing the Bless - ed
2. To - day I a - rise, By strength of Christ and his
3. To - day I a - rise, By ser - aphs serv - ing the
4. To - day I a - rise, By splen-dour of sun and
5. To - day I a - rise, With God my steers - man,
9. To - day I a - rise, In - vok - ing the Bless - ed

Tri - ni - ty, Con - fess - ing the Bless - ed
mys - tic Birth, By his Pas - sion and Tri - umph's
Lord a - bove, By truths his an - cient
flam - ing brand, By rush - ing wind, by
stay and guide, To guard, to coun-sel, to
Tri - ni - ty, Con - fess - ing the Bless - ed

U - ni - ty, Cre - a - tor of all the things that be.
sav - ing worth, By his com - ing a-gain to judge the earth.
her - alds prove, By saints in pur - i - ty, la - bour, love.
light - ning grand, By depth of sea, by strength of land.
hear, to bide, His way be - fore, his hosts be - side —
U - ni - ty, Sav - iour, on us Sal - va - tion be!

358

AFFIRMATION

CULRATHAIN Irregular

Adapted from a Traditional Irish Melody
by JAMES MOORE

6. Pro - tect-ing me now From craft - y wiles of
7. Lord Je - sus the Christ, To - day_ sur - round me
8. Di - rect and con - trol The minds of all_ who

de - mon crew, From foe - men, be _ they ma-ny or
with thy might; Be - fore, be - hind, on left _ and
think on me, The lips_ of all_ who speak to

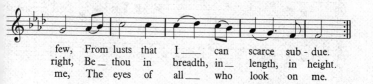

few, From lusts that I _ can scarce sub - due.
right, Be _ thou in breadth, in_ length, in height.
me, The eyes of all_ who look on me.

St. Patrick, 372–466; tr. Robert Alexander Stewart Macalister, 1870–1950

402 ST. PATRICK D.L.M.

Irish Traditional Melody

Acompiug inoiu niupc cpen

I BIND unto myself today
  The strong Name of the Trinity,
By invocation of the same,
  The Three in One, and One in Three.

2 I bind this day to me for ever,
    By power of faith, Christ's Incarnation;
  His baptism in the Jordan river;
    His death on cross for my salvation;
  His bursting from the spicèd tomb;
    His riding up the heavenly way;
  His coming at the day of doom:
    I bind unto myself today.

3 I bind unto myself today
    The virtues of the star-lit heaven,
  The glorious sun's life-giving ray,
    The whiteness of the moon at even,
  The flashing of the lightning free,
    The whirling wind's tempestuous shocks,
  The stable earth, the deep salt sea
    Around the old eternal rocks.

4 I bind unto myself today
   The power of God to hold and lead,
His eye to watch, his might to stay,
   His ear to hearken to my need,
The wisdom of my God to teach,
   His hand to guide, his shield to ward,
The word of God to give me speech,
   His heavenly host to be my guard.

6 *I bind unto myself the Name,*
   The strong Name of the Trinity,
By invocation of the same,
   The Three in One, and One in Three,
Of whom all nature hath creation,
   Eternal Father, Spirit, Word.
Praise to the Lord of my salvation:
   Salvation is of Christ the Lord. Amen.

St. Patrick, 372–466; version by Cecil Frances Alexander, 1818–95

CLONMACNOISE 8888. D   Mode I, transposed. Ancient Irish Melody

5. Christ be with me, Christ with-in me, Christ be-hind me, Christ be-fore me, Christ be-side me, Christ to win me, Christ to com-fort and re-store me, Christ be-neath me, Christ a-bove me, Christ in qui-et, Christ in dan-ger, Christ in hearts of all that love me, Christ in mouth of friend and stran-ger.

see previous page for v. 6

403 HAMBLEDEN 8989. D   WALTER KENDALL STANTON

THEE will I love, my God and King,
    Thee will I sing, my strength and tower:
For evermore thee will I trust,
    O God most just of truth and power;
Who all things hast in order placed,
    Yea, for thy pleasure hast created;
And on thy throne, unseen, unknown,
    Reignest alone in glory seated.

2 Set in my heart thy love I find;
    My wandering mind to thee thou leadest:
My trembling hope, my strong desire
    With heavenly fire thou kindly feedest.
Lo, all things fair thy path prepare,
    Thy beauty to my spirit calleth,
Thine to remain in joy or pain,
    And count it gain whate'er befalleth.

3 O more and more thy love extend,
    My life befriend with heavenly pleasure;
That I may win thy paradise,
    Thy pearl of price, thy countless treasure;
Since but in thee I can go free
    From earthly care and vain oppression,
This prayer I make for Jesus' sake,
    That thou me take in thy possession.

Robert Bridges, 1844–1930
Yattendon Hymnal, 1899

AFFIRMATION

404 CHRISTUS DER IST MEIN LEBEN
(BREMEN) 7676

MELCHIOR VULPIUS,
c. 1560–1615

* *If this tune is sung to No. 693, My soul there is a country, for which it is given as an
alternative, the dotted slurs should be observed in v. 3*

GOD is my strong salvation;
 What foe have I to fear?
In darkness and temptation
 My light, my help is near.

2 Though hosts encamp around me,
 Firm to the fight I stand;
What terror can confound me,
 With God at my right hand?

3 Place on the Lord reliance;
 My soul, with courage wait;
His truth be thine affiance,
 When faint and desolate.

4 His might thine heart shall strengthen,
 His love thy joy increase;
Mercy thy days shall lengthen;
 The Lord will give thee peace.

James Montgomery, 1771–1854. From Psalm 27

405 (i) MEINE HOFFNUNG
8787 337
Joachim Neander's *Alpha und Omega*, 1680

(ii) MICHAEL 8787 337
HERBERT HOWELLS

(iii) GROESWEN 8787 337
JOHN AMBROSE LLOYD, 1815-74

AFFIRMATION

Meine Hoffnung stehet feste

ALL my hope on God is founded;
   He doth still my trust renew.
Me through change and chance he guideth,
   Only good and only true.
      God unknown,
      He alone
Calls my heart to be his own.

2 Pride of man and earthly glory,
   Sword and crown betray his trust;
What with care and toil he buildeth,
   Tower and temple, fall to dust.
      But God's power,
      Hour by hour,
Is my temple and my tower.

3 God's great goodness aye endureth,
   Deep his wisdom passing thought:
Splendour, light, and life attend him,
   Beauty springeth out of naught.
      Evermore,
      From his store
New-born worlds rise and adore.

*4 Daily doth the Almighty Giver
   Bounteous gifts on us bestow;
His desire our soul delighteth,
   Pleasure leads us where we go.
      Love doth stand
      At his hand;
Joy doth wait on his command.

5 Still from man to God eternal
   Sacrifice of praise be done,
High above all praises praising
   For the gift of Christ his Son.
      Christ doth call
      One and all:
Ye who follow shall not fall.

Robert Bridges, 1844–1930,
based on Joachim Neander, 1650–80

* *This verse may be omitted*

406 & 407

EIN' FESTE BURG
8787 66667

MARTIN LUTHER, 1483-1546

406

Ein' feste Burg ist unser Gott

A SAFE stronghold our God is still,
    A trusty shield and weapon;
He'll help us clear from all the ill
    That hath us now o'ertaken.
      The ancient prince of hell
      Hath risen with purpose fell;
      Strong mail of craft and power
      He weareth in this hour;
    On earth is not his fellow.

2 With force of arms we nothing can,
    Full soon were we down-ridden;
But for us fights the proper Man,
    Whom God himself hath bidden.
      Ask ye who is this same?
      Christ Jesus is his Name,
      The Lord Sabaoth's Son;
      He, and no other one,
    Shall conquer in the battle.

3 And were this world all devils o'er,
    And watching to devour us,
We lay it not to heart so sore;
    Not they can overpower us.
      And let the prince of ill
      Look grim as e'er he will,
      He harms us not a whit;
      For why his doom is writ;
    A word shall quickly slay him.

4 God's word, for all their craft and force,
    One moment will not linger,
But, spite of hell, shall have its course;
    'Tis written by his finger.
      And, though they take our life,
      Goods, honour, children, wife,
      Yet is their profit small;
      These things shall vanish all:
    The city of God remaineth.

Martin Luther, 1483-1546; tr. Thomas Carlyle, 1795-1881

407

Ein' feste Burg ist unser Gott

A FORTRESS sure is God our King,
  A shield that ne'er shall fail us;
His sword alone shall succour bring,
  When evil doth assail us.
    With craft and cruel hate
    Doth Satan lie in wait,
      And, armed with deadly power,
      Seeks whom he may devour;
    On earth where is his equal?

2 O who shall then our champion be,
    Lest we be lost for ever?
  One sent by God—from sin 'tis he
    The sinner shall deliver;

And dost thou ask his Name?
'Tis Jesus Christ—the same
  Of Sabaoth the Lord,
  The Everlasting Word;
'Tis he must win the battle.

3 God's word remaineth ever sure,
    To us his goodness showing;
  The Spirit's gifts, of sin the cure,
    Each day he is bestowing.
    Though naught we love be left,
    Of all, e'en life, bereft,
      Yet what shall Satan gain?
      God's kingdom doth remain,
    And shall be ours for ever.

Martin Luther, 1483-1546; tr. Godfrey Thring, 1823-1903

408 BINCHESTER C.M.   WILLIAM CROFT, 1678-1727

O quam iuvat fratres, Deus

HAPPY are they, they that love God,
  Whose hearts have Christ confessed,
Who by his cross have found their life,
  And 'neath his yoke their rest.

2 Glad is the praise, sweet are the songs,
    When they together sing;
  And strong the prayers that bow the ear
  Of heaven's eternal King.

3 Christ to their homes giveth his peace,
    And makes their loves his own;
  But ah, what tares the evil one
  Hath in his garden sown!

4 Sad were our lot, evil this earth,
    Did not its sorrows prove
  The path whereby the sheep may find
    The fold of Jesus' love.

5 Then shall they know, they that love him,
    How all their pain was good;
  And death itself cannot unbind
    Their happy brotherhood.

Robert Bridges, 1844-1930,
Yattendon Hymnal, 1899, based on Charles Coffin, 1676-1749

409 SURREY (CAREY'S) 8888 88   HENRY CAREY, c. 1687–1743

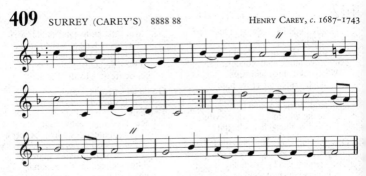

AND can it be, that I should gain
    An interest in the Saviour's blood?
Died he for me, who caused his pain—
    For me, who him to death pursued?
Amazing love! how can it be
That thou, my God, shouldst die for me?

2 He left his Father's throne above,—
    So free, so infinite his grace—
Emptied himself of all but love,
    And bled for Adam's helpless race:
'Tis mercy all, immense and free;
For, O my God, it found out me!

3 No condemnation now I dread;
    Jesus, and all in him, is mine!
Alive in him, my living Head,
    And clothed in righteousness divine,
Bold I approach the eternal throne,
And claim the crown, through Christ my own.

Charles Wesley, 1707-88

410 ST. BRIDE S.M.   SAMUEL HOWARD, 1710–82
                                   Parochial Harmony, 1762

[For No. 74]

A - men.

NOT what these hands have done
Can save this guilty soul;
Not what this toiling flesh has borne
Can make my spirit whole.

2 Not what I feel or do
Can give me peace with God;
Not all my prayers, and sighs, and tears
Can bear my heavy load.

3 Thy work alone, O Christ,
Can ease this weight of sin;
Thy blood alone, O Lamb of God,
Can give me peace within.

4 Thy love to me, O God,
Not mine, O Lord, to thee,
Can rid me of this dark unrest,
And set my spirit free.

5 Thy grace alone, O God,
To me can pardon speak;
Thy power alone, O Son of God,
Can this sore bondage break.

6 I bless the Christ of God,
I rest on life divine,
And with unfaltering lip and heart,
I call this Saviour mine.

Horatius Bonar, 1808-89 (altered)

411 BUTE L.M. and refrain

JOHN CURRIE

MY hope is built on nothing less
Than Jesus' blood and righteousness;
I dare not trust my sweetest frame,
But wholly lean on Jesus' Name.
    On Christ, the solid rock, I stand;
    All other ground is sinking sand.

2 When darkness seems to veil his face,
I rest on his unchanging grace;
In every high and stormy gale,
My anchor holds within the veil:

3 His oath, his covenant, and blood,
Support me in the whelming flood;
When all around my soul gives way,
He then is all my hope and stay:

Edward Mote, 1797-1874

412 WILL YOUR ANCHOR HOLD?
10 9 10 9 and refrain   WILLIAM JAMES KIRKPATRICK, 1838–1921

WILL your anchor hold in the storms of life,
When the clouds unfold their wings of strife?
When the strong tides lift, and the cables strain,
Will your anchor drift, or firm remain?
    We have an anchor that keeps the soul
    Steadfast and sure while the billows roll;
    Fastened to the Rock which cannot move,
    Grounded firm and deep in the Saviour's love!

2 Will your anchor hold in the straits of fear,
When the breakers roar and the reef is near?
While the surges rave, and the wild winds blow,
Shall the angry waves then your bark o'erflow?

3 Will your anchor hold in the floods of death,
When the waters cold chill your latest breath?
On the rising tide you can never fail,
While your anchor holds within the veil:

4 Will your eyes behold through the morning light
The city of gold and the harbour bright?
Will you anchor safe by the heavenly shore,
When life's storms are past for evermore?

Priscilla Jane Owens, 1829–1907

413 WARRINGTON L.M.

RALPH HARRISON, 1748–1810
Sacred Harmony, 1784

JESUS shall reign where'er the sun
Does his successive journeys run;
His Kingdom stretch from shore to shore,
Till moons shall wax and wane no more.

2 People and realms of every tongue
Dwell on his love with sweetest song;
And infant voices shall proclaim
Their early blessings on his Name.

3 Blessings abound where'er he reigns:
The prisoner leaps to lose his chains,
The weary find eternal rest,
And all the sons of want are blest.

4 Let every creature rise and bring
Peculiar honours to our King,
Angels descend with songs again,
And earth repeat the long Amen.

Isaac Watts, 1674–1748

414 LÜBECK 7777

Simplified form of a melody in
Freylinghausen's *Geistreiches Gesangbuch*, 1704

A - men.

Wir glauben all' an einen Gott

WE believe in one true God,
Father, Son, and Holy Ghost,
Ever present help in need,
Praised by all the heavenly host;

2 We believe in Jesus Christ,
Son of God and Mary's Son,
Who descended from his throne,
And for us salvation won;

3 We confess the Holy Ghost,
Who from both fore'er proceeds;
Who upholds and comforts us
In all trials, fears, and needs.

4 *Blest and Holy Trinity,*
Praise forever be to thee!
By whose mighty power alone
All is made and wrought and done.
Amen.

Tobias Clausnitzer, 1619–84
Tr. Catherine Winkworth, 1827–78 (altered)

415 NORMANDY 11 11 11 11

Basque Carol Melody, collected and extended
by CHARLES EDGAR PETTMAN, 1866–1943

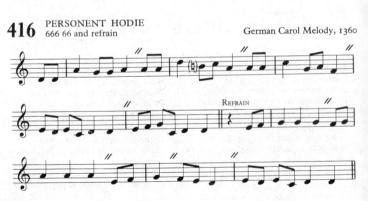

THE great love of God is revealed in the Son,
Who came to this earth to redeem every one.
That love, like a stream flowing clear to the sea,
Makes clean every heart that from sin would be free.

2 It binds the whole world, every barrier it breaks,
The hills it lays low, and the mountains it shakes.
It's yours, it is ours, O how lavishly given!
The pearl of great price, and the treasure of heaven!

Daniel Thambyrajah Niles, 1908–70

416 PERSONENT HODIE
666 66 and refrain

German Carol Melody, 1360

AFFIRMATION

For children

GOD is love: his the care,
Tending each, everywhere.
God is love—all is there!
Jesus came to show him,
That mankind might know him:
   Sing aloud, loud, loud!
   Sing aloud, loud, loud!
     God is good!
     God is truth!
   God is beauty! Praise him!

2 None can see God above;
All have here man to love;
Thus may we Godward move,
Finding him in others,
Holding all men brothers:

3 Jesus lived here for men,
Strove and died, rose again,
Rules our hearts, now as then;
For he came to save us
By the truth he gave us:

4 To our Lord praise we sing—
Light and life, friend and king,
Coming down love to bring,
Pattern for our duty,
Showing God in beauty:

Percy Dearmer, 1867–1936

417 ST. CYRIL   6575

PHILIPP BLISS, 1838–76
The Charm, 1871

For younger children

GOD is always near me,
Hearing what I say,
Knowing all my thoughts and deeds,
All my work and play.

2 God is always near me;
  In the darkest night
He can see me just the same
  As by mid-day light.

3 God is always near me,
  Though so young and small;
Not a look or word or thought,
  But God knows it all.

Philipp Bliss, 1838–76
The Charm, 1871

418 (i) GAELIC LULLABY 7777 and refrain   Gaelic Traditional Melody

For younger children

> JESUS loves me! this I know,
> For the Bible tells me so;
> Little ones to him belong;
> They are weak, but he is strong.
>> *Yes! Jesus loves me, loves me, loves me!*
>> *Yes! Jesus loves me,*
>> *For the Bible tells me so.*

2 Jesus loves me! he who died
Heaven's gate to open wide;
He will wash away my sin,
Let his little child come in:

3 Jesus loves me! he will stay
Close beside me all the way;
Then his little child will take
Up to heaven, for his dear sake:

Anna Bartlett Warner, 1820–1915

(ii)   JESUS LOVES ME
7777 and refrain   WILLIAM BATCHELDER BRADBURY, 1816–68

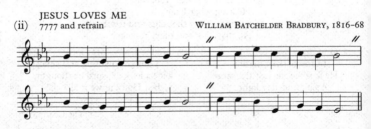

AFFIRMATION

Yes! Je-sus loves me! Yes! Je-sus loves me!
Yes! Je-sus loves me! The Bi-ble tells me so.

For younger children

JESUS loves me! this I know,
For the Bible tells me so;
Little ones to him belong;
They are weak, but he is strong.
  Yes! Jesus loves me!
  Yes! Jesus loves me!
  Yes! Jesus loves me!
  The Bible tells me so.

2 Jesus loves me! he who died
Heaven's gate to open wide;
He will wash away my sin,
Let his little child come in:

3 Jesus loves me! he will stay
Close beside me all the way;
Then his little child will take
Up to heaven, for his dear sake:

Anna Bartlett Warner, 1820–1915

419 NEWBURY C.M.

English Traditional Melody

Alternative tune, KINGS LANGLEY, No. 618

For younger children

LORD, I would own thy tender care,
And all thy love to me;
The food I eat, the clothes I wear,
Are all bestowed by thee.

2 'Tis thou preservest me from death
And dangers every hour;
I cannot draw another breath
Unless thou give me power.

3 Kind angels guard me every night,
As round my bed they stay;
Nor am I absent from thy sight
In darkness or by day.

4 My health and friends and parents
dear
To me by God are given;
I have not any blessing here
But what is sent from heaven.

5 Such goodness, Lord, and constant care
A child can ne'er repay;
But may it be my daily prayer
To love thee and obey.

Jane Taylor, 1783–1824

420 AURELIA 7676. D   SAMUEL SEBASTIAN WESLEY, 1810–76

THE Church's one foundation
  Is Jesus Christ her Lord:
She is his new creation
  By water and the word;
From heaven he came and sought her
  To be his holy bride;
With his own blood he bought her,
  And for her life he died.

2 Elect from every nation,
  Yet one o'er all the earth,
Her charter of salvation
  One Lord, one faith, one birth:
One holy Name she blesses,
  Partakes one holy food,
And to one hope she presses,
  With every grace endued.

3 'Mid toil and tribulation,
  And tumult of her war,
She waits the consummation
  Of peace for evermore,
Till with the vision glorious
  Her longing eyes are blest,
And the great Church victorious
  Shall be the Church at rest.

4 Yet she on earth hath union
  With God the Three in One,
And mystic sweet communion
  With those whose rest is won.
O happy ones and holy!
  Lord, give us grace that we,
Like them, the meek and lowly,
  On high may dwell with thee.

Samuel John Stone, 1839–1900

421 AUSTRIAN HYMN
8787. D

FRANZ JOSEPH HAYDN, 1732–1809,
based on a Croatian folk song

GLORIOUS things of thee are
    spoken,
  Zion, city of our God;
He whose word cannot be broken
  Formed thee for his own abode.
On the Rock of Ages founded,
  What can shake thy sure repose?
With salvation's walls surrounded,
  Thou may'st smile at all thy foes.

2 See! the streams of living waters,
    Springing from eternal love,
  Well supply thy sons and daughters,
    And all fear of want remove.
  Who can faint while such a river
    Ever flows their thirst to assuage,—
  Grace, which, like the Lord the Giver,
    Never fails from age to age?

3 Round each habitation hovering,
    See! the cloud and fire appear,
  For a glory and a covering,
    Showing that the Lord is near.
  Blest inhabitants of Zion,
    Washed in the Redeemer's blood,
  Jesus, whom their souls rely on,
    Makes them kings and priests to God.

4 Saviour, if of Zion's city
    I, through grace, a member am,
  Let the world deride or pity,
    I will glory in thy Name.
  Fading is the worldling's pleasure,
    All his boasted pomp and show;
  Solid joys and lasting treasure
    None but Zion's children know.

John Newton, 1725–1807

422 RICHMOND C.M.

THOMAS HAWEIS, 1734–1820, as adapted
by SAMUEL WEBBE, the younger, *c.* 1770–1843

CITY of God, how broad and far
    Outspread thy walls sublime!
The true thy chartered freemen are,
    Of every age and clime.

2 One holy Church, one army strong,
    One steadfast, high intent;
One working band, one harvest-song,
    One King omnipotent.

3 How purely hath thy speech come down
    From man's primeval youth!
How grandly hath thine empire grown,
    Of freedom, love and truth!

4 How gleam thy watch-fires through the night
    With never-fainting ray!
How rise thy towers, serene and bright,
    To meet the dawning day!

5 In vain the surge's angry shock,
    In vain the drifting sands:
Unharmed upon the eternal Rock
    The eternal City stands.

Samuel Johnson, 1822–82

423 MARCHING 8787   MARTIN SHAW, 1875-1958

Igjennem Nat og Trængsel

THROUGH the night of doubt and sorrow
   Onward goes the pilgrim band,
Singing songs of expectation,
   Marching to the promised land.

2 Clear before us, through the darkness,
   Gleams and burns the guiding light;
Brother clasps the hand of brother,
   Stepping fearless through the night;

3 One the light of God's own presence,
   O'er his ransomed people shed,
Chasing far the gloom and terror,
   Brightening all the path we tread;

4 One the object of our journey,
   One the faith which never tires,
One the earnest looking forward,
   One the hope our God inspires;

5 One the strain that lips of thousands
   Lift as from the heart of one;
One the conflict, one the peril,
   One the march in God begun;

6 One the gladness of rejoicing
   On the far eternal shore,
Where the one Almighty Father
   Reigns in love for evermore.

Bernhardt Severin Ingemann, 1789-1862
Tr. Sabine Baring-Gould, 1834-1924

424 THORNBURY 7676 767 and refrain BASIL HARWOOD, 1859–1949

REFRAIN

One Church, one Faith, one Lord. _____

THY hand, O God, has guided
  Thy flock, from age to age;
The wondrous tale is written,
  Full clear, on every page;
Our fathers owned thy goodness,
  And we their deeds record;
And both of this bear witness,
  One Church, one Faith, one Lord.

2 Thy heralds brought glad tidings
  To greatest, as to least;
They bade men rise, and hasten
  To share the great King's feast;
And this was all their teaching,
  In every deed and word,
To all alike proclaiming,

3 Through many a day of darkness,
  Through many a scene of strife,
The faithful few fought bravely
  To guard the nation's life.
Their Gospel of redemption,
  Sin pardoned, man restored,
Was all in this enfolded,

4 Thy mercy will not fail us,
  Nor leave thy work undone;
With thy right hand to help us,
  The victory shall be won;
And then, by men and angels,
  Thy Name shall be adored,
And this shall be their anthem:

Edward Hayes Plumptre, 1821–91

425 PITYOULISH C.M. REGINALD BARRETT-AYRES

IN Christ there is no East or West,
   In him no South or North,
But one great fellowship of love
   Throughout the whole wide earth.

2 In him shall true hearts everywhere
   Their high communion find,
His service is the golden cord
   Close-binding all mankind.

3 Join hands, then, brothers of the
     Faith,
   Whate'er your race may be:
Who serves my Father as a son
   Is surely kin to me.

4 In Christ now meet both East and
     West,
   In him meet South and North,
All Christlike souls are one in him,
   Throughout the whole wide earth.

John Oxenham, 1852-1941

426 ST. MAGNUS
(NOTTINGHAM) C.M.

Probably by
JEREMIAH CLARKE, *c.* 1673-1707

For children

A GLORIOUS company we sing,
The Master and his men,
He sent them forth to tell his love
By voice and hand and pen.

2 A loving company we sing,
When Jesus sent to save
All sick and blind and hungry folk,
The outcast and the slave.

3 We join this glorious company
   Of Jesus and his friends,
To spread throughout this troubled world
   His love that never ends.

Albert Frederick Bayly

The following are also suitable

No.
140   The Lord doth reign
139   I to the hills
167   His large and great dominion
333   Thou shalt arise
151   God, who made the earth
324   Blest is the man, O God

American Cowboy Melody
from an Irish folk tune
collected by JOHN A. LOMAX

427 LAREDO 12 10 12 11 irregular

For younger children

THE Church is wherever God's people are praising,
Singing their thanks for joy on this day.
The Church is wherever disciples of Jesus
Remember his story and walk in his way.

2 The Church is wherever God's people are helping,
Caring for neighbours in sickness and need.
The Church is wherever God's people are sharing
The words of the Bible in gift and in deed.

Carol Rose Ikeler

DEDICATION AND DISCIPLESHIP

428 SLANE 10 11 11 11 irregular

Irish Traditional Melody

LORD of creation, to thee be all praise!
Most mighty thy working, most wondrous thy ways!
Who reignest in glory no tongue can e'er tell,
Yet deign'st in the heart of the humble to dwell.

2 Lord of all power, I give thee my will,
In joyful obedience thy tasks to fulfil.
Thy bondage is freedom; thy service is song;
And, held in thy keeping, my weakness is strong.

3 Lord of all wisdom, I give thee my mind,
Rich truth that surpasseth man's knowledge to find.
What eye hath not seen and what ear hath not heard
Is taught by thy Spirit and shines from thy Word.

4 Lord of all bounty, I give thee my heart;
I praise and adore thee for all that thou art;
Thy love to inflame me, thy counsel to guide,
Thy presence to shield me, whate'er may betide.

5 Lord of all being, I give thee my all;
If e'er I disown thee, I stumble and fall;
But, sworn in glad service thy word to obey,
I walk in thy freedom to the end of the way.

Jack Copley Winslow,
1882–1974

429 ST. JAMES C.M.

Select Psalms and Hymns, 1697
Probably by RAPHAEL COURTEVILLE, ?1677–1772

A - men.

MY God, accept my heart this day
And make it always thine,
That I from thee no more may stray,
No more from thee decline.

2 Before the cross of him who died,
Behold, I prostrate fall;
Let every sin be crucified,
And Christ be all in all.

3 Anoint me with thy heavenly grace,
And seal me for thine own;
That I may see thy glorious face,
And worship near thy throne.

4 Let every thought and work and word
To thee be ever given;
Then life shall be thy service, Lord,
And death the gate of heaven.

5 *All glory to the Father be,*
All glory to the Son,
All glory, Holy Ghost, to thee,
While endless ages run. Amen.

Matthew Bridges, 1800–94

430 BRESLAU L.M.

German Traditional Melody,
in form used by MENDELSSOHN (1836)

'TAKE up thy cross,' the Saviour said,
'If thou wouldst my disciple be;
Take up thy cross, with willing heart,
And humbly follow after me.'

2 Take up thy cross; let not its weight
Fill thy weak soul with vain alarm;
His strength shall bear thy spirit up,
And brace thy heart, and nerve thine arm.

3 Take up thy cross, nor heed the shame,
And let thy foolish pride be still:
The Lord refused not e'en to die
Upon a cross, on Calvary's hill.

4 Take up thy cross, then, in his strength,
And calmly every danger brave;
'Twill guide thee to a better home,
And lead to victory o'er the grave.

5 Take up thy cross, and follow Christ,
Nor think till death to lay it down;
For only he who bears the cross
May hope to wear the glorious crown.

Charles William Everest, 1814–77

431 HEATHLANDS 7777 77

HENRY SMART, 1813–79

JESUS, Master, whose I am,
  Purchased, thine alone to be,
By thy blood, O spotless Lamb,
  Shed so willingly for me,
Let my heart be all thine own,
Let me live to thee alone.

2 Jesus, Master, I am thine:
  Keep me faithful, keep me near;
Let thy presence in me shine,
  All my homeward way to cheer.
Jesus, at thy feet I fall,
O be thou my All in All.

3 Jesus, Master, whom I serve,
  Though so feebly and so ill,
Strengthen hand and heart and nerve
  All thy bidding to fulfil;
Open thou mine eyes to see
All the work thou hast for me.

4 Jesus, Master, wilt thou use
  One who owes thee more than all?
As thou wilt! I would not choose;
  Only let me hear thy call.
Jesus, let me always be
In thy service glad and free.

Frances Ridley Havergal, 1836–79

432 VIGIL 8785   GEORGE THALBEN-BALL

MAY the mind of Christ my Saviour
  Live in me from day to day,
By his love and power controlling
  All I do or say.

2 May the word of God dwell richly
  In my heart from hour to hour,
So that all may see I triumph
  Only through his power.

3 May the peace of God my Father
  Rule my life in everything,
That I may be calm to comfort
  Sick and sorrowing.

4 May the love of Jesus fill me,
  As the waters fill the sea;
Him exalting, self abasing,
  This is victory.

5 May I run the race before me,
  Strong and brave to face the foe,
Looking only unto Jesus
  As I onward go.

Kate Barclay Wilkinson, 1859–1928

433 (i) PETTRONSEN Irregular   MARTIN DALBY

God be in my head, and in my un-der-stand-ing;

God be in mine eyes, and in my look-ing;

God be in my mouth, and in my speak-ing;

God be in my heart, and in my think-ing;

God be at mine end, and at my de-part-ing.

Book of Hours (1514)

(ii) GOD BE IN MY HEAD Irregular   WALFORD DAVIES, 1869–1941

God be in my head,

and in my un-der-stand-ing; God be in mine

eyes, and in my look-ing; God be in my mouth, and in my

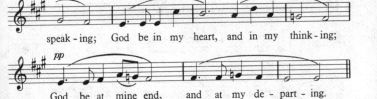

speak - ing; God be in my heart, and in my think - ing;

pp

God be at mine end, and at my de - part - ing.

Book of Hours (1514)

434 THORNBURY 7676. D BASIL HARWOOD, 1859–1949

O JESUS, I have promised
  To serve thee to the end;
Be thou for ever near me,
  My Master and my Friend:
I shall not fear the battle
  If thou art by my side,
Nor wander from the pathway
  If thou wilt be my Guide.

2 O let me feel thee near me:
  The world is ever near;
I see the sights that dazzle,
  The tempting sounds I hear;
My foes are ever near me,
  Around me and within;
But, Jesus, draw thou nearer,
  And shield my soul from sin.

3 O let me hear thee speaking
  In accents clear and still,
Above the storms of passion,
  The murmurs of self-will;
O speak to reassure me,
  To hasten or control;
O speak, and make me listen,
  Thou Guardian of my soul.

4 O Jesus, thou hast promised,
  To all who follow thee,
That where thou art in glory
  There shall thy servant be;
And, Jesus, I have promised
  To serve thee to the end;
O give me grace to follow,
  My Master and my Friend.

John Ernest Bode, 1816–74

435 UNIVERSITY C.M.

Randall's *Psalm and Hymn Tunes*, 1794
Probably by CHARLES COLLIGNON, 1725–85

LORD, in the fullness of my might,
　I would for thee be strong:
While runneth o'er each dear delight,
　To thee should soar my song.

2 I would not give the world my heart,
　And then profess thy love;
I would not feel my strength depart,
　And then thy service prove.

3 I would not with swift-wingèd zeal
　On the world's errands go,
And labour up the heavenly hill
　With weary feet and slow.

4 O not for thee my weak desires,
　My poorer, baser part!
O not for thee my fading fires,
　The ashes of my heart!

5 O choose me in my golden time:
　In my dear joys have part!
For thee the glory of my prime,
　The fullness of my heart!

Thomas Hornblower Gill, 1819–1906

436 MELCOMBE L.M.

SAMUEL WEBBE, the elder, 1740–1816
An Essay on the Church Plain-Chant, 1782

O MASTER, let me walk with thee
In lowly paths of service free;
Thy secret tell; help me to bear
The strain of toil, the fret of care.

2 Help me the slow of heart to move
By some clear winning word of love;
Teach me the wayward feet to stay,
And guide them in the homeward way.

3 Teach me thy patience; still with thee
In closer, dearer company,
In work that keeps faith sweet and strong,
In trust that triumphs over wrong,

4 In hope that sends a shining ray
Far down the future's broadening way,
In peace that only thou canst give,
With thee, O Master, let me live.

Washington Gladden, 1836–1918

437 HYFRYDOL 8787. D

ROWLAND HUGH PRICHARD, 1811–87
Haleliwiah Drachefn, Carmarthen, 1855

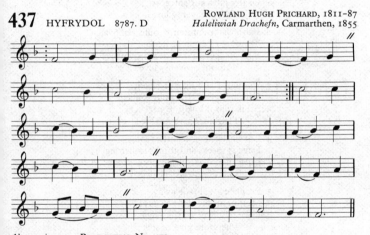

Alternative tune, BLAENWERN, No. 473

LOVE Divine, all loves excelling,
Joy of heaven, to earth come down,
Fix in us thy humble dwelling,
All thy faithful mercies crown.
Jesus, thou art all compassion,
Pure, unbounded love thou art;
Visit us with thy salvation,
Enter every trembling heart.

2 Come, almighty to deliver;
Let us all thy life receive;
Suddenly return, and never,
Never more thy temples leave.

Thee we would be always blessing,
Serve thee as thy hosts above,
Pray, and praise thee, without ceasing,
Glory in thy perfect love.

3 Finish then thy new creation:
Pure and spotless let us be;
Let us see thy great salvation,
Perfectly restored in thee,
Changed from glory into glory,
Till in heaven we take our place,
Till we cast our crowns before thee,
Lost in wonder, love, and praise.

Charles Wesley, 1707–88

438 CAPETOWN 7775

Adapted from a melody in
Filitz' *Choralbuch*, 1847

GRACIOUS Spirit, Holy Ghost,
Taught by thee, we covet most,
Of thy gifts at Pentecost,
　　Holy, heavenly love.

2 Faith that mountains could remove,
Tongues of earth or heaven above,
Knowledge, all things, empty prove
　　Without heavenly love.

3 Though I as a martyr bleed,
Give my goods the poor to feed,
All is vain if love I need;
　　Therefore give me love.

4 Love is kind, and suffers long;
Love is meek, and thinks no wrong,
Love than death itself more strong;
　　Therefore give us love.

5 Prophecy will fade away,
Melting in the light of day;
Love will ever with us stay;
　　Therefore give us love.

6 Faith and hope and love we see,
Joining hand in hand, agree;
But the greatest of the three,
　　And the best, is love.

Christopher Wordsworth, 1807-85
From 1 Corinthians 13

439 FARNHAM
C.M.

From an English Traditional Melody,
collected by RALPH VAUGHAN WILLIAMS, 1872-1958

O LORD and Master of us all,
    Whate'er our name or sign,
We own thy sway, we hear thy call,
    We test our lives by thine.

2 Thou judgest us: thy purity
    Doth all our lusts condemn;
The love that draws us nearer thee
    Is hot with wrath to them.

3 Our thoughts lie open to thy sight;
    And naked to thy glance
Our secret sins are, in the light
    Of thy pure countenance.

4 Yet, weak and blinded though we be,
    Thou dost our service own;
We bring our varying gifts to thee,
    And thou rejectest none.

5 Apart from thee all gain is loss,
    All labour vainly done;
The solemn shadow of thy cross
    Is better than the sun.

6 Our Friend, our Brother, and our Lord,
    What may thy service be?
Nor name, nor form, nor ritual word,
    But simply following thee.

7 We faintly hear; we dimly see;
    In differing phrase we pray;
But, dim or clear, we own in thee
    The Light, the Truth, the Way.

John Greenleaf Whittier, 1807-92

440 WOODLANDS 10 10 10 10   WALTER GREATOREX, 1877–1949

'LIFT up your hearts!' We lift them, Lord, to thee;
Here at thy feet none other may we see:
'Lift up your hearts!' E'en so, with one accord,
We lift them up, we lift them to the Lord.

2 Above the level of the former years,
The mire of sin, the slough of guilty fears,
The mist of doubt, the blight of love's decay,
O Lord of light, lift all our hearts today!

3 Lift every gift that thou thyself hast given;
Low lies the best till lifted up to heaven:
Low lie the bounding heart, the teeming brain,
Till, sent from God, they mount to God again.

4 Then, as the trumpet-call, in after years,
'Lift up your hearts!' rings pealing in our ears,
Still shall those hearts respond with full accord,
'We lift them up, we lift them to the Lord!'

Henry Montagu Butler, 1833–1918

441 FROM STRENGTH TO STRENGTH
D.S.M.   EDWARD WOODALL NAYLOR, 1867-1934

SOLDIERS of Christ! arise,
  And put your armour on,
Strong in the strength which God supplies
  Through his eternal Son;
  Strong in the Lord of hosts,
  And in his mighty power;
Who in the strength of Jesus trusts
  Is more than conqueror.

2   Stand, then, in his great might,
       With all his strength endued;
   And take, to arm you for the fight,
       The panoply of God.
       To keep your armour bright
       Attend with constant care,
   Still walking in your Captain's sight,
       And watching unto prayer.

3   From strength to strength go on;
       Wrestle, and fight, and pray;
   Tread all the powers of darkness down,
       And win the well-fought day,—
       That, having all things done,
       And all your conflicts passed,
   Ye may o'ercome through Christ alone,
       And stand complete at last.

                    Charles Wesley, 1707-88

442 (i) DUKE STREET
L.M.

Boyd's *Psalm and Hymn Tunes*, 1793,
later attributed to JOHN HATTON, d. 1793

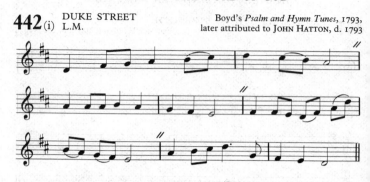

(ii) CANNOCK L.M.

WALTER KENDALL STANTON

FIGHT the good fight with all thy might;
Christ is thy strength, and Christ thy right;
Lay hold on life, and it shall be
Thy joy and crown eternally.

2 Run the straight race through God's good grace,
Lift up thine eyes, and seek his face;
Life with its path before us lies;
Christ is the way, and Christ the prize.

3 Cast care aside; and on thy Guide
Lean, and his mercy will provide,—
Lean, and the trusting soul shall prove
Christ is its life, and Christ its love.

4 Faint not, nor fear; his arm is near;
He changeth not, and thou art dear;
Only believe, and thou shalt see
That Christ is all in all to thee.

John Samuel Bewley Monsell, 1811-75

443 MONKS GATE
6565 6665

Adapted by RALPH VAUGHAN WILLIAMS,
1872-1958, from an English Traditional Melody

WHO would true valour see,
    Let him come hither;
One here will constant be,
        Come wind, come weather;
There's no discouragement
Shall make him once relent
His first avowed intent
    To be a pilgrim.

2 Whoso beset him round
    With dismal stories,
Do but themselves confound;
        His strength the more is.
No lion can him fright,
He'll with a giant fight,
But he will have a right
    To be a pilgrim.

3 Hobgoblin nor foul fiend
    Can daunt his spirit;
He knows he at the end
        Shall life inherit.
Then fancies fly away;
He'll fear not what men say;
He'll labour night and day
    To be a pilgrim.

John Bunyan, 1628-88

444 PETERSHAM D.C.M.   CLEMENT WILLIAM POOLE, 1828–1924

I FEEL the winds of God today;
    Today my sail I lift,
Though heavy oft with drenching spray,
    And torn with many a rift;
If hope but light the water's crest,
    And Christ my bark will use,
I'll seek the seas at his behest,
    And brave another cruise.

2 It is the wind of God that dries
    My vain regretful tears,
Until with braver thoughts shall rise
    The purer, brighter years;
If cast on shores of selfish ease
    Or pleasure I should be,
Lord, let me feel thy freshening breeze,
    And I'll put back to sea.

3 If ever I forget thy love
    And how that love was shown,
Lift high the blood-red flag above:
    It bears thy Name alone.
Great Pilot of my onward way,
    Thou wilt not let me drift;
I feel the winds of God today,
    Today my sail I lift.

Jessie Adams, 1863–1954

445 ICH HALTE TREULICH STILL
D.S.M.

Schemelli's *Musikalisches
Gesangbuch*, 1736
Thought to be by JOHANN SEBASTIAN BACH, 1685-1750

MAKE me a captive, Lord,
  And then I shall be free;
Force me to render up my sword,
  And I shall conqueror be.
  I sink in life's alarms
  When by myself I stand;
Imprison me within thine arms,
  And strong shall be my hand.

2 My heart is weak and poor
    Until it master find;
  It has no spring of action sure—
    It varies with the wind.
    It cannot freely move
    Till thou hast wrought its chain;
  Enslave it with thy matchless love,
    And deathless it shall reign.

3 My power is faint and low
    Till I have learned to serve;
  It wants the needed fire to glow,
    It wants the breeze to nerve;
    It cannot drive the world,
    Until itself be driven;
  Its flag can only be unfurled
    When thou shalt breathe from heaven.

4 My will is not my own
    Till thou hast made it thine;
  If it would reach a monarch's throne
    It must its crown resign;
    It only stands unbent,
    Amid the clashing strife,
  When on thy bosom it has leant
    And found in thee its life.

George Matheson, 1842-1906

446 TRURO L.M.

Williams' *Psalmodia Evangelica*, 1789

* LAND of our Birth, we pledge to thee
  Our love and toil in the years to be;
  When we are grown and take our place,
  As men and women with our race.

2 Father in heaven, who lovest all,
  O help thy children when they call;
  That they may build from age to age
  An undefilèd heritage.

3 Teach us to bear the yoke in youth,
  With steadfastness and careful truth;
  That, in our time, thy grace may give
  The truth whereby the nations live.

4 Teach us to rule ourselves alway,
  Controlled and cleanly night and day;
  That we may bring, if need arise,
  No maimed or worthless sacrifice.

5 Teach us to look, in all our ends,
  On thee for Judge, and not our friends;
  That we, with thee, may walk uncowed
  By fear or favour of the crowd.

6 Teach us the strength that cannot seek,
  By deed or thought, to hurt the weak;
  That, under thee, we may possess
  Man's strength to succour man's distress.

7 Teach us delight in simple things,
  And mirth that has no bitter springs;
  Forgiveness free of evil done,
  And love to all men 'neath the sun!

*8 Land of our Birth, our faith, our pride,
  For whose dear sake our fathers died;
  O Motherland, we pledge to thee,
  Head, heart, and hand through the years to be!

Rudyard Kipling, 1865–1936

* *The complete poem is given here, but verses 1 and 8 should be omitted unless the occasion warrants their use.*

447 SUSSEX 8787

Adapted by RALPH VAUGHAN WILLIAMS, 1872–1958, from an English Traditional Melody

DEDICATION AND DISCIPLESHIP

LORD and Master, who hast called us
All our days to follow thee,
We have heard thy clear commandment,
'Bring the children unto Me.'

2 So we come to thee, the teacher,
At thy feet we kneel to pray:
We can only lead the children
When thyself shalt show the way.

3 Teach us thy most wondrous method,
As of old in Galilee
Thou didst show thy chosen servants
How to bring men unto thee.

4 Give us store of wit and wisdom,
Give us love which never tires,
Give us thine abiding patience,
Give us hope which aye inspires.

5 Mighty Wisdom of the Godhead,
Thou the One eternal Word,
Thou the counsellor, the teacher,
Fill us with thy fullness, Lord.

Florence Margaret Smith, 1886-1958

448 SAFFRON WALDEN 8886   ARTHUR HENRY BROWN, 1830-1926

For young people

JUST as I am, thine own to be,
Friend of the young, who lovest me,
To consecrate myself to thee,
    O Jesus Christ, I come.

2 In the glad morning of my day,
My life to give, my vows to pay,
With no reserve and no delay,
    With all my heart I come.

3 I would live ever in the light,
I would work ever for the right,
I would serve thee with all my might,
    Therefore to thee I come.

4 Just as I am, young, strong and free,
To be the best that I can be
For truth, and righteousness, and thee,
    Lord of my life, I come.

Marianne Farningham, 1834-1909

The following are also suitable
No.
211 Jesus calls us! O'er the tumult
88 God of grace and God of glory

399

449 AVE VIRGO VIRGINUM 7676. D

Horn's *Gesangbuch*, 1544
(rhythm slightly altered)

For children

LOOKING upward every day,
    Sunshine on our faces;
Pressing onward every day
    Toward the heavenly places;
Growing every day in awe,
    For thy Name is holy;
Learning every day to love
    With a love more lowly;

2 Walking every day more close
    To our Elder Brother;
Growing every day more true
    Unto one another;
Leaving every day behind
    Something which might hinder;
Running swifter every day;
    Growing purer, kinder,—

3 Lord, so pray we every day:
    Hear us in thy pity,
That we enter in at last
    To the holy city.
Looking upward every day,
    Sunshine on our faces;
Press we onward every day
    Toward the heavenly places.

Mary Butler, 1841-1916

450 BUCKLAND 7777   LEIGHTON GEORGE HAYNE, 1836-83

For children

SAVIOUR, teach me, day by day,
Love's sweet lesson to obey;
Sweeter lesson cannot be,
Loving him who first loved me.

2 With a child's glad heart of love
At thy bidding may I move,
Prompt to serve and follow thee,
Loving him who first loved me.

3 Teach me thus thy steps to trace,
Strong to follow in thy grace,
Learning how to love from thee,
Loving him who first loved me.

4 Love in loving finds employ,
In obedience all her joy;
Ever new that joy will be,
Loving him who first loved me.

5 Thus may I rejoice to show
That I feel the love I owe;
Singing, till thy face I see,
Of his love who first loved me.

Jane Eliza Leeson, 1809-81

STEWARDSHIP AND SERVICE

451 CHILTON FOLIAT 10 10 10 10 GEORGE CLEMENT MARTIN, 1844–1916

ALMIGHTY Father of all things that be,
Our life, our work, we consecrate to thee,
Whose heavens declare thy glory from above,
Whose earth below is witness to thy love.

2 For well we know this weary, soilèd earth
Is yet thine own by right of its new birth,
Since that great cross upreared on Calvary
Redeemed it from its fault and shame to thee.

3 Thine still the changeful beauty of the hills,
The purple valleys flecked with silver rills,
The ocean glistening 'neath the golden rays;
They all are thine, and voiceless speak thy praise.

4 Thou dost the strength to workman's arm impart;
From thee the skilled musician's mystic art,
The grace of poet's pen or painter's hand
To teach the loveliness of sea and land.

5 Then grant us, Lord, in all things thee to own,
To dwell within the shadow of thy throne,
To speak and work, to think, and live, and move,
Reflecting thine own nature, which is love;

6 That so, by Christ redeemed from sin and shame,
And hallowed by thy Spirit's cleansing flame,
Ourselves, our work, and all our powers may be
A sacrifice acceptable to thee.

Ernest Edward Dugmore, 1843–1925

452 BANGOR C.M.   Tans'ur's *Harmony of Zion*, 1734

GOD, who hast given us power to sound
　　Depths hitherto unknown;
To probe earth's hidden mysteries,
　　And make their might our own;

2 Great are thy gifts: yet greater far
　　This gift, O God, bestow,
That as to knowledge we attain
　　We may in wisdom grow.

3 Let wisdom's godly fear dispel
　　All fears that hate impart;
Give understanding to the mind,
　　And with new mind new heart.

4 So for thy glory and man's good
　　May we thy gifts employ,
Lest, maddened by the lust of power,
　　Man shall himself destroy.

George Wallace Briggs, 1875-1959

453 CARRICK D.C.M.

JOHN CURRIE

BEHOLD us, Lord, a little space
  From daily tasks set free,
And met within thy holy place
  To rest awhile with thee.
Yet these are not the only walls
  Wherein thou mayst be sought;
On homeliest work thy blessing falls,
  In truth and patience wrought.

2 Thine is the loom, the forge, the mart,
  The wealth of land and sea,
The worlds of science and of art,
  Revealed and ruled by thee.
Work shall be prayer, if all be wrought
  As thou wouldst have it done,
And prayer, by thee inspired and taught,
  Itself with work be one.

John Ellerton, 1826–93

454 (i) PSALM 42 8787. D

French-Genevan Psalter, 1551

(ii) IN BABILONE 8787. D

Dutch Traditional Melody
Collected by JULIUS RÖNTGEN, 1855-1932

SON of God, eternal Saviour,
  Source of life and truth and grace,
Son of Man, whose birth incarnate
  Hallows all our human race;
Thou, our Head, who, throned in glory,
  For thine own dost ever plead,
Fill us with thy love and pity,
  Heal our wrongs, and help our need.

2 As thou, Lord, hast lived for others,
    So may we for others live;
  Freely have thy gifts been granted,
    Freely may thy servants give.
  Thine the gold and thine the silver,
    Thine the wealth of land and sea,
  We but stewards of thy bounty,
    Held in solemn trust for thee.

3 Come, O Christ, and reign among us,
    King of Love, and Prince of Peace;
  Hush the storm of strife and passion,
    Bid its cruel discords cease.
  Ah, the past is dark behind us,
    Strewn with wrecks and stained with blood;
  But before us gleams the vision
    Of the coming brotherhood.

4 See the Christlike host advancing,
    High and lowly, great and small,
  Linked in bonds of common service
    For the common Lord of all.
  Thou who prayedst, thou who willest
    That thy people should be one,
  Grant, O grant our hope's fruition:
    Here on earth thy will be done.

Somerset Corry Lowry, 1855-1932

455 (i)   ARTHOG   8585 843

GEORGE THALBEN-BALL

A-men.

(ii)   ANGEL VOICES   8585 843

EDWIN GEORGE MONK, 1819–1900

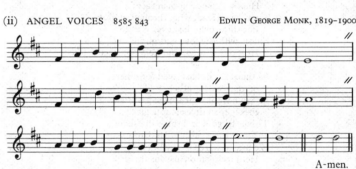

A-men.

ANGEL voices, ever singing
    Round thy throne of light,
Angel harps, for ever ringing,
    Rest not day nor night;
Thousands only live to bless thee,
    And confess thee
      Lord of might.

2 Yea, we know that thou rejoicest
    O'er each work of thine;
Thou didst ears and hands and voices
    For thy praise design;
Craftsman's art and music's measure
    For thy pleasure
      All combine.

3 In thy house, great God, we offer
    Of thine own to thee,
And for thine acceptance proffer,
    All unworthily,
Hearts and minds and hands and
      voices,
    In our choicest
      Psalmody.

4 *Honour, glory, might, and merit*
    Thine shall ever be,
Father, Son, and Holy Spirit,
    Blessèd Trinity.
Of the best that thou hast given,
    Earth and heaven
      Render thee. Amen.

Francis Pott, 1832–1909

456 NARENZA S.M.

Catholicum Hymnologium Germanicum, 1504
Adapted by WILLIAM HENRY HAVERGAL, 1793-1870

WE give thee but thine own,
  Whate'er the gift may be;
All that we have is thine alone,
  A trust, O Lord, from thee.

2 May we thy bounties thus
    As stewards true receive,
And gladly, as thou blessest us,
  To thee our first-fruits give.

3 O hearts are bruised and dead,
    And homes are bare and cold,
And lambs for whom the Shepherd
    bled
Are straying from the fold.

4 To comfort and to bless,
    To find a balm for woe,
To tend the lone and fatherless,
  Is angels' work below.

5 The captive to release,
    To God the lost to bring,
To teach the way of life and peace,
  It is a Christ-like thing.

6 And we believe thy word,
    Though dim our faith may be,—
Whate'er for thine we do, O Lord,
  We do it unto thee.

William Walsham How, 1823-97

457 ABBEY C.M.

Melody from *Scottish Psalter*, 1615

Alternative tune, RICHMOND, No. 422

FILL thou our life, O Lord our God,
  In every part with praise,
That our whole being may proclaim
  Thy being and thy ways.

2 Not for the lip of praise alone,
  Nor ev'n the praising heart
We ask, but for a life made up
  Of praise in every part.

3 Praise in the common things of life,
  Its goings out and in;
Praise in each duty and each deed,
  However small and mean.

4 So shalt thou, gracious Lord, receive
  From us the glory due;
And so shall we begin on earth
  The song for ever new.

5 So shall no part of day or night
  From sacredness be free;
But all our life, in every step,
  Be fellowship with thee.

Horatius Bonar, 1808-89 (altered)

458 SURSUM CORDA 10 10 10 10 ALFRED MORTON SMITH, 1879–1971

LORD of all good, our gifts we bring to thee,
Use them thy holy purpose to fulfil;
Tokens of love and pledges they shall be
That our whole life is offered to thy will.

2 Father, whose bounty all creation shows,
Christ, by whose willing sacrifice we live,
Spirit, from whom all life in fullness flows,
To thee with grateful hearts ourselves we give.

Albert Frederick Bayly

459 PRAETORIUS C.M.
Harmoniae Hymnorum
Scholiae Gorlicensis, Görlitz, 1599
Possibly by MICHAEL PRAETORIUS, 1571–1621

FOUNTAIN of good, to own thy love
Our thankful hearts incline;
What can we render, Lord, to thee,
When all the worlds are thine?

2 But thou hast needy brethren here,
Partakers of thy grace,
Whose names thou wilt thyself confess
Before the Father's face.

3 And in their accents of distress
　　Thy pleading voice is heard;
　In them thou mayst be clothed and fed,
　　And visited and cheered.

4 Thy face, with reverence and with love,
　　We in thy poor would see;
　O may we minister to them,
　　And in them, Lord, to thee.

Philip Doddridge, 1702–51

460 INTERCESSOR
11 10 11 10　　　　CHARLES HUBERT HASTINGS PARRY, 1848–1918

O BROTHER man, fold to thy heart thy brother!
　Where pity dwells, the peace of God is there;
To worship rightly is to love each other,
　Each smile a hymn, each kindly deed a prayer.

2 For he whom Jesus loved hath truly spoken:
　The holier worship which he deigns to bless
Restores the lost, and binds the spirit broken,
　And feeds the widow and the fatherless.

3 Follow with reverent steps the great example
　Of him whose holy work was doing good;
So shall the wide earth seem our Father's temple,
　Each loving life a psalm of gratitude.

4 Then shall all shackles fall; the stormy clangour
　Of wild war-music o'er the earth shall cease;
Love shall tread out the baleful fire of anger,
　And in its ashes plant the tree of peace.

John Greenleaf Whittier, 1807–92

461 ISLEWORTH 8886   SAMUEL HOWARD, 1710-82

Alternative tune, CHILDHOOD, No. 156

O GOD of mercy, God of might,
In love and pity infinite,
Teach us, as ever in thy sight,
  To live our life to thee.

2 And thou, who cam'st on earth to die
That fallen man might live thereby,
O hear us, for to thee we cry,—
  In hope, O Lord, to thee.

3 Teach us the lesson thou hast
    taught,
To feel for those thy blood hath
    bought,
That every word and deed and
    thought
  May work a work for thee.

4 For all are brethren, far and wide,
Since thou, O Lord, for all hast died;
Then teach us, whatsoe'er betide,
  To love them all in thee.

5 In sickness, sorrow, want, or care,
Whate'er it be, 'tis ours to share;
May we, where help is needed, there
  Give help as unto thee.

6 And may thy Holy Spirit move
All those who live, to live in love,
Till thou shalt greet in heaven above
  All those who give to thee.

Godfrey Thring, 1823-1903

462 LÜBECK 7777   Simplified form of a melody in Freylinghausen's *Geistreiches Gesangbuch*, 1704

TAKE my life, and let it be
Consecrated, Lord, to thee.
Take my moments and my days;
Let them flow in ceaseless praise.

2 Take my hands, and let them move
At the impulse of thy love.
Take my feet, and let them be
Swift and beautiful for thee.

3 Take my voice, and let me sing
  Always, only, for my King.
Take my intellect, and use
  Every power as thou shalt choose.

4 Take my will, and make it thine;
  It shall be no longer mine.
Take my heart—it is thine own;
  It shall be thy royal throne.

5 Take my love; my Lord, I pour
  At thy feet its treasure-store.
Take myself, and I will be
  Ever, only, all for thee.

Frances Ridley Havergal, 1836–79 (altered)

463 SONG 34
     (ANGELS' SONG) L.M.
                             ORLANDO GIBBONS,
                             1583–1625 (rhythm altered)

FORTH in thy Name, O Lord, I go,
  My daily labour to pursue,
Thee, only thee, resolved to know
  In all I think, or speak, or do.

2 The task thy wisdom hath assigned
  O let me cheerfully fulfil,
In all my works thy presence find,
  And prove thy good and perfect
    will.

3 Thee may I set at my right hand,
    Whose eyes mine inmost substance see,
And labour on at thy command,
    And offer all my works to thee.

4 Give me to bear thy easy yoke,
    And every moment watch and pray,
And still to things eternal look,
    And hasten to thy glorious day;

5 For thee delightfully employ
    Whate'er thy bounteous grace hath given,
And run my course with even joy,
    And closely walk with thee to heaven.

Charles Wesley, 1707–88 (altered)

464 TYROLESE 7676. D   Tyrolean Carol Melody

For children

THE wise may bring their learning,
  The rich may bring their wealth,
And some may bring their greatness,
  And some their strength and
    health:
We too would bring our treasures
  To offer to the King;
We have no wealth or learning,
  What gifts then shall we bring?

2 We'll bring the many duties
  We have to do each day;
We'll try our best to please him,
  At home, at school, at play:
And better are these treasures
  To offer to our King
Than richest gifts without them;
  Yet these we all may bring.

3 We'll bring him hearts that love him,
  We'll bring him thankful praise,
And souls for ever striving
  To follow in his ways:
And these shall be the treasures
  We offer to the King,
And these are gifts that ever
  Our grateful hearts may bring.

Book of Praise for Children (1881) *and Compilers
of* The BBC Hymn Book

465 WINCHMORE 7779   HILDA MARGARET DODD

For younger children

HANDS to work and feet to run—
    God's good gifts to me and you;
Hands and feet he gave to us
    To help each other the whole day
        through.

2 Eyes to see and ears to hear—
    God's good gifts to me and you;
Eyes and ears he gave to us
    To help each other the whole day
        through.

3 Minds to think and hearts to love—
    God's good gifts to me and you;
Minds and hearts he gave to us
    To help each other the whole day through.

Hilda Margaret Dodd

466 SOUTHWELL   S.M.   Damon's *The Psalmes of David*, 1579 (altered)

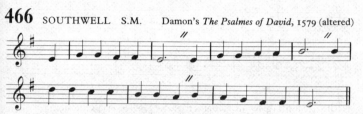

A version with an earlier form of rhythm is at No. 80

For younger children

OUR thoughts go round the world
    To children everywhere;
So much of joy is ours, O God,
    Help us to love and share.

Jessie Eleanor Moore, 1886–1969

467 EVENING PRAYER   8787   JOHN STAINER, 1840–1901

For younger children

TAKE our gifts, O loving Jesus,
    Use them in some lovely way,
For the happiness and comfort
    Of the whole wide world today.

2 Let us be allowed to help you,
    In some plan of loving care,
In some venture for the kingdom,
    By our pence and by our prayer.

Margaret Cropper

WITNESS AND ENCOURAGEMENT

468 IST GOTT FÜR MICH 7676. D

Lutheran Chorale in
Augsburg Gesangbuch, 1609

SPEAK forth thy word, O Father,
Men's hungry minds to feed:
The people starve and perish,
Unconscious of their need;
For so, Lord, thou hast made us
That not alone by bread,
But by thy word of comfort
Our hunger must be fed.

2 The secrets of the atom,
The universe of light,
All wonders of creation
Proclaim thy boundless might:
But only through the witness
From man to man passed on
Dost thou reveal in fullness
The Gospel of thy Son.

3 To each man in his language,
To each man in his home,
By many paths and channels
The faith of Christ may come:
How shall men hear its message
If there be none to preach?
How shall they learn its lesson
If there be none to teach?

4 Take us, then, Lord, and use us
Thy messengers to be:
Our prayers, our gifts, our service
We offer here to thee,
That every man and nation
May learn what we have heard,
And all the minds of millions
Shall feed upon thy word.

Charles Jeffries

414

469 DIEU, NOUS AVONS VU TA GLOIRE
12 12 and refrain

JEAN LANGLAIS

God, your glor-y we have seen in your Son, Full of truth, full of heav'n-ly grace: In Christ make us live,— his love shine on our face, And the na-tions shall see in us the tri-umph you have won. won.

Continue to vv. 2-6

Fine

verses 2-6

2. In the fields of this world his good news he has sown, And sends us out to reap till the har-vest is done.

D.%

3 In his love like a fire that consumes he passed by.
The flame has touched our lips; let us shout, 'Here am I'.

4 He was broken for us, God-forsaken his cry,
And still the bread he breaks; to ourselves we must die.

5 He has trampled the grapes of new life on his cross.
Now drink the cup and live; he has filled it for us.

6 He has founded a kingdom that none shall destroy;
The corner-stone is laid. Go to work: build with joy!

Didier Rimaud
Refrain tr. Ronald Johnson; verses tr. Brian Wren

* *Verse 1 is repeated as a refrain after each verse*

470 ASHTON 9999 7 irregular   REGINALD BARRETT-AYRES

GO ye, said Jesus, and preach the word,
All through the world let its voice be heard,
Publish the tidings o'er land and sea,
Tell men the truth that shall make them free
And carry the Gospel on!

2 Lo, I am with you the whole way through,
Blessing and guiding in all that you do,
Go ye wherever man's feet have trod,
Bearing the gift of the word of God
And carry the Gospel on!

3 Swiftly and surely the truth shall spread,
Winning its way as the word is read,
Lifting the nations till old and young,
Hearing God's voice in their native tongue,
Shall carry the Gospel on!

4 Saviour, obeying thy great command,
Safe in the grasp of thy guiding hand,
Strong in the faith of thy holy word,
Gladly we answer our risen Lord,
And carry the Gospel on!

George Osborne Gregory, 1881–1972

471(i) WINCHESTER OLD C.M.   Este's *Psalter*, 1592

A version with the earlier form of rhythm is at No. 138

(ii) WARWICK C.M.   SAMUEL STANLEY, 1767–1822

LIFT up your heads, ye gates of
brass,
  Ye bars of iron, yield,
And let the King of Glory pass;
  The cross is in the field.

2 Ye armies of the living God,
  His sacramental host,
Where hallowed footstep never trod,
  Take your appointed post.

3 Follow the cross; the ark of peace
  Accompany your path,
To slaves and rebels bring release
  From bondage and from wrath.

4 Though few and small and weak
your bands,
  Strong in your Captain's strength,
Go to the conquest of all lands;
  All must be his at length.

5 O fear not, faint not, halt not now;
  Quit you like men, be strong;
To Christ shall every nation bow,
  And sing with you this song:

6 'Uplifted are the gates of brass;
  The bars of iron yield;
Behold the King of Glory pass!
  The cross hath won the field.'

James Montgomery, 1771–1854

472 PSALM 36 (PSALM 68) 887 887. D *Strasbourg Psalter*, 1539

472 (i) *Verzage nicht, du Häuflein klein*

FEAR not, thou faithful Christian
    flock;
God is thy shelter and thy rock;
Fear not for thy salvation.
Though fierce the foe and dark the
    night,
The Lord of hosts shall be thy
    might,
Christ thine illumination.

Arise! Arise! thy foe defy!
Call on the Name of God most high,
With heavenly succour arm you!
'Gainst world and flesh and powers
    of hell,
Now for his honour quit you well.
Lo! there is naught can harm you.

*Robert Bridges, 1844-1930, based on
Johann Michael Altenburg, 1584-1640
v. 2 omitted*

472 (ii)

FAITH of our fathers, taught of old
By faithful shepherds of the fold,
    The hallowing of our nation;
Thou wast through many a wealthy
    year,
Through many a darkened day of
    fear,
    The rock of our salvation.

Arise, arise, good Christian men,
Your glorious standard raise again,
    The cross of Christ who calls you;
Who bids you live and bids you die
For his great cause, and stands on
    high
    To witness what befalls you.

2 Our fathers held the faith received,
By saints declared, by saints believed,
　By saints in death defended;
Through pain of doubt and bitterness,
Through pain of treason and distress,
　They for the right contended.

Arise, arise, good Christian men,
Your glorious standard raise again,
　The cross of Christ who bought you;
Who leads you forth in this new age,
With long-enduring hearts to wage
　The warfare he has taught you.

Thomas Alexander Lacey, 1853–1931
vv. 2, 4 omitted

473 BLAENWERN 8787. D　　WILLIAM PENFRO ROWLANDS, 1860–1937

Alternative tune, HYFRYDOL, No. 381

LORD, who in thy perfect wisdom
Times and seasons dost arrange,
Working out thy changeless purpose
In a world of ceaseless change;
Thou didst form our ancient nation,
Guiding it through all the days,
To unfold in it thy purpose
To thy glory and thy praise.

2 To our shores remote, benighted,
Barrier of the western waves,
Tidings in thy love thou sentest,
Tidings of the cross that saves.
Saints and heroes strove and suffered
Here thy gospel to proclaim;
We, the heirs of their endeavour,
Tell the honour of their name.

3 Still thine ancient purpose standeth
Every change and chance above;
Still thine ancient Church remaineth,
Witness to thy changeless love.
Grant us vision, Lord, and courage
To fulfil thy work begun;
In the Church and in the nation,
King of kings, thy will be done.

Timothy Rees, 1874–1939 (altered)

419

474 DELHI 888   EDWARD FRANCIS RIMBAULT, 1816–76 (adapted)

CHRIST is the King! O friends rejoice;
Brothers and sisters, with one voice
Make all men know he is your choice.

2 O magnify the Lord, and raise
Anthems of joy and holy praise
For Christ's brave saints of ancient days,

3 Who with a faith for ever new
Followed the King, and round him drew
Thousands of faithful men and true.

4 Let Love's unconquerable might
Your scattered companies unite
In service to the Lord of light:

5 So shall God's will on earth be done,
New lamps be lit, new tasks begun,
And the whole Church at last be one.

George Kennedy Allen Bell, 1883–1958

475 LIMPSFIELD 7373 7773   JOSIAH BOOTH, 1852–1929

WE have heard a joyful sound,—
'Jesus saves!'
Spread the gladness all around:
'Jesus saves!'
Bear the news to every land,
Climb the steeps and cross the waves;
Onward!—'tis our Lord's command.
Jesus saves!

2 Waft it on the rolling tide:
'Jesus saves!'
Tell to sinners far and wide,
'Jesus saves!'
Sing, ye islands of the sea;
Echo back, ye ocean caves;
Earth shall keep her jubilee:
Jesus saves!

3 Sing above the battle's strife
'Jesus saves!'
By his death and endless life
'Jesus saves!'
Sing it softly through the gloom,
When the heart for mercy craves;
Sing in triumph o'er the tomb,
'Jesus saves!'

4 Give the winds a mighty voice,
'Jesus saves!'
Let the nations now rejoice:
Jesus saves!
Shout salvation full and free
To every strand that ocean laves,—
This our song of victory,
'Jesus saves!'

Priscilla Jane Owens, 1829-1907

476 BISHOPGARTH 8787. D   ARTHUR SEYMOUR SULLIVAN, 1842–1900

'FOR my sake and the Gospel's, go
  And tell redemption's story';
His heralds answer, 'Be it so,
  And thine, Lord, all the glory!'
They preach his birth, his life, his cross,
  The love of his atonement
For whom they count the world but loss,
  His Easter, his enthronement.

2 Hark! hark! the trump of jubilee
  Proclaims to every nation,
From pole to pole, by land and sea,
  Glad tidings of salvation.
Still on and on the anthems spread,
  Of alleluia voices;
In concert with the holy dead,
  The warrior Church rejoices.

3 He comes whose advent-trumpet drowns
    The last of time's evangels,
  Immanuel, crowned with many crowns,
    The Lord of saints and angels.
  O Life, Light, Love, the great I AM
    Triune, who changest never,
  The throne of God and of the Lamb
    Is thine, and thine for ever.

Edward Henry Bickersteth, 1825–1906 (*altered*)

477 CARLISLE S.M.   CHARLES LOCKHART, 1745–1815

RISE up, O men of God!
  Have done with lesser things;
Give heart and soul and mind and
    strength
  To serve the King of kings.

2 Rise up, O men of God!
  His Kingdom tarries long;
Bring in the day of brotherhood,
  And end the night of wrong.

3 Rise up, O men of God!
  The Church for you doth wait:
His strength shall make your spirit
    strong,
  Her service make you great.

4 Lift high the cross of Christ!
  Tread where his feet have trod;
As brothers of the Son of Man
  Rise up, O men of God!

William Pierson Merrill, 1867-1954 (altered)

478 ORIENTIS PARTIBUS 7777   Medieval French Melody (adapted)

SOLDIERS of the cross, arise!
  Gird you with your armour
    bright;
Mighty are your enemies,
  Hard the battle ye must fight.

2 O'er a faithless fallen world
  Raise your banner in the sky;
Let it float there wide unfurled;
  Bear it onward; lift it high.

3 'Mid the homes of want and woe,
  Strangers to the living word,
Let the Saviour's herald go,
  Let the voice of hope be heard.

4 Where the shadows deepest lie,
  Carry truth's unsullied ray;
Where are crimes of blackest dye,
  There the saving sign display.

5 To the weary and the worn
  Tell of realms where sorrows
    cease;
To the outcast and forlorn
  Speak of mercy and of peace.

6 Guard the helpless; seek the
    strayed;
  Comfort troubles; banish grief;
In the might of God arrayed,
  Scatter sin and unbelief.

7 Be the banner still unfurled,
  Still unsheathed the Spirit's sword,
Till the kingdoms of the world
  Are the Kingdom of the Lord.

William Walsham How, 1823-97

479 (i) ARMAGEDDON 6565 Ter.

German Melody,
perhaps by LUISE REICHARDT, 1853,
adapted by JOHN GOSS, 1800–80

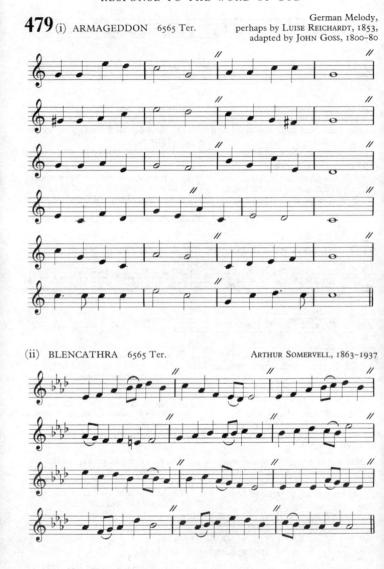

(ii) BLENCATHRA 6565 Ter.

ARTHUR SOMERVELL, 1863–1937

WHO is on the Lord's side?
  Who will serve the King?
Who will be his helpers
  Other lives to bring?
Who will leave the world's side?
  Who will face the foe?
Who is on the Lord's side?
  Who for him will go?
    By thy call of mercy,
      By thy grace divine,
    We are on the Lord's side;
      Saviour, we are thine.

2 Jesus, thou hast bought us,
    Not with gold or gem,
  But with thine own life-blood,
    For thy diadem.
  With thy blessing filling
    Each who comes to thee,
  Thou hast made us willing,
    Thou hast made us free.
      By thy grand redemption,
        By thy grace divine,
      We are on the Lord's side;
        Saviour, we are thine.

3 Fierce may be the conflict,
    Strong may be the foe,
  But the King's own army
    None can overthrow.
  Round his standard ranging,
    Victory is secure,
  For his truth unchanging
    Makes the triumph sure.
      Joyfully enlisting,
        By thy grace divine,
      We are on the Lord's side;
        Saviour, we are thine.

4 Chosen to be soldiers
    In an alien land,
  Chosen, called, and faithful,
    For our Captain's band,
  In the service royal
    Let us not grow cold;
  Let us be right loyal,
    Noble, true, and bold.
      Master, thou wilt keep us,
        By thy grace divine,
      Always on the Lord's side,
        Saviour, always thine.

Frances Ridley Havergal, 1836–79

480 ST. GERTRUDE
6565. D and refrain

ARTHUR SEYMOUR SULLIVAN, 1842–1900

REFRAIN

ONWARD! Christian soldiers,
    Marching as to war,
With the cross of Jesus
    Going on before.
Christ, the Royal Master,
    Leads against the foe;
Forward into battle,
    See! his banners go:
        Onward! Christian soldiers,
        Marching as to war,
        With the cross of Jesus
        Going on before.

2 At the sign of triumph
    Satan's legions flee;
On then, Christian soldiers,
    On to victory!
Hell's foundations quiver
    At the shout of praise;
Brothers, lift your voices,
    Loud your anthems raise:

3 Like a mighty army
    Moves the Church of God;
Brothers, we are treading
    Where the saints have trod.
We are not divided,
    All one body we,
One in hope, in doctrine,
    One in charity:

4 Crowns and thrones may perish,
    Kingdoms rise and wane,
But the Church of Jesus
    Constant will remain;
Gates of hell can never
    'Gainst that Church prevail;
We have Christ's own promise,
    And that cannot fail:

5 Onward, then, ye people!
    Join our happy throng;
Blend with ours your voices
    In the triumph song:
'Glory, laud, and honour
    Unto Christ the King!'
This, through countless ages,
    Mén and angels sing:

Sabine Baring-Gould, 1834–1924

481 MORNING LIGHT 7676. D GEORGE JAMES WEBB, 1803–87

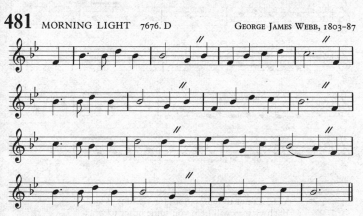

STAND up! stand up for Jesus,
    Ye soldiers of the cross!
Lift high his royal banner;
    It must not suffer loss.
From victory to victory
    His army he shall lead,
Till every foe is vanquished,
    And Christ is Lord indeed.

2 Stand up! stand up for Jesus!
    The trumpet-call obey;
Forth to the mighty conflict
    In this his glorious day!
Ye that are men, now serve him
    Against unnumbered foes;
Your courage rise with danger,
    And strength to strength oppose.

3 Stand up! stand up for Jesus!
    Stand in his strength alone;
The arm of flesh will fail you;
    Ye dare not trust your own.
Put on the gospel armour,
    Each piece put on with prayer;
Where duty calls, or danger,
    Be never wanting there.

4 Stand up! stand up for Jesus!
    The strife will not be long;
This day the noise of battle,
    The next the victor's song.
To him that overcometh
    A crown of life shall be;
He with the King of Glory
    Shall reign eternally.

George Duffield, 1818–88

482 FORTITUDE
11 11 11 12 and refrain

HORATIO RICHMOND PALMER, 1834-1907

YIELD not to temptation, for yielding is sin;
Each victory will help you some other to win;
Fight manfully onward; dark passions subdue;
Look ever to Jesus, he will carry you through.
> *Ask the Saviour to help you,*
> *Comfort, strengthen, and keep you;*
> *He is willing to aid you;*
> *He will carry you through.*

2 Shun evil companions; bad language disdain;
God's Name hold in reverence, nor take it in vain;
Be thoughtful and earnest, kind-hearted and true;
Look ever to Jesus, he will carry you through.

3 To him that o'ercometh God giveth a crown;
Through faith we shall conquer, though often cast down;
He who is our Saviour our strength will renew;
Look ever to Jesus, he will carry you through.

Horatio Richmond Palmer, 1834-1907

483 DEUS TUORUM MILITUM
(GRENOBLE) L.M.

Grenoble Antiphoner, 1753

[For No. 257]

A - men.

GO, labour on: spend and be spent,
    Thy joy to do the Father's will;
It is the way the Master went;
    Should not the servant tread it still?

2 Go, labour on while it is day:
    The world's dark night is hastening on;
Speed, speed thy work; cast sloth away;
    It is not thus that souls are won.

3 Men die in darkness at thy side,
    Without a hope to cheer the tomb;
Take up the torch and wave it wide,
    The torch that lights time's thickest gloom.

4 Toil on, faint not, keep watch, and pray;
    Be wise the erring soul to win;
Go forth into the world's highway,
    Compel the wanderer to come in.

5 Toil on, and in thy toil rejoice;
    For toil comes rest, for exile home;
Soon shalt thou hear the Bridegroom's voice,
    The midnight peal, 'Behold, I come!'

Horatius Bonar, 1808-89

484 (i) NORMAN 8787. D

Dole's *Verstimmiges Choralbuch*,
Leipzig, 1785

(ii) COURAGE, BROTHER 8787. D   ARTHUR SEYMOUR SULLIVAN, 1842-1900

Trust in God,

Trust in God,   Trust in God, and   do the right.

COURAGE, brother! do not stumble,
   Though thy path be dark as night;
There's a star to guide the humble:
   'Trust in God, and do the right.'
Let the road be rough and dreary,
   And its end far out of sight,
Foot it bravely; strong or weary,
   *Trust in God, and do the right.

2 Perish policy and cunning,
   Perish all that fears the light!
Whether losing, whether winning,
   Trust in God, and do the right.

Some will hate thee, some will love
   thee,
   Some will flatter, some will slight;
Cease from man, and look above thee:
   Trust in God, and do the right.

3 Simple rule, and safest guiding,
   Inward peace, and inward might,
Star upon our path abiding,—
   Trust in God, and do the right.
Courage, brother! do not stumble,
   Though thy path be dark as night;
There's a star to guide the humble:
   'Trust in God, and do the right.'

Norman Macleod, 1812–72

* *When this hymn is sung to Tune* (ii) COURAGE BROTHER, *the words 'Trust in God'
must be sung three times in the last line of each verse*

485(i) WARRINGTON
L.M.   RALPH HARRISON, 1748–1810, *Sacred Harmony*, 1784

(ii) LLEF L.M.   GRIFFITH HUGH JONES (GUTYN ARFON), 1849–1919

LORD, speak to me, that I may speak
  In living echoes of thy tone;
As thou hast sought, so let me seek
  Thy erring children lost and lone.

2 O lead me, Lord, that I may lead
  The wandering and the wavering
    feet;
O feed me, Lord, that I may feed
  Thy hungering ones with manna
    sweet.

3 O strengthen me, that, while I stand
  Firm on the rock, and strong in
    thee,
I may stretch out a loving hand
  To wrestlers with the troubled sea.

4 O teach me, Lord, that I may teach
  The precious things thou dost
    impart;
And wing my words, that they may
    reach
  The hidden depths of many a heart.

5 O give thine own sweet rest to me,
  That I may speak with soothing
    power
A word in season, as from thee,
  To weary ones in needful hour.

6 O fill me with thy fullness, Lord,
  Until my very heart o'erflow
In kindling thought and glowing
    word,
  Thy love to tell, thy praise to show.

7 O use me, Lord, use even me,
  Just as thou wilt, and when, and where,
Until thy blessèd face I see,
  Thy rest, thy joy, thy glory share.

Frances Ridley Havergal, 1836–79

431

486 HEADINGTON 11 6 11 6   KENNETH LEIGHTON

LOVER of souls and Lord of all the living,
    Whose service maketh free,
Hear us who once again ourselves are giving
    Thy servants sure to be.

2 Thou who dost bear the whole world's tribulation
    Upon thy heart alone,
Thou who hast bought us by thy cross and passion,
    And chos'n us for thine own,

3 Show us thyself, that we may know their sorrow
    Who have not seen thy face;
Show us their darkness, and the radiant morrow
    Of thine eternal grace.

4 Show us the love wherewith thy heart is burning,
    The travail of thy soul:
Grant us to share thy heart's desire and yearning
    That thou mightst make them whole.

*5 Make strong our hands, by thine own great hand grasping,
    Avail and guide our youth;
Grant to us now life that is everlasting,
    And then to know thy truth.

        * *This verse may be omitted*

                    Helen Waddell, 1889–1965

487 JERUSALEM D.L.M.   CHARLES HUBERT HASTINGS PARRY, 1848–1918

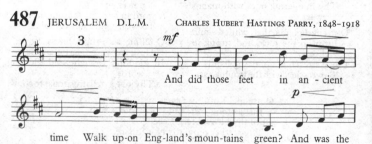

And did those feet in an-cient time Walk up-on Eng-land's moun-tains green? And was the

ho - ly Lamb of God On Eng-land's plea-sant pas - tures seen? And did the coun - te-nance di - vine Shine forth up - on our cloud-ed hills? And was Je - ru - sa-lem build-ed here Among these dark sa - tan - ic mills?

Bring me my bow of burn - ing gold! Bring me my ar-rows of de - sire! Bring me my spear! O clouds, un - fold! Bring me my cha - ri - ot of fire! I will not cease from men - tal fight, Nor shall my sword sleep in my hand, Till we have built Je - ru - sa - lem In Eng-land's green and plea - sant land.

William Blake, 1757–1827

488 LUMETTO 10 11 10 10   DAVID EVANS, 1874–1948

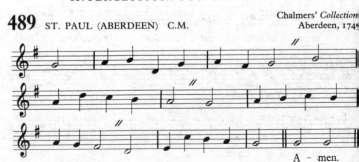

For younger children

JESUS bids us shine with a pure, clear light,
Like a little candle burning in the night.
In this world is darkness; so let us shine,
You in your small corner, and I in mine.

2 Jesus bids us shine, first of all for him;
Well he sees and knows it, if our light grows dim:
He looks down from heaven to see us shine,
You in your small corner, and I in mine.

3 Jesus bids us shine, then, for all around;
Many kinds of darkness in the world are found—
Sin, and want, and sorrow; so we must shine,
You in your small corner, and I in mine.

Susan Warner, 1819–85

INTERCESSION: FOR THE CHURCH

489 ST. PAUL (ABERDEEN) C.M.   Chalmers' *Collection*
                                          Aberdeen, 1749

A - men.

A version with the later form of rhythm is at No. 72 (i)

INTERCESSION: FOR THE CHURCH

I JOY'D when to the house of God,
  Go up, they said to me.
Jerusalem, within thy gates
  Our feet shall standing be.

2 Pray that Jerusalem may have
  Peace and felicity:
Let them that love thee and thy
    peace
Have still prosperity.

3 Therefore I wish that peace may still
  Within thy walls remain,
And ever may thy palaces
  Prosperity retain.

4 Now, for my friends' and brethren's
    sakes,
  Peace be in thee, I'll say.
And for the house of God our Lord,
  I'll seek thy good alway.

5 *To Father, Son, and Holy Ghost,*
  The God whom we adore,
  Be glory, as it was, and is,
  And shall be evermore. Amen.

490 HELFER MEINER ARMEN SEELE
777 and refrain
Heilige Seelenlust, 1657

We beseech thee, hear us.

JESUS, with thy Church abide;
Be her Saviour, Lord, and Guide,
While on earth her faith is tried:
  We beseech thee, hear us.

2 Keep her life and doctrine pure;
Grant her patience to endure,
Trusting in thy promise sure:

3 May she one in doctrine be,
One in truth and charity,
Winning all to faith in thee:

4 May her scattered children be
From reproach of evil free,
Blameless witnesses for thee:

5 May she thus all glorious be,
Spotless and from wrinkle free,
Pure and bright, and worthy thee:

Thomas Benson Pollock, 1836–96

491 ISTE CONFESSOR
(POITIERS) 11 11 11 5

Poitiers Vesperale, 1746

Alternative tune, DIVA SERVATRIX, No. 568

Christe, du Beistand deiner Kreuzgemeine

LORD of our life, and God of our salvation,
Star of our night, and Hope of every nation,
Hear and receive thy Church's supplication,
    Lord God Almighty.

2 See round thine ark the hungry billows curling;
See how thy foes their banners are unfurling;
Lord, while their darts envenomed they are hurling,
    Thou canst preserve us.

3 Lord, thou canst help when earthly armour faileth;
Lord, thou canst save when deadly sin assaileth;
Lord, o'er thy rock nor death nor hell prevaileth;
    Grant us thy peace, Lord.

4 Grant us thy help till foes are backward driven;
Grant them thy truth that they may be forgiven;
Grant peace on earth, and, after we have striven,
    Peace in thy heaven.

*Philip Pusey, 1799–1855;
based on Matthäus Apelles von Löwenstern, 1594–1648*

492 SONG 1   10 10 10 10   10 10

ORLANDO GIBBONS, 1583–1625

INTERCESSION: FOR THE CHURCH

O THOU, who at thy Eucharist didst pray
    That all thy Church might be for ever one,
Grant us at every Eucharist to say,
    With longing heart and soul, 'Thy will be done.'
O may we all one bread, one body be,
One through this sacrament of unity.

2 For all thy Church, O Lord, we intercede;
    Make thou our sad divisions soon to cease;
Draw us the nearer each to each, we plead,
    By drawing all to thee, O Prince of Peace;
Thus may we all one bread, one body be,
One through this sacrament of unity.

3 We pray thee too for wanderers from thy fold;
    O bring them back, good Shepherd of the sheep,
Back to the faith which saints believed of old,
    Back to the Church which still that faith doth keep;
Soon may we all one bread, one body be,
One through this sacrament of unity.

4 So, Lord, at length when sacraments shall cease,
    May we be one with all thy Church above,
One with thy saints in one unbroken peace,
    One with thy saints in one unbounded love:
More blessèd still, in peace and love to be
One with the Trinity in Unity.

William Harry Turton, 1856-1938
based on St. John 17: 11

INTERCESSION: FOR THE CHURCH'S MISSION

493 NARENZA S.M.

Catholicum Hymnologium Germanicum, 1504
Adapted by WILLIAM HENRY HAVERGAL, 1793–1870

A - men.

PSALM 67

LORD, bless and pity us,
  Shine on us with thy face:
That the earth thy way, and
    nations all
  May know thy saving grace.

2 Let people praise thee, Lord;
  Let people all thee praise.
O let the nations all be glad,
  In songs their voices raise:

3 Thou wilt justly people judge,
  On earth rule nations all.
Let people praise thee, Lord; let
    them
  Praise thee, both great and small.

4 The earth her fruit shall yield,
  Our God shall blessing send.
God shall us bless; men shall him
    fear
  Unto earth's utmost end.

5 *To thee be glory, Lord,*
  Whom heaven and earth adore,
To Father, Son, and Holy Ghost,
  One God for evermore. Amen.

494 MOSCOW 664 6664

FELICE DE GIARDINI, 1716–96

THOU whose almighty word
Chaos and darkness heard
 And took their flight,
Hear us, we humbly pray,
And, where the gospel day
Sheds not its glorious ray,
 Let there be light.

2 Thou who didst come to bring,
On thy redeeming wing,
 Healing and sight,
Health to the sick in mind,
Sight to the inly blind,
O now to all mankind
 Let there be light.

3 Spirit of truth and love,
Life-giving, holy Dove,
 Speed forth thy flight;
Move o'er the waters' face,
Bearing the lamp of grace,
And in earth's darkest place
 Let there be light.

4 Blessèd and holy Three,
Glorious Trinity,
 Wisdom, Love, Might,
Boundless as ocean's tide
Rolling in fullest pride,
Through the world far and wide
 Let there be light.

John Marriott, 1780–1825

495 HAMPTON S.M.   Williams' *Psalmody in Miniature, c. 1770*

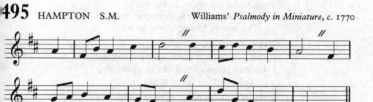

O LORD our God, arise!
The cause of truth maintain,
And wide o'er all the peopled world
Extend her blessèd reign.

2 Thou Prince of Life, arise!
Nor let thy glory cease;
Far spread the conquests of thy grace,
And bless the earth with peace.

3 Thou Holy Ghost, arise!
Expand thy quickening wing,
And o'er a dark and ruined world
Let light and order spring.

4 All on the earth, arise!
To God the Saviour sing;
From shore to shore, from earth to heaven,
Let echoing anthems ring.

Ralph Wardlaw, 1779–1853

496 WINCHESTER NEW
(CRASSELIUS) L.M.

Adapted from a melody in
Musikalisches Hand-Buch, Hamburg, 1690

O SPIRIT of the living God,
  In all thy plenitude of grace,
Where'er the foot of man hath trod,
  Descend on our apostate race.

2 Give tongues of fire and hearts of love,
  To preach the reconciling word;
Give power and unction from above,
  Whene'er the joyful sound is heard.

3 Be darkness, at thy coming, light;
  Confusion order, in thy path;
Souls without strength inspire with might;
  Bid mercy triumph over wrath.

4 O Spirit of the Lord, prepare
  All the round earth her God to meet;
Breathe thou abroad like morning air,
  Till hearts of stone begin to beat.

5 Baptize the nations; far and nigh
  The triumphs of the cross record;
The Name of Jesus glorify,
  Till every kindred call him Lord.

James Montgomery, 1771-1854

497 RATISBON
7777 77

Werner's *Choralbuch*, Leipzig, 1815

Alternative tune, HEATHLANDS, No. 236

440

GOD of mercy, God of grace,
Show the brightness of thy face;
Shine upon us, Saviour, shine,
Fill thy Church with light divine,
And thy saving health extend
Unto earth's remotest end.

2 Let the people praise thee, Lord;
Be by all that live adored;
Let the nations shout and sing
Glory to their Saviour King,
At thy feet their tribute pay,
And thy holy will obey.

3 Let the people praise thee, Lord;
Earth shall then her fruits afford,
God to man his blessing give,
Man to God devoted live—
All below and all above,
One in joy and light and love.

Henry Francis Lyte, 1793–1847

498 TRURO L.M.   Williams' *Psalmodia Evangelica, 1789*

ARM of the Lord, awake, awake!
Put on thy strength, the nations shake,
And let the world, adoring, see
Triumphs of mercy wrought by thee.

2 Say to the heathen from thy throne,
'I am Jehovah, God alone';
Thy voice their idols shall confound,
And cast their altars to the ground.

3 Let Zion's time of favour come;
O bring the tribes of Israel home;
And let our wondering eyes behold
Gentiles and Jews in Jesus' fold.

4 Almighty God, thy grace proclaim
In every clime of every name;
Let adverse powers before thee fall,
And crown the Saviour Lord of all.

William Shrubsole, 1759–1829

499 DURROW D.C.M.   Irish Traditional Melody

ETERNAL God, whose power
  upholds
  Both flower and flaming star,
To whom there is no here nor there,
  No time, no near nor far,
No alien race, no foreign shore,
  No child unsought, unknown,
O send us forth, thy prophets true,
  To make all lands thine own!

2 O God of love, whose spirit wakes
  In every human breast,
Whom love, and love alone, can
  know,
  In whom all hearts find rest,
Help us to spread thy gracious reign,
  Till greed and hate shall cease,
And kindness dwell in human hearts,
  And all the earth find peace!

3 O God of truth, whom science seeks
  And reverent souls adore,
Who lightest every earnest mind
  Of every clime and shore,
Dispel the gloom of error's night,
  Of ignorance and fear,
Until true wisdom from above
  Shall make life's pathway clear!

4 O God of beauty, oft revealed
  In dreams of human art,
In speech that flows to melody,
  In holiness of heart;
Teach us to ban all ugliness
  That blinds our eyes to thee,
Till all shall know the loveliness
  Of lives made fair and free.

5 O God of righteousness and grace,
  Seen in the Christ, thy Son,
Whose life and death reveal thy face,
  By whom thy will was done,
Inspire thy heralds of good news
  To live thy life divine,
Till Christ is formed in all mankind,
  And every land is thine!

Henry Hallam Tweedy, 1868–1953

500 MILTON ABBAS 664 6664   Eric Harding Thiman

CHRIST for the world we sing!
The world to Christ we bring
  With fervent prayer;
The wayward and the lost,
By restless passions tossed,
Redeemed at countless cost
  From dark despair.

2 Christ for the world we sing!
The world to Christ we bring
  With one accord;
With us the work to share,
With us reproach to dare,
With us the cross to bear,
  For Christ our Lord.

3 Christ for the world we sing!
The world to Christ we bring
  With joyful song;
The new-born souls, whose days,
Reclaimed from error's ways,
Inspired with hope and praise,
  To Christ belong.

Samuel Wolcott, 1813–86

501 DUNBLANE CATHEDRAL
10 10 10 10

ARCHIE FAIRBAIRN BARNES, 1878–1960
(altered)

For children

FAR round the world thy children sing their song:
From East and West their voices sweetly blend,
Praising the Lord in whom young lives are strong,
Jesus our Guide, our Hero, and our Friend.

2 Where thy wide ocean, wave on rolling wave,
Beats through the ages, on each island shore,
They praise their Lord, whose hand alone can save,
Whose sea of love surrounds them evermore.

3 Still there are lands where none have seen thy face,
Children whose hearts have never shared thy joy;
Yet thou wouldst pour on these thy radiant grace,
Give thy glad strength to every girl and boy.

4 All round the world let children sing thy song:
From East and West their voices sweetly blend,
Praising the Lord in whom young lives are strong,
Jesus our Guide, our Hero, and our Friend.

Basil Joseph Mathews, 1879–1951

444

502 SHIPSTON 8787

English Traditional Melody,
collected by LUCY BROADWOOD, 1858–1929

For children

GOD of heaven, hear our singing;
   Only little ones are we,
Yet, a great petition bringing,
   Father, now we come to thee.

2 Let thy Kingdom come, we pray thee;
   Let the world in thee find rest;
Let all know thee, and obey thee,
   Loving, praising, blessing, blest.

3 Let the sweet and joyful story
   Of the Saviour's wondrous love,
Wake on earth a song of glory,
   Like the angels' song above.

4 Father, send the glorious hour,
   Every heart be thine alone,
For the Kingdom, and the power,
   And the glory are thine own.

Frances Ridley Havergal, 1836–79

INTERCESSION: FOR THE WORLD

503 NORTHBROOK
11 10 11 10
REGINALD SPARSHATT THATCHER, 1888-1957

THY love, O God, has all mankind created,
 And led thy people to this present hour:
In Christ we see love's glory consummated;
 Thy Spirit manifests his living power.

2 We bring thee, Lord, in fervent intercession
 The children of thy world-wide family:
With contrite hearts we offer our confession,
 For we have sinned against thy charity.

3 From out the darkness of our hope's frustration;
 From all the broken idols of our pride;
We turn to seek thy truth's illumination;
 And find thy mercy waiting at our side.

4 In pity look upon thy children's striving
 For life and freedom, peace and brotherhood;
Till, at the fullness of thy truth arriving,
 We find in Christ the crown of every good.

5 Inspire thy Church, mid earth's discordant voices,
 To preach the gospel of her Lord above;
Until the day this warring world rejoices
 To hear the mighty harmonies of love,

6 Until the tidings men have long awaited,
 From north to south, from east to west shall ring;
And all mankind, by Jesus liberated,
 Proclaims in jubilation, Christ is King!

Albert Frederick Bayly

504 ST. VENANTIUS L.M. *Paris Antiphoner, 1681*

Alternative tune, MELCOMBE, No. 436

O GOD of love, O King of peace,
Make wars throughout the world to cease;
The wrath of sinful man restrain:
Give peace, O God, give peace again.

2 Remember, Lord, thy works of old,
The wonders that our fathers told;
Remember not our sin's dark stain:
Give peace, O God, give peace again.

3 Whom shall we trust but thee, O Lord?
Where rest but on thy faithful word?
None ever called on thee in vain:
Give peace, O God, give peace again.

4 Where saints and angels dwell above,
All hearts are knit in holy love;
O bind us in that heavenly chain:
Give peace, O God, give peace again.

Henry Williams Baker, 1821–77

447

505 RINKART (KOMMT SEELEN)
6767 6666

JOHANN SEBASTIAN BACH, 1685–1750

Alternative tune, NUN DANKET, No. 368

CHRIST is the world's true light,
  Its captain of salvation,
The daystar clear and bright
  Of every man and nation;
New life, new hope awakes,
  Where'er men own his sway:
Freedom her bondage breaks,
  And night is turned to day.

2 In Christ all races meet,
    Their ancient feuds forgetting,
  The whole round world complete,
    From sunrise to its setting:
  When Christ is throned as Lord,
    Men shall forsake their fear,
  To ploughshare beat the sword,
    To pruning-hook the spear.

3 One Lord, in one great name
    Unite us all who own thee;
  Cast out our pride and shame
    That hinder to enthrone thee;
  The world has waited long,
    Has travailed long in pain;
  To heal its ancient wrong,
    Come, Prince of Peace, and reign.

George Wallace Briggs, 1875–1959

506 O AMOR QUAM ECSTATICUS
L.M.

Rouen Antiphoner, 1728,
adapted by BASIL HARWOOD, 1859-1949

O GOD of our divided world,
Light up thy way where our ways part.
Restore the kinship of our birth,
Revive in us a single heart—

2 A heart that sees in Christ its goal
And cares with Christ for every man,
That seeks beyond all outward forms
The brotherhood of God's own plan.

3 Where we have failed to understand
Our brother's heart, O Lord forgive.
Grant us the confidence to share
The lights whereby our brothers live.

4 Then shall we know a richer world
Where all divisions are disowned,
Where heart joins heart and hand joins hand,
Where man is loved and Christ enthroned.

Alan Norman Phillips

507 OLD 124TH
11 10 11 10 and refrain

French–Genevan Psalter, 1551
(rhythm altered)

REFRAIN

FATHER Eternal, Ruler of Creation,
  Spirit of Life, which moved ere form was made,
Through the thick darkness covering every nation,
  Light to man's blindness, O be thou our aid!
  Thy Kingdom come, O Lord, thy will be done.

2 Races and peoples, lo! we stand divided,
    And, sharing not our griefs, no joy can share;
  By wars and tumults Love is mocked, derided,
    His conquering cross no kingdom wills to bear;

3 Envious of heart, blind-eyed, with tongues confounded,
    Nation by nation still goes unforgiven;
  In wrath and fear, by jealousies surrounded,
    Building proud towers which shall not reach to heaven.

4 Lust of possession worketh desolations;
    There is no meekness in the sons of earth.
  Led by no star, the rulers of the nations
    Still fail to bring us to the blissful birth.

5 How shall we love thee, holy, hidden Being,
    If we love not the world which thou hast made?
  O, give us brother-love, for better seeing
    Thy Word made flesh and in a manger laid.

Laurence Housman, 1865–1959

508 FINNART L.M.   KENNETH GEORGE FINLAY

ALMIGHTY Father, who dost give
The gift of life to all who live,
Look down on all earth's sin and strife,
And lift us to a nobler life.

2 Lift up our hearts, O King of kings,
To brighter hopes and kindlier things,
To visions of a larger good,
And holier dreams of brotherhood.

3 Thy world is weary of its pain,
Of selfish greed and fruitless gain,
Of tarnished honour, falsely strong,
And all its ancient deeds of wrong.

4 Hear thou the prayer thy servants pray,
Uprising from all lands today,
And o'er the vanquished powers of sin
O bring thy great salvation in.

John Howard Bertram Masterman, 1867–1933

509 SANCTA CIVITAS 8686 86   HERBERT HOWELLS

1. O Ho - ly Ci - ty, seen of John, Where
2. O shame to us who rest con - tent While
3. Give us, O God, the strength to build The
4. Al - rea - dy in the mind of God That

Christ, the Lamb, doth reign, With - in whose four-square
lust and greed for gain In street and shop and
Ci - ty that hath stood Too long a dream, whose
Ci - ty ri - seth fair: Lo, how its splen - dour

walls shall come No night, nor need, nor pain, And
ten - e - ment Wring gold from hu - man pain, And
laws are love, Whose ways are bro - ther - hood, And
chal - len - ges The souls that great - ly dare Yea,

where the tears are wiped from eyes That
bit - ter lips in blind des - pair Cry,
where the sun that shi - neth is God's
bids us seize the whole of life And

shall not weep a - gain!
'Christ hath died in vain!'
grace for hu - man good.
build its glor - y there.

Walter Russell Bowie, 1882-1969
(Suggested by St. John's vision in Revelation 21)

510 RUSTINGTON
8787 87 and refrain

CHARLES HUBERT HASTINGS PARRY, 1848–1918

Alternative tune, BLAENWERN, No. 473

LORD of light, whose Name outshineth
    All the stars and suns of space,
Deign to make us thy co-workers
    In the Kingdom of thy grace;
Use us to fulfil thy purpose
    In the gift of Christ thy Son:
Father, as in highest heaven,
    So on earth thy will be done.

2 By the toil of lowly workers
    In some far outlying field;
By the courage where the radiance
    Of the cross is still revealed;
By the victories of meekness,
    Through reproach and suffering
        won,—

3 Grant that knowledge, still increas-
        ing,
    At thy feet may lowly kneel;
With thy grace our triumphs hallow,
    With thy charity our zeal;
Lift the nations from the shadows
    To the gladness of the sun:

4 By the prayers of faithful watchmen,
    Never silent day or night;
By the cross of Jesus bringing
    Peace to men, and healing light;
By the love that passeth knowledge,
    Making all thy children one:

Howell Elvet Lewis, 1860–1953

511 HILLSBOROUGH S.M.   JOHN GARDNER

O DAY of God, draw nigh
In beauty and in power,
Come with thy timeless judgment now
To match our present hour.

2 Bring to our troubled minds,
Uncertain and afraid,
The quiet of a steadfast faith,
Calm of a call obeyed.

3 Bring justice to our land,
That all may dwell secure,
And finely build for days to come
Foundations that endure.

4 Bring to our world of strife
Thy sovereign word of peace,
That war may haunt the earth no more
And desolation cease.

5 O Day of God, draw nigh
As at creation's birth;
Let there be light again, and set
Thy judgments in the earth.

Robert Balgarnie Young Scott

512 O JESU MI DULCISSIME
L.M.   *Clausener Gesangbuch*, 1653

Alternative tune, BRESLAU, No. 430

WHERE cross the crowded ways of life,
Where sound the cries of race and clan,
Above the noise of selfish strife,
We hear thy voice, O Son of Man.

2 In haunts of wretchedness and need,
On shadowed thresholds dark with fears,
From paths where hide the lures of greed,
We catch the vision of thy tears.

3 From tender childhood's helplessness,
   From woman's grief, man's burdened toil,
 From famished souls, from sorrow's stress,
   Thy heart has never known recoil.

4 The cup of water given for thee
   Still holds the freshness of thy grace;
 Yet long these multitudes to see
   The sweet compassion of thy face.

5 O Master, from the mountain side
   Make haste, to heal these hearts of pain;
 Among these restless throngs abide,
   O tread the city's streets again:

6 Till sons of men shall learn thy love,
   And follow where thy feet have trod;
 Till glorious from thy heaven above,
   Shall come the City of our God.

Frank Mason North, 1850–1935

513 SEARCHING FOR LAMBS
C.M.

English Traditional Carol Melody
(adapted)

GOD of the pastures, hear our prayer,
Lord of the growing seed,
Bless thou the fields, for to thy care
We look in all our need.

2 God of the rivers in their course,
Lord of the swelling sea,
Where man must strive with nature's force,
Do thou his guardian be.

3 God of the dark and sombre mine,
Lord of its hard-won store,
In toil and peril all be thine;
Thy help and strength are sure.

4 God of the city's throbbing heart,
Lord of its industry,
Bid greed and base deceit depart,
Give true prosperity.

5 God of authority and right,
Lord of all earthly power,
To those who rule us grant thy light,
Thy wisdom be their dower.

6 God of the nations, King of men,
Lord of each humble soul,
We seek thy gracious aid again,
Come down and make us whole.

Thomas Charles Hunter Clare

514   SONG 1   10 10 10 10   10 10   ORLANDO GIBBONS, 1583-1625

ETERNAL Ruler of the ceaseless round
    Of circling planets singing on their way,
Guide of the nations from the night profound
    Into the glory of the perfect day:
Rule in our hearts, that we may ever be
Guided and strengthened and upheld by thee.

2 We are of thee, the children of thy love,
    The brothers of thy well-belovèd Son;
Descend, O Holy Spirit, like a dove,
    Into our hearts, that we may be as one;
As one with thee, to whom we ever tend;
As one with him, our Brother and our Friend.

3 We would be one in hatred of all wrong,
    One in our love of all things sweet and fair,
One with the joy that breaketh into song,
    One with the grief that trembleth into prayer,
One in the power that makes thy children free
To follow truth, and thus to follow thee.

4 O clothe us with thy heavenly armour, Lord,
    Thy trusty shield, thy sword of love divine;
Our inspiration be thy constant word;
    We ask no victories that are not thine:
Give or withhold, let pain or pleasure be;
Enough to know that we are serving thee.

John White Chadwick, 1840-1904

456

515 QUEM PASTORES
LAUDAVERE 888 7

From a German MS. of 1410 (adapted)

A version with the original form of rhythm is at No. 175

FATHER, who on man dost shower
Gifts of plenty from thy dower,
To thy people give the power
    All thy gifts to use aright.

2 Give pure happiness in leisure,
Temperance in every pleasure,
Holy use of earthly treasure,
    Bodies clear and spirits bright.

3 Lift from this and every nation
All that brings us degradation;
Quell the forces of temptation;
    Put thine enemies to flight.

4 Be with us, thy strength supplying,
That with energy undying,
Every foe of man defying,
    We may rally to the fight.

5 Thou who art our Captain ever,
Lead us on to great endeavour;
May thy Church the world deliver:
    Give us wisdom, courage, might.

6 Father, who hast sought and found us,
Son of God, whose love has bound us,
Holy Ghost, within us, round us—
    Hear us, Godhead infinite.

Percy Dearmer, 1867-1936

The following are also suitable
No.
340   Spirit of Light—Holy
214   Thine arm, O Lord, in days of old
322   Thy Kingdom come, O God

INTERCESSION: FOR THE NATION

516 & 517 RUSSIA (REPHIDIM)
11 10 11 9 Irregular   ALEXIS FEODOROVITCH LVOV, 1799–1871

516
GOD the Omnipotent! King, who ordainest
　Great winds thy clarions, lightnings thy sword:
Show forth thy pity on high where thou reignest;
　Give to us peace in our time, O Lord.

2 God the All-merciful! earth hath forsaken
　Meekness and mercy, and slighted thy word;
Bid not thy wrath in its terrors awaken;
　Give to us peace in our time, O Lord.

3 God the All-righteous One! man hath defied thee;
　Yet to eternity standeth thy word;
Falsehood and wrong shall not tarry beside thee;
　Give to us peace in our time, O Lord.

4 God the All-wise! by the fire of thy chastening,
　Earth shall to freedom and truth be restored;
Through the thick darkness thy Kingdom is hastening;
　Thou wilt give peace in thy time, O Lord.

5 So shall thy children, with thankful devotion,
　Praise him who saved them from peril and sword,
Singing in chorus, from ocean to ocean,
　Peace to the nations, and praise to the Lord.

Henry Fothergill Chorley, 1808–72, and John Ellerton, 1826–93

517
GOD of Eternity, Lord of the Ages,
　Father and Spirit and Saviour of men!
Thine is the glory of time's numbered pages;
　Thine is the power to revive us again.

2 Thankful, we come to thee, Lord of the nations,
　Praising thy faithfulness, mercy, and grace
Shown to our fathers in past generations,
　Pledge of thy love to our people and race.

*3 Far from our ancient home, sundered by oceans,
    Zion is builded, and God is adored:
    Lift we our hearts in united devotions!
    Ends of the earth, join in praise to the Lord!

*4 Beauteous this land of ours, bountiful Giver!
    Brightly the heavens thy glory declare;
    Streameth the sunlight on hill, plain, and river,
    Shineth thy cross over fields rich and fair.

5 Pardon our sinfulness, God of all pity,
    Call to remembrance thy mercies of old;
    Strengthen thy Church to abide as a city
    Set on a hill for a light to thy fold.

6 Head of the Church on earth, risen, ascended!
    Thine is the honour that dwells in this place:
    As thou hast blessed us through years that have ended,
    Still lift upon us the light of thy face.

Ernest Northcroft Merrington, 1876-1953

* v. 3 for use overseas
  v. 4 for use in the Southern Hemisphere; the reference is to the Southern Cross

518 ST. PAUL (ABERDEEN)
C.M.   Chalmers' *Collection*, Aberdeen, 1749

A version with the earlier form of rhythm is at No. 395 (ii)

LORD, while for all mankind we
    pray,
  Of every clime and coast,
O hear us for our native land,
  The land we love the most.

2 Our fathers' sepulchres are here,
    And here our kindred dwell,
  Our children too; how should we
    love
  Another land so well?

3 O guard our shores from every foe;
    With peace our borders bless;
  With prosperous times our cities
    crown,
  Our fields with plenteousness.

4 Unite us in the sacred love
    Of knowledge, truth, and thee;
  And let our hills and valleys shout
    The songs of liberty.

5 Lord of the nations, thus to thee
    Our country we commend;
  Be thou her refuge and her trust,
    Her everlasting Friend.

John Reynell Wreford, 1800-81

519 RHUDDLAN 8787 87   Welsh Traditional Melody

Alternative tune, PICARDY, No. 256(ii)

JUDGE Eternal, throned in splendour,
   Lord of lords and King of kings,
With thy living fire of judgment
   Purge this land of bitter things;
Solace all its wide dominion
   With the healing of thy wings.

2 Still the weary folk are pining
   For the hour that brings release;
And the city's crowded clangour
   Cries aloud for sin to cease;
And the homesteads and the woodlands
   Plead in silence for their peace.

3 Crown, O God, thine own endeavour;
   Cleave our darkness with thy sword;
Feed the faithless and the hungry
   With the richness of thy word;
Cleanse the body of this Nation
   Through the glory of the Lord.

Henry Scott Holland, 1847–1918 *(altered)*

520 PASSION CHORALE 7676. D   HANS LEO HASSLER, 1564–1612

INTERCESSION: FOR THE NATION

O GOD of earth and altar,
  Bow down and hear our cry;
Our earthly rulers falter,
  Our people drift and die;
The walls of gold entomb us,
  The swords of scorn divide,
Take not thy thunder from us,
  But take away our pride.

2 From all that terror teaches,
    From lies of tongue and pen,
  From all the easy speeches
    That comfort cruel men,

From sale and profanation
  Of honour and the sword,
From sleep and from damnation,
  Deliver us, good Lord!

3 Tie in a living tether
    The prince and priest and thrall;
  Bind all our lives together,
    Smite us and save us all;
  In ire and exultation,
    Aflame with faith, and free,
  Lift up a living nation,
    A single sword to thee.

Gilbert Keith Chesterton, 1874–1936

---

521 NATIONAL ANTHEM 664 6664

Origin uncertain
First popularized in 1745

GOD save our gracious Queen,
Long live our noble Queen;
  God save the Queen!
Send her victorious,
Happy and glorious,
Long to reign over us:
  God save the Queen!

2 Thy choicest gifts in store
  On her be pleased to pour;
    Long may she reign;
  May she defend our laws,
  And ever give us cause
  To sing with heart and voice,
    'God save the Queen!'

From the version of 1745

461

INTERCESSION: FOR THE FAMILY

522 RHOSYMEDRE (LOVELY)
6666 888

JOHN DAVID EDWARDS, 1805–85
Original Sacred Music, c. 1840

OUR FATHER, by whose Name
　All fatherhood is known,
　Who dost in love proclaim
　Each family thine own,
Bless thou all parents, guarding well,
With constant love as sentinel,
The homes in which thy people dwell.

2 O Christ, thyself a child
　Within an earthly home,
　With heart still undefiled,
　Thou didst to manhood come;
Our children bless, in ev'ry place,
That they may all behold thy face,
And knowing thee may grow in grace.

3 O Spirit, who dost bind
　Our hearts in unity,
　Who teachest us to find
　The love from self set free,
In all our hearts such love increase,
That ev'ry home by this release,
May be the dwelling place of peace.

Francis Bland Tucker

523 NORTHBROOK 11 10 11 10 REGINALD SPARSHATT THATCHER, 1888–1957

O selig Haus, wo man dich aufgenommen

O HAPPY home, where thou art loved the dearest,
    Thou loving Friend, and Saviour of our race,
And where among the guests there never cometh
    One who can hold such high and honoured place!

2 O happy home, where two in heart united
    In holy faith and blessèd hope are one,
Whom death a little while alone divideth,
    And cannot end the union here begun!

3 O happy home, whose little ones are given
    Early to thee, in humble faith and prayer,—
To thee, their Friend, who from the heights of heaven
    Dost guide and guard with more than mother's care!

4 O happy home, where each one serves thee, lowly,
    Whatever his appointed work may be,
Till every common task seems great and holy,
    When it is done, O Lord, as unto thee!

5 O happy home, where thou art not forgotten
    When joy is overflowing, full and free:
O happy home, where every wounded spirit
    Is brought, Physician, Comforter, to thee:

6 Until at last, when earth's day's work is ended,
    All meet thee in the blessèd home above,
From whence thou camest, where thou hast ascended,
    Thy everlasting home of peace and love!

Karl Johann Philipp Spitta, 1801–59
Tr. Sarah Laurie Findlater, 1823–1907

524 HERONGATE L.M. English Traditional Melody

THY Kingdom come; yea, bid it come,
But, when thy Kingdom first began
On earth, thy Kingdom was a home,
A child, a woman, and a man.

2 The child was in the midst thereof,
O blessèd Jesus, holiest one!
The centre and the fount of love,
Mary and Joseph's little Son.

3 Wherever on this earth shall be
A child, a woman, and a man,
The image of that trinity
Wherewith thy Kingdom first began,

4 Establish there thy Kingdom! Yea,
And o'er that trinity of love
Send down, as in thy appointed day,
The brooding spirit of thy Dove.

Katharine Tynan Hinkson, 1861-1931

INTERCESSION: FOR THE MINISTRY OF HEALING

525 NUN DANKET ALL C.M.

Crüger's *Praxis Pietatis Melica*
(1647 edition)

FROM thee all skill and science flow,
   All pity, care, and love,
All calm and courage, faith and hope;
   O pour them from above.

2 And part them, Lord, to each and all,
   As each and all shall need,
To rise like incense, each to thee,
   In noble thought and deed.

3 And hasten, Lord, that perfect day
   When pain and death shall cease,
And thy just rule shall fill the earth
   With health, and light, and peace;

4 When ever blue the sky shall gleam,
   And ever green the sod;
And man's rude work deface no more
   The Paradise of God.

Charles Kingsley, 1819–75

526 TALLIS' ORDINAL C.M.

THOMAS TALLIS, *c.* 1505–85

FATHER, whose will is life and good
   For all of mortal breath,
Bind strong the bond of brotherhood
   Of those who fight with death.

2 Empower the hands and hearts and wills
   Of friends in lands afar,
Who battle with the body's ills,
   And wage thy holy war.

3 Where'er they heal the maimed and blind,
   Let love of Christ attend:
Proclaim the good Physician's mind,
   And prove the Saviour friend.

4 For still his love works wondrous charms,
   And, as in days of old,
He takes the wounded to his arms,
   And bears them to the fold.

5 O Father, look from heaven and bless,
   Where'er thy servants be,
Their works of pure unselfishness,
   Made consecrate to thee!

Hardwicke Drummond Rawnsley, 1851–1920

INTERCESSION: FOR TRAVELLERS AND THE ABSENT

527 MELITA 8888 88   JOHN BACCHUS DYKES, 1823–76

ETERNAL Father, strong to save,
Whose arm hath bound the restless
   wave,
Who bidd'st the mighty ocean deep
Its own appointed limits keep:
   O hear us when we cry to thee
   For those in peril on the sea.

2 O Christ, whose voice the waters
   heard,
And hushed their raging at thy word,
Who walkedst on the foaming deep,
And calm amid the storm didst
   sleep:
   O hear us when we cry to thee
   For those in peril on the sea.

3 O Holy Spirit, who didst brood
Upon the waters dark and rude,
And bid their angry tumult cease,
And give, for wild confusion, peace:
   O hear us when we cry to thee
   For those in peril on the sea.

4 O Trinity of love and power,
Our brethren shield in danger's
   hour;
From rock and tempest, fire and foe,
Protect them wheresoe'er they go:
   Thus evermore shall rise to thee
   Glad hymns of praise from land
   and sea.

William Whiting, 1825–78

528 ST. JOHN 6666 88   *The Parish Choir*, Vol. iii, 1851
Perhaps by WILLIAM HENRY HAVERGAL, 1793–1870

THOU who dost rule on high,
   Our Father and our Friend,
All those who ride the sky
   We now to thee commend.
For though among the stars they move,
They cannot rise beyond thy love.

2 Alone in boundless space,
   May they be still with thee;
The glory of thy face
   Among the heavens see;
For thou, by land and sea and air,
Art with thy children everywhere.

3 When tempests loose their power
   And dangers gather round,
In thee, in that dread hour,
   May their defence be found;
O may that peace possess their mind
Which all thy trusting children find.

4 And soon from pole to pole,
   Thy Kingdom, Lord, arise;
And peace alone control
   The commerce of the skies;
Till all the gifts thou givest men,
We to thy glory give again.

Robert Wesley Littlewood

529 WESTRIDGE 8583   MARTIN SHAW, 1875-1958

HOLY Father, in thy mercy,
   Hear our anxious prayer;
Keep our loved ones, now far distant,
   'Neath thy care.

2 Jesus, Saviour, let thy presence
   Be their light and guide;
Keep, O keep them, in their weakness,
   At thy side.

3 When in sorrow, when in danger,
   When in loneliness,
In thy love look down and comfort
   Their distress.

4 May the joy of thy salvation
   Be their strength and stay;
May they love and may they praise thee
   Day by day.

5 Holy Spirit, let thy teaching
   Sanctify their life;
Send thy grace that they may conquer
   In the strife.

6 Father, Son, and Holy Spirit,
   God the One in Three,
Bless them, guide them, save them, keep them
   Near to thee.

Isabel Stephana Stevenson, 1843-90

THE CHURCH TRIUMPHANT

530 BISHOPTHORPE
C.M.

Select Portions of the Psalms, 1786
Probably by JEREMIAH CLARKE, *c.* 1673-1707

PARAPHRASE 61

BLEST be the everlasting God,
　The Father of our Lord!
Be his abounding mercy praised,
　His majesty adored!

2 When from the dead he raised his
　　Son,
　And called him to the sky,
He gave our souls a lively hope
　That they should never die.

3 To an inheritance divine
　He taught our hearts to rise;
'Tis uncorrupted, undefiled,
　Unfading in the skies.

4 Saints by the power of God are kept,
　Till the salvation come:
We walk by faith as strangers here
　But Christ shall call us home.

Scottish Paraphrases, 1781
From 1 Peter 1: 3-5

531 ST. NICHOLAS C.M.

Holdroyd's *The Spiritual Man's*
Companion, 1753, as adapted
in *Scottish Psalmody*, 1854

PARAPHRASE 59, verses 1-4, 13

BEHOLD what witnesses unseen
　Encompass us around;
Men, once like us, with suffering
　tried,
　But now with glory crowned.

2 Let us, with zeal like theirs inspired,
　Begin the Christian race,
And, freed from each encumbering
　weight,
　Their holy footsteps trace.

3 Behold a witness nobler still,
Who trod affliction's path,
Jesus, at once the finisher
And author of our faith.

4 He for the joy before him set,
So generous was his love,
Endured the cross, despised the shame,
And now he reigns above.

5 Then let our hearts no more despond,
Our hands be weak no more;
Still let us trust our Father's love,
His wisdom still adore.

Scottish Paraphrases, 1781
From Hebrews Chapter 12

532 ST. MAGNUS (NOTTINGHAM)
C.M.

Probably by JEREMIAH CLARKE,
c. 1673-1707

A - men.

PARAPHRASE 65, verses 5, 6, 8, 9, 11

HARK how the adoring hosts above
With songs surround the throne!
Ten thousand thousand are their tongues;
But all their hearts are one.

2 Worthy the Lamb that died, they cry,
To be exalted thus;
Worthy the Lamb, let us reply;
For he was slain for us.

3 Thou hast redeemed us with thy blood,
And set the prisoners free;
Thou mad'st us kings and priests to God,
And we shall reign with thee.

4 From every kindred, every tongue,
Thou brought'st thy chosen race;
And distant lands and isles have shared
The riches of thy grace.

5 *To him who sits upon the throne,*
The God whom we adore,
And to the Lamb that once was slain,
Be glory evermore. Amen.

Scottish Paraphrases, 1781
From Revelation 5: 11-14

533 ST. ASAPH
D.C.M.

Smith's *Sacred Music*, Edinburgh, 1825
Possibly by GIOVANNI MARIE GIORNOVICHI, 1745-1804

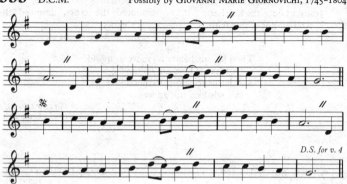

D.S. for v. 4

PARAPHRASE 66

HOW bright these glorious spirits
    shine!
  Whence all their white array?
How came they to the blissful seats
  Of everlasting day?
Lo! these are they, from sufferings
    great
  Who came to realms of light,
And in the blood of Christ have
    washed
  Those robes which shine so bright.

2 Now, with triumphal palms they
    stand
  Before the throne on high,
And serve the God they love, amidst
  The glories of the sky.
His presence fills each heart with joy,
  Tunes every mouth to sing:
By day, by night, the sacred courts
  With glad hosannas ring.

3 Hunger and thirst are felt no more,
  Nor suns with scorching ray;
God is their sun, whose cheering
    beams
  Diffuse eternal day.
The Lamb who dwells amidst the
    throne
  Shall o'er them still preside,
Feed them with nourishment divine,
  And all their footsteps guide.

*4 'Mong pastures green he'll lead his
    flock,
  Where living streams appear;
And God the Lord from every eye
  Shall wipe off every tear.

Scottish Paraphrases, 1781
From Revelation 7: 13-end

* *verse 4 is sung to the second half of the tune*

534 SINE NOMINE
10 10 10 and alleluias

RALPH VAUGHAN WILLIAMS, 1872-1958

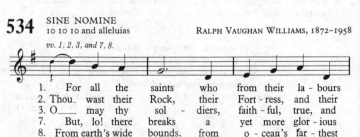

1.	For all	the	saints	who	from their	la -	bours
2. Thou	wast their	Rock,	their		Fort - ress,	and their	
3. O	may thy	sol -	diers,		faith - ful,	true, and	
7.	But, lo! there	breaks	a		yet	more glor -	ious
8. From earth's wide	bounds,	from			o - cean's	far - thest	

rest, Who thee by faith be-
Might; Thou, Lord, their Cap tain
bold, Fight as the saints who
day; The saints tri um phant
coast, Through gates of pearl streams

-fore the world con fessed, Thy Name, O
in the well-fought fight; Thou, in the
no-bly fought of old, And win, with
rise in bright ar ray; The King of
in the count-less host, Sing ing to

Je - sus, be for ev - er blest.
dark - ness drear, their one true Light.
them, the vic tor's crown of gold. } Al-
Glor - y pas ses on his way.
Fa - ther, Son, and Ho-ly Ghost,

- le - lu - ia! Al - le - lu - ia!

vv. 4, 5, & 6.

4. O blest com - mu - nion, fel - low-ship di - vine!
5. And when the strife is fierce, the war - fare long,
6. The gol - den even - ing bright-ens in the west;

(Small notes v. 6.)

We fee - bly strug - gle, they in glor - y shine; Yet
Steals on the ear the dis - tant tri - umph song, And
Soon, soon to faith - ful war - riors com - eth rest;

all are one in thee, for all are thine.
hearts are brave a - gain, and arms are strong. } Al-
Sweet is the calm of Pa - ra - dise the blest.

(Turn back for vv. 7 & 8.)

- le - lu - ia! Al - le - lu - ia!

William Walsham How, 1823-97

471

535 O QUANTA QUALIA
(REGNATOR ORBIS) 10 10 10 10

Paris Antiphoner, 1681

A - men.

O quanta, qualia sunt illa sabbata

O WHAT their joy and their glory must be,
Those endless Sabbaths the blessèd ones see!
Crown for the valiant; to weary ones rest;
God shall be all, and in all ever blest.

2 What are the Monarch, his court, and his throne?
What are the peace and the joy that they own?
Tell us, ye blest ones, that in it have share,
If what ye feel ye can fully declare.

3 Truly Jerusalem name we that shore,
'Vision of peace', that brings joy evermore!
Wish and fulfilment can severed be ne'er,
Nor the thing prayed for come short of the prayer.

4 We, where no trouble distraction can bring,
Safely the anthems of Zion shall sing;
While for thy grace, Lord, their voices of praise
Thy blessèd people shall evermore raise.

5 *Low before him with our praises we fall,*
Of whom, and in whom, and through whom are all;
Of whom, the Father; and through whom, the Son;
In whom, the Spirit, with these ever One. Amen.

Pierre Abelard, 1079–1142
Tr. John Mason Neale, 1818–66

536 MENDIP C.M.

English Traditional Melody, collected and
adapted by CECIL SHARP, 1859-1924

THERE is a land of pure delight,
　Where saints immortal reign;
Infinite day excludes the night,
　And pleasures banish pain;

2 There everlasting spring abides,
　And never-withering flowers:
Death, like a narrow sea, divides
　This heavenly land from ours.

3 Sweet fields beyond the swelling flood
　Stand dressed in living green;
So to the Jews old Canaan stood,
　While Jordan rolled between.

4 But timorous mortals start and shrink
　To cross this narrow sea,
And linger, shivering on the brink,
　And fear to launch away.

5 O could we make our doubts remove—
　Those gloomy doubts that rise—
And see the Canaan that we love,
　With unbeclouded eyes;

6 Could we but climb where Moses stood,
　And view the landscape o'er,
Not Jordan's stream, nor death's cold flood,
　Should fright us from the shore.

Isaac Watts, 1674-1748

537 EWING 7676. D   ALEXANDER EWING, 1830–95

A-men.

Urbs Sion aurea, patria lactea

JERUSALEM the golden,
  With milk and honey blest,
Beneath thy contemplation
  Sink heart and voice oppressed:
I know not, O I know not
  What social joys are there,
What radiancy of glory,
  What light beyond compare.

2 They stand, those halls of Zion,
  Conjubilant with song,
And bright with many an angel,
  And all the martyr throng:
The Prince is ever in them;
  The daylight is serene;
The pastures of the blessèd
  Are decked in glorious sheen.

3 There is the throne of David,
  And there, from care released,
The shout of them that triumph,
  The song of them that feast;
And they who, with their Leader,
  Have conquered in the fight,
For ever and for ever
  Are clad in robes of white.

4 O sweet and blessèd country,
  The home of God's elect!
O sweet and blessèd country,
  That eager hearts expect!
Jesus, in mercy bring us
  To that dear land of rest,
Who art, with God the Father
  And Spirit, ever blest. Amen.

vv. 1–3 Bernard of Cluny, 12th century
Tr. John Mason Neale, 1818–66
v. 4 Compilers of Hymns Ancient and Modern, 1861

538 RIPPONDEN 8884   NORMAN COCKER, 1889–1953

Alternative tune, ES IST KEIN TAG, No. 145 (i)

FOR those we love within the veil,
　　Who once were comrades of our way,
We thank thee, Lord; for they have won
　　To cloudless day;

2 And life for them is life indeed,
　　The splendid goal of earth's strait race;
And where no shadows intervene
　　They see thy face.

3 Not as we knew them any more,
　　Toilworn, and sad with burdened care,—
Erect, clear-eyed, upon their brows
　　Thy Name they bear.

4 Free from the fret of mortal years,
　　And knowing now thy perfect will,
With quickened sense and heightened joy
　　They serve thee still.

5 O fuller, sweeter is that life,
　　And larger, ampler is the air:
Eye cannot see nor heart conceive
　　The glory there;

6 Nor know to what high purpose thou
　　Dost yet employ their ripened powers,
Nor how at thy behest they touch
　　This life of ours.

7 There are no tears within their eyes;
　　With love they keep perpetual tryst;
And praise and work and rest are one,
　　With thee, O Christ.

William Charter Piggott, 1872–1943

539 UNIVERSITY COLLEGE 7777　　　HENRY JOHN GAUNTLETT, 1805–76

A - men.

Caelestis aulae principes

CAPTAINS of the saintly band,
Lights who lighten ev'ry land,
Princes who with Jesus dwell,
Judges of his Israel,

2 On the nations sunk in night
Ye have shed the Gospel light;
Sin and error flee away,
Truth reveals the promised day.

3 Not by warrior's spear and sword,
Not by art of human word,
Preaching but the cross of shame,
Rebel hearts for Christ ye tame.

4 Earth, that long in sin and pain
Groaned in Satan's deadly chain,
Now to serve its God is free
In the law of liberty.

5 Distant lands with one acclaim
Tell the honour of your name,
Who, wherever man has trod,
Teach the mysteries of God.

6 *Glory to the Three in One*
While eternal ages run,
Who from deepest shades of night
Called us to his glorious light. Amen.

Jean-Baptiste de Santeüil, 1630–97
Tr. Henry Williams Baker, 1821–77

540 AETERNA CHRISTI MUNERA
L.M.

Later form of plainsong melody as
given in Guidetti's *Directorium Chori*, 1582

Aeterna Christi munera

THE eternal gifts of Christ the King,
The apostles' glorious deeds, we sing;
And while due hymns of praise we pay,
Our thankful hearts cast grief away.

2 The Church in these her princes boasts,
These victor chiefs of warrior hosts;
The soldiers of the heavenly hall,
The lights that rose on earth for all.

3 'Twas thus the yearning faith of saints,
The unconquered hope that never faints,
The love of Christ that knows not shame,
The prince of this world overcame.

4 In these the Father's glory shone;
In these the will of God the Son;
In these exults the Holy Ghost;
Through these rejoice the heavenly host.

5 Redeemer, hear us of thy love,
That, with this glorious band above,
Hereafter, of thine endless grace,
Thy servants also may have place.

Attributed to St. Ambrose (c. 340–97)
Tr. John Mason Neale, 1818–66, and others

541 ELLACOMBE D.C.M.

18th century German melody, adapted
as in St. Gall *Gesangbuch*, 1863

THE Son of God goes forth to war,
    A kingly crown to gain;
His blood-red banner streams afar:
    Who follows in his train?
Who best can drink his cup of woe,
    Triumphant over pain,
Who patient bears his cross below,
    He follows in his train.

2 The martyr first, whose eagle eye
    Could pierce beyond the grave,
Who saw his Master in the sky,
    And called on him to save;
Like him, with pardon on his tongue
    In midst of mortal pain,
He prayed for them that did the wrong:
    Who follows in his train?

3 A glorious band, the chosen few
    On whom the Spirit came,
Twelve valiant saints, their hope they knew,
    And mocked the cross and flame;
They climbed the steep ascent of heaven,
    Through peril, toil, and pain:
O God, to us may grace be given
    To follow in their train.

Reginald Heber, 1783–1826

542 ST. SEBASTIAN
10 10 and refrain

PERCY CARTER BUCK, 1871–1947

An end - less Al - - le - lu - ia.

Alleluia piis edite laudibus

SING Alleluia forth in duteous praise,
Ye citizens of heaven; O sweetly raise
An endless Alleluia.

2 Ye powers, who stand before the eternal Light,
In hymning choirs re-echo to the height:

3 Ye who have gained at length your palms in bliss,
Victorious ones, your chant shall still be this:

4 There, in one grand acclaim, for ever ring
The strains which tell the honour of your King:

5 While thee, by whom were all things made, we praise
For ever, and tell out in sweetest lays:

6 Almighty Christ, to thee our voices sing
Glory for evermore; to thee we bring:

Mozarabic Breviary, 5th–8th century
Tr. John Ellerton, 1826–93

543 FRENCH (DUNDEE)
C.M.

Scottish Psalter, 1615 (later form of rhythm)

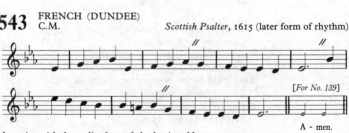

[For No. 139]

A - men.

A version with the earlier form of rhythm is at No. 139

THE CHURCH TRIUMPHANT

LET saints on earth in concert sing
  With those whose work is done;
For all the servants of our King
  In earth and heaven are one.

2 One family, we dwell in him,
    One Church, above, beneath;
  Though now divided by the stream,
    The narrow stream of death.

3 One army of the living God,
    To his command we bow;
  Part of his host hath crossed the
    flood,
  And part is crossing now.

4 Even now to their eternal home
    There pass some spirits blest,
  While others to the margin come,
    Waiting their call to rest.

5 Jesus, be thou our constant Guide;
  Then, when the word is given,
  Bid Jordan's narrow stream divide,
  And bring us safe to heaven.

Charles Wesley, 1707-88

544 CRUGYBAR 9898. D

Old Welsh Hymn Melody,
as in *Moliant Seion*, 1883

O fryniau Caersalem ceir gweled

FROM heavenly Jerusalem's
    towers,
  The path through the desert they
    trace;
And every affliction they suffered
  Redounds to the glory of grace;
Their look they cast back on the
    tempests,
  On fears, on grim death and the
    grave,
Rejoicing that now they're in safety,
  Through him that is mighty to
    save.

2 And we, from the wilds of the
    desert,
  Shall flee to the land of the blest;
Life's tears shall be changed to
    rejoicing,
  Its labours and toil into rest:
There we shall find refuge eternal,
  From sin, from affliction, from
    pain,
And in the sweet love of the Saviour,
  A joy without end shall attain.

David Charles, 1762-1834
Tr. Lewis Edwards, 1809-87

545 MOAB 6565 6665

JOHN ROBERTS (IEUAN GWYLLT), 1822–77
Llyfr Tonau Cynulleidfaol, 1870

FAR off I see the goal—
   O Saviour, guide me;
I feel my strength is small—
   Be thou beside me;
With vision ever clear,
With love that conquers fear,
And grace to persevere,
   O Lord, provide me.

2 Whene'er thy way seems strange,
   Go thou before me;
And, lest my heart should change,
   O Lord, watch o'er me;
But, should my faith prove frail,
And I through blindness fail,
O let thy grace prevail,
   And still restore me.

3 Should earthly pleasures wane,
   And joy forsake me,
And lonely hours of pain
   At length o'ertake me,—
My hand in thine hold fast
Till sorrow be o'er-past,
And gentle death at last
   For heaven awake me.

4 There, with the ransomed throng
   Who praise for ever
The love that made them strong
   To serve for ever,
I, too, would see thy face,
Thy finished work re-trace,
And magnify thy grace,
   Redeemed for ever.

Robert Rowland Roberts, 1865–1945

The following are also suitable

No.
14 We come unto our fathers' God
473 Lord, who in thy perfect wisdom

IV

THE SACRAMENTS

———

THE SACRAMENTS

HOLY BAPTISM

THE APOSTLES' CREED

546 I believe in

GOD THE FATHER ALMIGHTY, MAKER OF HEAVEN AND EARTH

and in

JESUS CHRIST HIS ONLY SON OUR LORD

who was conceived by the Holy Ghost,
born of the Virgin Mary,
suffered under Pontius Pilate,
was crucified, dead, and buried;
he descended into hell.
The third day he rose again from the dead,
he ascended into heaven, and sitteth on
the right hand of God the Father Almighty;
from thence he shall come to judge the quick and the dead.

I believe in

the HOLY GHOST;
the HOLY CATHOLIC CHURCH;
the COMMUNION OF SAINTS;
the FORGIVENESS OF SINS;
the RESURRECTION OF THE BODY;
and the LIFE EVERLASTING. Amen.

547 CAITHNESS C.M.   *Scottish Psalter, 1635*

A - men.

PSALM 78, verses 4(b)–7

THE praises of the Lord our God,
  And his almighty strength,
The wondrous works that he hath
    done,
  We will show forth at length.

2 His testimony and his law
  In Israel he did place,
And charged our fathers it to show
  To their succeeding race;

3 That so the race which was to come
  Might well them learn and know;

And sons unborn, who should arise,
  Might to their sons them show:

4 That they might set their hope in
    God,
  And suffer not to fall
His mighty works out of their mind,
  But keep his precepts all.

5 *To Father, Son, and Holy Ghost,*
  The God whom we adore,
Be glory, as it was, and is,
  And shall be evermore. Amen.

483

548 TALLIS' ORDINAL C.M.   THOMAS TALLIS, *c.* 1505-85

A - men.

PARAPHRASE 47, verses 2-4

WHEN to the sacred font we came,
　　Did not the rite proclaim,
That, washed from sin, and all its stains,
　　New creatures we became?

2 With Christ the Lord we died to sin;
　　With him to life we rise,
To life which, now begun on earth,
　　Is perfect in the skies.

3 Too long enthralled to Satan's sway,
　　We now are slaves no more;
For Christ hath vanquished death and sin,
　　Our freedom to restore.

4 *To Father, Son, and Holy Ghost,*
　　The God whom we adore,
Be glory, as it was, and is,
　　And shall be evermore. **Amen.**

Scottish Paraphrases, 1781
From Romans 6: 3-7

549 (i) ST. PETER C.M.   ALEXANDER ROBERT REINAGLE, 1799-1877
Psalm Tunes for the Voice and the Pianoforte, 1830

HOLY BAPTISM

(ii) BELMONT C.M.

Severn's *Psalms and Hymn Tunes*, 1854, possibly
from a melody in Gardiner's *Sacred Melodies*, 1812

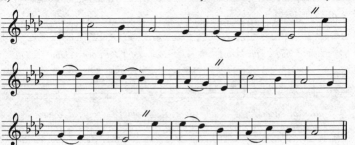

OUR children, Lord, in faith and prayer,
  We now devote to thee;
Let them thy covenant mercies share,
  And thy salvation see.

2 Such helpless babes thou didst embrace,
    While dwelling here below;
To us and ours, O God of grace,
    The same compassion show.

3 O thou whose infant feet were found
    Within thy Father's shrine,
Whose years, with changeless virtue crowned,
    Were all alike divine,

4 Dependent on thy bounteous breath,
    We seek thy grace alone,
In childhood, manhood, age, and death,
    To keep us still thine own.

vv. 1-2 Thomas Haweis, 1734-1820
vv. 3-4 Reginald Heber, 1783-1826

550 CRUCIFER 10 10 and refrain   SYDNEY HUGO NICHOLSON, 1875-1947

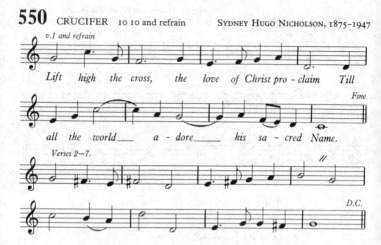

v.1 and refrain

Lift high the cross, the love of Christ pro-claim Till all the world___ a-dore___ his sa-cred Name.

Verses 2—7.

* LIFT high the cross, the love of Christ proclaim
  Till all the world adore his sacred Name.

2 Come, brethren, follow where our Captain trod,
  Our King victorious, Christ the Son of God:

3 Led on their way by this triumphant sign,
  The hosts of God in conquering ranks combine:

4 Each new-born soldier of the Crucified
  Bears on his brow the seal of him who died:

5 This is the sign which Satan's legions fear
  And angels veil their faces to revere:

6 O Lord, once lifted on the glorious tree,
  As thou hast promised, draw men unto thee:

7 From farthest regions let them homage bring,
  And on his cross adore their Saviour King:

Michael Robert Newbolt, 1874-1956,
based on George William Kitchin, 1827-1912

* Verse 1 is repeated as a refrain after each verse

551 COMMANDMENTS L.M.   From a melody in *La Forme des Prières et Chants Ecclésiastiques*, Strasbourg, 1545 (rhythm altered)

A LITTLE child the Saviour came,
The Mighty God was still his Name,
And angels worshipped as he lay
The seeming infant of a day.

2 He who, a little child, began
The life divine to show to man,
Proclaims from heaven the message free,
'Let little children come to me.'

3 We bring them, Lord, and with the sign
Of sprinkled water name them thine:

Their souls with saving grace endow;
Baptize them with thy Spirit now.

4 O give thine angels charge, good Lord,
Them safely in thy way to guard;
Thy blessing on their lives command,
And write their names upon thy hand.

5 O thou who by an infant's tongue
Dost hear thy perfect glory sung,
May these, with all the heavenly host,
Praise Father, Son, and Holy Ghost.

William Robertson, 1820-64

552 LIEBSTER JESU (DESSAU) 7878 88

JOHANN RODOLPH AHLE, 1625-73

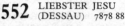

Liebster Jesu, wir sind hier

BLESSÈD Jesus, here we stand,
  Met to do as thou hast spoken;
And this child, at thy command,
  Now we bring to thee in token
That to Christ it here is given,
For of such shall be his heaven.

2 Therefore hasten we to thee;
  Take the pledge we bring, O take it;
Let us here thy glory see,
  And in tender pity make it
Now thy child, and leave it never—
Thine on earth, and thine for ever.

3 Make it, Head, thy member now;
  Shepherd, take thy lamb and feed it;

Prince of Peace, its peace be thou;
  Way of life, to heaven O lead it;
Vine, this branch may nothing sever,
Grafted firm in thee for ever.

4 Now upon thy heart it lies,
  What our hearts so dearly treasure;
Heavenward lead our burdened sighs;
  Pour thy blessing without measure;
Write the name we now have given,
Write it in the book of heaven.

Benjamin Schmolk, 1672-1737
Tr. Catherine Winkworth, 1827-78

553 SUSSEX CAROL 8888 88   English Traditional Melody

Alternative tune, SURREY, No. 16

O FATHER, in thy father-heart
We know our children have their part;
We sign them in thy threefold Name,
And by the sprinkled water claim
Thy covenant in Christ revealed,
To us and to our children sealed:

2 Name of the Father, pledge that we
Our inmost being draw from thee;
Name of the Son, whereby we know
The Father's love to men below;
Name of the Spirit, blessèd sign
That now we share the life divine.

Ella Sophia Armitage, 1841–1931

554 & 555 O WALY, WALY L.M.   English Traditional Melody

Alternative tune, COMMANDMENTS, No. 551

554

O GOD, thy life-creating love
   This sacred trust to parents gave.
In Christ thou camest from above
   Thy children's souls to claim and save.

2 Help us who now our pledges give
    The young to train and guard and guide,
To learn of Christ, and so to live
    That they may in thy love abide.

3 Grant, Lord, as strength and wisdom grow,
    That every child thy truth may learn.
Impart thy light, that each may know
    Thy will and life's true way discern.

4 Then home and child, kept in thy peace,
    And guarded, Father, by thy care,
Will in the grace of Christ increase,
    And all thy Kingdom's blessings share.

Albert Frederick Bayly

555

After Baptism

O LOVING Father, to thy care
    We give again this child of thine,
Baptized and blessed with faithful prayer
    And sealed with Love's victorious sign.

2 As Christ, thy Son, did not refuse
    The homage of the children's cry,
So teach *him* childhood's gifts to use
    Thy Name to praise and magnify.

3 Through youth and age, through shine and shade,
    Grant *him* to run *his* earthly race,
Forgetting not that man was made
    To show thy glory and thy grace:

4 Till, at the last, before thy throne
    He lays *his* earthly armour down,
His task of loving service done,
    And, in thy mercy, takes *his* crown.

Cyril Argentine Alington, 1872–1955

The following are also suitable

No.
402 I bind unto myself today *vv. 1, 2, 4, 6*
420 The Church's one foundation *vv. 1, 2*
421 Glorious things of thee are spoken *vv. 1–3*
429 My God accept my heart this day

556 (i) LILLE

Anonymous

The Lord bless you, and keep you: The Lord make his face to shine up-on you, and be grac-ious un-to you: The Lord lift up his count-en-ance up-on you,___ and give you peace.

(ii)

Tone ii ending I

The Lord bless you, and keep you: The Lord make his face to shine up-on you, and be grac-ious un-to you: The Lord lift up his countenance up-on you, and give you peace.

(iii) HEATON

THOMAS WILSON

Org.

The Lord bless you, and keep you: – The Lord make his face to shine up-on you, and be

490

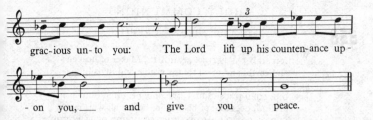

gracious un-to you: The Lord lift up his counten-ance up-

-on you, ___ and give you peace.

557 BATTISHILL 7777   Simplified version of a melody by
JONATHAN BATTISHILL, 1738–1801

For Cradle Roll

FATHER, hear us as we pray
For these little ones today:
Good and gentle may they be;
Early may they come to thee.

2 Bless, we pray thee, Saviour dear,
All whose names are written here;
Guard and keep them safe from harm;
Hold them with thy loving arm.

Edith Florence Boyle MacAlister, 1873–1950

HOLY COMMUNION

THE NICENE CREED

558

WE believe in
    ONE GOD THE FATHER ALMIGHTY, Maker of heaven
    and earth, and of all things visible and invisible:
and in
    ONE LORD JESUS CHRIST, the only begotten Son
    of God, begotten of his Father before all worlds,
    GOD OF GOD, LIGHT OF LIGHT, VERY GOD OF VERY GOD,
    begotten, not made, being of one substance with
    the Father, by whom all things were made:
        WHO, for us men, and for our salvation, came
    down from heaven, and was incarnate by the
    Holy Ghost of the Virgin Mary, AND WAS MADE
    MAN, and was crucified also for us under
    Pontius Pilate.
        HE suffered and was buried; and the
    third day he rose again according to the
    Scriptures, and ascended into heaven, and
    sitteth on the right hand of the Father. And he
    shall come again with glory to judge both
    the quick and the dead, whose Kingdom shall
    have no end.
And we believe in
    THE HOLY GHOST, the Lord and Giver
    of Life, who proceedeth from the Father
    and the Son; who with the Father and the
    Son together is worshipped and glorified; who
    spake by the prophets.
And we believe
    ONE HOLY CATHOLIC AND APOSTOLIC CHURCH.
We acknowledge
    ONE BAPTISM for the remission of sins.
And we look for
    THE RESURRECTION OF THE DEAD,
    and the LIFE OF THE WORLD TO COME. Amen.

559

SALUTATION

Minister. The Lord be with you;
People.   *And with thy spirit.*

SURSUM CORDA

Minister. Lift up your hearts;
People.   *We lift them up unto the Lord.*

Minister. Let us give thanks unto our Lord God;
People.   *It is meet and right so to do.*

560 SANCTUS KENNETH LEIGHTON

With a slow swing

Ho - - - ly, Ho - - ly, Ho - - - ly, Lord God of Hosts, Hea-ven and earth are full of thy glor-y. Glor-y be to thee, O Lord Most High. A - men.

561 BENEDICTUS QUI VENIT KENNETH LEIGHTON

Slow and sustained

Bless - ed is he that com-eth in the Name of the Lord: Ho - san - na, Ho - san - na, Ho - san - na in the high - est.

562

THE LORD'S PRAYER

FIRST FORM

OUR Father which art in heaven,
Hallowed be thy Name.
Thy Kingdom come.
Thy will be done in earth, as it is in heaven.
Give us this day our daily bread.
And forgive us our debts, as we forgive our debtors.
And lead us not into temptation, but deliver us from evil:
For thine is the Kingdom, and the power, and the glory, for ever. Amen.

SECOND FORM

OUR Father, who art in heaven,
Hallowed be thy Name.
Thy Kingdom come.
Thy will be done, on earth as it is in heaven.
Give us this day our daily bread.
And forgive us our trespasses, as we forgive those who trespass against us.
And lead us not into temptation, but deliver us from evil:
For thine is the Kingdom, the power, and the glory, for ever and ever. Amen.

St. Matthew 6: 9–13

563 AGNUS DEI KENNETH LEIGHTON

Very slow and expressive

O Lamb of God, that tak-est a-way the sins of the world, have mer-cy up-on us.

O Lamb of God, that tak-est a-way the sins of the world, have mer-cy up-on us.

O Lamb of God, that tak-est a-way the sins of the world, grant us thy peace.

564 ST. JAMES C.M.

Select Psalms and Hymns, 1697
Probably by Raphael Courteville, ?1677–1772

A - men.

PSALM 26, verses 6–8

MINE hands in innocence, O Lord,
    I'll wash and purify;
So to thine holy altar go,
    And compass it will I:

2 That I, with voice of thanksgiving,
    May publish and declare,
And tell of all thy mighty works,
    That great and wondrous are.

3 The habitation of thy house,
    Lord, I have lovèd well;
Yea, in that place I do delight
    Where doth thine honour dwell.

4 *To Father, Son, and Holy Ghost,*
    The God whom we adore,
Be glory, as it was, and is,
    And shall be evermore. Amen.

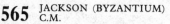

565 JACKSON (BYZANTIUM)
C.M.

THOMAS JACKSON, 1715–81
Twelve Psalm Tunes, 1780

A - men.

PSALM 116, verses 13, 14, 17–19

I'LL of salvation take the cup,
    On God's name will I call:
I'll pay my vows now to the Lord
    Before his people all.

2 Thank-offerings I to thee will give,
    And on God's name will call.
I'll pay my vows now to the Lord
    Before his people all;

3 Within the courts of God's own house,
    Within the midst of thee,
O city of Jerusalem.
    Praise to the Lord give ye.

4 *To Father, Son, and Holy Ghost,*
    The God whom we adore,
Be glory, as it was, and is,
    And shall be evermore. Amen.

566(i) ST. MATTHEW
D.C.M.

Later form of a tune in
A Supplement to the New Version, 1708
Probably by WILLIAM CROFT, 1678–1727

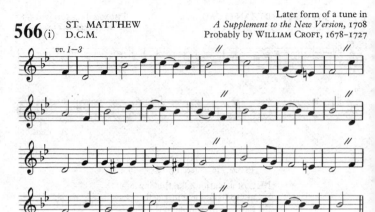

PSALM 24

THE earth belongs unto the Lord,
    And all that it contains;
The world that is inhabited,
    And all that there remains.
For the foundations of the same
    He on the seas did lay,
And he hath it establishèd
    Upon the floods to stay.

2 Who is the man that shall ascend
    Into the hill of God?
Or who within his holy place
    Shall have a firm abode?

Whose hands are clean, whose heart
    is pure,
    And unto vanity
Who hath not lifted up his soul,
    Nor sworn deceitfully.

3 This is the man who shall receive
    The blessing from the Lord;
The God of his salvation shall
    Him righteousness accord.
This is the generation who
    Do after him inquire;
They Jacob are, who seek thy face
    With their whole hearts' desire.

(ii) ST. GEORGE'S, EDINBURGH
D.C.M. Irregular

ANDREW MITCHELL THOMSON, 1778–1831

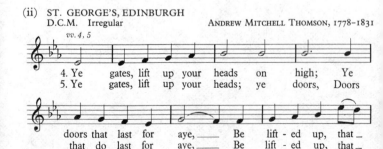

4. Ye gates, lift up your heads on high; Ye
5. Ye gates, lift up your heads; ye doors, Doors

doors that last for aye, __ Be lift-ed up, that _
that do last for aye, __ Be lift-ed up, that _

so the King Of___ glor - y en - ter may.
so the King Of___ glor - y en - ter may.

v. 4 to 'But who' 1st time
v. 5 to 'But who' 2nd time

4. But who of glor - y is the King? The

migh - ty Lord is this; Ev'n that same Lord that

great___ in___ might And strong in bat - tle is. Ev'n

D.C. for v. 5

that same Lord that great in___ might And strong in___ bat - tle is.

5. But who is he that is the King, The King of

glor - y? who is this? The Lord of hosts, and

none___ but___ he, ___ The King of glor - y is. The

Lord of hosts, and none but___ he, The King of ___ glor - y is.

CODA

Al - le - lu - ia! al - le - lu - ia! al - le - lu - ia! al - le - lu - ia!

al - le - lu - ia! A - men, A - men, A - men.

THE SACRAMENTS

567 SCHMÜCKE DICH 8888. D — Crüger's *Geistliche Kirchen-Melodien*, 1649

Schmücke dich, o liebe Seele

DECK thyself, my soul, with gladness,
Leave the gloomy haunts of sadness,
Come into the daylight's splendour,
There with joy thy praises render
Unto him whose grace unbounded
Hath this wondrous banquet founded;
High o'er all the heavens he reigneth,
Yet to dwell with thee he deigneth.

2 Hasten as a bride to meet him,
And with loving reverence greet him,
For with words of life immortal
Now he knocketh at thy portal;
Haste to ope the gates before him,
Saying, while thou dost adore him,
'Suffer, Lord, that I receive thee,
And I never more will leave thee.'

3 Sun, who all my life dost brighten;
Light, who dost my soul enlighten;
Joy, the sweetest man e'er knoweth;
Fount, whence all my being floweth:
At thy feet I cry, my Maker,
Let me be a fit partaker
Of this blessèd food from heaven,
For our good, thy glory, given.

4 Jesus, Bread of Life, I pray thee,
Let me gladly here obey thee;
Never to my hurt invited,
Be thy love with love requited:
From this banquet let me measure,
Lord, how vast and deep its treasure;
Through the gifts thou here dost give me,
As thy guest in heaven receive me.

Johann Franck, 1618–77
Tr. Catherine Winkworth, 1827–78

568 DIVA SERVATRIX 11 11 11 5 — *Bayeux Antiphoner*, 1739

A - - - men.

FATHER most loving, listen to thy children
Who as thy family joyfully for-gather,
Singing the praises of thy Son, our Brother,
Jesus beloved!

2 We stand attentive, listening to God's Gospel,
Welcoming Jesus as he speaks among us,
Mind and heart open, ready to receive him,
Lips to proclaim him!

3 Father in heaven, bless the gifts we offer,
Signs of our true love, hearts in homage given!
Make them the one gift that is wholly worthy,
Christ, spotless victim!

4 Father, we thank thee for thy Son's dear presence,
Coming to feed us as the Bread of heaven,
Making us one with him in sweet communion,
One with each other!

5 *Praised be our Father, lovingly inviting*
Guests to this banquet, praised the Son who feeds us,
Praised too the Spirit, sent by Son and Father,
Making us Christ-like! Amen.

James Quinn

救世之身爲眾生擘

569 SHENG EN (GOD'S GRACE)
Irregular
SU YIN-LAN, 1934

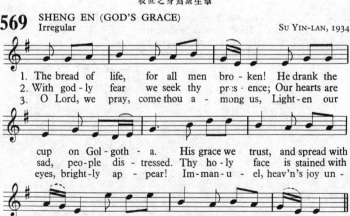

1. The bread of life, for all men bro-ken! He drank the
2. With god-ly fear we seek thy pres-ence; Our hearts are
3. O Lord, we pray, come thou a-mong us, Light-en our

cup on Gol-goth-a. His grace we trust, and spread with
sad, peo-ple dis-tressed. Thy ho-ly face is stained with
eyes, bright-ly ap-pear! Im-man-u-el, heav'n's joy un-

rev'-rence This ho-ly feast, and thus re-mem-ber.
bit-ter tears, Our hu-man pain still bear-est thou with us.
end-ing, Our life with thine for ev-er blend-ing.

Timothy Tingfang Lew, 1891-1947; tr. Walter Reginald Oxenham Taylor

501

570 WIGTOWN C.M.   *Scottish Psalter*, 1635

I AM not worthy, holy Lord,
   That thou shouldst come to me;
Speak but the word; one gracious word
   Can set the sinner free.

2 I am not worthy; cold and bare
   The lodging of my soul;
How canst thou deign to enter there?
   Lord, speak, and make me whole.

3 I am not worthy; yet, my God,
   How can I say thee nay,—
Thee, who didst give thy flesh and blood
   My ransom price to pay?

4 O come, in this sweet morning* hour,
   Feed me with food divine;
And fill with all thy love and power
   This worthless heart of mine.

Henry Williams Baker, 1821–77

* *Or* evening.

571 (i) JESU DULCIS MEMORIA
L.M.

Catholische Geistliche Gesänge,
Andernach, 1608

(ii) WAREHAM L.M.

WILLIAM KNAPP, 1698-1768
A Sett of New Psalm Tunes, 1738

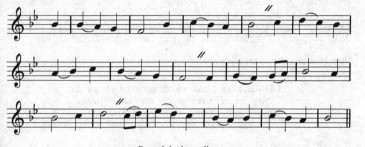

Jesu, dulcedo cordium

JESUS, thou Joy of loving hearts,
    Thou Fount of life, thou Light of men,
From the best bliss that earth imparts
    We turn unfilled to thee again.

2 Thy truth unchanged hath ever stood;
    Thou savest those that on thee call:
To them that seek thee thou art good,
    To them that find thee, all in all.

3 We taste thee, O thou living Bread,
    And long to feast upon thee still;
We drink of thee, the Fountain-head,
    And thirst our souls from thee to fill.

4 Our restless spirits yearn for thee,
    Where'er our changeful lot is cast,—
Glad when thy gracious smile we see,
    Blest when our faith can hold thee fast.

5 O Jesus, ever with us stay;
    Make all our moments calm and bright;
Chase the dark night of sin away;
    Shed o'er the world thy holy light.

12th century
Tr. Ray Palmer, 1808-87

572 STONER HILL 10 10 10 10   WILLIAM HENRY HARRIS, 1883-1973

Alternative tune, SONG 22, No. 573

COME, risen Lord, and deign to be our guest;
  Nay, let us be thy guests; the feast is thine;
Thyself at thine own board make manifest,
  In thine own sacrament of bread and wine.

2 We meet, as in that upper room they met;
  Thou at the table, blessing, yet dost stand;
'This is my body': so thou givest yet;
  Faith still receives the cup as from thy hand.

3 One body we, one body who partake,
  One Church united in communion blest;
One name we bear, one bread of life we break,
  With all thy saints on earth and saints at rest.

4 One with each other, Lord, for one in thee,
  Who art one Saviour and one living Head;
Then open thou our eyes, that we may see;
  Be known to us in breaking of the bread.

George Wallace Briggs, 1875-1959

573 SONG 22 10 10 10 10   ORLANDO GIBBONS, 1583-1625
(rhythm altered)

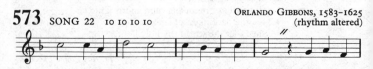

Alternative tune, STONER HILL, No. 572

Before Communion

HERE, O my Lord, I see thee face to face;
   Here would I touch and handle things unseen,
Here grasp with firmer hand the eternal grace,
   And all my weariness upon thee lean.

2 Mine is the sin, but thine the righteousness;
   Mine is the guilt, but thine the cleansing blood;
Here is my robe, my refuge, and my peace—
   Thy blood, thy righteousness, O Lord my God.

3 Here would I feed upon the bread of God,
   Here drink with thee the royal wine of heaven;
Here would I lay aside each earthly load,
   Here taste afresh the calm of sin forgiven.

4 This is the hour of banquet and of song;
   This is the heavenly table spread for me;
Here let me feast, and, feasting, still prolong
   The hallowed hour of fellowship with thee.

After Communion

5 Too soon we rise; the symbols disappear;
   The feast, though not the love, is past and gone;
The bread and wine remove, but thou art here,
   Nearer than ever, still my Shield and Sun.

6 I have no help but thine; nor do I need
   Another arm save thine to lean upon;
It is enough, my Lord, enough indeed;
   My strength is in thy might, thy might alone.

7 Feast after feast thus comes and passes by,
   Yet, passing, points to the glad feast above,
Giving sweet foretaste of the festal joy,
   The Lamb's great bridal feast of bliss and love.

Horatius Bonar, 1808–89
(verse order altered)

574 PSALM 118
(RENDEZ À DIEU) 9898. D

French–Genevan Psalter, 1551

Alternative tune, LES COMMANDEMENS DE DIEU, No. 586

BREAD of the world, in mercy broken,
  Wine of the soul, in mercy shed,
By whom the words of life were spoken,
  And in whose death our sins are dead:
Look on the heart by sorrow broken,
  Look on the tears by sinners shed;
And be thy feast to us the token
  That by thy grace our souls are fed.

Reginald Heber, 1783–1826

575 CHRISTUS DER IST MEIN LEBEN
(BREMEN) 7676

MELCHIOR VULPIUS, c. 1560–1615

A - men.

THOU standest at the altar,
  Thou offerest every prayer;
In faith's unclouded vision
  We see thee ever there.

2 Out of thy hand the incense
  Ascends before the throne,
Where thou art interceding,
  Lord Jesus, for thine own.

3 And, through thy blood accepted,
  With thee we keep the feast:
Thou art the one Oblation;
  Thou only art the Priest.

4 We come, O only Saviour;
  On thee, the Lamb, we feed:
Thy flesh is bread from heaven;
  Thy blood is drink indeed.

5 *To thee, Almighty Father;*
   Incarnate Son, to thee;
   To thee, Anointing Spirit,—
   All praise and glory be. Amen.

Edward Wilton Eddis, 1825–1905
(altered)

576(i) COLINTON 8987   KENNETH LEIGHTON

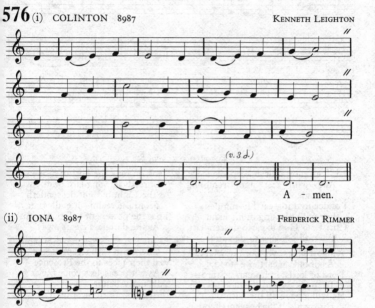

(ii) IONA 8987   FREDERICK RIMMER

O CHRIST, who sinless art alone,
   Our frailty and our sin who knowest,
We stand in thee before the throne
   And plead the death thou showest.

2 O Christ, our sacrifice and Priest,
   Who in the glory intercedest,
We in the shadow keep the feast
   And show the death thou pleadest.

3 *To thee in endless life enthroned,*
   O Christ, eternal praise be given,
   With Holy Ghost and Father owned
   One God in earth and heaven. Amen.

Arthur Wellesley Wotherspoon, 1853–1936

577 PICARDY 8787 87   French Carol Melody

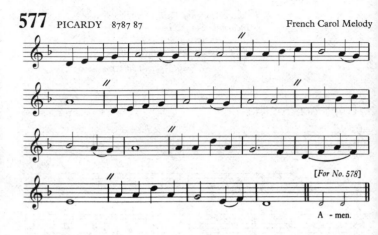

[For No. 578]

A - men.

Σιγησάτω πᾶσα σὰρξ βροτεία

LET all mortal flesh keep silence,
   And with fear and trembling
     stand;
Ponder nothing earthly-minded,
   For with blessing in his hand
Christ our God to earth descendeth,
   Our full homage to demand.

2 King of kings, yet born of Mary,
   As of old on earth he stood,
Lord of lords, in human vesture—
   In the body and the blood—
He will give to all the faithful
   His own self for heavenly food.

3 Rank on rank the host of heaven
   Spreads its vanguard on the way,
As the Light of light descendeth
   From the realms of endless day,
That the powers of hell may vanish
   As the darkness clears away.

4 At his feet the six-winged Seraph;
   Cherubim with sleepless eye,
Veil their faces to the Presence,
   As with ceaseless voice they cry,
'Alleluia, Alleluia,
   Alleluia, Lord most high'.

Liturgy of St. James
Tr. Gerard Moultrie, 1829–85

578 (i)   PANGE LINGUA
        8787 87   Plainsong Melody (Sarum form), Mode iii

A - men.

578 (ii) PICARDY (*see No. 577*)

Pange lingua gloriosi Corporis mysterium

* NOW, my tongue, the mystery telling
Of the glorious Body sing,
And the Blood, all price excelling,
Which the Gentiles' Lord and King,
In a Virgin's womb once dwelling,
Shed for this world's ransoming.

2 That last night, at supper lying,
'Mid the Twelve, his chosen band,
Jesus, with the law complying,
Keeps the feast its rites demand;
Then, more precious food supplying,
Gives himself with his own hand.

3 Word-made-flesh, true bread he maketh
By his word his Flesh to be,
Wine his Blood; which whoso taketh
Must from carnal thoughts be free;
Faith alone, though sight forsaketh,
Shows true hearts the mystery.

*   *   *   *   *

†4 Therefore we, before him bending,
This great sacrament revere;
Types and shadows have their ending,
For the newer rite is here;
Faith, our outward sense befriending,
Makes our inward vision clear.

5 *Unto God be praise and honour:*
To the Father, to the Son,
To the mighty Spirit, glory—
Ever Three and ever One:
Power and glory in the highest
While eternal ages run. Amen.

St. Thomas Aquinas, c. 1227-74
Tr. Edward Caswall, 1814-78 and
Compilers of Hymns Ancient and Modern, 1861

* *The pointing is for use with Tune* (i) PANGE LINGUA *only*
† *vv. 4, 5 may be sung to* TANTUM ERGO SACRAMENTUM, *No. 373*

579 AETERNA CHRISTI MUNERA
L.M.

Later form of plainsong melody,
as given in Guidetti's *Directorium Chori*, 1582

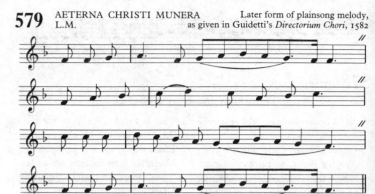

Alternative tune, SOLEMNIS HAEC FESTIVITAS, No. 610

ALMIGHTY Father, Lord most high,
Who madest all, who fillest all,
Thy Name we praise and magnify,
For all our needs on thee we call.

2 We offer to thee of thine own,
Ourselves and all that we can bring,
In bread and cup before thee shown,
Our universal offering.

3 All that we have we bring to thee,
Yet all is naught when all is done,
Save that in it thy love can see
The sacrifice of thy dear Son.

4 By his command in bread and cup
His body and his blood we plead;
What on the cross he offered up
Is here our sacrifice indeed.

5 For all thy gifts of life and grace,
Here we thy servants humbly pray
That thou wouldst look upon the face
Of thine anointed Son today.

Vincent Stuckey Stratton Coles, 1845-1929

580 SONG 1 10 10.10 10 10 10   ORLANDO GIBBONS, 1583–1625

AND now, O Father, mindful of the love
    That bought us, once for all, on Calvary's Tree,
And having with us him that pleads above,
    We here present, we here spread forth to thee
That only offering perfect in thine eyes,
The one true, pure, immortal sacrifice.

2 Look, Father, look on his anointed face,
    And only look on us as found in him;
Look not on our misusings of thy grace,
    Our prayer so languid, and our faith so dim:
For lo! between our sins and their reward
We set the Passion of thy Son our Lord.

3 And then for those, our dearest and our best,
    By this prevailing presence we appeal;
O fold them closer to thy mercy's breast,
    O do thine utmost for their souls' true weal;
From tainting mischief keep them white and clear,
And crown thy gifts with strength to persevere.

4 And so we come: O draw us to thy feet,
    Most patient Saviour, who canst love us still;
And by this food, so awesome and so sweet,
    Deliver us from every touch of ill:
In thine own service make us glad and free,
And grant us never more to part with thee.

William Bright, 1824–1901, based
on Unde et memores, Domine, nos servi tui

581 DAS WALT' GOTT VATER
L.M.

Probably by DANIEL VETTER, c. 1713

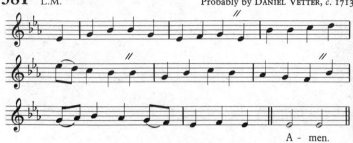

A - men.

Alternative tune, VERBUM SUPERNUM, No. 116

Verbum supernum prodiens, nec Patris

FORTH from on high the Father sends
His Son, who yet stays by his side.
The Word made man for man then spends
His life till life's last eventide.

2 While Judas plans the traitor's sign,
The mocking kiss that Love betrays,
Jesus in form of bread and wine
His loving sacrifice displays.

3 He gives himself that faith may see
The heavenly Food on which men feed,
That flesh and blood of man may be
Fed by his flesh and blood indeed.

4 By birth he makes himself man's kin;
As Food before his guests he lies;
To death he bears man's cross of sin;
In heaven he reigns as man's blest prize.

5 O Priest and Victim, Lord of Life,
Throw wide the gates of Paradise!
We face our foes in mortal strife;
Thou art our strength! O heed our cries!

6 *To Father, Son, and Spirit blest,*
One only God, be ceaseless praise!
May he in goodness grant us rest
In heaven, our home, for endless days! Amen.

James Quinn
From the Latin of
St. Thomas Aquinas, 1227–74

582 SONG 22 10 10 10 10   ORLANDO GIBBONS, 1583-1625 (rhythm altered)

A-men.

IN love, from love, thou camest forth, O Lord,
Sent from the Father, his incarnate Word:
That in that perfect Name, by thee confessed,
Our hearts with thine might find their perfect rest.

2 Within the veil, thy mortal travail o'er,
Thou livest unto God to die no more;
And now, made sons of God, with thee we stand,
Girt with the grace of thy confirming hand.

3 Thou art our Royal Priest before the throne;
Our priesthood is in thee, from thee alone;
In thee we offer at our Father's feet
The offering pure, with holy incense sweet.

4 The sacred rite its ordered course hath run,
All that thy Love ordained our love hath done,
Still showing forth before our Father's eyes
The one, pure, perfect, filial sacrifice.

5 And now, O Lord, from out thy chosen place
Thy voice proclaims anew the feast of grace.
Cleanse thou us, Lord, in this most holy hour
By thine own breath of resurrection power.

6 Lord of the living and the tranquil dead,
Reveal thyself, our one all-glorious Head;
And through these hallowed gifts of bread and wine
Feed thy one Body with the Life divine.

7 O perfect Brother, and true Son of God,
Impart to us thy Body and thy Blood,
That through communion of one mind, one heart,
We may advance to see thee as thou art.

8 *Jesus, Immanuel, evermore adored,*
At thy great Name we bow, we own thee Lord:
Glory be thine, O Father, thine, O Son,
And thine, O Holy Spirit, ever One. Amen.

John MacLeod, 1840-98

513

583 TREDEGAR 8787 87   GUTHRIE FOOTE, 1897–1972

Alternative tune, HELMSLEY, No. 316 *(with threefold Alleluia)*

LORD, enthroned in heavenly splendour,
    First-begotten from the dead,
Thou alone, our strong defender,
    Liftest up thy people's head.
        Alleluia! Alleluia!
    Jesus, true and living Bread.

2 Here our humblest homage pay we;
    Here in loving reverence bow;
Here for faith's discernment pray we,
    Lest we fail to know thee now.
        Alleluia! Alleluia!
    Thou art here, we ask not how.

3 Though the lowliest form doth veil thee,
    As of old in Bethlehem,
Here as there thine angels hail thee,
    Branch and Flower of Jesse's stem.
        Alleluia! Alleluia!
    We in worship join with them.

4 Paschal Lamb, thine offering, finished
    Once for all when thou wast slain,
In its fullness undiminished
    Shall for evermore remain,
        Alleluia! Alleluia!
    Cleansing souls from every stain.

5 Life-imparting, heavenly Manna,
    Stricken Rock with streaming side,
Heaven and earth with loud hosanna
    Worship thee, the Lamb who died,
        Alleluia! Alleluia!
    Risen, ascended, glorified.

George Hugh Bourne, 1840–1925

584 (i) ADORO TE 10 10 10 10

Paris Processionale, 1740

In free rhythm

(ii) *For antiphonal singing (upper and lower voices)*

Adoro te devote, latens Deitas

THEE we adore, O hidden Saviour, thee,
Who in thy sacrament dost deign to be:
Both flesh and spirit at thy presence fail,
Yet here thy presence we devoutly hail.

2 O blest memorial of our dying Lord!
Thou living Bread, who life dost here
afford,
O may our souls for ever live by thee,
And thou to us for ever precious be.

3 Fountain of goodness, Jesus, Lord, and
God,
Cleanse us, unclean, with thy most
cleansing blood;
Make us in thee devoutly to believe,
In thee to hope, to thee in love to cleave.

4 O Christ, whom now beneath a veil we
see,
May what we thirst for soon our portion be,
There in the glory of thy dwelling-place
To gaze on thee unveiled, and see thy
face.

St. Thomas Aquinas, 1227-74
From the translation by
James Russell Woodford, 1820-85

585 ST. FLAVIAN C.M.

Melody of Psalm 132 in *English Psalter*, 1562
(first half only), adapted 1599 and later

A version with the later form of rhythm is at No. 8

ACCORDING to thy gracious
 word,
  In meek humility,
This will I do, my dying Lord,
  I will remember thee.

2 Thy body, broken for my sake,
  My bread from heaven shall be;
Thy testamental cup I take,
  And thus remember thee.

3 Gethsemane can I forget?
  Or there thy conflict see,
Thine agony and bloody sweat,
  And not remember thee?

4 When to the cross I turn mine eyes,
  And rest on Calvary,
O Lamb of God, my sacrifice,
  I must remember thee,—

5 Remember thee, and all thy pains,
  And all thy love to me;
Yea, while a breath, a pulse remains,
  Will I remember thee.

6 And when these failing lips grow dumb,
  And mind and memory flee,
When thou shalt in thy Kingdom come,
  Jesus, remember me.

James Montgomery, 1771–1854

586 LES COMMANDEMENS DE DIEU
9898

From a melody in *La Forme des
Prières et Chants Ecclésiastiques*,
Strasbourg, 1545 (rhythm simplified)

FATHER, we thank thee who hast planted
 Thy holy name within our hearts.
Knowledge and faith and life immortal
 Jesus thy Son to us imparts.

2 Thou, Lord, didst make all for thy pleasure,
   Didst give man food for all his days,
Giving in Christ the bread eternal;
   Thine is the power, be thine the praise.

3 Watch o'er thy Church, O Lord, in mercy,
   Save it from evil, guard it still,
Perfect it in thy love, unite it,
   Cleansed and conformed unto thy will.

4 As grain, once scattered on the hillsides,
   Was in the bread we break made one,
So may thy world-wide Church be gathered
   Into thy Kingdom by thy Son.

From prayers in the DIDACHE,
probably second century
Tr. and versified by Francis Bland Tucker (altered)

587 DOLGELLEY (DOLGELLAU)
6666 88

Welsh Hymn Melody from
Haleliwiah Drachefn, Carmarthen, 1855

AUTHOR of life divine,
   Who hast a table spread,
Furnished with mystic wine
   And everlasting bread,
Preserve the life thyself hast given,
And feed and train us up for heaven.

2   Our needy souls sustain
      With fresh supplies of love,
   Till all thy life we gain,
      And all thy fullness prove,
   And, strengthened by thy perfect grace,
   Behold without a veil thy face.

Charles Wesley, 1707-88

588 ACH GOTT UND HERR
8787

Andachts Zymbeln, Freiburg, 1655

نبلا عَنْ اِنوا وِهنهت

STRENGTHEN for service, Lord, the hands
    That holy things have taken;
Let ears that now have heard thy songs
    To clamour never waken.

2 Lord, may the tongues which 'Holy' sang
    Keep free from all deceiving;
The eyes which saw thy love be bright,
    Thy blessèd hope perceiving.

3 The feet that tread thy holy courts
    From light do thou not banish;
The bodies by thy body fed
    With thy new life replenish.

LITURGY OF MALABAR
Tr. Charles William Humphreys, 1840–1921,
Percy Dearmer, 1867–1936, and others

589 DANIEL L.M.

Irish Traditional Melody

[For No. 601]

A - men.

FORTH in the peace of Christ we go;
Christ to the world with joy we bring;
Christ in our minds, Christ on our lips,
Christ in our hearts, the world's true King.

2 King of our hearts, Christ makes us kings;
Kingship with him his servants gain;
With Christ, the Servant-Lord of all,
Christ's world we serve to share Christ's reign.

3 Priests of the world, Christ sends us forth
  The world of time to consecrate,
  The world of sin by grace to heal,
  Christ's world in Christ to re-create.

4 Christ's are our lips, his word we speak;
  Prophets are we whose deeds proclaim
  Christ's truth in love that we may be
  Christ in the world, to spread Christ's name.

5 We are the Church; Christ bids us show
  That in his Church all nations find
  Their hearth and home where Christ restores
  True peace, true love, to all mankind.

James Quinn

590 MORAVIA C.M.

Adapted from a melody in Wolder's
Gesangbuch, Hamburg, 1598

A - men.

PARAPHRASE 38, verses 8, 10, 11

NOW, Lord! according to thy word,
  Let me in peace depart;
Mine eyes have thy salvation seen,
  And gladness fills my heart.

2 This great salvation, long prepared,
    And now disclosed to view,
  Hath proved thy love was constant
      still,
    And promises were true.

3 That Sun I now behold, whose light
    Shall heathen darkness chase,
  And rays of brightest glory pour
    Around thy chosen race.

4 *To Father, Son, and Holy Ghost,*
    The God whom we adore,
  Be glory, as it was, and is,
    And shall be evermore. Amen.

Scottish Paraphrases, 1781
From St. Luke 2: 29-32

The following are also suitable

No.
  7   O send thy light forth and thy truth
351   O thou my soul, bless God the Lord
391   God will I bless all times
492   O thou who at thy Eucharist didst pray
307   'Lift up your hearts'

V

OTHER ORDINANCES

———

V

OTHER ORDINANCES

CONFIRMATION

591 JACKSON (BYZANTIUM)
C.M.

THOMAS JACKSON, 1715–81
Twelve Psalm Tunes, 1780 (simplified)

PARAPHRASE 54

I'M not ashamed to own my Lord,
Or to defend his cause,
Maintain the glory of his cross,
And honour all his laws.

2 Jesus, my Lord! I know his Name,
His Name is all my boast;
Nor will he put my soul to shame,
Nor let my hope be lost.

3 I know that safe with him remains,
Protected by his power,
What I've committed to his trust,
Till the decisive hour.

4 Then will he own his servant's name
Before his Father's face,
And in the New Jerusalem
Appoint my soul a place.

Scottish Paraphrases, 1781
From 2 Timothy 1: 12

592 CHRISTCHURCH 6666 88   CHARLES STEGGALL, 1826–1905

WE come, O Christ, to thee,
   True Son of God and man,
By whom all things consist,
   In whom all life began:
In thee alone we live and move,
And have our being in thy love.

2 Thou art the way to God,
   Thy blood our ransom paid;
In thee we face our Judge
   And Maker unafraid.
Before the throne absolved we stand:
Thy love has met thy law's demand.

3 Thou art the living truth!
   All wisdom dwells in thee,
Thou source of every skill,
   Eternal verity!
Thou great I AM! In thee we rest,
True answer to our every quest.

4 Thou only art true life,
   To know thee is to live
The more abundant life
   That earth can never give:
O risen Lord! We live in thee
And thou in us eternally!

5 We worship thee, Lord Christ,
   Our Saviour and our King,
To thee our youth and strength
   Adoringly we bring:
So fill our hearts that men may see
Thy life in us and turn to thee!

Edith Margaret Clarkson

593 ABBOT'S LEIGH 8787. D   CYRIL VINCENT TAYLOR

Alternative tune, HYFRYDOL, No. 381 (in G), and 437 (in F)

YE that know the Lord is gracious,
 Ye for whom a Corner-stone
Stands, of God elect and precious,
 Laid that ye may build thereon,
See that on that sure foundation
 Ye a living temple raise,
Towers that may tell forth salvation,
 Walls that may re-echo praise.

2 Living stones, by God appointed
 Each to his allotted place,
Kings and priests, by God anointed,
 Shall ye not declare his grace?

Ye, a royal generation,
 Tell the tidings of your birth,
Tidings of a new creation
 To an old and weary earth.

3 Tell the praise of him who called
 you
 Out of darkness into light,
Broke the fetters that enthralled you,
 Gave you freedom, peace and
 sight:
Tell the tale of sins forgiven,
 Strength renewed and hope
 restored,
Till the earth, in tune with heaven,
 Praise and magnify the Lord!

Cyril Argentine Alington, 1872–1955
From 1 Peter 2: 3–10

594 ARDEN C.M.   GEORGE THALBEN-BALL

WITNESS, ye men and angels, now,
 Before the Lord we speak;
To him we make our solemn vow,
 A vow we dare not break;

2 That, long as life itself shall last,
 Ourselves to Christ we yield;
Nor from his cause will we depart,
 Or ever quit the field.

3 We trust not in our native strength,
 But on his grace rely,
That, with returning wants, the Lord
 Will all our need supply.

4 O guide our doubtful feet aright,
 And keep us in thy ways;
And while we turn our vows to
 prayers,
 Turn thou our prayers to praise.

Benjamin Beddome, 1717–95

595 ASCENDIT DEUS
887. D

JOHANN GOTTFRIED SCHICHT, 1753–1823
Allgemeines Choralbuch, Leipzig, 1819

WE magnify thy Name, O God,
That to thy people thou hast given
  A covenant sign eternal.
Baptized into the Triune Name
Of Father, Son, and Holy Ghost
  Thou didst them seal for ever.

2 Nurtured within thy family,
  Thy servants now proclaim to all
    Their faith in Christ their Saviour.
  Confirm and strengthen them, O
    God,
  Increase in them the Spirit's grace;
    Grant them thy benediction.

3 May they, at Christ's own Table, be
  Partakers of his flesh and blood
    With grateful adoration.
  May they in all things live like Christ,
  And thereby witness to all men
    That he is Lord eternal.

John Monteith Barkley

The following are also suitable

No.
629 Fair waved the golden corn
342 Come, Holy Ghost
550 Lift high the cross

Also, Hymns of Affirmation, Dedication, Stewardship, Witness (*Section III*)

ORDINATION

596 PRAETORIUS C.M.

Harmoniae Hymnorum Scholiae
Gorlicensis, Görlitz, 1599
Possibly by MICHAEL PRAETORIUS, 1571-1621

A - men.

PSALM 103, verses 19-22

THE Lord preparèd hath his throne
  In heavens firm to stand;
And every thing that being hath
  His kingdom doth command.

2 O ye his angels, that excel
    In strength, bless ye the Lord;
  Ye who obey what he commands,
    And hearken to his word.

3 O bless and magnify the Lord,
    Ye glorious hosts of his;
  Ye ministers, that do fulfil
    Whate'er his pleasure is.

4 O bless the Lord, all ye his works,
    Wherewith the world is stored
  In his dominions everywhere.
    My soul, bless thou the Lord.

5 *To Father, Son, and Holy Ghost,*
    The God whom we adore,
  Be glory, as it was, and is,
    And shall be evermore. Amen.

597 WINCHESTER NEW
(CRASSELIUS) L.M.

Adapted from a melody in
Musikalisches Hand-Buch, Hamburg, 1690

POUR out thy Spirit from on high;
    Lord, thine ordainèd servants
        bless;
Graces and gifts to each supply,
    And clothe thy priests with right-
        eousness.

2 Within thy temple when they stand,
    To teach the truth, as taught by
        thee,
    Saviour, like stars in thy right hand
    The angels of the churches be!

3 Wisdom and zeal and faith impart,
    Firmness with meekness, from above,
    To bear thy people on their heart,
    And love the souls whom thou dost love.

4 To watch and pray, and never faint;
    By day and night strict guard to keep;
    To warn the sinner, cheer the saint,
    Nourish thy lambs, and feed thy sheep;

5 Then, when their work is finished here,
    In humble hope their charge resign.
    When the Chief Shepherd shall appear,
    O God, may they and we be thine.

James Montgomery, 1771–1854

MARRIAGE

598 (i)

WALFORD DAVIES, 1869–1941

(ii)

SAMUEL WESLEY, 1766–1837

PSALM 67

GOD be merciful unto'us and'bless us:
  and cause his'face to'shine up-'on us:
That thy way may be'known upon'earth:
  thy saving'health a-'mong all'nations.

2 Let the people'praise thee O'God:
  let'all the'people'praise thee:
O let the nations be glad and'sing for'joy:
  for thou shalt judge the people righteously and'govern the'nations
  up·on'earth.

3 Let the people'praise thee O'God:
  let'all the'people'praise thee:
Then shall the earth'yield her'increase:
  and God even'our own'God shall'bless us.

† God'shall'bless us:
  and all the'ends of the'earth shall'fear him.

Glory'be to the'Father:
  and to the Son'and to the'Holy'Ghost:
As it'was in the be-'ginning:
  is now and ever shall be   'world without'end. A-'men.

    † *These two lines should be sung to the second half of the chant*

529

599 TALLIS' CANON
L.M.

THOMAS TALLIS, c. 1505-85
As shortened by THOMAS RAVENSCROFT, *Psalter*, 1621

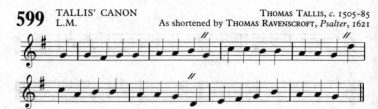

O FATHER, by whose sovereign sway
  The sun and stars in order move,
Yet who hast made us bold to say
  Thy nature and thy Name is love:

2 O royal Son, whose every deed
  Showed love and love's divinity,
Yet didst not scorn the humblest need
  At Cana's feast in Galilee:

3 O Holy Spirit, who dost speak
  In saint and sage since time began,
Yet givest courage to the weak
  And teachest love to selfish man:

4 Be present in our hearts today,
  All powerful to bless, and give
To these thy children grace that they
  May love, and through their loving live.

Cyril Argentine Alington, 1872–1955

600 AURELIA 7676. D

SAMUEL SEBASTIAN WESLEY, 1810-76

O FATHER, all creating,
  Whose wisdom, love, and power
First bound two lives together
  In Eden's primal hour,
The lives of these thy children
  With thy best gifts endue,
A home by thee made happy,
  A love by thee kept true.

2 O Saviour, Guest most bounteous
  Of old in Galilee,
Vouchsafe today thy presence
  With these who call on thee;
Their store of earthly gladness
  Transform to heavenly wine,
And teach them, in the tasting,
  To know the gift is thine.

3 O Spirit of the Father,
 Breathe on them from above,
So mighty in thy pureness,
 So tender in thy love;
That, guarded by thy presence,
 From sin and strife kept free,
Their lives may own thy guidance,
 Their hearts be ruled by thee.

4 Except thou build it, Father,
 The house is built in vain;
Except thou, Saviour, bless it,
 The joy will turn to pain;
But naught can break the union
 Of hearts in thee made one;
And love thy Spirit hallows
 Is endless love begun.

John Ellerton, 1826–93 (altered)

601 MELCOMBE L.M.

SAMUEL WEBBE, the elder, 1740–1816
An Essay on the Church Plain-Chant, 1782

A - men.

Alternative tune, DANIEL, Nos. 589, 691

O GOD, whose loving hand has led
Thy children to this joyful day,
We pray that thou wilt bless them now
As, one in thee, they face life's way.

2 Grant them the will to follow Christ
Who graced the Feast in Galilee,
And through his perfect life of love
Fulfilment of their love to see.

3 Give them the power to make a home
Where peace and honour shall abide,
Where Christ shall be the gracious Head,
The trusted Friend, the constant Guide.

4 *To Father, Son, and Holy Ghost,*
 The God whom heaven and earth adore,
 Be glory, as it was of old,
 Is now, and shall be evermore. Amen.

John Boyd Moore

531

602 CHILDHOOD 8886

WALFORD DAVIES, 1869–1941
A Students' Hymnal, 1923

O GOD of Love, to thee we bow,
And pray for these before thee now,
That, closely knit in holy vow,
   They may in thee be one.

2 When days are filled with pure
      delight,
When paths are plain and skies are
      bright,
Walking by faith and not by sight,
    May they in thee be one.

3 When stormy winds fulfil thy will,
And all their good seems turned to ill,
Then, trusting thee completely, still
    May they in thee be one.

4 Whate'er in life shall be their share
Of quickening joy or burdening care,
In power to do and grace to bear,
    May they in thee be one.

5 Eternal Love, with them abide;
In thee for ever may they hide,
For even death cannot divide
    Those whom thou makest one.

William Vaughan Jenkins, 1868–1920

The following are also suitable

No.
634 May the grace of Christ our Saviour
9 Praise to the Lord, the Almighty
115 Come down, O Love Divine
368 Now thank we all our God
388 The King of Love my Shepherd is
457 Fill thou our life
360 Praise, my soul, the King of heaven

OTHER ORDINANCES

FUNERAL SERVICES

603 KILMARNOCK C.M.

NEILL DOUGALL, 1776–1862
Clarke's *Parochial Psalmody*, 2nd edition, 1831

A - men.

PSALM 103, verses 13-17

SUCH pity as a father hath
  Unto his children dear;
Like pity shows the Lord to such
  As worship him in fear.

2 For he remembers we are dust,
  And he our frame well knows.
Frail man, his days are like the grass,
  As flower in field he grows:

3 For over it the wind doth pass,
  And it away is gone;
And of the place where once it was
  It shall no more be known.

4 But unto them that do him fear
  God's mercy never ends;
And to their children's children still
  His righteousness extends.

5 *To Father, Son, and Holy Ghost,*
  The God whom we adore,
Be glory, as it was, and is,
  And shall be evermore. Amen.

604 LES COMMANDEMENS DE DIEU
9898

From a melody in *La Forme des
Prières et Chants Ecclésiastiques,*
Strasbourg, 1545 (rhythm simplified)

GO, happy soul, thy days are ended,
  Thy pilgrimage on earth below:
Go, by angelic guard attended,
  To God's own Paradise now go.

2 Go; Christ, the Shepherd good,
    befriend thee,
  Who gave his life thy soul to win;
'Tis even he that shall defend thee,
  Thy going out and coming in.

3 Go forth in peace: farewell to sadness:
    May rest in Paradise be thine;
  In Jesus' presence there is gladness:
    Light everlasting on thee shine.

*George Ratcliffe Woodward, 1849-1934,
and Compilers of* The BBC Hymn Book

605 ST. ALBINUS
7878 and Alleluia

HENRY JOHN GAUNTLETT, 1805-76

Jesus lebt, mit ihm auch ich

JESUS lives! thy terrors now
  Can, O Death, no more appal us;
Jesus lives! by this we know
  Thou, O grave, canst not enthral us.
      Alleluia!

2 Jesus lives! henceforth is death
  But the gate of life immortal;
This shall calm our trembling breath
  When we pass its gloomy portal.

3 Jesus lives! for us he died;
  Then, alone to Jesus living,
Pure in heart may we abide,
  Glory to our Saviour giving.

4 Jesus lives! our hearts know well
  Naught from us his love shall sever;
Life, nor death, nor powers of hell
  Tear us from his keeping ever.

5 Jesus lives! to him the throne
  Over heaven and earth is given;
May we go where he is gone,
  Live and reign with him in heaven.

Christian Fürchtegott Gellert, 1715-69
Tr. Frances Elizabeth Cox, 1812-97

606 VULPIUS (GELOBT SEI GOTT)
888 and Alleluias

Vulpius' *Gesangbuch*, 1609

FUNERAL SERVICES

Al - le - lu - ia! Al - le - lu - ia! Al - le - lu - ia!

O LORD of life, where'er they be,
Safe in thine own eternity,
Our dead are living unto thee.
 Alleluia! Alleluia! Alleluia!

2 All souls are thine, and, here or
 there,
They rest within thy sheltering care;
One providence alike they share.

3 Thy word is true, thy ways are just;
Above the requiem, 'Dust to dust',
Shall rise our psalm of grateful
 trust,

4 O happy they in God who rest,
No more by fear and doubt
 oppressed;
Living or dying, they are blest:

Frederick Lucian Hosmer, 1840–1929

607 VATER UNSER
 (OLD 112TH) 8888 88   *Geistliche Lieder, Leipzig, 1539*

GOD of the living, in whose eyes
Unveiled thy whole creation lies,
All souls are thine; we must not say
That those are dead who pass away;
From this our world of flesh set free,
We know them living unto thee.

2 Released from earthly toil and strife,
With thee is hidden still their life;
Thine are their thoughts, their works, their powers,
All thine, and yet most truly ours;
For well we know, where'er they be,
Our dead are living unto thee.

John Ellerton, 1826–93

608 ANNUE CHRISTE 12 12 12 12   *Paris Antiphoner, 1736*

A - men.

THERE is a blessèd home beyond this land of woe,
Where trials never come, nor tears of sorrow flow;
Where faith is lost in sight, and patient hope is crowned,
And everlasting light its glory throws around.

2 O joy all joys beyond! to see the Lamb who died,
For ever there enthroned, for ever glorified;
To give to him the praise of every triumph won,
And sing, through endless days, the great things he hath done.

3 *There is a land of peace; the angels know it well;*
Glad songs that never cease within its portals swell;
Around its glorious throne ten thousand saints adore
Christ, with the Father one and Spirit, evermore. Amen.

Henry Williams Baker, 1821–77

DEDICATION OF CHURCH BUILDINGS

609 & 610 SOLEMNIS HAEC FESTIVITAS L.M.   *Paris Gradual, 1685*

609

THIS stone to thee in faith we lay;
    We build the temple, Lord, to thee:
Thine eye be open, night and day,
    To guard this house and sanctuary.

2 Here, when thy people seek thy face,
    And dying sinners pray to live,
Hear, thou, in heaven thy dwelling-place,
    And when thou hearest, O forgive!

3 Here, when thy messengers proclaim
    The blessèd Gospel of thy Son,
Still, by the power of his great Name,
    Be mighty signs and wonders done.

4 'Hosanna!' to their heavenly King
    When children's voices raise that song,
'Hosanna!' let their angels sing,
    And heaven, with earth, the strain prolong.

5 But will the eternal Father deign
    Here to abide, no transient guest?
Will here the world's Redeemer reign,
    And here the Holy Spirit rest?

6 That glory never hence depart!
    Yet choose not, Lord, this house alone;
Thy Kingdom come to every heart:
    In all the world be thine the throne.

James Montgomery, 1771–1854 (altered)

610

ALL things are thine; no gift have we,
Lord of all gifts, to offer thee:
And hence with grateful hearts today,
Thine own before thy feet we lay.

2 Thy will was in the builders' thought;
Thy hand unseen amidst us wrought;
Through mortal motive, scheme and plan,
Thy wise eternal purpose ran.

3 In weakness and in want we call
On thee for whom the heavens are small;
Thy glory is thy children's good,
Thy joy thy tender Fatherhood.

4 O Father, deign these walls to bless;
Fill with thy love their emptiness;
And let their door a gateway be
To lead us from ourselves to thee.

John Greenleaf Whittier, 1807–92

The following is also suitable

No. 10   Christ is made the sure foundation

VI

TIMES AND SEASONS

———

TIMES AND SEASONS

NEW YEAR

611 ST. ANNE C.M.

Modern form of a melody from
A Supplement to the New Version, 1708
Probably by WILLIAM CROFT, 1678–1727

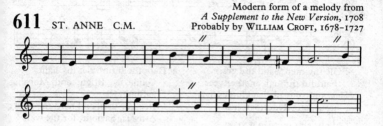

O GOD, our help in ages past,
  Our hope for years to come,
Our shelter from the stormy blast,
  And our eternal home!

2 Under the shadow of thy throne
    Thy saints have dwelt secure;
  Sufficient is thine arm alone,
    And our defence is sure.

3 Before the hills in order stood,
    Or earth received her frame,
  From everlasting thou art God,
    To endless years the same.

4 A thousand ages in thy sight
    Are like an evening gone;
  Short as the watch that ends the night
    Before the rising sun.

5 Time, like an ever-rolling stream,
    Bears all its sons away;
  They fly forgotten, as a dream
    Dies at the opening day.

6 O God, our help in ages past,
    Our hope for years to come,
  Be thou our guard while troubles last,
    And our eternal home.

Isaac Watts, 1674–1748

541

612 ORIENTIS PARTIBUS 7777   Medieval French Melody (adapted)

FOR thy mercy and thy grace,
   Faithful through another year,
Hear our song of thankfulness;
   Jesus, our Redeemer, hear.

2 Lo! our sins on thee we cast,
   Thee, our perfect sacrifice,
And, forgetting all the past,
   Press towards our glorious prize.

3 Dark the future; let thy light
   Guide us, Bright and Morning
     Star;
Fierce our foes, and hard the fight;
   Arm us, Saviour, for the war.

4 In our weakness and distress,
   Rock of strength, be thou our stay;
In the pathless wilderness
   Be our true and living way.

5 Keep us faithful, keep us pure,
   Keep us evermore thine own;
Help, O help us to endure;
   Fit us for the promised crown.

Henry Downton, 1818–85

613 WAREHAM L.M.

WILLIAM KNAPP, 1698–1768
A Sett of New Psalm Tunes, 1738

[For No. 617]

A - men.

GREAT God, we sing that mighty
   hand
By which supported still we stand;
The opening year thy mercy shows,
And mercy crowns its lingering
   close.

2 By day, by night, at home, abroad,
Still are we guarded by our God,
By his incessant bounty fed,
By his unerring counsel led.

3 With grateful hearts the past we
    own;
  The future, all to us unknown,
  We to thy guardian care commit,
  And peaceful leave before thy feet.

4 In scenes exalted or depressed
  Thou art our joy, and thou our rest;
  Thy goodness all our hopes shall
    raise,
  Adored through all our changing
    days.

5 When death shall interrupt these songs,
  And seal in silence mortal tongues,
  Our helper God, in whom we trust,
  Shall keep our souls and guard our dust.

Philip Doddridge, 1702-51

614 RHOSYMEDRE (LOVELY) JOHN DAVID EDWARDS, 1805-85
6666 88(8) *Original Sacred Music, c. 1840 (slightly altered)*

Alternative tune, CHRISTCHURCH, No. 592

MARCH on, my soul, with strength,
  March forward, void of fear;
He who hath led will lead,
  While year succeedeth year;
And as thou goest on thy way,
*His hand shall hold thee day by day.

2 March on, my soul, with strength,
  In ease thou dar'st not dwell;
High duty calls thee forth;
  Then up, and quit thee well!
Take up thy cross, take up thy sword,
And fight the battles of thy Lord!

3 March on, my soul, with strength,
    With strength, but not thine own;
  The conquest thou shalt gain,
    Through Christ thy Lord alone;
  His grace shall nerve thy feeble arm,
  His love preserve thee safe from harm.

4 March on, my soul, with strength,
    From strength to strength march on;
  Warfare shall end at length,
    All foes be overthrown.
  Then, O my soul, if faithful now,
  The crown of life awaits thy brow.

William Wright, 1859-1924

* *The last line of each verse is repeated*

615 RUSTINGTON 8787. D   CHARLES HUBERT HASTINGS PARRY, 1848–1918

Alternative tune, BLAENWERN, No. 473

HEAVENLY Father, thou hast brought us
    Safely to the present day,
Gently leading on our footsteps,
    Watching o'er us all the way.
Friend and Guide through life's long journey,
    Grateful hearts to thee we bring;
But for love so true and changeless
    How shall we fit praises sing?

2 Mercies new and never-failing
    Brightly shine through all the past,
Watchful care and loving-kindness,
    Always near from first to last,
Tender love, divine protection
    Ever with us day and night;
Blessings more than we can number
    Strew the path with golden light.

3 Shadows deep have crossed our pathway;
    We have trembled in the storm;
Clouds have gathered round so darkly
    That we could not see thy form;
Yet thy love hath never left us
    In our griefs alone to be,
And the help each gave the other
    Was the strength that came from thee.

4 Many that we loved have left us,
    Reaching first their journey's end;
Now they wait to give us welcome—
    Brother, sister, child, and friend.
When at last our journey's over,
    And we pass away from sight,
Father, take us through the darkness
    Into everlasting light.

Hester Periam Hawkins, 1846–1928

616 AUSTRIAN HYMN
8787. D

FRANZ JOSEPH HAYDN, 1732–1809,
based on a Croatian folk song

AT thy feet, our God and Father,
    Who hast blessed us all our days,
We with grateful hearts would gather,
    To begin the year with praise,—
Praise for light so brightly shining
    On our steps from heaven above,
Praise for mercies daily twining
    Round us golden cords of love.

2 Jesus, for thy love most tender,
    On the cross for sinners shown,
We would praise thee, and surrender
    All our hearts to be thine own.
With so blest a Friend provided,
    We upon our way would go,
Sure of being safely guided,
    Guarded well from every foe.

3 Every day will be the brighter
    When thy gracious face we see;
Every burden will be lighter
    When we know it comes from thee.
Spread thy love's broad banner o'er us;
    Give us strength to serve and wait,
Till the glory breaks before us,
    Through the city's open gate.

James Drummond Burns, 1823–64

617 WINCHESTER NEW (CRASSELIUS) L.M.

Adapted from a melody in *Musikalisches Hand-Buch*, Hamburg, 1690

A-men.

Alternative tune, WAREHAM, No. 613

PSALM 145 (ii), verses 9, 10 15, 16

GOOD unto all men is the Lord:
O'er all his works his mercy is.
Thy works all praise to thee afford:
Thy saints, O Lord, thy Name shall bless.

2 The eyes of all things, Lord, attend,
And on thee wait that here do live,
And thou, in season due, dost send
Sufficient food them to relieve.

3 Yea, thou thine hand dost open wide,
And every thing dost satisfy
That lives, and doth on earth abide,
Of thy great liberality.

4 *To Father, Son, and Holy Ghost,*
The God whom earth and heaven adore,
Be glory, as it was of old,
Is now, and shall be evermore. Amen.

618 KING'S LANGLEY C.M.

English Traditional May-Day Carol Melody, collected by LUCY BROADWOOD, 1858-1929

SPRING

THE glory of the spring how sweet!
  The new-born life how glad!
What joy the happy earth to greet,
  In new, bright raiment clad!

2 Divine Renewer, thee I bless;
  I greet thy going forth;
I love thee in the loveliness
  Of thy renewèd earth.

3 But O these wonders of thy grace,
  These nobler works of thine,
These marvels sweeter far to trace,
  These new births more divine,

4 This new-born glow of faith so
    strong,
  This bloom of love so fair,
This new-born ecstasy of song,
  And fragrancy of prayer!

5 Creator Spirit, work in me
  These wonders sweet of thine;
Divine Renewer, graciously
  Renew this heart of mine.

Thomas Hornblower Gill, 1819–1906

619 SUSSEX 8787

Adapted by RALPH VAUGHAN WILLIAMS, 1872–1958,
from an English Traditional Melody

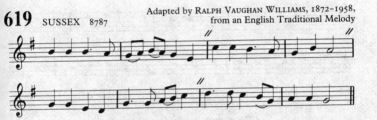

BY the rutted roads we follow,
  Fallow fields are rested now;
All along the waking country
  Soil is waiting for the plough.

2 In the yard the plough is ready,
  Ready to the ploughman's hand,
Ready for the crow-straight furrow,
  Farmer's sign across God's land.

3 God, in this good land you lend us,
  Bless the service of the share;
Light our thinking with your wisdom,
  Plant your patience in our care.

4 This is first of all man's labours,
  Man must always plough the earth;
God, be with us at the ploughing,
  Touch our harvest at its birth.

John Arlott

620 WIR PFLÜGEN
7676. D and refrain

JOHANN ABRAHAM PETER SCHULZ, 1747-1800

Wir pflügen und wir streuen

WE plough the fields, and scatter
    The good seed on the land,
But it is fed and watered
    By God's almighty hand;
He sends the snow in winter,
    The warmth to swell the grain,
The breezes and the sunshine
    And soft refreshing rain.
        All good gifts around us
        Are sent from heaven above;
        Then thank the Lord, O thank the Lord,
        For all his love.

2 He only is the Maker
    Of all things near and far;
He paints the wayside flower,
    He lights the evening star;
The winds and waves obey him,
    By him the birds are fed;
Much more to us, his children,
    He gives our daily bread.

3 We thank thee then, O Father,
　For all things bright and good,
The seed-time and the harvest,
　Our life, our health, our food.
Accept the gifts we offer
　For all thy love imparts,
And, what thou most desirest,
　Our humble, thankful hearts.

Matthias Claudius, 1740–1815
Tr. Jane Montgomery Campbell, 1817–78

621 SEVEN JOYS OF MARY
7575 and refrain

English Traditional Carol Melody

For younger children

SEE the farmer sow the seed
　While the field is brown;
See the furrows deep and straight
　Up the field and down:
　　Farmer, farmer, sow your seed
　　Up the field and down;
　　God will make the golden corn
　　Grow where all is brown.

2 Wait awhile and look again
　Where the field was bare;
See how God has sent the corn
　Growing golden there:

Frederick Arthur Jackson, 1867–1942

622 LONGWALL 7676   KENNETH DONALD SMITH

For younger children

IN the lanes and in the parks
    Little flowers are showing;
God, who made and loves the flowers,
    Watches o'er their growing.

2 In the bushes and the trees,
    Birdsong is beginning;
God, who made and loves the birds,
    Listens to their singing.

M. Temple Frere

SUMMER

623 FOREST GREEN D.C.M.   English Traditional Melody

THE summer days are come again;
    Once more the glad earth yields
Her golden wealth of ripening grain,
    And breath of clover fields,
And deepening shade of summer
    woods,
    And glow of summer air,
And winging thoughts, and happy
    moods,
    Of love and joy and prayer.

2 The summer days are come again;
    The birds are on the wing;
God's praises, in their loving strain,
    Unconsciously they sing.
We know who giveth all the good
    That doth our cup o'erbrim;
For summer joy in field and wood,
    We lift our song to him.

Samuel Longfellow, 1819–92

624 KING'S WESTON 6565. D   RALPH VAUGHAN WILLIAMS, 1872–1958

SUMMER suns are glowing
  Over land and sea;
Happy light is flowing,
  Bountiful and free.
Everything rejoices
  In the mellow rays;
All earth's thousand voices
  Swell the psalm of praise.

2 God's free mercy streameth
  Over all the world,
And his banner gleameth,
  Everywhere unfurled.
Broad and deep and glorious,
  As the heaven above,
Shines in might victorious
  His eternal love.

3 Lord, upon our blindness
  Thy pure radiance pour;
For thy loving-kindness
  Make us love thee more.
And, when clouds are drifting
  Dark across our sky,
Then, the veil uplifting,
  Father, be thou nigh.

4 We will never doubt thee,
  Though thou veil thy light;
Life is dark without thee;
  Death with thee is bright.
Light of light, shine o'er us
  On our pilgrim way;
Go thou still before us,
  To the endless day.

William Walsham How, 1823–97

625 SAVEZ-VOUS 7676   French Folk Melody

For younger children

LET us sing our song of praise;
  Thank you, God! Thank you, God!
For the happy summer days,
  Thank you, God! Thank you, God!

2 For the sunshine and the showers,
  Thank you, God! Thank you,
    God!
Bringing us the lovely flowers,
  Thank you, God! Thank you,
    God!

3 For the green and shady trees,
  Thank you, God! Thank you, God!
For the gentle cooling breeze,
  Thank you, God! Thank you, God!

Winifred Eva Barnard

SEEDTIME AND HARVEST

626 COLCHESTER
C.M.   Tans'ur's *Harmony of Zion*, 1734
                  (later form of rhythm)

A - men.

PSALM 65, verses 9, 11–13

EARTH thou dost visit, water-
  ing it,
  Making it rich to grow
With thy full flood, providing corn;
  Thou hast prepared it so.

2 So thou the year most liberally
  Dost with thy goodness crown;
And all thy paths abundantly
  On us drop fatness down.

3 They drop upon the pastures wide,
 That do in deserts lie;
The little hills on every side
 Rejoice right pleasantly.

4 With flocks the pastures clothèd be,
 The vales with corn are clad;
And now they shout and sing to
  thee,
 For thou hast made them glad.

5 *To Father, Son, and Holy Ghost,*
 The God whom we adore,
Be glory, as it was, and is,
 And shall be evermore. **Amen.**

627 ST. GEORGE'S, WINDSOR 7777. D GEORGE JOB ELVEY, 1816-93

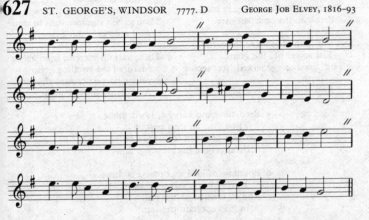

COME, ye thankful people, come,
Raise the song of harvest-home:
All is safely gathered in,
Ere the winter storms begin;
God, our Maker, doth provide
For our wants to be supplied:
Come to God's own temple, come,
Raise the song of harvest-home.

2 All this world is God's own field,
Fruit unto his praise to yield;
Wheat and tares together sown,
Unto joy or sorrow grown;
First the blade, and then the ear,
Then the full corn shall appear:
Lord of harvest, grant that we
Wholesome grain and pure may be.

3 For the Lord our God shall come,
And shall take his harvest home;
From his field shall in that day
All offences purge away;
Give his angels charge at last
In the fire the tares to cast;
But the fruitful ears to store
In his garner evermore.

4 Even so, Lord, quickly come;
Bring thy final harvest home:
Gather thou thy people in,
Free from sorrow, free from sin;
There, for ever purified,
In thy garner to abide:
Come, with all thine angels, come,
Raise the glorious harvest-home!

Henry Alford, 1810-71

628 UNIVERSITY
C.M.

Randall's *Psalm and Hymn Tunes*, 1794
Probably by CHARLES COLLIGNON, 1725-85

FOUNTAIN of mercy, God of love,
  How rich thy bounties are!
The rolling seasons, as they move,
  Proclaim thy constant care.

2 When in the bosom of the earth
  The sower hid the grain,
Thy goodness marked its secret birth,
  And sent the early rain.

3 The spring's sweet influence was thine;
  The plants in beauty grew;
Thou gavest summer suns to shine,
  And mild refreshing dew.

4 These various mercies from above
  Matured the swelling grain;
A yellow harvest crowns thy love,
  And plenty fills the plain.

5 Seed-time and harvest, Lord, alone
  Thou dost on man bestow;
Let him not then forget to own
  From whom his blessings flow.

6 Fountain of love, our praise is thine;
  To thee our songs we'll raise,
And all created nature join
  In glad exultant praise.

Alice Flowerdew, 1759-1830 (altered)

Also suitable
Creation and Providence (*Section II*)

629 HILLSBOROUGH
S.M.

JOHN GARDNER

Alternative tune, SANDYS, No. 153

FAIR waved the golden corn
In Canaan's pleasant land,
When full of joy, some shining morn,
Went forth the reaper band.

2 To God, so good and great,
Their cheerful thanks they pour,
Then carry to his temple gate
The choicest of their store.

3 For thus the holy word,
Spoken by Moses, ran:
'The first ripe ears are for the Lord,
The rest he gives to man.'

4 Like Israel, Lord, we give
Our earliest fruits to thee,
And pray that, long as we shall live,
We may thy children be.

5 Thine is our youthful prime,
And life and all its powers;
Be with us in our morning time,
And bless our evening hours.

6 In wisdom let us grow,
As years and strength are given,
That we may serve thy Church below,
And join thy saints in heaven.

John Hampden Gurney, 1802-62

630 KING'S LANGLEY
C.M.

English Traditional May-Day Carol Melody,
collected by LUCY BROADWOOD, 1858-1929

For children

THE fields and vales are thick with corn,
The reapers now are there,
They gather in the sheaves where once
The earth was brown and bare.

2 The empty barns will soon be filled
With ripe and golden grain,
For God has given the harvest fruit,
Who gave the sun and rain.

Frederick Arthur Jackson, 1867-1942

631 CHILDHOOD 8886

WALFORD DAVIES, 1869–1941
A Students' Hymnal, 1923

For younger children

WE thank thee, Lord, for all thy gifts
Of sunshine warm, and showers of rain
That ripened all the lovely fruits
And fields of golden grain.

2 We thank thee for the joy that comes
To us, when harvest gifts we bring—
That others, too, may know thy love,
Which speaks through everything.

3 O give us loving, thankful hearts,
For all thy goodness, love, and care;
And help us always to be glad
To give away and share.

Jessie Margaret Macdougall Ferguson,
1895–1964 (altered)

WINTER

632 O WALY WALY L.M.

English Traditional Melody

'TIS winter now; the fallen snow
   Has left the heavens all coldly clear;
Through leafless boughs the sharp winds blow,
   And all the earth lies dead and drear.

2 And yet God's love is not withdrawn;
   His life within the keen air breathes;
His beauty paints the crimson dawn,
   And clothes the boughs with glittering wreaths.

3 And though abroad the sharp winds blow,
   And skies are chill, and frosts are keen,
Home closer draws her circle now,
   And warmer glows her light within.

4 O God! who giv'st the winter's cold,
   As well as summer's joyous rays,
Us warmly in thy love enfold,
   And keep us through life's wintry days.

Samuel Longfellow, 1819–92

633 ST. AIDAN 7575   HERBERT POPPLE, 1891–1965

For younger children

LITTLE birds in winter time
Hungry are and poor;
Feed them, for the Father's sake,
Till the winter's o'er.

2 Throw them crumbs that you can spare
Round about your door;
Feed them, for the Father's sake,
Till the winter's o'er.

Frederick Arthur Jackson, 1867–1942

VII

CLOSE OF SERVICE

———

CLOSE OF SERVICE

634 GOTT DES HIMMELS (WALTHAM) 8787

HEINRICH ALBERT, 1604-51
Adapted by BACH in *The Christmas Oratorio*

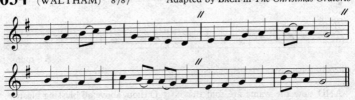

MAY the grace of Christ our Saviour,
  And the Father's boundless love,
With the Holy Spirit's favour,
  Rest upon us from above.

2 Thus may we abide in union
    With each other and the Lord,
  And possess in sweet communion
    Joys which earth cannot afford.

John Newton, 1725-1807
Based on 2 Corinthians 13: 14

635 DUNFERMLINE C.M.

Scottish Psalter, 1615

ALMIGHTY God, thy word is cast
  Like seed into the ground;
Now let the dew of heaven descend,
  And righteous fruits abound.

2 Let not the foe of Christ and man
    This holy seed remove,
  But give it root in every heart
    To bring forth fruits of love.

3 Let not the world's deceitful cares
    The rising plant destroy,
  But let it yield a hundredfold
    The fruits of peace and joy.

4 Oft as the precious seed is sown,
    Thy quickening grace bestow,
  That all whose souls the truth receive
    Its saving power may know.

John Cawood, 1775-1852

636 SALISBURY C.M.

Ravenscroft's *Psalter*, 1621

A - men.

Alternative tune, MARTYRDOM, No. 667

AND now the wants are told that brought
Thy children to thy knee;
Here lingering still, we ask for naught,
But simply worship thee.

2 For thou art God, the One, the Same,
O'er all things high and bright;
And round us, when we speak thy Name,
There spreads a heaven of light.

3 O thou, above all blessing blest,
O'er thanks exalted far,
Thy very greatness is a rest
To weaklings as we are;

4 For when we feel the praise of thee
A task beyond our powers,
We say, 'A perfect God is he,
And he is fully ours'.

5 *All glory to the Father be,*
All glory to the Son,
All glory, Holy Ghost, to thee,
While endless ages run. Amen.

William Bright, 1824-1901

637 WHITEHALL L.M.

HENRY LAWES, 1596-1662

A - men.

Alternative tune, TALLIS' CANON, No. 641

CLOSE OF SERVICE

COME, dearest Lord, descend and dwell
  By faith and love in every breast;
Then shall we know, and taste, and feel
  The joys that cannot be expressed.

2 Come, fill our hearts with inward strength,
    Make our enlargèd souls possess
  And learn the height and breadth and length
    Of thine unmeasurable grace.

3 *Now to the God whose power can do*
    More than our thoughts or wishes know,
  Be everlasting honours done
    By all the Church, through Christ his Son. Amen.

Isaac Watts, 1674–1748

638 ORIEL 8787 87   Ett's *Cantica Sacra*, 1840

LORD, dismiss us with thy blessing;
  Fill our hearts with joy and peace;
Let us each, thy love possessing,
  Triumph in redeeming grace;
  O refresh us, O refresh us,
  Travelling through this wilderness.

2 Thanks we give and adoration
    For thy Gospel's joyful sound;
  May the fruits of thy salvation
    In our hearts and lives abound;
    May thy presence, may thy presence
    With us evermore be found.

John Fawcett, 1740–1817

563

639 KEINE SCHÖNHEIT HAT DIE WELT
7777

GEORG JOSEPH,
c. 1650, in Scheffler's *Heilige Seelenlust,* 1657

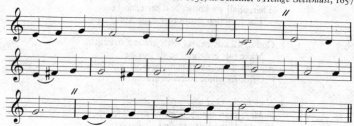

NOW may he who from the dead
   Brought the Shepherd of the sheep,
Jesus Christ, our King and Head,
   All our souls in safety keep.

2 May he teach us to fulfil
   What is pleasing in his sight,
Perfect us in all his will,
   And preserve us day and night.

3 To that dear Redeemer's praise,
   Who the covenant sealed with blood,
Let our hearts and voices raise
   Loud thanksgivings to our God.

John Newton, 1725–1807

640 OLD 124TH 10 10 10 10 10

French–Genevan Psalter, 1551
(rhythm altered)

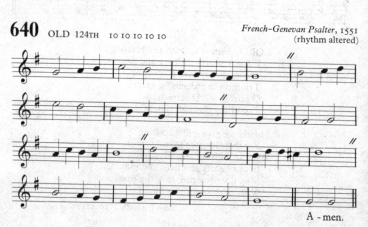

A - men.

CLOSE OF SERVICE

Αἰνεῖτε, παῖδες, Κύριον

PRAISE ye the Lord, ye servants of the Lord:
Praise ye his name; his lordly honour sing:
Thee we adore; to thee glad homage bring;
Thee we acknowledge; God to be adored
For thy great glory, Sovereign, Lord, and King.

2 *Father of Christ—of him whose work was done,*
When by his death he took our sins away—
To thee belongeth worship, day by day,
Yea, Holy Father, everlasting Son,
And Holy Ghost, all praise be thine for aye! Amen.

Apostolic Constitutions (*3rd century*)
Tr. George Ratcliffe Woodward, 1849–1934,
and Compilers of The BBC Hymn Book

The following are also suitable

No.
204 Lord, now lettest thou thy servant
463 Forth in thy Name, O Lord, I go

EVENING

641 TALLIS' CANON
L.M.

THOMAS TALLIS, *c.* 1505–85
As shortened by THOMAS RAVENSCROFT, *Psalter*, 1621

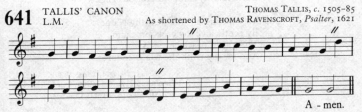

A - men.

ALL praise to thee, my God, this night,
For all the blessings of the light!
Keep me, O keep me, King of kings,
Beneath thy own almighty wings.

2 Forgive me, Lord, for thy dear Son,
The ill that I this day have done,
That with the world, myself, and thee,
I, ere I sleep, at peace may be.

3 Teach me to live, that I may dread
The grave as little as my bed;
Teach me to die, that so I may
Rise glorious at the awesome day.

4 O may my soul on thee repose,
And may sweet sleep mine eyelids close,—
Sleep that may me more vigorous make
To serve my God when I awake.

5 When in the night I sleepless lie,
My soul with heavenly thoughts supply;
Let no ill dreams disturb my rest,
No powers of darkness me molest.

6 *Praise God, from whom all blessings flow;*
Praise him, all creatures here below;
Praise him above, ye heavenly host;
Praise Father, Son, and Holy Ghost.
Amen.

Thomas Ken, 1637–1711

642 ACH BLEIB BEI UNS
(CALVISIUS) L.M.

Geistliche Lieder, Leipzig, 1589

Ach bleib bei uns, Herr Jesu Christ

NOW cheer our hearts this eventide,
Lord Jesus Christ, and with us bide;
Thou that canst never set in night,
Our heavenly Sun, our glorious Light.

2 May we and all who bear thy Name
By gentle love thy cross proclaim,
Thy gift of peace on earth secure,
And for thy truth the world endure.

Robert Bridges, 1844–1930,
Yattendon Hymnal, 1899, *based*
on Nicolaus Selnecker, 1532–92

643 DIVA SERVATRIX 11 11 11 5

Bayeux Antiphoner, 1739

[For No. 568]

A - - men.

EVENING

Die Nacht ist kommen, drin wir ruhen sollen

NOW God be with us, for the night is closing;
The light and darkness are of his disposing,
And 'neath his shadow here to rest we yield us,
    For he will shield us.

2 Let evil thoughts and spirits flee before us;
Till morning cometh, watch, Protector, o'er us;
In soul and body thou from harm defend us;
    Thine angels send us.

3 Let holy thoughts be ours when sleep o'ertakes us;
Our earliest thoughts be thine when morning wakes us;
All day serve thee, in all that we are doing
    Thy praise pursuing.

4 We have no refuge, none on earth to aid us,
Save thee, O Father, who thine own hast made us;
But thy dear Presence will not leave them lonely
    Who seek thee only.

5 Father, thy Name be praised, thy Kingdom given,
Thy will be done on earth as 'tis in heaven;
Keep us in life, forgive our sins, deliver
    Us now and ever.

Petrus Herbert, ?–1571
Tr. Catherine Winkworth, 1827–78

644   CAPETOWN   777 5   Adapted from a tune in
Filitz' *Choralbuch*, 1847

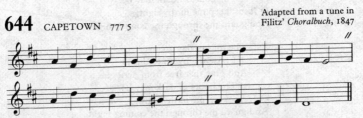

HOLY Father, cheer our way
With thy love's perpetual ray;
Grant us, every closing day,
    Light at evening time.

2 Holy Saviour, calm our fears
When earth's brightness disappears;
Grant us in our latter years
    Light at evening time.

3 Holy Spirit, be thou nigh
When in mortal pains we lie;
Grant us, as we come to die,
    Light at evening time.

4 Holy, blessèd Trinity,
Darkness is not dark to thee;
Those thou keepest always see
    Light at evening time.

Richard Hayes Robinson, 1842–92

645

HOMINUM AMATOR
7676 88

WILLIAM HAROLD FERGUSON, 1874–1950

Τὴν ἡμέραν διελθών

THE day is past and over:
　　All thanks, O Lord, to thee;
　　I pray thee now that sinless
　　The hours of dark may be.
O Jesus, keep me in thy sight,
And guard me through the coming night.

2　　　The joys of day are over:
　　　I lift my heart to thee,
　　　And pray thee that offenceless
　　　The hours of dark may be.
O Jesus, keep me in thy sight,
And guard me through the coming night.

3　　　The toils of day are over:
　　　I raise the hymn to thee,
　　　And pray that free from peril
　　　The hours of dark may be.
O Jesus, keep me in thy sight,
And guard me through the coming night.

4　　　Be thou my soul's Preserver,
　　　O God, for thou dost know
　　　How many are the perils
　　　Through which I have to go.
Lover of men, O hear my call,
And guard and save me from them all.

6th century
Tr. John Mason Neale, 1818–66

646 (i) LES COMMANDEMENS DE DIEU
9898

From a melody in *La Forme des Prières et Chants Ecclésiastiques*, Strasbourg, 1545 (rhythm simplified)

(ii) ST. CLEMENT 9898   CLEMENT COTTERILL SCHOLEFIELD, 1839–1904

THE day thou gavest, Lord, is ended;
    The darkness falls at thy behest;
To thee our morning hymns ascended,
    Thy praise shall sanctify our rest.

2 We thank thee that thy Church unsleeping,
    While earth rolls onward into light,
Through all the world her watch is keeping,
    And rests not now by day or night.

3 As o'er each continent and island
    The dawn leads on another day,
The voice of prayer is never silent,
    Nor dies the strain of praise away.

4 The sun that bids us rest is waking
    Our brethren 'neath the western sky,
And hour by hour fresh lips are making
    Thy wondrous doings heard on high.

5 So be it, Lord! thy throne shall never,
    Like earth's proud empires, pass away;
Thy Kingdom stands and grows for ever,
    Till all thy creatures own thy sway.

John Ellerton, 1826–93

647 CONNOLLY L.M.

MARTIN DALBY

SUN of my soul, thou Saviour dear,
It is not night if thou be near:
O may no earth-born cloud arise
To hide thee from thy servant's
    eyes.

2 Abide with me from morn till eve,
For without thee I cannot live;
Abide with me when night is nigh,
For without thee I dare not die.

3 Watch by the sick; enrich the poor
With blessings from thy boundless
    store;
Be every mourner's sleep to-night,
Like infant's slumbers, pure and
    light.

4 Come near and bless us when we
    wake,
Ere through the world our way we
    take,
Till in the ocean of thy love
We lose ourselves in heaven above.

John Keble, 1792–1866

648 THANET 8 33 6

JOSEPH JOWETT, 1784–1856
Parochial Psalmody, 1832

ERE I sleep, for every favour
    This day showed
    By my God,
I will bless my Saviour.

2 O my Lord, what shall I render
    To thy Name,
    Still the same,
Gracious, good, and tender?

3 Visit me with thy salvation;
    Let thy care
    Now be near,
Round my habitation.

4 Thou my Rock, my Guard, my
    Tower,
    Safely keep,
    While I sleep,
Me, with all thy power.

5 So, whene'er in death I slumber,
    Let me rise
    With the wise,
Counted in their number.

John Cennick, 1718–55

649 (i) FARLEY CASTLE 10 10 10 10   HENRY LAWES, 1596–1662

(ii) ELLERS 10 10 10 10   EDWARD JOHN HOPKINS, 1818–1901

SAVIOUR, again to thy dear Name we raise
With one accord our parting hymn of praise.
Guard thou the lips from sin, the hearts from shame,
That in this house have called upon thy Name.

2 Grant us thy peace, Lord, through the coming night;
Turn thou for us its darkness into light;
From harm and danger keep thy servants free;
For dark and light are both alike to thee.

3 Grant us thy peace throughout our earthly life;
Peace to thy Church from error and from strife;
Peace to our land, the fruit of truth and love;
Peace in each heart, thy Spirit from above:

4 Thy peace in sorrow, balm of every pain;
Thy peace in death, the hope to rise again;
Then, when thy voice shall bid our conflict cease,
Call us, O Lord, to thine eternal peace.

John Ellerton, 1826–93

650 SEELENBRÄUTIGAM
(ARNSTADT) 55 88 55

Geistreiches Gesangbuch, Darmstadt, 1698
Attributed to ADAM DRESE, 1620–1701

ROUND me falls the night;
Saviour, be my light:
Through the hours in darkness shrouded
Let me see thy face unclouded;
Let thy glory shine
In this heart of mine.

2 Earthly work is done,
Earthly sounds are none;
Rest in sleep and silence seeking,
Let me hear thee softly speaking;
In my spirit's ear
Whisper, 'I am near'.

3 Blessèd, heavenly Light,
Shining through earth's night;
Voice that oft of love hast told me;
Arms so strong to clasp and hold me;
Thou thy watch wilt keep,
Saviour, o'er my sleep.

William Romanis, 1824–99

651 TREWEN 8888. D

DAVID EMLYN EVANS, 1843–1913

A SOVEREIGN Protector I have,
   Unseen, yet for ever at hand,
Unchangeably faithful to save,
   Almighty to rule and command.
He smiles, and my comforts abound;
   His grace as the dew shall descend,
And walls of salvation surround
   The soul he delights to defend.

2 Inspirer and Hearer of prayer,
   Thou Shepherd and Guardian of
     thine,
My all to thy covenant care
   I sleeping and waking resign.
If thou art my Shield and my Sun,
   The night is no darkness to me;
And, fast as my moments roll on,
   They bring me but nearer to thee.

Augustus Montague Toplady, 1740–78

652   JESU NOSTRA REDEMPTIO   L.M.   *Antiphonale Romanum*

A - men.

Alternative tune, TALLIS' CANON, No. 641

Christe, qui lux es et dies

O CHRIST who art the Light and
   Day,
Thou drivest darksome night away.
We know thee as the Light of light,
Illuminating mortal sight.

2 All holy Lord, we pray to thee,
Keep us tonight from danger free,
Grant us, dear Lord, in thee to rest,
So be our sleep in quiet blest.

3 And while the eyes soft slumber take,
   Still be the heart to thee awake,
   Be thy right hand upheld above
   Thy servants resting in thy love.

4 Yes, our Defender, be thou nigh
   To bid the powers of darkness fly,
   Keep us from sin, and guide for good
   Thy servants purchased by thy blood.

5 *All praise to God the Father be,*
   All praise, eternal Son, to thee,
   Whom with the Spirit we adore,
   For ever and for evermore. Amen.

6th century
Verses 1–4 tr. Richard Runciman Terry, 1865–1938
Verse 5 tr. William John Copeland, 1804–85

573

653 EUDOXIA 6565   SABINE BARING-GOULD, 1834–1924

A-men.

Alternative tune, AU CLAIR DE LA LUNE, No. 58

For younger children

NOW the day is over,
    Night is drawing nigh,
Shadows of the evening
    Steal across the sky.

2 Now the darkness gathers,
    Stars begin to peep,
Birds, and beasts, and flowers
    Soon will be asleep.

3 Jesus, give the weary
    Calm and sweet repose;
With thy tender blessing
    May mine eyelids close.

4 Grant to little children
    Visions bright of thee;
Guard the sailors tossing
    On the deep blue sea.

5 Comfort every sufferer
    Watching late in pain;
Those who plan some evil
    From their sin restrain.

6 Through the long night-watches,
    May thine angels spread
Their white wings above me,
    Watching round my bed.

7 When the morning wakens,
    Then may I arise
Pure, and fresh, and sinless
    In thy holy eyes.

8 *Glory to the Father,*
    Glory to the Son,
And to thee, blest Spirit,
    Whilst all ages run. Amen.

Sabine Baring-Gould, 1834–1924

654 CASSEL 7777 77

Thommen's *Gesangbuch*,
Basle, 1745, adapted 1889

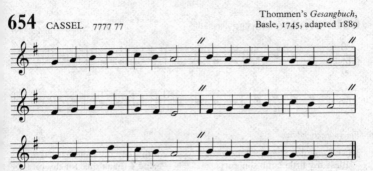

For younger children

GENTLE Jesus, hear our prayer,
Keep us in thy loving care;
And when evening shadows fall,
Casting darkness over all,
Loving Jesus, be thou near,
For with thee we have no fear.

Jessie Margaret Macdougall Ferguson, 1895–1964

655 INTO THY KEEPING 6564

GUTHRIE FOOTE, 1897–1972

For younger children

INTO thy loving care,
Into thy keeping,
Lord, who art everywhere,
Take us, we pray.

Author unknown

656 EVENING PRAYER 8787

JOHN STAINER, 1840-1901

For younger children

JESUS, tender Shepherd, hear me;
  Bless thy little lamb tonight;
Through the darkness be thou near
    me;
  Watch my sleep till morning light.

2 All this day thy hand has led me,
  And I thank thee for thy care;
Thou hast clothed me, warmed and
    fed me;
  Listen to my evening prayer.

3 Let my sins be all forgiven;
  Bless the friends I love so well;
Take me, when I die, to heaven,
  Happy there with thee to dwell.

Mary Lundie Duncan, 1814-40

DOXOLOGIES

657 REGENT SQUARE 8787 447

HENRY SMART, 1813-79

A -men.

NOW to him who loved us, gave us
  Every pledge that love could give,
Freely shed his blood to save us,
  Gave his life that we might live,
    Be the Kingdom
    And dominion
  And the glory evermore. Amen.

Samuel Miller Waring, 1792-1827

658 OLD 100TH L.M. *French–Genevan Psalter, 1551*

A - men.

PRAISE God, from whom all blessings flow;
Praise him, all creatures here below;
Praise him above, ye heavenly host;
Praise Father, Son, and Holy Ghost. Amen.

Thomas Ken, 1637–1711

659 NUN DANKET 6767 6666 Later form of a melody in Crüger's
Praxis Pietatis Melica (1647 edn.)

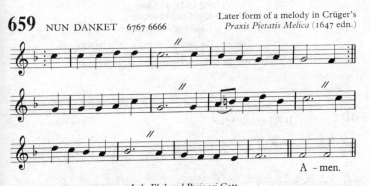

A - men.

Lob, Ehr' und Preis sei Gott

ALL praise and thanks to God
    The Father now be given,
The Son, and him who reigns
    With them in highest heaven,—
The one, eternal God,
    Whom earth and heaven adore;
    For thus it was, is now,
And shall be evermore. Amen.

Martin Rinkart, 1586–1649
Tr. Catherine Winkworth, 1827–78

577

660 TANTUM ERGO SACRAMENTUM
(GRAFTON) 8787 87

French Church Melody from
*Chants Ordinaires de l'Office
Divin*, Paris, 1881

A -men.

Gloria et honor Deo

UNTO God be praise and honour:
To the Father, to the Son,
To the mighty Spirit, glory—
Ever Three and ever One:
Power and glory in the highest
While eternal ages run. Amen.

*Venantius Fortunatus, c. 530–609
Tr. William Mair, 1830–1920, and
Arthur Wellesley Wotherspoon, 1853–1936*

661 WESTMINSTER ABBEY
(BELVILLE) 8787 87

From the concluding Alleluias in a
Purcell anthem,
The Psalmist, 1842

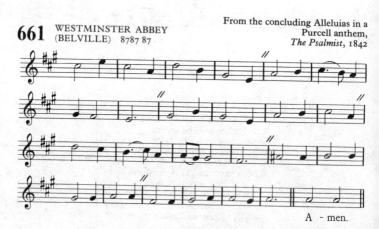

A - men.

DOXOLOGIES

Gloria et honor Deo

LAUD and honour to the Father,
Laud and honour to the Son,
Laud and honour to the Spirit,
Ever Three and ever One,
One in might, and One in glory,
While unending ages run. Amen.

7th or 8th century
Tr. John Mason Neale, 1818–66

The following Doxologies are included elsewhere in the book:

HYMN NO.	
1, v. 5 *(and elsewhere)*	To Father, Son, and Holy Ghost (L.M.)
5, v. 6 *(and elsewhere)*	To Father, Son, and Holy Ghost (C.M.)
30, v. 7	Let all things their Creator bless
70, v. 3 *(lines 5–8)*	Now glory be to God
74, v. 6	To thee be glory, Lord
135, v. 6	To God the Father, Son
198, v. 5	Christ to thee, with God the Father
301, v. 4	Glory to God the Father, The unbegotten One
392, v. 5	Glory to God the Father, God the Son

The following hymns also end in Doxologies:

31, 37, 43, 56, 75, 118, 182, 189, 199, 208, 209, 223, 257, 264, 305, 329, 330, 348, 352, 358, 366, 400, 402, 414, 429, 455, 493, 532, 535, 539, 568, 575, 576, 581, 582, 636, 637, 640, 652, 653.

Gloria Patri appears at No. 344

662 AMENS

(i) Perfect cadence

A-men.

(ii) Plagal cadence

A-men.

(iii)

A — men.

(iv)

A — men.

(v) PERCY CARTER BUCK, 1871–1947

A — — men.

(vi) Dresden   JOHANN NAUMAN, 1741–1801

A — — men.

662 (cont.)

(vii)

ORLANDO GIBBONS, 1583–1625

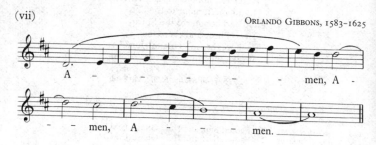

A - - - - - men, A - - men, A - - - men.

VIII

PERSONAL FAITH
AND
DEVOTION

———

663–695

663 WINDSOR (DUNDEE)
C.M.

Damon's Psalter, *The Booke of the Musicke*, 1591. Rhythm as in *Scottish Psalter*, 1615

Alternative tune, CAITHNESS, No. 395 (i)

O FOR a closer walk with God,
    A calm and heavenly frame,
A light to shine upon the road
    That leads me to the Lamb!

2 Where is the blessedness I knew
    When first I saw the Lord?
Where is the soul-refreshing view
    Of Jesus and his word?

3 What peaceful hours I once enjoyed!
    How sweet their memory still!
But they have left an aching void
    The world can never fill.

4 Return, O Holy Dove! return,
    Sweet messenger of rest!
I hate the sins that made thee mourn,
    And drove thee from my breast.

5 The dearest idol I have known,
    Whate'er that idol be,
Help me to tear it from thy throne,
    And worship only thee.

6 So shall my walk be close with God,
    Calm and serene my frame;
So purer light shall mark the road
    That leads me to the Lamb.

William Cowper, 1731–1800

583

664 ST. LEONARD C.M.   HENRY SMART, 1813-79

O FOR a faith that will not shrink,
  Though pressed by many a foe,
That will not tremble on the brink
  Of poverty or woe,

2 That will not murmur nor complain
  Beneath the chastening rod,
But, in the hour of grief or pain,
  Can lean upon its God;

3 A faith that shines more bright and
    clear
  When tempests rage without,
That when in danger knows no fear,
  In darkness feels no doubt;

4 A faith that keeps the narrow way
  Till life's last spark is fled,
And with a pure and heavenly ray
  Lights up a dying bed!

5 Lord, give me such a faith as this,
  And then, whate'er may come,
I taste even now the hallowed bliss
  Of an eternal home.

William Hiley Bathurst, 1796-1877

665 WAINWRIGHT L.M.   RICHARD WAINWRIGHT, 1758-1825 (altered)

O GOD, thou art my God alone,
  Early to thee my soul shall cry,
A pilgrim in a land unknown,
  A thirsty land whose springs are
    dry.

2 O that it were as it hath been
  When, praying in the holy place,
Thy power and glory I have seen,
  And marked the footsteps of thy
    grace!

3 Yet through this rough and thorny maze
  I follow hard on thee, my God;
Thine hand unseen upholds my ways;
  I safely tread where thou hast trod.

4 Thee, in the watches of the night,
   When I remember on my bed,
Thy presence makes the darkness light;
   Thy guardian wings are round my head.

5 Better than life itself thy love,
   Dearer than all beside to me;
For whom have I in heaven above,
   Or what on earth, compared with thee?

6 Praise, with my heart, my mind, my voice,
   For all thy mercy I will give;
My soul shall still in God rejoice;
   My tongue shall bless thee while I live.

James Montgomery, 1771-1854

666 HELSINGFORS 6 88 6   HUGO NYBERG, 1873-1935

O THOU, my Judge and King—
   My broken heart, my voiceless
      prayer,
My poverty, and blind despair,
To thee, O Christ, I bring.

2 O thou, my Judge and King—
   My treason to thy love most sweet,
   My pride that pierced thy weary
      feet,
   To thee, O Christ, I bring.

3 O thou, my Judge and King—
   My tearful hope, my faith's distress,
   For thee to pardon and to bless,
   To thee, O Christ, I bring.

4 O thou, my Judge and King—
   With no excuse, for thou art just,
   My sins, that set me in the dust,
   To thee, O Christ, I bring.

5 O thou, my Judge and King—
   My soul, from depths of my disgrace,
   To seek for mercy at thy face,
   To thee, O Christ, I bring.

Lauchlan MacLean Watt, 1867-1957

667 MARTYRDOM C.M.

HUGH WILSON, 1766–1824

[For No. 636]

A – men.

APPROACH, my soul, the mercy-seat,
 Where Jesus answers prayer;
There humbly fall before his feet,
 For none can perish there.

2 Thy promise is my only plea;
 With this I venture nigh:
Thou callest burdened souls to thee,
 And such, O Lord, am I.

3 Bowed down beneath a load of sin,
 By Satan sorely pressed,
By war without and fears within,
 I come to thee for rest.

4 Be thou my Shield and Hiding-place,
 That, sheltered near thy side,
I may my fierce accuser face,
 And tell him thou hast died.

5 O wondrous love! to bleed and die,
 To bear the cross and shame,
That guilty sinners, such as I,
 Might plead thy gracious Name!

John Newton, 1725–1807

668 NEUMARK 9898 88

GEORG NEUMARK, 1621–81
(Form adopted by MENDELSSOHN in *St. Paul*, 1836)

Wer nur den lieben Gott lässt walten

IF thou but suffer God to guide thee,
  And hope in him through all thy ways,
He'll give thee strength, whate'er betide thee,
  And bear thee through the evil days;
Who trusts in God's unchanging love
Builds on the rock that naught can move.

2 What can these anxious cares avail thee,
  These never-ceasing moans and sighs?
What can it help if thou bewail thee
  O'er each dark moment as it flies?
Our cross and trials do but press
The heavier for our bitterness.

3 Only be still, and wait his leisure
  In cheerful hope, with heart content
To take whate'er thy Father's pleasure
  And all-discerning love have sent;
Nor doubt our inmost wants are known
To him who chose us for his own.

4 Sing, pray, and keep his ways unswerving;
  So do thine own part faithfully,
And trust his word,—though undeserving,
  Thou yet shalt find it true for thee;
God never yet forsook at need
The soul that trusted him indeed.

Georg Neumark, 1621–81
Tr. Catherine Winkworth, 1827–78

669 ICH HALTE TREULICH STILL
D.S.M.

Schemelli's *Musikalisches Gesangbuch*, 1736. Thought to be by JOHANN SEBASTIAN BACH, 1685-1750

Befiehl du deine Wege

PUT thou thy trust in God,
In duty's path go on;
Walk in his strength with faith and hope,
So shall thy work be done.
Give to the winds thy fears;
Hope, and be undismayed;
God hears thy sighs and counts thy tears,
God shall lift up thy head

2   Through waves, and clouds, and storms
He gently clears thy way;
Wait thou his time; so shall this night
Soon end in joyous day.
Leave to his sovereign sway
To choose and to command;
So shalt thou, wondering, own his way
How wise, how strong his hand.

3   Thou seest our weakness, Lord;
Our hearts are known to thee:
O lift thou up the sinking hand,
Confirm the feeble knee.
Let us, in life, in death,
Thy steadfast truth declare,
And publish, with our latest breath,
Thy love and guardian care.

Paul Gerhardt, 1607-76
Par. John Wesley, 1703-91, and others

670 MARTYRS C.M.   *Scottish Psalter, 1615 (1635 rhythm)*

Alternative tune, LONDON NEW, No. 147

WORKMAN of God! O lose not heart,
    But learn what God is like,
And, in the darkest battle-field,
    Thou shalt know where to strike.

2 Thrice blest is he to whom is given
    The instinct that can tell
That God is on the field when he
    Is most invisible.

3 He hides himself so wondrously,
    As though there were no God;
He is least seen when all the powers
    Of ill are most abroad.

4 Ah! God is other than we think;
    His ways are far above,
Far beyond reason's height, and reached
    Only by childlike love.

5 Then learn to scorn the praise of men,
    And learn to lose with God;
For Jesus won the world through shame,
    And beckons thee his road.

6 For right is right, since God is God,
    And right the day must win;
To doubt would be disloyalty,
    To falter would be sin.

Frederick William Faber, 1814–63

671 WEM IN LEIDENSTAGEN
(CASWALL) 6565

FRIEDRICH FILITZ, 1804-76

Wem in Leidenstagen

O LET him whose sorrow
No relief can find,
Trust in God, and borrow
Ease for heart and mind.

2 Where the mourner, weeping,
Sheds the secret tear,
God his watch is keeping,
Though none else be near.

3 God will never leave thee;
All thy wants he knows,
Feels the pains that grieve thee,
Sees thy cares and woes.

4 If in grief thou languish,
He will dry the tear,
Who his children's anguish
Soothes with succour near.

5 All thy woe and sadness,
In this world below,
Balance not the gladness
Thou in heaven shalt know,

6 When thy gracious Saviour,
In the realms above,
Crowns thee with his favour,
Fills thee with his love.

Heinrich Siegmund Oswald, 1751-1834
Tr. Frances Elizabeth Cox, 1812-97

672 MAYFIELD 66 6565

KENNETH LEIGHTON

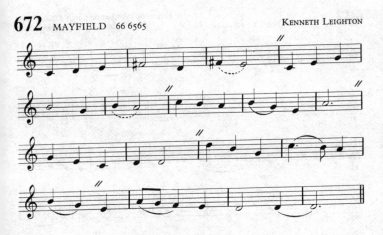

CHRIST who knows all his sheep
Will all in safety keep,
 He will not lose one soul,
  Nor ever fail us;
Nor we the promised goal,
  Though hell assail us.

2 I know my God is just;
To him I wholly trust
 All that I have and am,
  All that I hope for:
All's sure and seen to him,
  Which here I grope for.

3 Lord Jesus, take this spirit:
We trust thy love and merit.
 Take home the wandering sheep,
  For thou hast sought it;
This soul in safety keep,
  For thou hast bought it.

Richard Baxter, 1615-91 (altered)

673 FINLANDIA 10 10 10 10 10 10

From the symphonic poem *Finlandia* by
JEAN SIBELIUS, 1865–1957

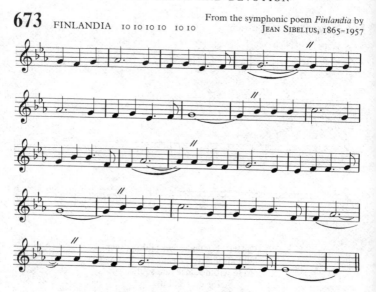

Stille, mein Wille; dein Jesus hilft siegen

BE still, my soul: the Lord is on thy side;
  Bear patiently the cross of grief or pain;
Leave to thy God to order and provide;
  In every change he faithful will remain.
Be still, my soul: thy best, thy heavenly Friend
Through thorny ways leads to a joyful end.

2 Be still, my soul: thy God doth undertake
    To guide the future as he has the past.
  Thy hope, thy confidence let nothing shake;
    All now mysterious shall be bright at last.
  Be still, my soul: the waves and winds still know
  His voice who ruled them while he dwelt below.

3 Be still, my soul: when dearest friends depart,
    And all is darkened in the vale of tears,
  Then shalt thou better know his love, his heart,
    Who comes to soothe thy sorrow and thy fears.
  Be still, my soul: thy Jesus can repay,
  From his own fullness, all he takes away.

4 Be still, my soul: the hour is hastening on
   When we shall be forever with the Lord,
When disappointment, grief, and fear are gone,
   Sorrow forgot, love's purest joys restored.
Be still, my soul: when change and tears are past,
All safe and blessèd we shall meet at last.

Katharina von Schlegel, 1697–?
Tr. Jane Laurie Borthwick, 1813–97

674 ST. BOTOLPH C.M.   GORDON SLATER

JESUS, these eyes have never seen
   That radiant form of thine;
The veil of sense hangs dark between
   Thy blessèd face and mine.

2 I see thee not, I hear thee not,
   Yet art thou oft with me;
And earth hath ne'er so dear a spot
   As where I meet with thee.

3 Like some bright dream that comes unsought,
   When slumbers o'er me roll,
Thine image ever fills my thought,
   And charms my ravished soul.

4 Yet, though I have not seen, and still
   Must rest in faith alone,
I love thee, dearest Lord, and will,
   Unseen but not unknown.

5 When death these mortal eyes shall seal,
   And still this throbbing heart,
The rending veil shall thee reveal
   All glorious as thou art.

Ray Palmer, 1808–87

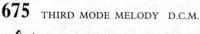

675 THIRD MODE MELODY D.C.M.

Thomas Tallis, *c.* 1505–85
(rhythm slightly simplified)

Alternative tune, WINDSOR (DUNDEE), No. 377(i)

'TWIXT gleams of joy and clouds of doubt
  Our feelings come and go;
Our best estate is tossed about
  In ceaseless ebb and flow.
No mood of feeling, form of thought,
  Is constant for a day;
But thou, O Lord, thou changest not:
  The same thou art alway.

2 I grasp thy strength, make it mine own,
  My heart with peace is blest;
I lose my hold, and then comes down
  Darkness, and cold unrest.
Let me no more my comfort draw
  From my frail hold of thee,
In this alone rejoice with awe—
  Thy mighty grasp of me.

3 Out of that weak, unquiet drift
  That comes but to depart,
To that pure heaven my spirit lift
  Where thou unchanging art.
Lay hold of me with thy strong grasp,
  Let thy almighty arm
In its embrace my weakness clasp,
  And I shall fear no harm.

4 Thy purpose of eternal good
  Let me but surely know;
On this I'll lean—let changing mood
  And feeling come or go—
Glad when thy sunshine fills my soul,
  Not lorn when clouds o'ercast,
Since thou within thy sure control
  Of love dost hold me fast.

John Campbell Shairp, 1819-85

676 SONG 13 7777   ORLANDO GIBBONS, 1583-1625

HARK, my soul! it is the Lord;
'Tis thy Saviour, hear his word;
Jesus speaks, and speaks to thee:
'Say, poor sinner, lov'st thou me?

2 'I delivered thee when bound,
And, when bleeding, healed thy wound;
Sought thee wandering, set thee right;
Turned thy darkness into light.

3 'Can a woman's tender care
Cease towards the child she bare?
Yes, she may forgetful be,
Yet will I remember thee.

4 'Mine is an unchanging love,
Higher than the heights above,
Deeper than the depths beneath,
Free and faithful, strong as death.

5 'Thou shalt see my glory soon,
When the work of grace is done;
Partner of my throne shalt be;
Say, poor sinner, lov'st thou me?'

6 Lord, it is my chief complaint
That my love is weak and faint;
Yet I love thee, and adore;
O for grace to love thee more!

William Cowper, 1731-1800

677 ST. MARGARET 88 886   ALBERT LISTER PEACE, 1844–1912

O LOVE that wilt not let me go,
  I rest my weary soul in thee:
I give thee back the life I owe,
That in thine ocean depths its flow
    May richer, fuller be.

2 O Light that followest all my way,
  I yield my flickering torch to thee:
My heart restores its borrowed ray,
That in thy sunshine's blaze its day
    May brighter, fairer be.

3 O Joy that seekest me through pain,
  I cannot close my heart to thee:
I trace the rainbow through the rain,
And feel the promise is not vain,
    That morn shall tearless be.

4 O Cross that liftest up my head,
  I dare not ask to fly from thee:
I lay in dust life's glory dead,
And from the ground there blossoms red
    Life that shall endless be.

George Matheson, 1842–1906

678 (i) KILLINCHY 8888 88   SEBASTIAN FORBES

(ii) DAS NEUGEBORNE KINDELEIN
8888 88

MELCHIOR VULPIUS, c. 1560-1615

Ich will Dich lieben, meine Stärke

THEE will I love, my Strength, my Tower;
   Thee will I love, my Joy, my Crown;
Thee will I love with all my power,
   In all thy works, and thee alone;
Thee will I love, till sacred fire
Fill my whole soul with pure desire.

2 I thank thee, uncreated Sun,
   That thy bright beams on me have shined;
I thank thee, who hast overthrown
   My foes, and healed my wounded mind;
I thank thee, whose enlivening voice
Bids my freed heart in thee rejoice.

3 Thee will I love, my Joy, my Crown;
   Thee will I love, my Lord, my God;
Thee will I love, beneath thy frown
   Or smile, thy sceptre or thy rod;
What though my flesh and heart decay,
Thee shall I love in endless day.

Johann Scheffler, 1624-77
Tr. John Wesley, 1703-91 (altered)

597

679 ASHWELL C.M.   EDRIC CUNDELL, 1893–1961

LORD, it belongs not to my care
  Whether I die or live;
To love and serve thee is my share,
  And this thy grace must give.

2 If life be long, I will be glad,
  That I may long obey;
If short, yet why should I be sad
  To welcome endless day?

3 Christ leads me through no darker rooms
  Than he went through before;
He that into God's Kingdom comes
  Must enter by this door.

4 Come, Lord, when grace hath made me meet
  Thy blessèd face to see;
For, if thy work on earth be sweet,
  What will thy glory be?

5 My knowledge of that life is small,
  The eye of faith is dim;
But 'tis enough that Christ knows all,
  And I shall be with him.

Richard Baxter, 1615–91

680 SWABIA S.M.   Adapted by WILLIAM HENRY HAVERGAL, 1793–1870,
          from a melody in Spiess' *Davids Harpffen-Spiel*,
          Heidelberg, 1745

MY times are in thy hand:
  My God, I wish them there;
My life, my friends, my soul I leave
  Entirely to thy care.

2 My times are in thy hand,
  Whatever they may be,
Pleasing or painful, dark or bright,
  As best may seem to thee.

3   My times are in thy hand:
     Why should I doubt or fear?
  My Father's hand will never cause
     His child a needless tear.

4   My times are in thy hand,
     Jesus, the Crucified;
  Those hands my cruel sins had
     pierced
     Are now my guard and guide.

5   My times are in thy hand:
     I'll always trust in thee;
  And, after death, at thy right hand
     I shall for ever be.

William Freeman Lloyd, 1791-1853

681 PENLAN 7676. D   DAVID JENKINS, 1849-1915

Alternative tune, DURROW, No. 397

IN heavenly love abiding,
   No change my heart shall fear;
And safe is such confiding,
   For nothing changes here:
The storm may roar without me,
   My heart may low be laid;
But God is round about me,
   And can I be dismayed?

2 Wherever he may guide me,
   No want shall turn me back;
My Shepherd is beside me,
   And nothing can I lack.

His wisdom ever waketh,
   His sight is never dim:
He knows the way he taketh,
   And I will walk with him.

3 Green pastures are before me,
   Which yet I have not seen;
Bright skies will soon be o'er me,
   Where the dark clouds have been.
My hope I cannot measure:
   My path to life is free:
My Saviour has my treasure,
   And he will walk with me.

Anna Laetitia Waring, 1820-1910

682 LUX BENIGNA 10 4 10 4 10 10   JOHN BACCHUS DYKES, 1823–76

LEAD, kindly Light, amid the encircling gloom,
    Lead thou me on;
The night is dark, and I am far from home;
    Lead thou me on.
Keep thou my feet; I do not ask to see
The distant scene,—one step enough for me.

2 I was not ever thus, nor prayed that thou
    Shouldst lead me on;
I loved to choose and see my path, but now
    Lead thou me on;
I loved the garish day, and, spite of fears,
Pride ruled my will: remember not past years.

3 So long thy power hath blest me, sure it still
    Will lead me on,
O'er moor and fen, o'er crag and torrent, till
    The night is gone,
And with the morn those angel faces smile,
Which I have loved long since, and lost awhile.

John Henry Newman, 1801–90

683 WELCOME VOICE S.M. and refrain   Lewis Hartsough, 1828–1919

I HEAR thy welcome voice
  That calls me, Lord, to thee,
For cleansing in thy precious blood
  That flowed on Calvary.
  I am coming, Lord,
    Coming now to thee;
  Wash me, cleanse me in the blood
    That flowed on Calvary.

2 'Tis Jesus calls me on
  To perfect faith and love,
To perfect hope and peace and trust,
  For earth and heaven above.

3 'Tis Jesus who confirms
  The blessèd work within,
By adding grace to welcomed grace,
  Where reigned the power of sin.

4 All hail, atoning blood!
  All hail, redeeming grace!
All hail, the gift of Christ our Lord,
  Our Strength and Righteousness!

Lewis Hartsough, 1828–1919

684 HELDER   7686 8686   BARTHOLOMAEUS HELDER, 1585-1635

BENEATH the cross of Jesus
   I fain would take my stand—
The shadow of a mighty rock
   Within a weary land;
A home within a wilderness,
   A rest upon the way,
From the burning of the noontide heat
   And the burden of the day.

2 O safe and happy shelter,
   O refuge tried and sweet,
O trysting-place where heaven's love
   And heaven's justice meet!
As to the exiled patriarch
   That wondrous dream was given,
So seems my Saviour's cross to me—
   A ladder up to heaven.

3 Upon that cross of Jesus,
   Mine eye at times can see
The very dying form of One
   Who suffered there for me;
And from my smitten heart, with tears,
   Two wonders I confess—
The wonder of his glorious love,
   And my own worthlessness.

4 I take, O cross, thy shadow
   For my abiding-place;
I ask no other sunshine than
   The sunshine of his face:
Content to let the world go by,
   To know no gain nor loss—
My sinful self my only shame,
   My glory all, the cross.

Elizabeth Cecilia Clephane, 1830–69

685 CUTTLE MILLS 8583   WILLIAM GRIFFITH, 1867–1929

I AM trusting thee, Lord Jesus,
   Trusting only thee,
Trusting thee for full salvation,
   Great and free.

2 I am trusting thee for pardon:
   At thy feet I bow,
For thy grace and tender mercy
   Trusting now.

3 I am trusting thee to guide me;
   Thou alone shalt lead,
Every day and hour supplying
   All my need.

4 I am trusting thee for power:
   Thine can never fail;
Words which thou thyself shalt give me
   Must prevail.

5 I am trusting thee, Lord Jesus;
   Never let me fall;
I am trusting thee for ever,
   And for all.

Frances Ridley Havergal, 1836–79

686 NORTH COATES 6565. D   TIMOTHY RICHARD MATTHEWS, 1826–1910

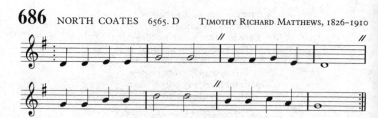

JESUS, I will trust thee,—
   Trust thee with my soul;
Guilty, lost, and helpless,
   Thou canst make me whole.
There is none in heaven
   Or on earth like thee;
Thou hast died for sinners—
   Therefore, Lord, for me.

2 Jesus, I will trust thee;
   Name of matchless worth,
Spoken by the angel
   At thy wondrous birth,
Written, and for ever,
   On thy cross of shame:
Sinners read and worship,
   Trusting in that Name.

3 Jesus, I will trust thee,
   Pondering thy ways
Full of love and mercy
   All thine earthly days.
Sinners gathered round thee,
   Lepers sought thy face,
None too vile or loathsome
   For a Saviour's grace.

4 Jesus, I will trust thee,
   Trust without a doubt;
Whosoever cometh
   Thou wilt not cast out.
Faithful is thy promise;
   Precious is thy blood;
These my soul's salvation,
   Thou my Saviour God!

Mary Jane Walker, 1816–78

687 ACH GOTT UND HERR
888 7
Andachts Zymbeln, Freiburg, 1655

I AM not skilled to understand
What God hath willed, what God hath planned;
I only know at his right hand
    Stands One who is my Saviour.

2 I take God at his word and deed:
  'Christ died to save me', this I read;
And in my heart I find a need
    Of him to be my Saviour.

3 And was there then no other way
For God to take?—I cannot say;
I only bless him, day by day,
    Who saved me through my Saviour.

4 That he should leave his place on high
And come for sinful man to die,
You count it strange?—so do not I,
    Since I have known my Saviour.

5 And O that he fulfilled may see
The travail of his soul in me,
And with his work contented be,
    As I with my dear Saviour!

6 Yea, living, dying, let me bring
My strength, my solace, from this spring,
That he who lives to be my King
    Once died to be my Saviour.

Dora Greenwell, 1821–82

688 BREAD OF LIFE 6464   ERIC HARDING THIMAN

I NEED thee every hour,
  Most gracious Lord;
No tender voice but thine
  Can peace afford.

2 I need thee every hour;
  Stay thou near by;
Temptations lose their power
  When thou art nigh.

3 I need thee every hour,
  In joy or pain;
Come quickly and abide,
  Or life is vain.

4 I need thee every hour;
  Teach me thy will;
And thy rich promises
  In me fulfil.

Annie Sherwood Hawks, 1835–1918

689 (i) WILMINGTON 6464 664   ERIK ROUTLEY

(ii) PROPIOR DEO 6464 664(4)   ARTHUR SEYMOUR SULLIVAN, 1842–1900

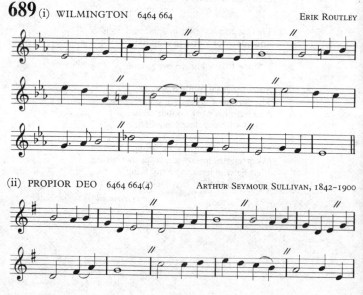

NEARER, my God, to thee,
  Nearer to thee!
E'en though it be a cross
  That raiseth me,
Still all my song would be,
'Nearer, my God, to thee,
  *Nearer to thee!'

2 Though, like the wanderer,
  The sun gone down,
Darkness be over me,
  My rest a stone,
Yet in my dreams I'd be
Nearer, my God, to thee,
  Nearer to thee!

3 There let the way appear
  Steps unto heaven,
All that thou send'st to me
  In mercy given,
Angels to beckon me
Nearer, my God, to thee,
  Nearer to thee!

4 Then, with my waking thoughts
  Bright with thy praise,
Out of my stony griefs
  Bethel I'll raise,
So by my woes to be
Nearer, my God, to thee,
  Nearer to thee!

5 Or if on joyful wing
  Cleaving the sky,
Sun, moon, and stars forgot,
  Upwards I fly,
Still all my song shall be,
'Nearer, my God, to thee,
  Nearer to thee!'

Sarah Flower Adams, 1805–48

* *When Tune* (ii) PROPIOR DEO *is used, the last line of each verse is repeated*

690 BLACKFORD 6464 6664 KENNETH LEIGHTON

TEACH me to serve thee, Lord,
I humbly pray.
Help me the path to tread
In thine own way.
As thou hast promised, Lord,
O let thy living Word
New strength to me afford
For every day.

2 Teach me, O Lord, to give,
Nor count the cost,
For what is given for thee
Is never lost.
Whate'er I lend to thee
Thou first didst give to me,
Thy debtor I must be
Till Jordan's crossed.

3 Teach me, O Lord, to fight,
Nor heed the pain:
Since he who fights for thee
Ne'er fights in vain.
Help me to stand for right,
Be thou my guiding light,
And daily by thy might
I shall attain.

4 Teach me to labour on,
Nor ask reward,
To toil, nor seek for rest
While sin's abroad.
And should I faithful be,
Grant I may dwell with thee,
Through all eternity,
My King, my Lord.

Edna Martha Phillips

691 DANIEL L.M. Irish Traditional Melody

[For No. 601]

A - men.

DEAR Master, in whose life I see
All that I would but fail to be,
Let thy clear light for ever shine,
To shame and guide this life of mine.

2 Though what I dream and what I do
In my weak days are always two,
Help me, oppressed by things undone,
O thou, whose deeds and dreams were one!

John Hunter, 1848–1917

692 SANDYS S.M.

English Traditional Carol Melody,
from Sandys' *Christmas Carols Ancient and
Modern*, 1833

TEACH me, my God and King,
In all things thee to see;
And what I do in anything,
To do it as for thee!

2   A man that looks on glass,
On it may stay his eye;
Or if he pleaseth, through it pass,
And then the heaven espy.

3   All may of thee partake;
Nothing can be so mean,
Which with this tincture, 'for thy sake',
Will not grow bright and clean.

4   A servant with this clause
Makes drudgery divine:
Who sweeps a room, as for thy laws,
Makes that and the action fine.

5   This is the famous stone
That turneth all to gold;
For that which God doth touch and own
Cannot for less be told.

George Herbert, 1593–1633

693 CHERRY TREE CAROL
7676 irregular

English Traditional Melody

Alternative tune, CHRISTUS DER IST MEIN LEBEN, No. 404

MY soul, there is a country
    Afar beyond the stars,
Where stands a wingèd sentry
    All skilful in the wars.

2 There, above noise, and danger,
    Sweet peace sits, crowned with smiles,
And One born in a manger
    Commands the beauteous files.

3 He is thy gracious friend,
    And—O my soul, awake!—
Did in pure love descend,
    To die here for thy sake.

4 If thou canst get but thither,
    There grows the flower of peace,
The rose that cannot wither,
    Thy fortress, and thy ease.

5 Leave then thy foolish ranges;
    For none can thee secure,
But One, who never changes,
    Thy God, thy Life, thy Cure.

Henry Vaughan, 1621-95

694 RUTHERFORD 7676 7675

CHRÉTIEN URHAN, 1790-1845,
as adapted in Rimbault's
Hymns for Divine Worship, 1867

THE sands of time are sinking;
   The dawn of heaven breaks;
The summer morn I've sighed for,
   The fair, sweet morn, awakes.
Dark, dark hath been the midnight,
   But dayspring is at hand,
And glory, glory dwelleth
     In Immanuel's land.

2 O Christ! He is the fountain,
   The deep, sweet well of love;
The streams on earth I've tasted
   More deep I'll drink above:
There to an ocean fullness
   His mercy doth expand,
And glory, glory dwelleth
     In Immanuel's land.

3 With mercy and with judgment
   My web of time he wove,
And aye the dews of sorrow
   Were lustred by his love;
I'll bless the hand that guided,
   I'll bless the heart that planned,
When throned where glory dwelleth
     In Immanuel's land.

4 I've wrestled on towards heaven,
   'Gainst storm and wind and tide;
Now, like a weary traveller
   That leaneth on his guide,
Amid the shades of evening,
   While sinks life's lingering sand,
I hail the glory dawning
     In Immanuel's land.

Anne Ross Cousin, 1824–1906

695 EVENTIDE 10 10 10 10   WILLIAM HENRY MONK, 1823–89

ABIDE with me: fast falls the eventide;
The darkness deepens; Lord, with me abide:
When other helpers fail, and comforts flee,
Help of the helpless, O abide with me.

2 Swift to its close ebbs out life's little day;
Earth's joys grow dim, its glories pass away;
Change and decay in all around I see:
O thou who changest not, abide with me.

3 I need thy presence every passing hour;
What but thy grace can foil the tempter's power?
Who like thyself my guide and stay can be?
Through cloud and sunshine, O abide with me.

4 I fear no foe with thee at hand to bless;
Ills have no weight, and tears no bitterness:
Where is death's sting? where, grave, thy victory?
I triumph still if thou abide with me.

5 Hold thou thy cross before my closing eyes,
Shine through the gloom, and point me to the skies;
Heaven's morning breaks, and earth's vain shadows flee:
In life and death, O Lord, abide with me.

Henry Francis Lyte, 1793–1847

INDEXES

ALPHABETICAL INDEX OF TUNES

Brackets round a number indicate words for which the tune is also suitable

INDEX OF CHANTS, PLAINSONG TONES, PLAINSONG MELODIES AND SETTINGS OF LITURGICAL ITEMS, ETC.

INDEX OF PSALMS

The metrical psalms have been taken from the *Scottish Metrical Psalter* of 1650 and the *Irish Metrical Psalter* of 1880.

Psalms taken from other sources are printed in *italic* and the sources are given.
AV = Authorized Version; NEB = New English Bible.

TABLE OF LITURGICAL ITEMS

INDEX OF FIRST LINES

Hymns for children are marked with an asterisk

INDEX OF FIRST LINES

INDEX OF FIRST LINES

INDEX OF FIRST LINES